Investments

Volume 1

Investments

Volume 1: Portfolio Theory and Asset Pricing

Edwin J. Elton
Martin Gruber

The MIT Press
Cambridge, Massachusetts
London, England

Second printing, 2000

This book was set in Palatino by Asco Typesetters, Hong Kong.
Printed and bound in the United States of America.

Library of Congress Cataloging-in-Publication Data

Elton, Edwin J.
Investments / Edwin J. Elton, Martin Gruber.
p. cm.
Includes bibliographical references and index.
Contents: v. 1. Portfolio theory and asset pricing —
v. 2. Securities prices and performance.
ISBN 0-262-05059-5 (v. 1, hardcover : alk. paper)
ISBN 0-262-05060-9 (v. 2, hardcover : alk. paper)
1. Portfolio management. 2. Investment analysis. I. Gruber, Martin Jay, 1937– . II. Title.
HG4529.5.E468 1999
332.6—dc21 98-51526
CIP

To our wives Diane Elton and Ellie Gruber,
To our children:

Annette Elton Bietel

Ned Elton

Kathryn Elton

John Elton

and

Jonathan Gruber

Stacey Gruber

Joelle Gruber

and to our grandchildren, the next generation of our readers:

Eric Bietel

Samuel Gruber

Jack Gruber

Contents

Foreword

Harry Markowitz

I recall viewing Mount Fuji from the bullet train on a cloudless day. It was an impressive sight: a single snowcapped volcanic cone towering above its surroundings. An impressive sight of a different sort is the view of the Andes from Santiago, Chile. That presents the viewer with an unending wall of huge mountains—any one of which would be magnificent on its own—with even taller mountains visible here and there behind the front row of giants.

Contemplating the works of Elton and Gruber is like viewing the Andes. There are so many towering works that one has difficulty keeping track of them all, or knowing what percent one has seen. The present two-volume set helps the reader in this matter by assembling in one place what the authors refer to as their "favorite articles." This is not their entire work; indeed, just beyond the cutoff for these two volumes are articles that the authors refer to as "almost our favorites"—like tall mountains not visible because of other mountains.

The two volumes are divided into seven parts with introductions summarizing their contents, plus an eighth, one-article part that needs no introduction. Taken together, the eight introductions constitute a definitive survey of Elton and Gruber's favorite works. I will not try to provide an alternate survey. Rather, I will focus on two related topics—namely, models of covariance and properties of mean-variance efficient sets—that occupy several of their papers. I will discuss the state of the art prior to the Elton and Gruber (and the Elton, Gruber, Padberg [EGP]) discoveries, and the impact of these discoveries.

I begin by reviewing what was known about mean-variance efficient sets prior to publication of the revolutionary EGP (1976). Markowitz (1952) defined mean-variance efficiency and illustrated the nature of mean-variance efficient sets in terms of 3- and 4-security diagrams (requiring

2- and 3-dimensional drawings). The only constraint set considered is what I now refer to as the "standard" constraint set

$$\sum_{i=1}^{n} X_i = 1 \tag{1a}$$

$$X_i \geqslant 0 \qquad i = 1, \ldots, n, \tag{1b}$$

where X_i is the fraction of the portfolio invested in the i-th of n securities. It was assumed that the covariance matrix is nonsingular. The 3-security examples illustrated that the set of efficient portfolios is piecewise linear —the successive pieces meeting at points called "corner portfolios." The nature of the lines connecting the successive corner portfolios is better seen in the 4-security case. Given any nonempty subset I of the numbers 1 through 4, that is, $I \subset \{1, 2, 3, 4\}$, we define a subspace s_I and a critical line ℓ_I. The subspace s_I consists of all points (X_1, X_2, X_3, X_4) in which $X_j = 0$ for j *not* in I. The other X_i are only required to satisfy $\sum X_i = 1$. The critical line ℓ_I is the locus of all points (portfolios) that minimize V for some given E among points in the subspace s_I. Under the given assumptions, the set of efficient portfolios

> may be traced out by starting at the point of minimum available variance, moving continuously along various $\ell_{a1,\ldots,a\alpha}$ according to definite rules, ending in a point which gives maximum E. Typically we proceed along a given critical line until either this line intersects one of a larger subspace or meets a boundary (and simultaneously the critical line of a lower dimensional subspace). In either of these cases the efficient [set] turns and continues along the new line. The efficient [set] terminates when a point with maximum E is reached. (Markowitz [1952], note 8)

The efficient sets can similarly be traced out starting with the efficient portfolio with maximum E and ending with the one with minimum V. This is the more frequent practice now.

While the preceding quote is correct qualitatively, Markowitz (1952) did not supply the formulas for the critical lines. These were supplied in Markowitz (1956), which presented the "critical line algorithm" for tracing out the set of efficient portfolios, under more general assumptions concerning the constraint set than the standard set (1) assumed in Markowitz (1952). Specifically, Markowitz (1956) permitted securities that might or might not be required to be nonnegative; might be subject to linear equality constraints in addition to, or instead of, (1a); and/or might be subject to linear inequality constraints (with weak inequalities $\leqslant$ or $\geqslant$ rather than strong ones, $>$ or $<$). These various cases cluttered the exposition. Markowitz (1959) notes that all these cases are handled if one simply treats the case in which the constraints are linear equalities in nonnegative variables. In matrix notation

$$\mathbf{AX} = \mathbf{b} \tag{2a}$$

$$\mathbf{X} \geqslant 0 \tag{2b}$$

where $\mathbf{A}$ is an m by n matrix, $\mathbf{b}$ an m component column vector, and $\mathbf{X}$ an n component portfolio vector. For example, a variable X_i that is allowed to be either positive or negative in the 1956 exposition is treated as the difference between two nonnegative variables, the positive and negative parts of X_i. Inequalities are transformed into equalities by the introduction of "slack" variables as in linear programming.

Another difference between Markowitz (1956) and Markowitz (1959) is that, while the former does not require the covariance matrix $\mathbf{C}$ to be nonsingular, it does require variance, $V = \mathbf{X}'\mathbf{C}\mathbf{X}$, to be a strictly convex function over the set of feasible $\mathbf{X}$; Markowitz (1959) dispenses with this assumption and allows any possible covariance matrix, that is, any positive semidefinite $\mathbf{C}$. In this case more than one feasible portfolio may have the same efficient mean and variance. But (provided the model is feasible and has efficient portfolios) there is always a set of efficient portfolios that meets the qualitative description quoted above. This then was the state of knowledge about the shapes and properties of efficient sets, and how to compute them, in 1959. It is approximately the state at present if efficient portfolios for all efficient EV combinations is sought (see Perold [1984]). In particular, the critical line algorithm in Markowitz (1987) differs from that in Markowitz (1959) only in the handling of some "funny cases," like unbounded E or more than one portfolio with maximum E.

Consider the case with the standard constraint set (1) and with a universe of securities consisting of n risky securities with nonsingular covariance matrix, plus one risk-free asset ("cash"). Tobin (1958) showed that the piecewise linear set of efficient portfolios consists of zero, one, or more pieces containing risky securities only, plus a final (lowest variance) piece consisting of mixtures of cash and one particular portfolio $\hat{\mathbf{X}}$ of risky securities. Thus all efficient portfolios that hold cash and risky assets hold the latter in the proportions $\hat{\mathbf{X}}$. Sharpe (1964) showed that if, in addition, the investor could borrow any desired amount at the risk-free rate r_f (equal to the rate paid by cash) then any efficient portfolio would consist of either cash only, or a mixture of $\hat{\mathbf{X}}$ and cash, or of $\hat{\mathbf{X}}$ and borrowing.

Thus (except for the cash-only portfolio) all efficient portfolios would contain risky securities in the proportions $\hat{\mathbf{X}}$.

EGP (1976) solves for $\hat{\mathbf{X}}$ when one of two models of covariance is assumed. One model for which they find $\hat{\mathbf{X}}$ is the one-factor model. Markowitz (1959) thought means and variances would be estimated by security analysts, but noted that there are too many covariances to expect an analyst team to estimate them individually. I suggested that a model of covariance is needed, and I proposed a model in which the return on the i-th security is

$$r_i = \alpha_i + \beta_i F + u_i, \tag{3}$$

where α_i and β_i are constants (which may vary between securities), F is a common random factor and the u_i are idiosyncratic random terms. The u_i are assumed to be uncorrelated with each other and with F. The one-factor model (3) is also referred to as the market model or the single index model, since F is usually interpreted as "the market," and the αs and βs usually estimated by regressions against some market index. It is also referred to as the "diagonal" model for reasons given below.

Sharpe (1963) backtested the one-factor model, as compared to using historical covariances as estimates, and cautiously concluded that the results were "too fragmentary to be considered conclusive but they do suggest that the diagonal model may be able to represent the relationships among securities rather well and thus that the value of portfolio analyses based on the model will exceed their rather nominal cost. For these reasons it appears to be an excellent choice for the initial practical applications of the Markowitz technique." Elton and Gruber (1973) backtested several methods of estimating covariance including the one-factor model and the "constant correlation" model, which assumes that all correlation coefficients (ρ_{ij} $i \neq j$) are the same. They concluded that "in particular, we have found that in the case of five-year estimates three average techniques [including the constant correlation model] outperformed all other techniques. The fact that these models consistently outperformed the SSI [i.e., one-factor] and Historical models, which have been the two most commonly used ways to generate input to portfolio analysis, has major implications for future empirical research."

By 1963 Bill Sharpe and I had observed that when the one-factor model is assumed, the critical line computation can be much simplified by use of a certain "gimmick." From equation (3) deduce that the return on the portfolio may be written as

$$R = \left(\sum \alpha_i X_i\right) + \left(\sum \beta_i X_i\right) F + \sum X_i u_i \tag{4}$$

Since F and all the u_i are uncorrelated

$$V(R) = \left(\sum \beta_i X_i\right)^2 V(F) + \sum X_i^2 V(u_i) \tag{5}$$

If we add an $(n+1)$st variable and a new constraint thus

$$X_{n+1} = \sum_{i=1}^{n} X_i \beta_i \tag{6a}$$

then

$$V = \sum_{i=1}^{n} V(u_i) X_i^2 + V(F) X_{n+1}^2 \tag{6b}$$

Thus V becomes a sum of squares. Only the diagonal elements of the covariance matrix are nonzero, whence the name "diagonal" model. The equations which describe a critical line, obtained by setting to zero the partial derivatives of a certain Lagrangian expression, are much simplified and easily solved.

A similar gimmick can be applied to the constant correlation model provided that ρ, the common correlation coefficient, is nonnegative. In general

$$V = \sum \sum X_i X_j \sigma_{ij} \tag{7}$$

From

$$\sigma_{ij} = \rho \sigma_i \sigma_j \qquad \text{for } i \neq j$$

$$\sigma_{ij} = \sigma_i^2 \qquad \text{for } i = j$$

$$= (1-\rho)\sigma_i^2 + \rho \sigma_i^2$$

we derive

$$V = (1-\rho) \sum X_i^2 \sigma_i^2 + \rho \left(\sum X_i \sigma_i\right)^2 \tag{8}$$

If we add a variable and constraint thus

$$X_{n+1} = \sum_{i=1}^{n} X_i \sigma_i \tag{9a}$$

then

$$V = \sum_{i=1}^{n} X_i^2((1-\rho)\sigma_i^2) + \rho X_{n+1}^2 \tag{9b}$$

Once again the model is diagonalized. In fact, the constant correlation model with $\rho \geqslant 0$ is equivalent to the one-factor model with the added condition that $\beta_i/\sigma(u_i)$ is the same for all i.[1]

Since the one-factor model is a special case of an arbitrary covariance matrix **C**, and the constant correlation model with nonnegative ρ is a special case of the one-factor model, if heaven supplied us true parameters there would never be an advantage to assuming the constant correlation model with nonnegative ρ rather than the one-factor model, or the one-factor model rather than an arbitrary **C**. But estimates have sampling error; and **C** probably varies over time. Therefore it is possible that estimates of the parameters of more complex models provide more noise than news, and that it is better in practice to use a simpler, more restrictive model. Sharpe concluded that this seemed to be the case for the one-factor model as compared to an arbitrary **C**; Elton and Gruber concluded the same for the constant correlation model as compared to the more general one-factor model.

The EGP (1976) discovery is not a faster way to trace out the whole efficient frontier; rather, it supplies a simple rule for finding the portfolio $\hat{\mathbf{X}}$. One benefit of this discovery was computational speed. The critical line algorithm traces out the frontier starting with the portfolio with maximum expected return as determined by the simplex algorithm of linear programming.[2] It determines in turn all the corner portfolios of the efficient frontier ending with $\hat{\mathbf{X}}$ next to the last, and finally the all-cash portfolio. Thus, if it is given that $\hat{\mathbf{X}}$, or a mixture of $\hat{\mathbf{X}}$ and cash, is the desired efficient portfolio then the critical line algorithm will generate a (possibly long) sequence of portfolios of which only the next to last one is of interest. This contrasts with the EGP procedure that directly computes $\hat{\mathbf{X}}$. (See also Christofi and Theodossiou [1995].)

But speed of computation is only part of the value of the EGP discovery. The other part is the insight it provides concerning the nature of $\hat{\mathbf{X}}$. For example, a basic lesson of portfolio theory is that one should think in terms of the portfolio as a whole. A portfolio which maximizes some criteria may or may not consist only of securities which have high or highest value of that criteria. For example, on the one hand (for the standard constraint set) the efficient portfolio that maximizes expected return E is a portfolio consisting of that security (or those securities) with maximum expected return; on the other hand the same is *not* true for geometric mean. (See Markowitz [1959], chapter 6.) But what can be said about the Sharpe ratio, $(E - r_f)/\sigma$? Does the portfolio that maximizes the latter necessarily consist of securities whose Sharpe ratios are greatest? What may we say to an investment manager who tries to maximize the Sharpe ratio of his or her portfolio by holding securities with maximum Sharpe ratio? Are there plausible assumptions that would make this optimum?

The efficient $\hat{\mathbf{X}}$ which mixes with cash is the one which maximizes the Sharpe ratio. EGP (1976) tells us that, when the constant correlation model holds, $\hat{\mathbf{X}}$ may be computed by ranking securities according to their Sharpe ratio, selecting all those above a certain cutoff point, then weighting them in the portfolio according to a formula that depends on more than the Sharpe ratio. Thus the manager who seeks a high Sharpe ratio for the portfolio by selecting securities with highest Sharpe ratio may be told that, implicitly at least, he or she is assuming the constant correlation model of covariance. He or she can also be advised to see EGP (1976) concerning where in the list of securities, ranked by Sharpe ratio, one should cut off, and how one should weight the securities selected.

But EGP (1976) also shows that it is not always true that the portfolio with highest Sharpe ratio contains securities with highest such. If the one-factor model is true then the EGP (1976) procedure starts by ranking securities according to $(E_i - r_f)/\beta_i$. In general this is not the same as ranking according to $(E_i - r_f)/\sigma_i$ unless β_i is proportional to σ_i.

EGP (1976) finds $\hat{\mathbf{X}}$ for a given r_f, and other parameters, for the one-factor and constant correlation models. EGP (1978) presents a procedure that traces out the entire efficient frontier by varying r_f and updating the EGP (1976) solution for that r_f. Personally, I am not convinced that the EGP (1978) procedure will compute the efficient frontier faster than the critical line algorithm taking full advantage of the diagonalized versions of the one-factor or constant correlation models.[3] The relative merits of the two algorithms on this problem remain to be determined.

Among the works in these two volumes, other than those cited above, my favorite is Elton, Gruber, and Rentzler (1989). Depending on tastes and interests, the reader will have her or his own favorites. The authors are to be thanked for assembling this collection so that we all can have our old favorites readily at hand, and have the opportunity to pursue new favorites. Also, the authors are to be much congratulated for a lifetime (more precisely, two lifetimes) of monumental contributions.

Notes

1. For, on the one hand, given any positive $\rho, \sigma_1, \sigma_2, \ldots \sigma_N$, equations (6) and (9) show that the one-factor model with $\sigma(u_i) = \sqrt{1-\rho}\sigma_i$, $V_F = \rho$ and $\beta_i = \sigma_i$ has the same relationship between the portfolio and its variance as does the constant correlation model with these parameters; and, conversely, if a one-factor model has

$$\beta_i = k\sigma(u_i) \qquad \text{for every } i$$

then $\text{cov}(r_i, r_j) = \beta_i\beta_j V_F$ for $i \neq j$, which is known for the one-factor model, and $\rho_{ij} = \text{cov}(r_i, r_j)/\sigma_i\sigma_j$, which is the definition of correlation, implies that all correlations are the same. We may always arrange for k to be nonnegative, by defining a new underlying factor $F^N = -F$, if necessary.

2. Special procedures must be instituted for starting the critical line algorithm if the simplex algorithm finds that feasible E is not bounded above, or that many portfolios maximize E. (See chapter 9 of Markowitz [1987]). Once thus started it proceeds as in the case of a unique E maximizing portfolio.

3. The diagonalized critical line calculation solves two linear equations in two unknowns to determine two Lagrangian multipliers. Given the latter, the formula for the critical line follows from a few arithmetic operations per "*IN*" variable. The coefficients of the two by two include sums such as $\sum_{i \in IN} \beta_i / Vu_i$. Note that the sum is over the i, which are "*IN*" on the particular critical line. Since only one i goes into or comes out of the *IN* set at each corner portfolio, these sums should be updated by adding or subtracting a term, rather than being added up from scratch, at each iteration. Since there is not too much else to do per iteration, this detail will materially affect the time required to compute the frontier for a large problem.

References

Christofi, A., and Theodossiou, P. (1995). "Simple Criteria for Optimal Portfolio Selection Revisited." *Advances in Mathematical Programming and Financial Planning* 4: 45–59.

Elton, E. J., Gruber, M. J. (1973). "Estimating the Dependence Structure of Share Prices—Implications for Portfolio Selection." *Journal of Finance* 28, no. 5 (December): 1203–1232.

Elton, E. J., Gruber, M. J., and Padberg, M. W. (1976). "Simple Criteria for Optimal Portfolio Selection." *Journal of Finance* 31, no. 5 (December): 1341–1357.

Elton, E. J., Gruber, M. J., and Padberg, M. W. (1978). "Simple Criteria for Optimal Portfolio Selection: Tracing Out the Efficient Frontier." *Journal of Finance* 33, no. 1 (March): 296–302.

Elton, E. J., Gruber, M. J., and Rentzler, J. (1989). "New Public Offerings, Information, and Investor Rationality: The Case of Publicly Offered Commodity Funds." *Journal of Business*, 62, no. 1: 1–16.

Markowitz, H. M. (1952). "Portfolio Selection." *Journal of Finance* 7, no. 1 (March): 77–91.

Markowitz, H. M. (1956). "The Optimization of a Quadratic Function Subject to Linear Constraints." *Naval Research Logistics Quarterly* 3: 111–133.

Markowitz, H. M. (1959). *Portfolio Selection: Efficient Diversification of Investments.* New Haven: Yale University Press, 1970.

Markowitz, H. M. (1987). *Mean-Variance Analysis in Portfolio Choice and Capital Markets.* New York: Basil Blackwell.

Perold, A. F. (1984). "Large-Scale Portfolio Optimization." *Management Science* 30, no. 10 (October): 1143–1160.

Sharpe, W. F. (1963). "A Simplified Model for Portfolio Analysis." *Management Science,* January.

Tobin, J. (1958). "Liquidity Preference as Behavior Towards Risk." *Review of Economic Studies,* February, 65–86.

Preface

We were very pleased when MIT Press approached us to put together a set of our favorite articles in the area of portfolio analysis and investments for this two-volume publication. We have written an introduction to each section of these volumes but decided to write a more personal overall introduction.

Many people have asked us about a collaboration that has lasted almost thirty-five years. We started working together in 1965, the year in which we both arrived at NYU, Marty from Columbia and Ned from Carnegie Mellon. NYU classes were primarily in the evening in those days, and a group of young faculty used to go to a local bar after teaching on Wednesday nights. Soon after we arrived the two of us had a major disagreement in the bar about the benefits of share repurchase. We each went home to write up our argument and this turned into our first article. By the way, in putting together these works we reread our first article and each of us still thinks he was right. This pattern has continued through our thirty-five years of working together. The partnership has remained productive because we approach problems differently and argue them through until both of us are convinced that we have the best answer. We discuss where we are going, work out theoretical problems, look at empirical results, and then divide up the writing of individual sections. We then attempt to rip each other's ideas apart. In a field where truth does not yet exist and there are only better answers and worse answers, we find that a collaboration of individuals with different attitudes and backgrounds who can remain friends through (at times) severe disagreements has been, and will continue to be, highly fruitful. Over the years we have published with several authors, many of them our Ph.D. students, who have enriched our research and made great contributions to our work. These include Vijay Bawa, Chris Blake, Jeff Busse, David Cho, Sanjiv Das, Seth Grossman, Mustafa Gultekin, Matt Hlavka, Paul Kleindorfer, Zvi

Lieber, John Lightstone, Roni Michaely, Suk Mo Koo, Prafulla Nabar, Manfred Padberg, Joel Rentzler, and Tom Urich.

We have also benefited from discussions with our doctoral students, with whom we did not directly collaborate. These include Dong-Hyun Ahn, George Allayannis, Andy Benartzy, Finbar Bradley, Lance Brofman, Lewis Chakrin, Tom Conine, Charles Ellis, Cheol Eun, Jim Farrell, Bob Ferguson, Jim Greenleaf, Allan Greenspan, George Handjinicolaou, Gabriel Hawawini, Jeff Heisler, Jingzhi Huang, Sung Wng Hwang, Alex Kane, Richard Kolodny, Mario Lavalee, Gerald Levin, Eric Lindenberg, Joshua Livnat, Massoud Mussavian, Jerry Pinto, William Remaley, Tavy Ronen, Meir Schneller, Jim Stanard, Olivier Tabutoni, Nick Travlos, and Irwin Vanderhoof.

We would like to thank Sue Cubberly for her excellent assistance in compiling the material for this book, Victoria Richardson at the MIT Press for her encouragement, and Depak Agrawal, George Comer, Chris Mann, and Barbara Remmers for help in preparation of the manuscript.

This book contains our favorite articles in the field of investments and portfolio management. We have not included the many articles that we wrote on corporate finance and regulation in the early days of our collaboration. We both started out teaching and doing research in corporate finance; over the years we switched to teaching investments. In the interest of space we have also had to exclude many articles on investments and portfolio analysis. In rereading our research we find that we still like almost all of the work we have published. In fact, each of us had forgotten some articles we wrote years ago; it was a pleasure to rediscover them.

We would like to thank some people who had a major impact on our work. Ned and Marty would like to thank our respective mentors, Kal Cohen and Rodger Murray, who first showed each of us the joys of financial research. Larry Ritter was Chairman when we arrived at NYU and, was a guide and major influence in shaping our professional careers. Finally, we would like to thank Harry Markowitz for discovering portfolio analysis, a field in which we have had so much fun.

We have divided our work into two volumes. Volume 1 contains papers on portfolio theory and management and asset pricing. Volume 2 contains papers on pricing of individual securities and performance evaluation.

Sources

1. "Estimating the Dependence Structure of Share Prices—Implications for Portfolio Selection." Reprinted with permission from the *Journal of Finance* 28, no. 5 (1973): 1203–1232.

2. "Are Betas Best?" Reprinted with permission from the *Journal of Finance* 33, no. 5 (1978): 1375–1384.

3. "A Multi-Index Risk Model of the Japanese Stock Market." Reprinted with permission from *Japan and the World Economy* 1, no. 1 (1988): 21–44.

4. "Do Investors Care About Sentiment?" Reprinted with permission from the *Journal of Business* 71, no. 4 (1998).

5. "Valuation and Asset Selection under Alternative Investment Opportunities." Reprinted with permission from the *Journal of Finance* 31, no. 2 (1976): 525–539.

6. "Simple Criteria for Optimal Portfolio Selection." Reprinted with permission from the *Journal of Finance* 31, no. 5 (1976): 1341–1357.

7. "Simple Criteria for Optimal Portfolio Selection: Tracing Out the Efficient Frontier." Reprinted with permission from the *Journal of Finance* 33, no. 1 (1978): 296–302.

8. "Simple Rules for Optimal Portfolio Selection: The Multi-Group Case." Reprinted with permission from the *Journal of Financial and Quantitative Analysis* 11, no. 3 (1977): 329–345.

9. "Simple Rules for Optimal Portfolio Selection in Stable Paretian Markets." Reprinted with permission from the *Journal of Finance* 34, no. 4 (1979): 1041–1047.

10. "Portfolio Analysis with Partial Information: The Case of Grouped Data." Reprinted with permission from *Management Science* 33, no. 10 (1987): 1238–1246.

11. "On the Maximization of the Geometric Mean with Log-Normal Return Distribution." Reprinted with permission from *Management Science* 21, no. 4 (1974): 483–488.

12. "Portfolio Theory When Investment Relatives Are Log-Normally Distributed." Reprinted with permission from the *Journal of Finance* 29, no. 4 (1974): 1265–1273.

13. "Optimal Investment Strategies with Investor Liabilities." Reprinted with permission from the *Journal of Banking and Finance* 16 (1992): 869–890.

14. "Portfolio Analysis with a Non-Normal Multi-Index Return Generating Process." Reprinted with permission from the *Review of Quantitative Finance and Accounting* 2 (1992): 5–16.

15. "Dynamic Programming Applications in Finance." Reprinted with permission from the *Journal of Finance* 26, no. 2 (1971): 473–506.

16. "On the Optimality of Some Multi-Period Portfolio Selection Criteria." Reprinted with permission from the *Journal of Business* 47, no. 2 (1974): 231–243.

17. "The Multi-Period Consumption Investment Problem and Single Period Analysis." Reprinted with permission from *Oxford Economic Papers* 26, no. 2 (1974): 289–301.

18. "Non-Standard C.A.P.M.s and the Market Portfolio." Reprinted with permission from the *Journal of Finance* 29, no. 3 (1984): 911–924.

19. "The Arbitrage Pricing Model and Returns on Assets under Uncertain Inflation." Reprinted with permission from the *Journal of Finance* 38, no. 2 (1983): 525–537.

20. "On the Robustness of the Roll and Ross Arbitrage Pricing Theory." Reprinted with permission from the *Journal of Financial and Quantitative Analysis* 19, no. 1 (1984): 1–10.

21. "Marginal Stockholder Tax Rates and the Clientele Effect." Reprinted with permission from the *Review of Economics and Statistics* 52, no. 1 (1970): 68–74.

22. "The Ex-Dividend Day Behavior of Stock Prices: A Re-Examination of the Clientele Effect: A Comment." Reprinted with permission from the *Journal of Finance* 39, no. 2 (1984): 551–556.

23. "A Simple Explanation of the Empirical Relationship between Dividend Yields and Deviations from the C.A.P.M." Reprinted with permission from the *Journal of Banking and Finance* 7 (1983): 135–146.

24. "Taxes and Portfolio Composition." Reprinted with permission from the *Journal of Financial Economics* 6 (1978): 399–410.

25. "Modern Portfolio Theory, 1950 to Date." Reprinted with permission from the *Journal of Banking and Finance* 21 (1997): 1743–1759.

I Inputs to Portfolio Management

In this section we explore some of our research on estimating inputs to the portfolio selection process. One type of input that is important in the portfolio area is estimates of the variance/covariance structure. We explore estimation of the variance/covariance matrix in the first chapter; at the time we wrote it, portfolio theory had rarely been implemented despite it having existed for many years. We felt that the principal hindrance to professionals we knew in portfolio manager positions was the difficult-to-impossible task of obtaining information. The covariance matrix was particularly troublesome. In this chapter we explored three types of models for estimating the covariance structure and the relationship of these models to each other. These classes of models are the full variance/covariance matrix, index models, and constant correlation models (either all correlations the same or the same within a subgroup). In estimating these models we continued our interest in using principal component solutions (see volume 2) to estimate index models. In this chapter and in our work in earnings (see volume 2), we pioneered its use in the finance area. There are several aspects that are worth special mention. First, we explored constructing groups of firms that behaved alike insofar as patterns of returns are concerned. This foreshadowed our latter work on clustering and creating pseudo industries (groups of firms that behave alike). Second, in comparing techniques we examined how the portfolios selected, using the different forecasting techniques, performed (at various risk levels) in addition to an examination of forecast errors per se. We found that the models that used constant correlation coefficients led to better portfolios than other types of models.

In the second chapter we concentrate on various alternative ways of estimating beta and the accuracy of these alternatives in forecasting the correlation coefficient between securities. There are two aspects that are worthy of special mention. First, forecast error was normally judged by simply looking at the significance of the mean forecasting error (either absolute value or squared error) between techniques. We introduced an alternative measure that relied on stochastic dominance. In particular, if for any size error, technique A has a lower probability of larger errors than technique B, then A can be said to dominate B. While this is a more stringent criterion than comparing mean errors, its advantage is that it does not depend on any specific preference function; it is just that smaller errors are better than larger. When mean squared errors or absolute errors are compared, an explicit preference function is being used (although rarely is this mentioned). We also showed that standard beta adjustment techniques such as Vasichek or Blume bias the mean of the distribution of forecasted correlations and that readjusting the mean of the forecasted correlations to historical levels improves the forecast.

The third and fourth chapters represent examples of our development of multi-index models for capturing return-generating processes. In the third chapter we used statistical techniques to extract factors for the Japanese stock market. Of special interest is how we examined the reasonableness of these factors. While we used several techniques, two stand out as particularly interesting. First, we examined the reasonableness by testing each model's performance in replicating an index using alternative numbers of securities. In particular, we compared the tracking error of the four-index model to simpler models in a forecast mode. Second, we were able to relate the factors to economic variables.

The fourth chapter examines the importance of a specific index, sentiment, in the return-generating process. There has been substantial research showing that the discount on closed-end mutual funds was a measure of investor sentiment and a priced factor. We show that using a multi-index model sentiment is not important and that it appeared important only because other indexes were not included. The second section discusses one of our valuation articles. We decided not to include most of our work in corporate finance because much of it was done in our early years. This chapter is one of the exceptions. We included it because the issues it deals with are still relevant, and there are no recent articles that are an improvement. In it we examine standard stock valuation models. We show that implicit in each model is an assumption about how the firm's investment schedule changes over time.

Dependence Structure

1

Estimating the Dependence Structure of Share Prices—Implications for Portfolio Selection

Edwin J. Elton and Martin J. Gruber

A well defined theoretical structure for portfolio analysis has existed since 1952 [18]. Yet despite the large amount of both theoretical and empirical research which followed Markowitz's pioneering work, portfolio theory has rarely been implemented.[1]

Perhaps the major reason for this lies in the nature of the inputs required for portfolio analysis. If *accurate* expectations about future mean returns for each security, the variance of the returns for each security, and the correlation of returns between each pair of securities could be obtained, then Markowitz's model, employing Quadratic Programming, would produce optimum portfolios.[2] The problem lies in obtaining accurate expectations of the three types of inputs needed for this model. This problem is particularly acute with respect to the matrix of correlations between securities. While the problem of estimating means and variances is not a trivial one, it is one that has received a lot of attention. The random walk literature specifies that the best estimate of future mean returns and variances for any stock is historical means and variances (the random walk theory assumes that the distribution of returns for any stock is stable over time).[3] On the other hand, most analysts believe that they can form expectations about future mean returns (how well a stock will perform) and variances (how sure they are about their forecasts).

While a great deal of attention has been paid to estimating means and variances, little attention has been paid to the problem of estimating correlations. The analyst has a difficult time producing direct estimates of correlations for two reasons. First, a large number of estimates are involved. To obtain efficient portfolios from among 200 stocks, 19,900 correlation coefficients would have to be produced. Second, and perhaps more important, there is no non-overlapping organizational structure that will allow security analysts to produce estimates of correlation coefficients between all pairs of stocks. Each analyst in a financial institution follows a subset of the stocks in which the institution has an interest. Who then can produce correlations between stocks followed by different analysts? The analyst also has a difficult time obtaining indirect estimates of correlation coefficients. For example, the analyst could obtain estimates of correlation coefficients by first estimating the parameters of a single or multi-index model. Contained in these estimates is an implied forecast of correlation coefficients. Although some organizations have made attempts in this direction, it seems unlikely that most analysts can think in these terms and even when they are trained to do so that their estimates will necessarily be superior to more mechanical procedures.[4] Despite these problems (except for some indirect tests of the Sharpe model [23]), the literature in finance has paid almost no attention to the accuracy of techniques used for estimating the correlation structure of share prices.[5]

In this paper, we shall be concerned with estimating the correlation matrix of stock returns. Because of the difficulties of getting subjective estimates, we shall be concerned with estimates prepared from historical data. Estimates will be compared both with respect to their ability to forecast correlation matrixes and with respect to their ability to choose portfolios which prove to be efficient in future periods.

This paper is divided into two sections. Section I discusses the general types of forecasting models that could be used, their characteristics, and the variants of each model we tested. Section II presents the empirical results.

I The Forecasting Models

This section presents three types of models which can be used for estimating future correlation coefficients: a full historical data model, index models and averaging models. The discussion will emphasize differences in the assumptions underlying each model as well as how each model can be used to forecast.

A A Full Historical Model

The simplest method of estimating future correlation coefficients using historical data is to assume that past values of these coefficients are useful estimates of their future values. In short, calculate each pairwise correlation coefficient over a historical period and use this value as an estimate of the future. No assumptions are made as to how or why any pair of securities might move together. Instead, the amount of their co-movement is estimated directly. This is one of the models we analyzed. In the discussion of results, it is referred to as the Historical Model.

An alternative to direct estimate of correlation coefficients is to assume a behavioral model of why securities move together; estimate the parameters of this model using historical data; and then use this behavioral model to estimate the future correlation coefficients.

B *Index Models*

Index models can usefully be classified according to whether returns are assumed to depend on one index or on a group of indices.

1 Single Index Models

The simplest behavioral model was developed by Sharpe [23], following a suggestion by Markowitz [19]. Sharpe assumes that securities move together only because of a common response to changes in an aggregate index. Let:

R_i be the return on security i;

I_1 be the return of the aggregate index;

A_i the return of a security i that is independent of changes in the aggregate index;

B_{i1} a measure of the responsiveness of security i to changes in the aggregate index;

e_i a variable with mean of zero and variance σ_i^2 which measures the variability of security i that is not attributable to changes in the aggregate index;

A_{N+1} a constant equal to the expected return of the aggregate index;

e_{N+1} a variable with mean of zero and variance of $\sigma_{N+1}^2 \cdot \sigma_{N+1}^2$ measures the variability of the aggregate index.

Then Sharpe's model can be written as:

$$R_i = A_i + B_{i1} I_1 + e_i$$

$$I_1 = A_{N+1} + e_{N+1}$$

$$E(e_{N+1} e_i) = 0 \qquad i = 1, \ldots, N$$

$$E(e_i e_j) = 0 \qquad i = 1, \ldots, N \text{ and } j = 1, \ldots, N \text{ and } i \neq j.$$

It is easy to show that estimates of the mean returns and variance of returns (for individual securities) produced by the Sharpe model are identical to those produced by a direct estimation of their level using historical data. Estimates of the correlation coefficient are, however, different. If $E[\ ]$ is the expected value operator, then the covariance between security i and security j using the Sharpe model can be expressed as:

$$E[(r_i - E(r_i))(r_j - E(r_j))] = B_{i1}B_{j1}\sigma^2_{N+1} + B_{i1}E(e_{N+1}e_j) + B_{j1}E(e_{N+1}e_i) + E(e_ie_j).$$

The correlation coefficient between security i and security j is the above divided by the product of the standard deviations of security i and security j. If the parameters of the model are estimated using least squares regression, then the second and third terms of the equation above are zero by construction, since the expected value of the residuals of a regression are independent of the value assumed by the independent variables. However, there is nothing in the estimation of the parameters that guarantees that the fourth term is zero. In fact, one would expect in general that it would be non-zero. The assumption that $E(e_ie_j) = 0$ is the only difference between estimation using the Sharpe model and estimation using full historical data. Insofar as the behavioral assumption made by Sharpe is a perfect representation of reality (i.e., $E(e_ie_j) = 0$) obtaining the returns, variances, and correlation coefficients directly or by estimating the behavioral model produces identical results. If, however, the behavioral model is an approximation but not perfect representation of reality, a choice exists. If that part of the correlation structure that is not captured by the Sharpe model

$$\frac{E(e_ie_j)}{\sigma_i\sigma_j}$$

is stable over time, then estimating this part of the matrix from past data might be useful. If it is unstable, then ignoring it might lead to better forecasts of future correlation coefficients (e.g., assuming that zero is a better estimate of its future value than the previous level). A third possibility exists. Perhaps the term $E(e_ie_j)$ has a stable component(s) plus random noise. This possibility will be discussed below under the heading of multi-index models.

Two versions of the single index model were tested. These differed in the choice of index. One choice was the Standard and Poor Industrial Index adjusted for dividends. This has appeal both because it is a broad based market index and because it is the index which has most commonly been used for single index models.[6] We have called this model the Standard Single Index or SSI model. The second single index model used an index that was specific to the sample of stocks used in this study. More specifically, we employed the first principal component of the historical correlation matrix. This is the index which best explains the variance in the past correlation matrix for our sample. This model is identified as F-1 throughout the remainder of the paper.

2 Multi-index Models

An alternative behavioral model assumes that securities move together, partly because of economy wide charges and partly because of their association with some subgroup in the economy.[7] These subgroups could be industries or they could be aggregate groups such as durables, nondurables, or other groupings. One version of a multi-index model is:

$$R_i = A_i + B_{i1}I_1 + B_{i2}I_2 + \cdots + B_{im}I_m + \varepsilon_i \qquad i = 1, \ldots, N$$

$$I_k = A_{N+k} + \varepsilon_{N+k} \qquad k = 1, \ldots, m$$

$$E(\varepsilon_i \varepsilon_{N+k}) = 0 \qquad i = 1, \ldots, N \text{ and } k = 1, \ldots, m$$

$$E(\varepsilon_i \varepsilon_j) = 0 \qquad i = 1, \ldots, N \text{ and } j = 1, \ldots, N \text{ and } i \neq j$$

$$E(\varepsilon_{N+k} \varepsilon_{N+p}) = 0 \qquad k = 1, \ldots, m \text{ and } p = 1, \ldots, m \text{ and } k \neq p$$

where:

B_{ki} is a measure of responsiveness of security i to changes in index k;

I_k is an aggregate index if $k = 1$ and is an index of subgroup movements otherwise;

ε_i is a variable with mean of zero and variance $\sigma_i^2 \cdot \sigma_i^2$ measures the variability of security i that is not attributable to changes in any index;

ε_{N+k} is a variable with mean of zero and variance $\sigma_{N+k}^2 \cdot \sigma_{N+k}^2$ measures the variability of the index k; and other terms as before.

Once again, estimates of expected returns and variances (for each security) produced by this model using historical estimation of the parameters would be identical to the estimates obtained using full historical estimation and therefore, would, of course, be equal to the estimates obtained from the Sharpe model. Again, letting $E[\ ]$ be the expected value operator, the covariance between security i and security j is:

$$\begin{aligned} E[(r_i - E(r_i))(r_j - E(r_j))] &= [B_{i1}B_{j1}\sigma^2_{N+1} + B_{i2}B_{j2}\sigma^2_{N+2} + \cdots + B_{im}B_{jm}\sigma^2_{N+m}] \\ &\quad + [B_{i1}B_{j2}E(\varepsilon_{N+1}\varepsilon_{N+2}) + B_{i1}B_{j3}E(\varepsilon_{N+1}\varepsilon_{N+3}) \\ &\quad + \cdots + B_{iN+k-1}B_{jN+k}E(\varepsilon_{N+k-1}\varepsilon_{N+k})] \\ &\quad + [B_{i1}E(\varepsilon_j\varepsilon_{N+1}) + \cdots + B_{iN}E(\varepsilon_j\varepsilon_{N+1}) \\ &\quad + B_{j1}E(\varepsilon_i\varepsilon_{N+1}) + \cdots + B_{jN}E(\varepsilon_j\varepsilon_{N+1})] + [E(\varepsilon_i\varepsilon_j)]. \end{aligned}$$

The correlation between security i and security j is the above divided by $\sigma_i\sigma_j$. The above expression has been divided by brackets into four types of terms. As before, the third set of terms is zero by construction if the parameter estimates are obtained by least squares regression. Furthermore, if the indices are constructed so they are orthogonal to one another (as we did in a manner to be discussed shortly), then the second set of bracketed terms is also zero by construction. In general, many of the first set of terms would be zero since a particular stock need not be related to all indices.

The final term need not be zero and, in fact, estimates of it using historical data would normally be non-zero. The assumption that $E(\varepsilon_i\varepsilon_j) = 0$ is the only difference between estimates from the multi-index model and estimates obtained directly from pair-wise calculations using full historical data. If the assumption were true in practice, then no difference would exist in any of the estimates produced by the two models. The multi-index model and the single index model differ in their assumption as to what is zero. The single index model assumes no interaction except that caused by a common market movement or $E(e_ie_j) = 0$. The multi-index model splits $E(e_ie_j)$ into interaction due to movements of subgroups $[B_{i2}B_{j2}\sigma^2_{N+2} + \cdots + B_{im}B_{jm}\sigma^2_{N+m}]$, and a residual $E(\varepsilon_i\varepsilon_j)$. Only the residual is assumed zero. These considerations are summarized in Table 1.1 below. Which of these models performs best will depend on whether zero or the historical level is a better estimate of the future values of the subgroup indexes and the residuals.

The multi-index models were obtained by extracting additional indexes from the principal components solution of the historical correlation matrix.[8] Three multi-index models were tested. The first two were a 3 and 8 index model which will be referred to as F-3 and F-8. These were selected because the per cent of variance explained dropped sharply with

Table 1.1
Correlation terms

1. Full historical (direct pairwise estimation)

$$\frac{[B_{i1}B_{j1}\sigma_{N+1}^2]}{\sigma_i\sigma_j} + \frac{[B_{i2}B_{j2}\sigma_{N+2}^2 + \cdots + B_{im}B_{jm}\sigma_{N+m}^2]}{\sigma_i\sigma_j} + \frac{[E(\varepsilon_i\varepsilon_j)]}{\sigma_i\sigma_j}$$

2. Multi-index

$$\frac{[B_{i1}B_{j1}\sigma_{N+1}^2]}{\sigma_i\sigma_j} + \frac{[B_{i2}B_{j2}\sigma_{N+2}^2 + \cdots + B_{im}B_{jm}\sigma_{N+m}^2]}{\sigma_i\sigma_j} + 0$$

3. Single index

$$\frac{[B_{i1}B_{j1}\sigma_{N+1}^2]}{\sigma_i\sigma_j} + 0 + 0$$

Table 1.2
Firms in sample by industry

2800	Chemical	18 firms
2830	Drug	10 firms
2912	Oil	12 firms
3310	Steel companies	17 firms
3550	Special machinery	7 firms
3560	General machinery	6 firms
3714	Automobile parts	6 firms
Total		76 firms

the fourth and again with the 9th index. In addition, the 8 index model is interesting because, as will be discussed shortly, we had 7 industries and an 8 index model is of the same dimensionality as a model including a market index and one index for each of the 7 industries. The final multi-index model was determined by preserving those components whose eigenvalue is greater than 1.[9] In all cases this left us with 17 or 18 indices.[10] (see Table 1.2) Results from this model will be referred to as F-max throughout the rest of the paper.

C *Mean Models*

An alternative to the models presented earlier is to argue that historical data only contain information concerning the mean correlation coefficients and that observed pair-wise differences are random or sufficiently unstable, so that zero is a better estimate (than their historical level) of their future value. The most aggregate averaging possible is to set every correlation coefficient equal to the average of all correlation coefficients. This is one of the models we tested and is referred to as the overall mean model. This type of aggregate averaging could be thought of as a naive model which can be used to evaluate the more complex models discussed earlier. The use of such a naive model is a common feature of much of the forecast evaluation literature (see Cragg and Malkiel [4], Elton and Gruber [5], and Kessel [15]). Alternatively, if the assumption of $E(e_i e_j) = 0$ in the single index model held, then the overall mean model is the same as a constrained form of the single index model where the correlation of every firm with the market is assumed to be the same. To understand what this implies, examine the single index model. The response of the firms return to a change in the return of the market is given by

$$B_{i1} = \frac{\rho_{iN+1}\sigma_i\sigma_{N+1}}{\sigma_{N+1}^2} = \frac{\rho_{iN+1}}{\sigma_{N+1}}\sigma_i$$

where ρ_{iN+1} is the correlation coefficient between the return on stock i and the market. All other symbols are as before. Setting ρ_{iN+1} equal to a constant for all firms means that B_{i1} is directly proportional to σ_i.[11] A more disaggregated mean model would be to assume that there is a common mean only within subgroups and that this mean could vary between subgroups. This latter pattern is represented pictorially in Figure 1.1.

The correlation data are partitioned into 3 groups. Consider group 1. Within the group all firms have a common correlation coefficient with one another represented by μ_1. The between group correlation between group 1 and any other group is also the same for all members of each group. It is given by μ_{12} between groups 1 and 2 and μ_{13} between groups 1 and 3. In short, firms within the same group have a common correlation structure with all other firms. We tested three forms of this model. First, we assumed the SIC industrial classification really represented homogeneous groups and averaged within and between these groups.[12] We called this the Traditional Mean Model. The last two averaging models are similar to the Traditional Mean averaging model except that, rather than accepting traditional industries as homogeneous groups, multi-variate techniques

	1	2	3
1	μ_1	μ_{12}	μ_{13}
2	μ_{12}	μ_2	μ_{23}
3	μ_{13}	μ_{23}	μ_3

Figure 1.1
Structure of mean models

were employed to determine which groups had behaved as homogeneous units. We called these homogeneous units pseudo-industries. As in the case of traditional industries, averaging was performed both within and between pseudo-industries. Two pseudo-industry models were tried.[13] One model contained three pseudo-industries (identified as Pseudo-3 or P-3) and one involved seven pseudo-industries (identified as Pseudo-7 or P-7).

To review, we have examined 10 models:

Name	Description
I. Historical Model	Assumes future correlation coefficients are identical to past coefficients.
II. Single Index	
A. SSI	Index is S&P index adjusted for dividends.
B. F-1	Index is first component of principal component solution.
III. Multiple Index	
A. F-3	Indices are first 3 components from principle component solution.
B. F-8	Indices are 8 components from principle component solution.
C. F-Max	Indices are first 17 or 18 components from principle component solution.
IV. Mean Model	
A. Overall Mean	Assumes same correlation coefficient between all firms.
B. Traditional Mean	Assumes same pattern of correlation coefficients within an industry.
C. P-3	Assumes same pattern of correlation coefficients within 3 pseudo-industries.
D. P-7	Assumes same pattern of correlation coefficients within 7 pseudo-industries.

II Empirical Results

In evaluating the accuracy of alternative forecasting techniques, one always has two criteria: statistical significance and economic significance. To evaluate statistical significance, the ability of each of our techniques

Table 1.3
Sample periods

Historical data	Forecast period
A. 5-year forecast	
1. June 1948–June 1958	June 1958–June 1963
2. June 1953–June 1963	June 1963–June 1968
B. 1-year forecast	
1. June 1948–June 1958	June 1958–June 1959
2. June 1953–June 1963	June 1963–June 1964
3. June 1956–June 1966	June 1966–June 1967

to forecast future correlation matrices will be examined. Economic significance will be analyzed by using the forecasted correlation coefficients as inputs to a portfolio selection model and examining the expost performance of portfolios to see if differences between techniques are of economic importance.

Because we are interested in testing forecasting accuracy over different time spans, both one and five year estimates of correlation matrices will be made. In order to see if our results are consistent over time, two separate five year and three separate one year forecasts will be studied. The time periods involved in each of these forecasts are shown in Table 1.3. In discussing the statistical significance of the forecasts, we will present results from each of these time periods as well as from a combined five year sample and a combined one year sample.

The sample employed for this study consisted of 240 monthly rate of return observations for each of 76 firms for the period of June 1948–June 1968.[14] These 76 firms were members of 7 traditional industries.[15]

A Five Year Results—Statistical Information

The first step in our analysis of performance is to examine directly how well each model actually forecasts future correlation matrices. To do so, we will primarily employ tests of the statistical significance of the difference in absolute forecast error between techniques (Tables 1.5 and 1.10), and comparisons of the cumulative frequency of forecast error (Tables 1.6, 1.7, and 1.8).[16]

The first model discussed above was the full Historical model. Before discussing the accuracy of forecasts produced by this model, it might be worthwhile to examine the Historical correlation to see if the order of data in its cells contains any information. To do this, 30 correlation matrices were formed for each of two five year forecast periods by randomly rearranging the entries in the Historical correlation matrix. The mean absolute error for each of these 30 matrices for each of the two five year forecast periods is presented in Table 1.4. Not only does each of the randomly arranged correlation matrices produce larger average absolute errors than the Historical correlation matrix, each produces forecasts which are considerably worse than any of the ten techniques under study. Thus, the Historical correlation matrix contains some useful information about the individual correlations between firms.[17] (See Tables 1.5, 1.6, 1.7, and 1.8.)

In each five year sample and in the combined sample, the SSI model outperformed the Full Historical model. The fact that SSI always beats the Historical correlation matrix (the difference being significant at the .05 level in two out of three cases) indicates that estimating that part of the correlation between stocks which is not due to common correlation with the market at zero is better than estimating it at its historical level.[20] This is quite interesting, for the SSI technique was originally defended on the grounds of computational efficiency under the assumption that it would lead to inferior forecasts. Here we see that it actually produces better forecasts of future correlation matrices than the full Historical correlation matrix.

Both SSI and F-1 consistently outperform the multi-index models (F-3, F-8, and F-max). The differences in the case of SSI are statistically significant in both five-year samples and the combined five-year sample. While the multi-index models explain a greater percentage of the historical correlation between the stocks in our sample (see note 10), they lead to worse predictions. It seems that all adding indices to a single index model does is pick up random noise. In other words, assuming that the correlation between stocks not due to common correlation with a single market index is zero, is better than trying to predict it from the *historical* correlation of the residuals.[21]

SSI consistently outperforms F-1 at a statistically significant level. The difference between these two single index techniques is that F-1 is based on that single index which best explains the historical correlation between the stocks in our sample rather than on a more broadly based market index. The fact that the more broadly based market index performed better indicates that the correlation between stocks is better estimated on the basis of broad market influences rather than influences which are specific to a sample of stocks.

Table 1.4
Average absolute error random portfolios

	First five-year	Second five-year	First one-year	Second one-year	Third one-year
1	0.1752	0.1780	0.3435	0.3124	0.2398
2	0.1762	0.1790	0.3406	0.3151	0.2432
3	0.1791	0.1789	0.3404	0.3167	0.2420
4	0.1786	0.1763	0.3461	0.3127	0.2420
5	0.1771	0.1800	0.3381	0.3130	0.2427
6	0.1784	0.1785	0.3410	0.3145	0.2456
7	0.1774	0.1785	0.3432	0.3163	0.2411
8	0.1795	0.1796	0.3436	0.3131	0.2417
9	0.1785	0.1785	0.3428	0.3154	0.2460
10	0.1798	0.1782	0.3415	0.3156	0.2440
11	0.1794	0.1786	0.3454	0.3155	0.2417
12	0.1791	0.1773	0.3403	0.3111	0.2446
13	0.1830	0.1778	0.3449	0.3090	0.2443
14	0.1803	0.1744	0.3420	0.3102	0.2425
15	0.1816	0.1797	0.3457	0.3139	0.2436
16	0.1800	0.1778	0.3451	0.3191	0.2411
17	0.1798	0.1776	0.3425	0.3149	0.2451
18	0.1762	0.1781	0.3401	0.3133	0.2399
19	0.1789	0.1765	0.3408	0.3140	0.2411
20	0.1764	0.1795	0.3396	0.3179	0.2455
21	0.1792	0.1789	0.3421	0.3123	0.2421
22	0.1793	0.1792	0.3425	0.3122	0.2443
23	0.1814	0.1770	0.3422	0.3149	0.2409
24	0.1794	0.1776	0.3461	0.3114	0.2431
25	0.1793	0.1780	0.3409	0.3135	0.2460
26	0.1767	0.1770	0.3401	0.3146	0.2404
27	0.1773	0.1783	0.3396	0.3160	0.2416
28	0.1796	0.1783	0.3450	0.3181	0.2429
29	0.1767	0.1814	0.3412	0.3160	0.2443
30	0.1778	0.1775	0.3409	0.3099	0.2413

Table 1.5
Five-year forecasts[18]: average absolute error (unadjusted)

First five-year		Second five-year		Combined five-year	
1 Industry mean	.1199	1 Pseudo-3	.1291	1 Industry mean	.1281
2 Pseudo-3	.1309	2 Pseudo-7	.1329	2 Pseudo-3	.1300
3 Overall mean	.1310	3 Overall mean	.1337	3 Overall mean	.1373
4 SSI	.1427	4 SSI	.1355	4 SSI	.1390
5 Full historical	.1440	5 Industry mean	.1363	5 Pseudo-7	.1391
6 Pseudo-7	.1454	6 F-1	.1477	6 F-1	.1467
7 F-1	.1458	7 F-3	.1485	7 Full historical	.1473
8 F-maximum	.1468	8 Full historical	.1506	8 F-3	.1502
9 F-3	.1520	9 F-8	.1521	9 F-maximum	.1506
10 F-8	.1594	10 F-maximum	.1543	10 F-8	.1558

Table 1.6
Dominance by cumulative frequency function[19]: first five-year

	F-8	F-3	F-17	F-1	Hist.	P-7	SSI	P-3	Ovrl.	Ind. mean
F-8	×									
F-3	25	×								
F-17	25	25	×							
F-1	25	25	$17\frac{1}{2}$	×						
Hist.	25	25	22	$18\frac{1}{2}$	×					
P-7	25	25	$18\frac{1}{2}$	20	$16\frac{1}{2}$	×				
SSI	25	25	22	19	19	18	×			
P-3	25	25	25	$22\frac{1}{2}$	25	24	24	×		
Overall	25	25	25	25	25	25	25	$21\frac{1}{2}$	×	
Ind. mean	25	25	25	25	25	25	25	25	25	×
Max.	25	25	25	25	25	25	25	25	25	25

Table 1.7
Dominance by cumulative frequency function[19]: second five-year

	F-18	F-8	Full hist.	F-3	F-1	Ind. mean	SSI	Ovr. mean	P-7	P-3
F-18										
F-8	19½									
Full historical	24	19								
F-3	23	21	22							
F-1	25	24½	23	18						
Industry mean	25	25	25	25	25					
SSI	25	25	25	25	25	16½				
Overall mean	25	25	25	25	25	23	21			
P-7	25	25	25	25	25	19	14	15		
P-3	25	25	25	25	25	25	24	18½	24	
Max.	25	25	25	25	25	25	25	25	25	25

Table 1.8
Dominance by cumulative frequency function: combined five-years

	F-8	F-max.	F-3	Full hist.	F-1	P-7	SSI	Ovrl. mean	P-3	Inds. mean
F-8										
F-max.	25									
F-3	25	15½								
Full historical	25	24	25							
F-1	25	24½	25	15½						
P-7	25	25	25	25	25					
SSI	25	25	25	25	25	16				
Overall mean	25	25	25	25	25	25	25			
P-3	25	25	25	25	25	25	25	22½		
Industry mean	25	25	25	25	25	25	25	24½	21½	
Max.	25	25	25	25	25	25	25	25	25	25

Table 1.9
Average correlation coefficient

	One-year			Five-year	
	First	Second	Third	First	Second
Actual	.1085	.1715	.2921	.3560	.2895
Overall mean	.3549	.3419	.3203	.3549	.3419
Industry mean	.3549	.3419	.3203	.3549	.3419
Pseudo-3	.3549	.3419	.3203	.3549	.3419
Pseudo-7	.3549	.3419	.3203	.3549	.3419
SSI	.3006	.2918	.2770	.3006	.2918
F-1	.3884	.3492	.3276	.3884	.3492
F-3	.3871	.3485	.3269	.3871	.3485
F-8	.3854	.3472	.3257	.3854	.3472
F-max	.3581	.3451	.3239	.3581	.3451
Historical	.3549	.3419	.3203	.3549	.3419

Three techniques produced better estimates of future correlation coefficients than SSI. These are: Overall Mean, P-3, and Traditional Mean. Overall Mean outperformed SSI in both 5-year samples and the combined samples (2 of the 3 being statistically significant).[22] In addition, the odds of an error of any size was always less with Overall Mean when the results from the two samples were combined.[23]

Allowing differences in the correlation between stocks to enter the model on either statistical grounds (Pseudo-3) or on the grounds of industrial structure (Traditional Mean) leads to an additional improvement in the results.[24] P-3 outperformed the Overall Mean model in all samples with the difference being statistically significant in the second 5-year and combined 5-year sample.[25] The Traditional Mean model performed better than Overall Mean at a statistically significant level in the first 5-year and combined samples, and while it performed slightly worse in the second 5-year sample, the result was not statistically significant.[26]

Before turning to 1-year forecasts, there is another point which should be discussed. Full Historic, Overall Mean, Industry Mean, P-3, and P-7 all make the same estimate of the average correlation between stocks. The same is not true of the remaining models. The mean correlation produced by these models can be below or above the mean historic correlation coefficient. Table 1.9 presents the average correlation coefficient predicted by each model for each forecast period. A forecast method might appear

Table 1.10
Five-year forecast errors[18]: average absolute error (adjusted)

First five-year		Second five-year		Combined five-year	
1 Industry mean	.1200	1 Pseudo-3	.1291	1 Industry mean	.1281
2 Pseudo-3	.1309	2 Pseudo-7	.1329	2 Pseudo-3	.1300
3 Overall mean	.1310	3 Overall mean	.1337	3 Overall mean	.1323
4 SSI	.1349	4 Industry mean	.1363	4 SSI	.1374
5 F-1	.1427	5 SSI	.1406	5 Pseudo-8	.1391
6 Full historical	.1440	6 F-1	.1460	6 F-1	.1443
7 Pseudo 7	.1455	7 F-3	.1468	7 Full historical	.1473
8 F-maximum	.1468	8 Full historical	.1506	8 F-3	.1481
9 F-3	.1494	9 F-8	.1507	9 F-max.	.1501
10 F-8	.1570	10 F-maximum	.1535	10 F-8	.1539

superior because it captures the mean level of the future correlation coefficients while doing a poor job of estimating differences in the correlation between firms. To test this we have constructed Table 1.10 (and Table 1.16) which is identical to Table 1.5 (and Table 1.14), except that the correlation matrix for each technique has been adjusted so that all techniques will forecast the same average correlation coefficients.[27]

For the 5-year forecasts, the relative performance of techniques is virtually the same as that described above whether the mean adjustment is made or not. The reason for this can easily be seen by examining the evident stability of 5-year average correlation coefficients (particularly as contrasted to 1-year average coefficients) presented in Tables 1.9 and 1.11.[28]

B *Five Year Results—Economic Significance*

Up to this point we have attempted to differentiate between forecasting techniques on their ability to produce accurate estimates of a future correlation matrix. Now we would like to differentiate between them on their ability to aid in the selection of more efficient portfolios.

In more detail, what we have done is to generate a set of predicted efficient portfolios using each of our estimates of the future correlation matrix plus actual ex-post values of returns and variances and then examined how efficient these portfolios really were in the ex-post period. Our procedure can be viewed as an answer to the following question: Given the

Table 1.11
Comparison of mean correlation coefficients

	Mean	Standard deviation	Range
1 year correlation	.3411	.088	.1085–.4882
5 year correlation	.3452	.033	.2903–.3820

best possible estimates of means and variances, which estimates of the correlation matrix gives rise to the selection of the most efficient portfolios?[29] The ordering of techniques in selecting ex-post efficient portfolios can be different from the ordering in predicting the ex-post correlation matrices, for only a small subset of the securities under study will enter into efficient portfolios.

For the 5-year forecasts, ex-post performances of portfolios in the efficient set, selected by each forecasting technique, are shown for various ex-post risk levels in Table 1.12. To aid in interpretation, Table 1.13 shows the relative rank of each technique at different risk levels. The ordering of techniques is similar to but not identical with the ordering obtained by directly comparing forecast errors.

The best three techniques are Overall Mean, Traditional Mean, and P-3. While the order of these three techniques is different from what it was in terms of forecast error (now Overall Mean is best with Traditional Mean and Pseudo-3 performing almost identically), the difference in return from employing any of these techniques is quite small. For example, at a risk level of .0375, the difference between return from the Overall Mean and the Traditional Mean is less than 30¢ per $100 invested per year, while between the Traditional Mean and Pseudo-3, it is less than 5¢ per $100 invested per year.[30] Thus, if we had chosen the Traditional Mean model which our earlier works indicated was best, we would have only sacrificed a return of 30¢ per $100 invested per year at the .0375 risk level. In fact, the largest return we would have sacrificed by choosing this criteria at any risk level was 50¢ per $100 per year.

The Sharpe technique is ranked fourth under both evaluation procedures. The difference between using the Sharpe technique and the worst of the three averaging techniques is much more significant ($5.40 per $100 per year at the .035 risk level or a percentage charge in return of 25%). While there is some crossing of performance for the four intermediate techniques (P-7, F-1, F-8, and F-3), the two worst techniques (Historic and F-Max) can be clearly identified. The fact that these techniques perform worse in selecting efficient portfolios than they do in forecasting the

Table 1.12
First five years

Risk level	Actual	Overall mean	Pseudo-3	Traditional mean	SSI	Pseudo-7	F-1	F-8	F-3	Historical	F-18
0.027500	1.011681										
0.028000	1.012232										
0.028500	1.012740										
0.029000	1.013213										
0.029500	1.013643	1.007590	1.007551								
0.030000	1.014044	1.008498	1.008404	1.008566							
0.030500	1.014421	1.009988	1.009322	1.009579							
0.031000	1.014773	1.010844	1.010218	1.010392							
0.031500	1.015102	1.011519	1.010958	1.011144	1.008681		1.007380				
0.032000	1.015415	1.012131	1.011678	1.011872	1.009150		1.008017	1.006814	1.006978		
0.032500	1.015713	1.012764	1.012306	1.012494	1.009696		1.008580	1.007634	1.007622	1.008667	
0.033000	1.015999	1.013400	1.012965	1.013050	1.010183	1.008212	1.009132	1.008279	1.008190	1.009080	
.033500	1.016274	1.013948	1.013556	1.013560	1.010631	1.008960	1.009644	1.008821	1.008705	1.009446	
0.034000	1.016542	1.014420	1.014061	1.014044	1.011053	1.009614	1.010106	1.009313	1.009216	1.009789	1.009374
0.034500	1.016802	1.014832	1.014509	1.014481	1.011456	1.010199	1.010530	1.009749	1.009738	1.010142	1.009661
0.035000	1.017054	1.015204	1.014918	1.014866	1.011838	1.010738	1.010979	1.010206	1.010243	1.010475	1.009929
0.035500	1.017299	1.015554	1.015291	1.015219	1.012235	1.011191	1.011406	1.010675	1.010697	1.010791	1.010182
0.036000	1.017538	1.015884	1.015635	1.015585	1.012644	1.011549	1.011810	1.011136	1.011126	1.011087	1.010423
0.036500	1.017772	1.016195	1.015962	1.015934	1.013038	1.011891	1.012202	1.011594	1.011539	1.011367	1.010683
0.037000	1.018001	1.016496	1.016269	1.016268	1.013419	1.012231	1.012583	1.012030	1.011963	1.011662	1.010935
0.037500	1.018225	1.016792	1.016556	1.016593	1.013788	1.012546	1.012949	1.012427	1.012380	1.011958	1.011178

0.038000	1.018445	1.017078	1.016834	1.016887	1.014148	1.012841	1.013296	1.012790	1.012778	1.012258	1.011399
0.038500	1.018661	1.017355	1.017105	1.017161	1.014498	1.013124	1.013633	1.013141	1.013163	1.012539	1.011597
0.039000	1.018874	1.017624	1.017368	1.017421	1.014840	1.013428	1.013961	1.013481	1.013535	1.012813	1.011809
0.039500	1.019084	1.017886	1.017625	1.017675	1.015176	1.013746	1.014281	1.013893	1.013895	1.013081	1.012031
0.040000	1.019291	1.018142	1.017876	1.017920	1.015504	1.014051	1.014596	1.014289	1.014246	1.013344	1.012260
0.040500	1.019495	1.018392	1.018205	1.018151	1.015834	1.014411	1.014904	1.014671	1.014588	1.013605	1.012505
0.041000	1.019696	1.018636	1.018518	1.018379	1.016149	1.014842	1.015207	1.015042	1.014923	1.013864	1.012743
0.041500	1.019896	1.018876	1.018813	1.018602	1.016432	1.015251	1.015506	1.015404	1.015251	1.014131	1.012989
0.042000	1.020093	1.019112	1.019058	1.018821	1.016692	1.015641	1.015799	1.015746	1.015573	1.014400	1.013241
0.042500	1.020288	1.019344	1.019297	1.019044	1.016948	1.016071	1.016084	1.016072	1.015881	1.014665	1.013488
0.043000	1.020481	1.019574	1.019527	1.019289	1.017198	1.016490	1.016363	1.016385	1.016250	1.014921	1.013734
0.043500	1.020672	1.019809	1.019753	1.019527	1.017438	1.016876	1.016635	1.016685	1.016647	1.015159	1.013979
0.044000	1.020860	1.020028	1.019973	1.019758	1.017673	1.017337	1.016980	1.016976	1.016950	1.015413	1.014237
0.044500	1.021043	1.020234	1.020188	1.019972	1.017904	1.017791	1.017338	1.017258	1.017242	1.015667	1.014506
0.045000	1.021221	1.020432	1.020399	1.020181	1.018132	1.018216	1.017631	1.017531	1.017528	1.015921	1.014770
0.045500	1.021397	1.020626	1.020600	1.020384	1.018375	1.018618	1.017916	1.017798	1.017806	1.016202	1.015029
0.046000	1.021569	1.020816	1.020788	1.020569	1.018616	1.019001	1.018195	1.018056	1.018078	1.016502	1.015289
0.046500	1.021738	1.021001	1.020971	1.020754	1.018848	1.019366	1.018469	1.018303	1.018344	1.016788	1.015548
0.047000	1.021905	1.021183	1.021151	1.020940	1.019164	1.019777	1.018739	1.018548	1.018605	1.017070	1.015800
0.047500	1.022069	1.021371	1.021327	1.021138	1.019638	1.020200	1.019007	1.018795	1.018862	1.017887	1.016145
0.048000	1.022230	1.021567	1.021501	1.021347	1.020109	1.020576	1.019275	1.019033	1.019115	1.018524	1.016480
0.048500	1.022389	1.021760	1.021671	1.021584	1.020512	1.020934	1.019543	1.019266	1.019425	1.019020	1.016792
0.049000	1.022547	1.021946	1.021839	1.021804	1.020864	1.021275	1.019806	1.019495	1.019733	1.019444	1.017253
0.049500	1.022702	1.022114	1.022005	1.022011	1.021154	1.021600	1.020153	1.019717	1.020042	1.019867	1.017879
0.050000	1.022856	1.022276	1.022169	1.022207	1.021427	1.021933	1.020503	1.019927	1.020339	1.020356	1.018646

Table 1.13
First five-year—ranks on efficient frontier

Risk level	Overall mean	P-3	Trdtn'l. mean	SSI	P-7	F-1	F-8	F-3	Hstrcl.	F-18
.0350	1	2	3	4	6	5	9	8	7	10
.0375	1	3	2	4	6	5	7	8	9	10
.0400	1	3	2	4	6	5	7	8	9	10
.0425	1	2	3	4	6	5	7	8	9	10
.0450	1	2	3	5	4	6	7	8	9	10
.0475	1	2	3	5	4	6	8	7	9	10
.0500	1	3	2	5	4	6	9	8	7	10
Average rank	1	2.4	2.6	4.4	5.1	5.4	7.7	7.9	8.4	10

correlation matrix would indicate that they do a relatively poorer job in estimating the correlation between stocks which are most promising for portfolios. Comparing the best of these two techniques, Historical, with the techniques which our direct predictions indicated was best, Traditional Mean, yields a significant difference in performance. The return from employing the Traditional Mean model is over 40% higher at the .035 risk level than the return from using the Historical technique and it is 25% higher than that produced by SSI.

In this section, we have shown that meaningful differences can be found in the performance of the forecasting techniques under study. Statistically significant differences existed in the forecast accuracy of the techniques and the ranking of techniques was consistent from one 5-year sample to another. Furthermore, these differences were of economic significance. The return on a portfolio could be increased by as much as 50% by selecting portfolios on the basis of these techniques which forecast most accurately.

C *One Year Results—Statistical Significance*

Let us start, as we did in the 5-year case, by comparing our forecasting techniques with the forecasting ability of 30 correlation matrices generated by randomly rearranging the elements in the Historical correlation matrix. As can be seen by comparing Tables 1.12 and 1.4, our forecasting techniques tend to outperform the random correlation matrices though the dominance does not appear to be as great as it was in the 5-year case. Since the techniques under study appear to contain some forecasting ability, it is worthwhile to examine forecast accuracy in more detail.

Table 1.14 is directly analogous to Table 1.5. The first item of importance to note is that the forecast error for 1-year forecasts is much higher than for 5-year forecasts. In fact, the average absolute forecast errors are two to three times as large for 1-year forecasts as they are for 5-year forecasts. This larger forecast error must be due to some combination of errors in forecasting the average correlation between all stocks and errors in forecasting pair-wise deviations from this average. Table 9 shows that a large part of this error was due to differences between the *average* correlation coefficient that was forecast and the actual (expost) average correlation coefficient. For example, in the first 1-year forecast period the Historical correlation coefficient was .3549, while the average correlation coefficient that materialized in the forecast period was .1085. The erratic nature of year to year changes in the average correlation coefficient can be seen from Table 1.11. This contrasts with the relative stability of 5-year correlation coefficients.[31] All of this suggests that much of the deterioration in estimating short run correlation coefficients is due to error in estimating the mean correlation coefficient.[32] Furthermore, the large error in mean prediction should also cause the ranking among techniques to be in large part a reflection of their ability to estimate the mean.

Because of this, let us start by examining the relative performance of forecasting techniques when all have been adjusted to produce the same average correlation coefficient. Table 1.16 shows that under this condition the techniques tend to have the same ranking from year to year and this ranking is very similar to the ranking for 5-year forecasts (both unadjusted and adjusted for mean). P-3, Industry Mean, and P-7 all provide better forecasts (in that order) than Overall Mean. SSI ranks next and beats Historical. The multi-index models prove inferior to the single index models.

When we compare forecasting techniques on the unadjusted data, we would expect the results to be more erratic. As Table 1.14 shows, not only is there more variance in the ordering of techniques from year to year, but that in any 1-year sample there are many fewer cases of statistical dominance. This can also be seen in Table 1.15 where an examination of the cumulative frequency functions of relative errors shows that there were eleven cases of complete dominance, where the corresponding 5-year period had twenty-seven.[33]

Table 1.14
One-year forecast errors[18]: average absolute error (unadjusted)

First one-year		Second one-year		Third one-year		Overall one-year	
1 SSI	.2921	1 SSI	.2747	1 Pseudo-3	.2100	1 SSI	.2624
2 Industry mean	.3125	2 Pseudo-3	.2816	2 Industry mean	.2124	2 Pseudo-3	.2692
3 Pseudo-3	.3162	3 Pseudo-7	.2823	3 Overall mean	.2134	3 Industry mean	.2698
4 Pseudo-7	.3188	4 Industry mean	.2845	4 Pseudo-7	.2159	4 Pseudo-7	.2723
5 Overall mean	.3193	5 Overall mean	.2904	5 F-1	.2201	5 Overall mean	.2743
6 Full historical	.3224	6 Full historical	.2927	6 SSI	.2205	6 Full historical	.2801
7 F-maximum	.3251	7 F-3	.2927	7 F-3	.2242	7 F-maximum	.2827
8 F-3	.3420	8 F-1	.2928	8 Full historical	.2254	8 F-1	.2855
9 F-1	.3435	9 F-8	.2940	9 F-8	.2263	9 F-3	.2863
10 F-8	.3454	10 F-maximum	.2956	10 F-maximum	.2274	10 F-8	.2885

Table 1.15
Dominance by cumulative frequency function[19]: second one-year

	F-18	F-8	F-1	Full hist.	F-3	Overall mean	Indus. mean	P-7	P-3	SSI
F-18										
F-8	23½									
F-1	25½	23½								
Full historical	34½	29½	23½							
F-3	31	26½	18	22						
Overall mean	37	28½	29½	23½	25½					
Industry mean	37½	35	35½	35	33½	33				
P-7	40	40	40	40	39	40	31½			
P-3	39	39	40	39	38	38	33½	21½		
SSI	40	40	40	40	39	40	38	32	32	
Max.	40	40	40	40	40	40	40	40	40	40

As discussed earlier, the ability of any technique to forecast the future 1-year correlation matrix should depend in large part on how well it forecasts the average level of future correlations. An illustration of this can be seen by examining Tables 1.9, 1.14 and 1.16. In the first 1-year sample, SSI moves from fifth place to first place as we remove the mean adjustment. From Table 1.9 we can see that this switch in position is due to a better forecast of the mean. On the other hand, in the third 1-year sample SSI moves from fifth to sixth place because it produces a poorer forecast of the average correlation coefficient.[34]

The techniques do not seem to show any consistency in their ability to forecast the mean. If we rank the techniques by the size of their forecast of the mean correlation coefficient, the ranking is preserved whether all the forecasts are too high or they are all too low. In short, the models under study do not exhibit a consistent differential ability to forecast the average correlation coefficient. Since their relative ability in forecasting correlation matrices depends so much on their ability to forecast the mean correlation coefficient, we expect the lack of consistency in results from year to year, the large forecast errors, and the lack of statistical difference in performance which are exhibited by Table 1.14. The size of the errors produced by every technique, together with the inability to tell the difference between most techniques on a statistically significant level, makes us

Table 1.16
One-year forecast errors[18]: average absolute error (adjusted)

First one-year		Second one-year		Third one-year		Combined one-year	
1 Industry mean	.3125	1 Pseudo-3	.2816	1 Pseudo-3	.2099	1 Pseudo-3	.2693
2 Pseudo-3	.3162	2 Pseudo-7	.2822	2 Industry mean	.2125	2 Industry mean	.2698
3 Pseudo-7	.3188	3 Industry mean	.2845	3 Overall mean	.2134	3 Pseudo-7	.2723
4 Overall mean	.3193	4 SSI	.2901	4 Pseudo-7	.2159	4 Overall mean	.2744
5 SSI	.3196	5 F-1	.2902	5 SSI	.2194	5 SSI	.2764
6 Full historical	.3224	6 F-3	.2903	6 F-1	.2198	6 F-1	.2780
7 F-3	.3231	7 Overall mean	.2904	7 F-3	.2238	7 F-3	.2791
8 F-maximum	.3233	8 F-8	.2920	8 Full historical	.2254	8 Full historical	.2801
9 F-1	.3240	9 Full historical	.2927	9 F-8	.2260	9 F-maximum	.2816
10 F-8	.3277	10 F-maximum	.2944	10 F-maximum	.2271	10 F-8	.2819

much more cautious of conclusions drawn from 1-year forecasts, particularly in comparison to 5-year forecasts.

D One Year Forecast—Economic Significance

As in the 5-year case, a set of efficient portfolios was generated using each of our estimates of the future correlation matrix plus actual ex-post values of return and variances. The ex-post performance of portfolios in the efficient set, selected by each forecasting technique, are shown for various ex-post risk levels in Tables 1.17 and 1.18. It is very difficult to discern any ordering of techniques in terms of portfolio performance. Five of the ten techniques perform best for some ex-post risk levels. The fact that there is no significant differences between the efficiency of portfolios formed on the basis of 1-year correlation forecasts is not surprising in light of our analysis of their forecast accuracy. Unlike the 5-year results, when forecasting for a 1-year period, very little can be said about the relative performance of techniques on either statistical or economic grounds.

IV Conclusion

In this paper we have shown that:

1. Some differences exist in the ability of different techniques to forecast 1-year correlation matrices. However, these differences are so small compared to the forecast error that one can't consistently differentiate between techniques on statistical or economic grounds.
2. Differences exist in the ability of techniques to forecast 5-year correlation matrices. These differences tend to be statistically significant and to persist over time. Furthermore, they are of economic importance for they can account for up to a 50% increase in the earned rate of return at certain risk levels.

In particular, we have found that in the case of 5-year estimates three averaging techniques (Traditional Industry Mean, Pseudo-3 and Overall Mean) outperformed all other techniques. The fact that these models consistently outperformed the SSI and Historical models, which have been the two most commonly used ways to generate input to portfolio analysis, has major implications for future empirical research.

Furthermore, since these models have a particularly simple structure, their good relative performance suggests that simplified portfolio algorithms

Table 1.17

	SSI	F-3	F-17	Traditional mean	P-7	Historical	F-8	P-3	Overall mean	F-1
0.017000	1.031744	0.024069			1.027249					
0.017500	1.034184	1.034666			1.029505	1.019942			1.022674	1.028330
0.018000	1.036485	1.037581	1.025607		1.030513	1.017838		1.024165	1.025561	1.030974
0.018500	1.037924	1.038857	1.032735	1.025375	1.031481	1.035785		1.026578	1.027559	1.033133
0.019000	1.039125	1.038873	1.034927	1.028325	1.032445	1.037278		1.028458	1.029462	1.034878
0.019500	1.040260	1.041224	1.036563	1.030359	1.033350	1.038562	1.030876	1.030203	1.031208	1.036077
0.020000	1.041480	1.043020	1.038335	1.032159	1.034249	1.040273	1.036684	1.031846	1.032921	1.037139
0.020500	1.042830	1.043990	1.039898	1.033875	1.035772	1.041635	1.038684	1.033409	1.034366	1.038143
0.021000	1.044447	1.044844	1.041154	1.035435	1.038214	1.042773	1.041157	1.034907	1.035423	1.039102
0.021500	1.045957	1.045665	1.042247	1.036894	1.040443	1.043800	1.043112	1.036169	1.036203	1.040021
0.022000	1.047170	1.046457	1.043236	1.038642	1.042326	1.044749	1.044633	1.037435	1.036975	1.041034
0.022500	1.048286	1.047226	1.044149	1.039969	1.043963	1.045639	1.046027	1.038530	1.037745	1.043524
0.023000	1.049200	1.047975	1.045007	1.041211	1.045443	1.046483	1.047110	1.039360	1.038513	1.045575
0.023500	1.049966	1.048705	1.045820	1.042385	1.046808	1.047290	1.047938	1.040174	1.039283	1.047507
0.024000	1.050718	1.049420	1.046597	1.043496	1.048089	1.048065	1.048742	1.040976	1.040040	1.048798
0.024500	1.051450	1.050300	1.047345	1.044559	1.049273	1.048816	1.049524	1.041764	1.040787	1.049880
0.025000	1.052163	1.051265	1.048068	1.045879	1.050345	1.049485	1.050362	1.042555	1.041523	1.050885
0.025500	1.052861	1.052176	1.048770	1.047431	1.051353	1.050080	1.051253	1.043546	1.042399	1.051830
0.026000	1.053546	1.053045	1.049453	1.048880	1.052307	1.050664	1.052120	1.044522	1.043300	1.052729
0.026500	1.054218	1.053878	1.050119	1.050247	1.053219	1.051238	1.052984	1.045465	1.044165	1.053588
0.027000	1.054879	1.054681	1.050772	1.051508	1.054083	1.051804	1.053823	1.046380	1.045088	1.054476
0.027500	1.055531	1.055477	1.051412	1.052704	1.054908	1.052361	1.054655	1.047270	1.045989	1.055464

0.028000	1.056173	1.056299	1.052485	1.053986	1.055701	1.053066	1.055483	1.048138	1.046869	1.056406
0.028500	1.056808	1.057099	1.053311	1.055346	1.056468	1.053936	1.056289	1.048986	1.048079	1.057310
0.029000	1.057433	1.057880	1.054055	1.056732	1.057212	1.054793	1.057659	1.049877	1.049567	1.058128
0.029500	1.058071	1.058644	1.054871	1.058040	1.057936	1.055608	1.058948	1.051224	1.050973	1.058773
0.030000	1.058820	1.059394	1.055642	1.059184	1.058642	1.056387	1.060164	1.052510	1.052313	1.059406
0.030500	1.059550	1.060003	1.056385	1.060295	1.059333	1.057297	1.061323	1.053746	1.053667	1.060027
0.031000	1.060267	1.060540	1.057111	1.061278	1.060010	1.058251	1.062433	1.054940	1.054969	1.060640
0.031500	1.060971	1.061069	1.057828	1.062176	1.060674	1.059165	1.063191	1.056090	1.056225	1.061322
0.032000	1.061663	1.061591	1.058531	1.063007	1.061326	1.060044	1.063710	1.057204	1.057441	1.061974
0.032500	1.062344	1.062104	1.059329	1.063790	1.061983	1.060895	1.064212	1.058172	1.058480	1.062602
0.033000	1.062995	1.062600	1.060095	1.064532	1.062659	1.061719	1.064700	1.058843	1.059484	1.063210
0.033500	1.063629	1.063080	1.060836	1.065241	1.063312	1.062495	1.065174	1.059666	1.060576	1.063799
0.034000	1.064255	1.063546	1.061643	1.065922	1.063953	1.063191	1.065639	1.060491	1.062144	1.064373
0.034500	1.064867	1.064000	1.062452	1.066579	1.064590	1.063890	1.066092	1.061323	1.063579	1.064934
0.035000	1.065466	1.064444	1.063264	1.067216	1.065210	1.064578	1.066536	1.062169	1.064815	1.065482
0.035500	1.066108	1.064877	1.064011	1.067834	1.065816	1.065228	1.066973	1.065622	1.066172	1.066019
0.036000	1.066686	1.065302	1.064707	1.068429	1.066408	1.065848	1.067401	1.068294	1.067606	1.066545
0.036500	1.067251	1.065718	1.065379	1.068988	1.067358	1.066442	1.067793	1.069995	1.068871	1.067084
0.037000	1.067804	1.066212	1.066011	1.069532	1.068433	1.066992	1.068110	1.071240	1.069991	1.067584
0.037500	1.068351	1.066741	1.066614	1.070084	1.069472	1.067520	1.068422	1.072278	1.070977	1.068015
0.038000	1.068921	1.067257	1.067190	1.070887	1.070414	1.068031	1.068769	1.073277	1.071872	1.068439
0.038500	1.069454	1.067763	1.067743	1.071649	1.071304	1.068526	1.069119	1.074327	1.072699	1.068855
0.039000	1.069952	1.068259	1.068266	1.072379	1.072153	1.069008	1.069459	1.075219	1.073472	1.069266
0.039500	1.070441	1.068746	1.068769	1.073082	1.072968	1.069477	1.069816	1.076003	1.074321	1.069671
0.040000	1.070923	1.069224	1.069256	1.073757	1.073764	1.069936	1.070165	1.076714	1.075101	1.070071

Table 1.18
First-year—rank for each risk level

	SSI	F-3	F-17	Tradit. mean	P-7	Hist.	F-8	P-3	Overall mean	F-1
.0200	2	1	4	8	5	3		9	7	6
.0225	1	2	5	8	6	4	3	9	10	7
.0250	1	2	6	8	$4\frac{1}{2}$	6	$4\frac{1}{2}$	9	10	3
.0275	1	2	8	6	4	7	5	9	10	3
.0300	5	3	8	4	6	7	1	9	10	2
.0325	4	5	8	2	6	7	1	10	9	3
.0350	4	8	9	1	5	7	2	10	6	3
.0375	6	9	10	3	4	8	5	1	2	7
.0400	5	$9\frac{1}{2}$	$9\frac{1}{2}$	$3\frac{1}{2}$	$3\frac{1}{2}$	7	6	1	2	8

might be possible and heuristics, which lead to optimum or near optimum portfolios, can be developed. As an illustration of the kind of simplification that can result from the use of these models, consider the following decision. Assume a portfolio manager has a fixed amount of money and has decided to use it to select one stock to add to his portfolio. If he accepts the Overall Mean model, the covariance between his present portfolio and any potential new investment is equal to a constant times the standard deviation of the potential investment. This constant is equal to the common correlation coefficient between all stocks times the standard deviation of the present portfolio. Thus, in selecting a stock to add to his portfolio, an investor need only consider each stock's return, its own variance, and a constant common to all stocks which determines the impact of the stock's own variance on the covariance between the stock and the existing portfolio. If either the Traditional Industry Mean model or Pseudo-3 is accepted, then the portfolio manager choosing among stocks in the same traditional or pseudo industry, has the same decision problem as he had with the Overall Mean model. This would be true whether the portfolio manager was considering adding or subtracting or replacing a given number of stocks in his portfolio.[35]

Appendix A: Tests of Statistical Significance

Each of the techniques examined in this paper produces for each time period studied an estimate of the value of each cell in the future (ex-post) correlation matrix. Thus, each technique for each period yields estimates of 2,850 different correlation coefficients. To measure differences in performances, the frequency function of the differences in absolute error between each pair of forecasting techniques is examined.[36] For example, one observation determining the frequency function for technique *A* versus technique *B* would be the absolute error in the forecast of a particular correlation coefficient by technique *A*, minus the absolute error in the forecast of the same correlation coefficient by technique *B*. Repeating this for all possible correlation coefficients produces one frequency function from which the comparative performance of techniques *A* and *B* can be judged. If the differences across all firms had the same sign, then this would indicate that technique *A* was superior to technique *B*. Given the sample size, this is unlikely to occur. What can and does happen is that some frequency functions have mostly positive or negative values and a mean at a statistically significant level different from zero. When the mean differs from zero at a statistically significant level, it is appropriate to conclude that one technique outperforms the other.

From the central limit theorem, the distribution of the mean of these frequency functions is normally distributed with mean equal to the mean of the frequency function. Thus, standard tests for means different from zero can be employed.[37] The results of these tests are presented in Tables 1.5 and 1.12.

In addition to examining differences in mean errors, it is instructive to examine the cumulative frequency function of absolute forecast errors. Cumulative frequency functions were calculated for each of the forecast techniques in each of the time periods. The cumulative frequency functions were divided into 25 intervals of .02 in the case of 5-year forecasts (.50, .48, .46, etc.) and 40 intervals of .02 in the case of 1-year forecasts. The number of times one technique had a larger cumulative frequency function than a second was then determined. These results are contained in Tables 6, 7, 8 and 13. Techniques could have significantly different mean errors without having the odds of any particular size error being less. Thus, the cumulative frequency function test is a more stringent test of dominance. It is a particularly interesting test because if one technique dominates another technique 25 out of 25 times, it will be preferred by all forecasters regardless of their loss functions.

Appendix B: Industry Membership

Name	Traditional	Pseudo-3	Pseudo-7
1 Abbot Laboratories	2	2	2
2 Allegheny Ludlum	4	1	1
3 Allied Chemical	1	2	2
4 American Chain & Cable	6	1	1
5 American Cyanamid	1	2	2
6 American Home Products	2	2	5
7 American Machinery & Foundry	5	1	3
8 Armco Steel	4	1	1
9 Atlas Chemical	1	1	1
10 Bethlehem Steel	4	1	1
11 Bliss and Laughlin	4	1	7
12 Borg-Warner	7	1	6
13 Brunswick Corp.	5	1	6
14 Cf. and I Steel	4	1	1
15 Celanese	1	2	2
16 Chemetron	1	1	7
17 Chicago Pneumatic	6	1	3
18 Cities Service	3	3	1
19 Clevite Corp.	7	1	1
20 Commercial Solvents	1	1	2
21 Continental Steel	4	1	1
22 Cooper Industries	6	1	4
23 Copperweld Steel	4	1	1
23 Crompton Knowles Corp.	5	3	3
24 Detroit Steel	4	1	1
25 Dow Chemical	1	2	2
26 Dupont	1	2	2
27 Eastman Kodak	1	2	2
28 Emhart	5	1	7
29 Federal Mogul	7	1	6
30 FMC Corporation	1	2	2
31 Gardner Denver	6	1	1
32 Getty Oil	3	3	3

Appendix B (continued)

Name	Traditional	Pseudo-3	Pseudo-7
33 Gillette Company	2	1	1
34 Granite City Steel Co.	4	1	1
35 Hercules	1	2	2
36 Ingersoll-Rand Co.	6	1	5
37 Inland Steel	4	1	1
38 Interlake Steel	4	1	1
39 Johnson & Johnson	2	2	2
40 Jones & Laughlin Steel	4	1	1
41 Kendall Company	2	1	1
42 Kerr McGee Corp.	3	3	6
43 Kappers Co.	1	1	1
44 Leesona Corporation	5	1	1
45 Libby-Owens Ford Glass	7	2	2
46 Lukens Steel	4	3	1
47 MacAndrews & Forbes	1	1	4
48 Marathon Oil	3	3	3
49 McLouth Steel Corp.	4	1	4
50 Merck & Co.	2	2	2
51 Mesta Machine	6	1	3
52 Midland Ross	5	1	6
53 Minnesota Mining & Manufac.	1	2	2
54 Monsanto Co.	1	2	2
55 National Lead	1	2	2
56 National Steel	4	1	1
57 Otis Elevator	5	2	5
58 Parke Davis	2	2	2
59 Pfizer Ochasid & Coct.	2	2	2
60 Phillips Petroleum	3	3	3
61 Plough Inc.	2	3	6
62 Purolator Products Inc.	7	1	1
63 Quaker State Oil	3	1	1
64 Republic Steel	4	1	1
65 Rohn/Haas Co.	1	2	2
66 Shell Oil	3	3	3
67 Skelly Oil	3	3	3

Appendix B (continued)

Name	Traditional	Pseudo-3	Pseudo-7
68 Smith Kline & French	2	1	6
69 Standard Oil (Indiana)	3	3	3
70 Standard Oil (Ohio)	3	3	3
71 Sun Oil Co.	3	3	3
72 Temken Roller Bearing	7	1	1
73 Union Carbide	1	2	2
74 Union Oil Co. of Cal.	3	3	3
75 U.S. Steel	4	1	1

Notes

The Institute for Quantative Research in Finance and TIAA-CREF provided research support for this project.

1. See Markowitz [18], [19], Sharpe [17] and Cohen and Pogue [3] for a discussion of some attempts to make portfolio analysis more amenable to implementation.

2. We are making the common assumption that comparison of portfolios in mean, standard deviation space is meaningful. For a discussion of the appropriateness of this criterion see Elton and Gruber [9], Tobin [26], Fama [10], and Feldstein [13].

3. See Osborne [12], Kendall [14], Mandelbrodt [17] and Fama [11]. Some proponents of the random walk (Fama [10] and [11]) would agree with stability but would replace the concept of variance in the portfolio framework with other risk measures because of a belief that variances are infinite.

4. It has been shown that even when forecasting a much more familiar concept, earnings, analysts haven't outperformed models based on extrapolation from historical data. See Elton and Gruber [7] and Cragg and Malkiel [4].

5. King [16] examined the correlation structure of share prices during a period of time, but he did not examine the stability or predictive value of this structure over time. Cohen and Pogue [3] examined the predictability of several portfolio models, but did not examine the accuracy of their correlation projections nor attempt to separate errors caused by misestimating correlation coefficients from errors in misestimating mean returns or variances. Blume [2] has analyzed the stability of Beta over time. Since Betas are related to correlation coefficients (see Section I), this is an indirect test of the predictability of the correlation coefficients produced by the Sharpe model. However, Blume's results cannot be used to directly estimate the errors in forecasting correlation coefficients.

6. See Sharpe [23] and Cohen and Pogue [3] and Smith [25].

7. Empirical tests of the capital asset pricing model have uniformly found that the single index model by itself was insufficient in explaining the return of a security. Douglas [5] and Miller and Scholes [20] and Lintner as reported by Douglas all found firms' returns significantly related to residual variation, as well as the systematic (with the market) risk. Black,

Jenson and Scholes [1] and Fama and MacBeth [12] find Beta related factors, and in the case of Fama and MacBeth [12], the firm's own variance improves the explanatory power. King [16], working with a completely different methodology, also found that multiple indices seem to have real explanatory power (though he did not study predictive power). In short, the empirical work of others strongly suggests the presence of influences beyond that captured by the single index model.

8. These components have the desirable properties of being orthogonal and being ordered by their ability to explain the historical correlation matrix.

9. The argument for 1 is that eigenvalues less than 1 mean that the index is explaining less that its proportionate share of the overall variance. For example, allowing n to stand for the original number of observations, this criterion eliminates from consideration all principal components that explain less than $1/n$. 100 per cent of the variance in the correlation data or in our case, 1.47%.

10. As we add more indices (from 1 to 3 to 8 to 17), the percentage of the variation in the original data or, alternatively, the accuracy with which the historical correlation matrix can be reproduced is always increased. On an average across our sample, it went from 36% to 45% to 61% to 75%. However, this does not mean that employing more indices will increase the predictive accuracy of the system. Additional indices may be measuring random influences (over time) in the correlation matrix and these influences may better be estimated at zero.

11. This model is not inconsistent with the capital asset pricing model. Returns and variances are still affected by market movements. The concept of efficiency still holds. Firms still have different covariances with each other and with the market. This model can be considered an alternative way of estimating B_{i1} where it is assumed proportional to a stock's standard deviation rather than estimated directly from historic values. If this model estimates well, it could explain some recent empirical findings [1], [5], [12], and [20] where rate of return was found to be more closely related to a stock's own variance than to B_{i1}. The stock's own variance may be serving as a proxy for (forecaster of) B_{i1} itself.

12. All firms in each industry had the same 4 digit company code (see Table 1.2).

13. The first step in our analysis was deciding on the number of pseudo-industries we wished to form. Since the first three principal components account for such a disproportionate amount of the variance in the return data, a solution involving three pseudo-industries was tried. Since the original data contained seven traditional industries, a solution involving seven pseudo-industries was tried. In each case (for three and seven principal components), a varimax rotation of the components was performed and firms were assigned to that rotated factor on which they had the largest loading. Appendix B contains a listing of the firms in our sample along with the traditional industry and each of the pseudo-industries (for the three pseudo-industry case and the seven pseudo-industry case) to which they belonged as of 1958.

14. Monthly return was defined as:

$$R_t = \frac{P_t - P_{t-1} + D_t}{P_{t-1}}$$

where P_t = price at end of month t

P_{t-1} = price at end of month $t-1$

D_t = cash dividends paid during month t.

Prices were adjusted for all stock splits and stock dividends.

15. Since we were interested in confining our analysis to relatively large companies (which might be suitable for institutional ownership), we selected our sample from the Compustat 950 stock tape. Because we were interested in studying industry effects, it was necessary to include in our sample several firms from each industry represented in our sample. We applied the following stratified sampling plan. Each industry on the Compustat tape which had less than six firms present for a 20 year period was eliminated from consideration. Seven industries were then selected at random from the remaining firms. All firms from each of these seven industries (which were included in the Compustat sample) were included in our sample. The industries selected for our sample along with their SIC codes and the number of firms included in each industry is shown in Table 1.2. Appendix *B* lists each firm and the traditional industry of which it is a member.

16. See Appendix A for a detailed discussion of the methodology underlying the construction of these tables and an explanation of the tests of statistical significance employed in this paper.

17. The average correlation coefficient produced by the historical correlation matrix is the same as that produced by randomly rearranging it. Thus a difference in performance cannot be due to a better forecast of the average level of correlation between all firms in our sample, but must be due to some ability on the part of the historical correlation matrix to differentiate between firms.

18. This table contains a ranking from best to worst of all ten forecasting techniques along with their average absolute forecast errors. The test of the mean difference in errors was applied to all forecasting techniques taken two at a time and the results are indicated in this table. A technique is statistically superior (at the 5% level) to all techniques following it and statistically inferior to all techniques preceding it, unless it is enclosed in brackets. All techniques enclosed in brackets are not statistically different at the 5% level. For example, in Table 5 in the first 5-year period, the Industry Mean model was superior at the 5% level to all other techniques. Pseudo-3 and Overall Mean, while superior to all remaining techniques at the 5% level, did not perform differently from each other at a .05 significance level. A detailed discussion of these tests are contained in Appendix B.

19. The number in the table indicates the number of times the technique on the left had a larger cummulative frequency function (and hence small errors) than the technique on the top. For example, in Table 1.6, the 25 in the cell next to Overall Mean indicates the odds of having an error less than any amount are always higher with Overall Mean than with F-8. Anything less than 25 indicates the cumulative frequency functions crossed. For example, crossing could occur if one technique had both many more small errors and large errors than a second. In all cases the techniques are ranked from worst to best. In cases where the number is much less than 25 (*e.g.* 18 or 17), the cumulative frequency functions were almost identical. Numbers close to 25 (24, 23, or 22) usually indicates that the techniques crossed at the end intervals.

20. The odds of getting an error less than any value was also higher for SSI in the combined 5 years.

21. Although our multi-index models are different from those used by Cohen and Pogue [3] our results are similar. They found that a single model outperformed their multi-index models.

22. It should be noted that with the Overall Mean model (constant correlation coefficients between stocks) individual securities will have different B_i's with the market. A stock's B_i depends on its standard deviation of return as well as its correlation with the market. As

shown in the previous section, with the Overall Mean model the stock's correlation coefficient with the market may be constant. The standard deviation of course need not be. Since stocks have non-zero and different B_i's, the return and variance of a stock (or a portfolio) will depend on market movements. Furthermore, the covariance between pairs of stock will neither be zero nor the same for all pairs of stocks; the idea of an efficient frontier is maintained.

23. It is also interesting to note that the Overall Mean model always outperforms the Full Historical model at a statistically significant level. Furthermore, the odds of getting an error smaller than any particular number is always less with Overall Mean. Since both models predict the same average correlation coefficient, differences in their performance are due to differences in their estimates of the deviation of individual correlation coefficients from the average. Overall Mean performing best implies that estimating these deviations at zero is better than estimating them at their historical level.

24. Pseudo-7 performed significantly more poorly than Pseudo-3 (in all cases), indicating that further disaggregation of data produced more noise than information. How much additional noise was introduced can be gauged by noting that Pseudo-7 also did worse than Overall Mean (this difference being significant in the second 5-year and combined cases). Thus, the further disaggregation led to the introduction of sufficient noise to negate the original information concerning firm differences. Even with this reduction in accuracy, Pseudo-7 still significantly outperformed Historical in the second 5-year and combined cases with no statistical difference being discernible in the first 5 years.

25. See Elton and Gruber [5] and [8] for a discussion of the ability of pseudo-industries to increase forecast accuracy as well as a test of their usefulness in forecasting earnings per share.

26. The usefulness of traditional industry groupings is consistent with King's results [15].

27. In more detail, all forecasting techniques had each forecast adjusted by the difference between that technique's mean forecast and the mean forecast from the historical correlation matrix.

28. Table 1.11 contains the mean, standard deviation and range of all 5 year and 1 year average correlation coefficients for non-overlapping time intervals over the period June 1948 to June 1968.

29. Because of the large amount of computational time involved in solving the quadratic programming program for each forecasting technique, a set of ex-ante efficient portfolios was generated only for the first 5-year and first 1-year forecast period.

30. Table 1.12 and Table 1.13 are presented in terms of one plus the monthly return. These returns have been converted to yearly returns for the discussion in the text.

31. Table 1.7 shows that the long run correlation coefficient is more stable than the short run correlation coefficient. The long run correlation coefficient can be considered an average (albeit not simple average) of short run correlation coefficients. If short run correlation coefficients have a stable mean plus random noise, the averaging underlying the calculation of long run correlation coefficients should produce a number closer to the underlying mean. Thus, the long run correlation coefficient should be more stable over time.

32. Although the increase in forecast error with 1-year forecasts can be explained in large part by the erratic behavior of the mean level of 1-year correlation coefficients, this is not the total explanation. Even though the average estimate of the mean correlation coefficient is better in the third 1-year than in the second 5-year case, the errors are much higher in the

1-year case. This suggests that part of the deterioration in forecast accuracy is due to a deterioration in estimating firm deviations from the mean, even though the major determinant would seem to be the erratic nature of the mean.

33. The cumulative frequency functions for the other 1-year forecasts were not included for they simply reemphasize the evidence of Table 1.9, that of a lack of statistical dominance among techniques.

34. In all samples, SSI produced lower estimates of the average correlation coefficient between securities than any other technique. This is consistent with the results of Cohen and Pogue [23].

35. Even in the Overall Mean Model the correlation coefficients would enter into the decision on the optimal size of the portfolio. In a forthcoming paper we shall explain decision rules for size and composition of optimum portfolios, given estimates of correlation coefficients arrived at by the three averaging techniques.

36. Before testing differences between individual forecasting techniques (e.g., between the forecast error for Pseudo-3 and that for F-1), it is necessary to determine whether all the forecast errors could have come from the same population (whether all methods in fact yield the same result).

Because the correlation between any pair of firms appears as an observation for each technique, the samples of the absolute value of the forecast errors for each technique are not independent, and the statistical tests must be appropriate for related samples. Under very stringent assumptions, namely that the standard errors are independently drawn from normally distributed populations, that the populations all have the same variance, and that the row and column effects are additive, analysis of variance tests could be employed. Because these assumptions appear unrealistic in this case, a non-parametric test, the Friedman two-way analysis of variance by ranks, is used. Friedman's test was applied to each of the two 5-year forecasts and to each of the three 1-year forecasts. In addition, the two 5-year forecasts were combined into one sample and the three 1-year forecasts were similarly combined. This gave us a total of seven samples. In each of the seven samples, the probability that all forecasting techniques did equally well was considerably less than one in one hundred.

Since significant differences exist in the forecasts produced by the techniques under study, it is appropriate to undertake a detailed examination of the performance of each technique against all other techniques. For further discussion, see Siegel [23], pp. 166–172. All 2850 correlation coefficients are not independent, so some adjustment has to be made to the degrees of freedom. The conclusions still hold after the adjustment.

37. That the frequency functions under question were derived from differencing two variables should not bother the reader. The central limit theorem states that as the number of observations increases, the distribution of the mean is normally distributed no matter what the original frequency function. A two-tailed normal test was used since we were not willing to assert in advance which technique would dominate.

References

1. F. Black, M. Jensen and M. Scholes. "The Capital Asset Pricing Model: Some Empirical Tests," in M. C. Jensen, ed., *Studies in the Theory of Capital Markets* (Praeger Press, New York, New York).

2. Marshall Blume. "On the Assessment of Risk," *Journal of Finance*, Vol. XXVI, No. 1, (March, 1971), pp. 1–10.

3. Kalman Cohen and Gerald Pogue. "An Empirical Evaluation of Alternative Portfolio-Selection Models," *Journal of Business*, (April, 1967), pp. 166–193.

4. John Cragg and Burton Malkiel. "The Consensus and Accuracy of Some Predictions of the Growth of Corporate Earnings," *Journal of Finance*, (March, 1968), pp. 67–84.

5. G. W. Douglas. "Risk in the Equity Markets: An Empirical Appraisal of Market Efficiency," *Yale Economic Essays*, Vol. 9, (Spring, 1969), pp. 3–45.

6. Edwin J. Elton and Martin J. Gruber. "Improved Forecasting Through the Design of Homogeneous Groups," *Journal of Business*, (October, 1971), pp. 432–450.

7. Edwin J. Elton and Martin J. Gruber. "Earnings Estimates and the Accuracy of Expectational Data," *Management Science*, (April, 1972), pp. B409–B424.

8. Edwin J. Elton and Martin J. Gruber. "Homogeneous Groups and the Testing of Economic Hypotheses," *Journal of Financial and Quantitative Analysis*, (January, 1970), pp. 581–602.

9. Edwin J. Elton and Martin J. Gruber. "Portfolio Theory When Investment Relatives are Lognormaly Distributed," forthcoming, *Journal of Finance*.

10. Eugene Fama. "Portfolio Analysis in a Stable Paretian Market," *Management Science*, (January, 1965), pp. 404–419.

11. Eugene Fama. "The Behavior of Stock Market Prices," *Journal of Business*, (January, 1965), pp. 34–105.

12. Eugene Fama and J. MacBeth. "Risk, Return and Equilibrium: Empirical Tests," unpublished manuscript, University of Chicago, (July, 1972).

13. M. Feldstein. "Mean Variance Analysis in the Theory of Liquidity Preference and Portfolio Selection," *Review of Economic Studies*, (1969), pp. 5–10.

14. M. G. Kendall. "The Analysis of Economic Time Series," *Journal of the Royal Statistical Society*, (1953), pp. 11–25.

15. Reuben Kessel. *The Cyclical Behavior of the Term Structure of Interest Rates*, Occasional Paper 91, (New York: National Bureau of Economic Research, 1965).

16. Benjamin King. "Market and Industry Factors in Stock Price Behavior," *Journal of Business, Supplement*, (January, 1966), pp. 139–190.

17. Benoit Mandelbrodt. "Forecasts of Future Prices, Unbiased Markets, and 'Martingale' Models," *Journal of Business*, (January, 1966), pp. 242–255.

18. Harry Markowitz. "Portfolio Selection," *The Journal of Finance*, (March, 1952), pp. 77–91.

19. Harry Markowitz. *Portfolio Selection*, (John Wiley and Sons, Inc., New York, 1959).

20. M. H. Miller and M. Scholes. "Rates of Return in Relation to Risk: A Re-examination of Some Recent Findings," in M. C. Jensen, ed., *Studies in the Theory of Capital Markets*, (Praeger Press, New York, New York).

21. Donald Morrison. *Multivariate Statistical Methods*, (McGraw-Hill: New York, 1967).

22. M. F. M. Osborne. "Periodic Structure in the Brownian Motion of Stock Prices," *Operations Research*, (May–June, 1962), pp. 345–379.

23. William Sharpe. "A Simplified Model for Portfolio Analysis," *Management Science*, (January, 1963), pp. 277–293.

24. Sidney Siegel. *Non-Parametric Statistics for the Behavioral Sciences*, (McGraw-Hill: New York, 1956).

25. Keith Smith. "Stock Price and Economic Indexes for Generating Efficient Portfolios," *Journal of Business*, (July, 1969), pp. 326–336.

26. J. Tobin. "Liquidity Preference as Behavior Towards Risk," *Review of Economic Studies*, (February, 1958), pp. 65–86.

2 Are Betas Best?

Edwin J. Elton, Martin J. Gruber,
and Thomas J. Urich

In 1973 Elton and Gruber (3) published an article in which they investigated the accuracy of forecasts of the correlation structure between securities produced by a group of alternative models. As pointed out in that article, while analysts may be capable of providing estimates of returns and variances, the development of estimates of correlation coefficients from anything other than models utilizing historical data is highly unlikely. The article after investigating the accuracy of certain forecasting techniques suggested that those techniques which provided the best forecasts could lead to a simplification of the portfolio problem. Elton, Gruber and Padberg in a series of subsequent articles (4), (5) and (6) have shown that if one accepts any of the assumptions underlying the models which worked best as forecasters in (3) then the optimal portfolio can be determined quickly and easily without the use of a computer.

In this paper we shall re-examine the forecasting ability of some of the techniques which provided the best set of forecasts in (3) as well as some new variations of these techniques. This re-examination is motivated by two factors. The first is that development of simple rules for optimal portfolio selection (4), (5), and (6) means that the likelihood of one or more of these techniques being used has been substantially increased, thus the choice between them becomes much more critical. The second is that some improvements in estimating the basic techniques have been reported in the literature and have gained acceptance in industry and it is worthwhile to compare the improved version of the basic models.

I Techniques

This section describes the alternative types of models we used for estimating future correlation coefficients: a historical model, single index models and a constant correlation model.

A A Full Historical Model

The simplest method of estimating future correlation coefficients using historical data is to assume that past values of these coefficients are the best estimates of their future values. In short calculate each pairwise correlation coefficient over a historical period and use this value as an estimate of the future. No assumption is made as to how or why securities move together. Instead, the amount of their co-movement is estimated directly. Several studies [e.g., (2) & (3)] have shown that while there is useful information contained in historical correlation coefficients, other techniques perform better. We have used the historical matrix in this study because it is common to all studies and can usefully serve as a benchmark against which other techniques can be evaluated. Historical correlation coefficients were calculated using the five years of data prior to the forecast period.

B Single Index Models

The single index model is the most widely used method of estimating correlation coefficients. As is well known the key assumption underlying its use is that securities systematically move together only because of a common response to a single index. We've used four variants of this model: unadjusted Betas, Vasicek adjustment to Betas, Blume's Beta adjustment and an assumed Beta of one for all stocks.

Unadjusted Betas are the Betas obtained from a least square regression of security returns on a market index during some historical period. These Betas are then used to estimate future correlation coefficients. Throughout this study we use as an index the S&P composite index adjusted for dividends. Unadjusted Betas were obtained by fitting a regression using data from the 5 years prior to the forecast period.

The Vasicek (See (11) for a detailed discussion) procedure consists of taking a weighted average of the unadjusted Beta and the average Beta for the sample of stocks under consideration. The weights add to one and depend on the standard error of the individual Beta and the standard deviation of the distribution of Betas in the sample. Once again the parameters were obtained by using data from the 5 years prior to the forecast period.

The Blume adjustment procedure consists of regressing Betas from one historical period on Betas from a prior period and then using this regression to adjust Betas for the forecast period (see Blume (1) for a detailed discussion of this procedure). Consider three sequential five year periods of data. Unadjusted Betas from the second period are regressed on unadjusted Betas from the first period. Unadjusted Betas from the second period are then substituted into this regression, as the independent variable to obtain an adjusted estimate of the Beta in the third period.

The final estimate of Beta was obtained by assuming that all Betas are one. The use of a Beta of one was motivated by Fisher and Kamin's (8) finding that this naive forecast performed surprisingly well compared to some more sophisticated techniques. Thus we have four estimates of future correlation coefficients using single index models.

Using standard symbols, estimates of correlation coefficients are obtained from Betas by noting that

$$\mathrm{Cov}(ij) = \rho_{ij}\sigma_i\sigma_j = \beta_i\beta_j\sigma_m^2$$

thus

$$\rho_{ij} = \frac{\beta_i\beta_j\sigma_m^2}{\sigma_i\sigma_j}$$

C Constant Correlation Model

An alternative to the single index models just presented is to assume that historical data only contains information concerning the mean correlation coefficients and that observed pair-wise differences from the average are random or sufficiently unstable, so that zero is a better estimate (than their historical level) of their future value. The most aggregate averaging possible is to set every correlation coefficient equal to the average of all correlation coefficients. In an earlier study we examined this technique primarily as a naive model against which to compare more sophisticated models. To our surprise it was among the models that produced the best forecasts, outperforming the unadjusted Beta and full historical model. Hence it is well worth continuing to examine it. We call this technique Overall Mean.

II Empirical Tests

The superiority of each of the techniques under consideration is judged by its ability to forecast the correlation matrix of security returns in a period subsequent to that over which the technique is fitted. Forecast accuracy will be judged over 5 year periods. In order to insure the robustness of our techniques, forecasts will be made for each of two 100 firm samples (as well as the combined sample) over two 5 year non-overlapping periods.[1] The first set of forecasts are prepared using data from 1956 to 1965 for the Blume technique and 1961 to 1965 for all other techniques and the forecasts are judged for accuracy against the actual correlation matrix for the years 1966 to 1970. For the second set of tests the parallel dates are 1961–1970, 1966–1970, and 1971–1975. An additional 5 year period is required for the Blume technique to parameterize the model.

Two types of tests were employed do judge differences in the forecasts produced by alternative techniques. First we examined the differences in the absolute forecast error between each pair of techniques. We judged one technique dominated the second, if the mean of these differences was, statistically, significantly different from zero. To be more precise, for each correlation coefficient, we computed the absolute value of the difference between the expost correlation coefficient and the forecast correlation coefficient produced by each technique. Then, taking the techniques two at a time (say technique A and B), the difference in the absolute values of the forecast errors was computed for each correlation coefficient. This allowed us to compute the distribution of the difference in the absolute value of the forecast error between technique A and B across all firms as well as the mean and standard deviation of this distribution. Technique A was said to dominate technique B if the mean of this distribution was negative and significantly different from zero at the 5% level.[2]

The second test we employed was to examine the distribution of the differences in absolute forecast errors and see if the probability of any size error was less with one technique then a second. We examined 10 intervals of .02. For example consider two of our techniques Overall Mean and Full Historical. We first examined the probability that overall mean would have an error greater than .20 larger than full historical. We then examined the probability that Full Historical would have an error .20 larger than overall mean. We continued this for .18 larger, .16 larger etc. If the odds of all size errors were consistently less for one technique than a second, then that technique dominates independent of the individuals loss function.[3] This test is a much more stringent test of dominance than the one discussed above. In some cases the mean error was smaller for one technique compared to a second and the difference was statistically significant but the first technique tended to have many large errors.

In examining the forecast accuracy of alternative models we felt it was worthwhile to look at the results both when the average forecast from each technique was adjusted to have the same value and when it was not.

Table 2.1
Average absolute error* (no adjustment)

First five years		Second five years		Combined	
1. Overall mean	.1169	1. Overall mean	.1415	1. Overall mean	.1292
2. Blume beta	.1270	2. Blume beta	.1499	2. Blume beta	.1385
3. Vasicek beta	.1289	[3. Unadjusted beta	.1539	3. Vasicek beta	.1419
4. Unadjusted beta	.1348	4. Full historical	.1545	4. Unadjusted beta	.1444
5. Beta = 1	.1378	5. Vasicek]	.1548	5. Full historical	.1491
6. Full historical	.1436	6. Beta = 1	.1776	6. Beta = 1	.1577

* All differences are statistically significant unless grouped by a bracket.

The forecast errors from each model are due in part to the error in forecasting the mean correlation coefficient and in part due to errors in forecasting differences from the mean. Several of the techniques can be expected to produce biased estimates of the means (as will be discussed in detail in section IV). Since the individual employing these techniques can easily adjust for differences in mean forecasts it is worthwhile examining forecast accuracy both with and without the mean adjustment. In the next section we examine unadjusted forecasts.

III Unadjusted Forecasts

As shown in Table 2.1, in each five year period, Overall Mean had a lower error at a statistically significant level than any other technique. In addition, as shown in Tables 2.2 and 2.3, for both time periods the probability of obtaining an error of any size is always smaller with the Overall Mean than with any other procedure except Blume. Overall mean dominates Blume for 9 of the 10 categories of error size in each time period. As another check on the dominance of overall mean we split each 200 firm sample into two 100 firm samples. Once again with one exception overall mean dominates all other techniques at a statistically significant level. The one exception is that in one sample for one time period, while Overall Mean produced a smaller error, the difference is not statistically significant.

The second best performing technique is the Blume procedure. It dominated all other techniques in terms of mean absolute error and all but the Vasicek procedure in terms of distributional properties. The dominance of the Blume procedure carried over to the subsamples. The Blume technique performed better than all other techniques and at a significant level except for the Vasicek technique in one subsample and the full historical in a second.

Table 2.2
Dominance by cumulative frequency function (unadjusted) first five years

	Full historical	Beta = 1	Unadjusted beta	Vasicek beta	Blume beta	Overall mean
Full historical	×					
Beta = 1	10	×				
Unadjusted beta	10	8	×			
Vasicek beta	10	8	5	×		
Blume beta	10	10	10	6	×	
Overall mean	10	10	10	10	9	×

The number in the table indicates the number of times the technique on the left had a larger cumulative frequency function (and hence small errors) than the technique on the top. For example, the 10 in the cell next to Overall Mean indicates the odds of having an error less than any amount are always higher with Overall Mean than with Full Historical.

Table 2.3
Dominance by cumulative frequency function (unadjusted) second five years

	Beta = 1	Vasicek beta	Full historical	Unadjusted beta	Blume beta	Overall mean
Beta = 1	×					
Vasicek beta	10	×				
Full historical	10	3	×			
Unadjusted beta	10	9	7	×		
Blume beta	10	10	10	10	×	
Overall mean	10	10	10	10	9	×

* See note to Table 2.2

The next best performing technique was the Vasicek adjustment to Beta. However, its ranking varied in the two five year periods. This variation was carried over in the subsamples.

The ranking among the remaining techniques also varied somewhat. In general the remaining techniques were (from best to worst) the unadjusted Beta, full historical, and Beta = 1.

IV Adjustment by the Mean Correlation Coefficient

Almost all of the models presented in this paper lead to different estimates of the average future correlation coefficient. The one exception is that the Overall Mean and the Full Historical technique give the same estimate.

Table 2.4
Forecast of average correlation coefficient

First five years		Second five years	
Blume beta	.354	Blume beta	.356
Full historical	.302	Full historical	.334
Overall mean	.302	Overall mean	.334
Beta = 1	.290	Beta = 1	.305
Unadjusted beta	.276	Unadjusted beta	.302
Vasicek beta	.275	Vasicek beta	.298
Realization	.334	Realization	.359

Thus any technique might appear superior (inferior) because of differences in estimating the mean correlation coefficient or because of differences in the estimation of the variation of each correlation coefficient from the mean. Alternative techniques will produce estimates of the future mean correlation coefficient that are either lower than or consistently higher than the historical mean correlation coefficient. Unless there is a reason to suspect a drift in the average correlation coefficient overtime, it is useful to judge the performance of any technique with the effect of bias in its mean forecast removed. We shall do so shortly but first we will discuss why each technique is likely to produce estimates of future correlation coefficients that tend to be above or below the average correlation in the sample on which the technique is fitted.

Table 2.4 presents the average correlation coefficient estimated by each of the forecasting techniques for each of the samples under study. Note that the mean estimate for the Full Historical Technique (and the Overall Mean Technique) is equal to the true mean from the sample.

The average correlation coefficient estimated by the Unadjusted Beta Method is smaller than the average correlation that existed over the period of time to which the model was fitted. The same result was found in Elton and Gruber (3) though a different sample of firms was employed over two different time periods. All of the Beta methods assume that the only correlation between securities arises because of common correlation with the market. To the extent that there are additional sources of correlation (e.g. industry affects) present, ignoring them will lead to downward biased estimates of the correlation coefficient.[4]

Yet despite the fact that the Beta technique ignores all sources of correlation except that associated with the market, the Blume technique produces higher estimates of the correlation coefficient than the sample to which it was fitted. There are two factors that account for this. One is that the average Beta in the sample was increasing in the periods under study. The Blume technique results in an extrapolation of this rise in Beta and thus for the period studied in higher estimates of Betas (and correlations) than the unadjusted Betas. This is easily seen from the fact that the Blume technique produced average Betas of 1.14 and 1.14 for the two periods while the unadjusted Betas for these two periods was 1.04 and 1.11. The second reason the Blume Betas result in higher correlations is because of the adjustment of all Betas towards the mean. Remember that the correlation coefficients depend on the product of the Betas for alternative securities. The average product of two Betas with the same mean but less dispersion around the mean will be higher than the average product of the unadjusted distribution.

The second (not the first) of these influences will also be present in the Vasicek technique. Why then does the Vasicek adjustment procedure result in lower Betas? The bias comes from the weighting procedure used to obtain the adjusted Beta. The adjusted Beta is a combination of the stocks own Beta and the average Beta in the sample. The weight placed on the stocks own Beta depends on the inverse of the variance of the stocks Beta. Since high Beta stocks tend to have high standard errors in their Beta estimate while low Beta stocks have low standard errors this procedure results in a large decrease in the Betas for high Beta stocks relative to the increase in the Beta for low Beta stocks. The net result is an estimate of average Beta below its unadjusted level and a low estimate of average correlation coefficient. For example, in the two periods under study, the average Beta from the Vasicek technique was 1.02 and 1.07 which is much lower than the estimates produced by the unadjusted Beta method or the Blume method.

The remaining method is to set all Betas equal to one.[5] This technique led to low estimates of the mean correlation coefficient because the average Betas in our two samples were 1.04 and 1.11.

Unless there is some reason why one of these techniques captures a nonrandom movement in the mean correlation coefficient, and the authors see no reason to suspect this is true, it is worthwhile to examine the forecast ability of these models when the forecasts are forced to have the same mean. We can consider this the ability of each model to forecast correlation coefficients when the forecast of the mean correlation coefficients is done exogenously. In particular two forecasts of the average future correlation coefficient will be tried. The first will assume that the average correlation coefficient follows a zero drift random walk. If this is true then the

Table 2.5
Average absolute errors* (historical adjustment)

First five years		Second five years		Combined	
1. Overall mean	.1169	1. Overall mean	.1415	1. Overall mean	.1292
2. Vasicek beta	.1231	2. Vasicek beta	.1458	2. Vasicek beta	.1345
3. Blume beta	.1275	3. Unadjusted beta	.1468	3. Unadjusted beta	.1372
4. Unadjusted beta	.1293	4. Blume beta	.1522	4. Blume beta	.1399
5. Beta = 1	.1358	5. Full historical	.1545	5. Full historical	.1491
6. Full historical	.1436	6. Beta = 1	.1720	6. Beta = 1	.1539

* All differences are statistically significant unless grouped by a bracket.

optimal forecast is the last observed average correlation coefficient.[6,7] Our second forecasting method will assume perfect knowledge and will adjust by the actual average correlation coefficient in the future period. In both cases each correlation coefficient estimated by some technique is adjusted by subtracting from it the mean correlation coefficient for that technique and adding the new estimate of the mean.

The results of adjusting all forecasts for the historic average correlation coefficient are presented in Table 2.5. The average absolute error of the Overall Mean and Full Historical technique are unchanged since their average forecast is unchanged. The average absolute error of every other technique except Blume Betas goes down in both periods. Blume does better on an unadjusted bases because it is upward biased and there was a continued upward movement in correlation coefficients over the period examined. The most striking result from Table 2.5 is that the Overall Mean continues to dominate all other techniques at a statistically significant level in both periods. This is true not only using the mean absolute error but also using the same cumulative frequency function as employed in Part I. Using this technique the Overall Mean dominates each other technique 10 out of 10 possible times. Thus, irrespective of an individuals loss function, the Overall Mean dominates.

Another interesting point is the improvement in the Vasicek technique. Correcting for its downward bias in estimating the mean made it the second best forecasting technique. It dominates all other techniques (but Overall Mean) at a statistically significant level in both periods. As mentioned above the Blume technique now performs worse than it did without the mean adjustment and is virtually indistinguishable from the unadjusted Beta technique. The fact that setting Beta equal to one performs worse than any other Beta technique when the mean adjustment is

Table 2.6
Rank of each technique in each subsample (rank on mean absolute error) historical adjustment

	First five years		Second five years	
Technique	Sample 1	Sample 2	Sample 1	Sample 2
Overall mean	1	1	1	1
Vasicek beta	2	2	3*	2
Unadjusted beta	3	4	2*	4*
Blume beta	4	3	4	3*
Full historical	6*	6*	5	5
Beta = 1	5*	5*	6	6

* Indicates that the two entries in the column were not different at a statistically significant level.

made indicates that differences between Betas, whether adjusted or not, convey real information about the future correlation structure. Finally the poor performance of the Full Historical correlation matrix indicates that pairwise correlation coefficients contain a lot of random noise. The Overall Mean and Beta techniques can be viewed as smoothing techniques, with the Overall Mean method involving the most stringent smoothing. The ordering of the techniques indicates that smoothing across correlation coefficients eliminates random noise and improves forecasting ability.

It is worth while examining how robust the relative performance of these techniques is across non-overlaping subsamples of firms. As mentioned earlier we prepared forecasts for each technique for each subsample in each of two periods. The rankings for each technique are shown in Table 2.6. Notice that the rankings are quite consistent between subsamples as well as for the overall sample. Overall Mean performs best in each subsample. The Vasicek Beta technique performs second best in three of the four subsamples. The one time it is third rather than second its difference from the second technique is not statistically significant. The next two techniques in performance are the Blume Beta and the Unadjusted Beta. They switch back and forth in ranking but are worse than the two previously mentioned techniques and better than the two remaining techniques. The two worst techniques are the Full Historical technique and the Beta equals one model. They are virtually indistinguishable from each other.

Table 2.7 presents the results of forecasting future correlation coefficients when the techniques are adjusted so that the average correlation

Table 2.7
Average absolute error* (future adjustment)

First five years		Second five years		Combined	
1. Overall mean	.1145	1. Overall mean	.1384	1. Overall mean	.1265
2. Vasicek beta	.1211	2. Vasicek beta	.1432	2. Vasicek beta	.1322
3. Blume beta	.1256	3. Unadjusted beta	.1443	3. Unadjusted beta	.1354
4. Unadjusted beta	.1275	4. Blume beta	.1497	4. Blume beta	.1377
5. Beta = 1	.1335	5. Full historical	.1521	5. Full historical	.1416
6. Full historical	.1414	6. Beta = 1	.1696	6. Beta = 1	.1516

* All differences are statistically significant unless grouped by a bracket.

coefficient predicted by each model is equal to the true future average correlation coefficient. Obviously this leads to an improvement in forecast accuracy. Of more interest is the fact that the ordering and statistical significance of results is identical to that obtained when the adjustment is made using the historic average correlation coefficient.

V Conclusion

In this paper we demonstrated that Overall Mean is a prefered method of forecasting future correlation coefficients in comparison to the best of the Beta time series techniques. In addition we discussed the bias, in the mean estimate produced by standard Beta estimating techniques. Correcting for this bias had no effect on the dominance of Overall Mean but did change the ranking within the Beta techniques.

Notes

The authors would like to thank the Institute for Quantitative Research in Finance for financial support.

1. To be more precise, we made forecasts on the basis of the 200 firm sample and we observed how well these forecasts did over two 100 firm subsamples as well as over the 200 firm sample.

2. From the central limit theorem, the distribution of the mean of these frequency functions is normally distributed with mean equal to the mean of the frequency function. Thus standard tests for means different from zero can be employed.

3. This follows directly from the principles of stochastic dominance.

4. Additional sources of correlation have been discussed and empirically demonstrated in (7) and (9).

5. The estimates from this technique might have improved if the Betas were set equal to the average in the sample rather then one. However given the poor performance of this technique this change is unlikely to effect any conclusions.

6. Since this number can easily be computed from historical data if this adjustment leads to better forecasts the user can easily incorporate the adjustment in his forecasting scheme.

7. By optimal forecast we mean unbiased since an individual's loss function could result in an optimal forecast that is biased.

References

1. Marshal Blume. "On The Assessment of Risk", *Journal of Finance* (March, 1971) pp. 1–10.

2. Kalmen Cohen and Jerry Pogue. "An Empirical Evaluation of Alternative Portfolio Selection Models" *Journal of Business* (April 1968) pp. 180–190.

3. Edwin J. Elton and Martin J. Gruber. "Estimating the Dependence Structure of Share Prices" *Journal of Finance* (December 1973) pp. 1203–1232.

4. Edwin J. Elton, Martin J. Gruber and Manfred W. Padberg. "Simple Criteria for Optimal Portfolio Selection" *Journal of Finance* (December 1976) pp. 1341–1357.

5. Edwin J. Elton, Martin J. Gruber and Manfred W. Padberg. "Simple Criteria for Optimal Portfolio Selection—with Upper Bounds" *Operations Research* (November–December 1978).

6. Edwin J. Elton, Martin J. Gruber and Manfred W. Padberg. "Simple Criteria for Optimal Portfolio Selection—Multi-Group Models *Journal of Financial and Quantitative Analysis* (March 1977), pp. 329–345.

7. James L. Farrel. "Analyzing Covariation of Returns to Determine Homogeneous Stock Groupings" *The Journal of Business* (April 1974), pp. 186–207.

8. Lawrence Fisher and J. Kamin. "Good Betas and Bad Betas", Paper for the Seminar on the Analysis of Security Prices, University of Chicago, November 1971.

9. B. King. "Market and Industry factors in Stock Price Behavior" *Journal of Business* (January 1966), pp. 139–190.

10. Robert C. Klenkosky and John D. Martin. "The Adjustment of Beta Forecasts", *Journal of Finance*, (September 1975), pp. 1123–1128.

11. O. Vasicek. "A Note on Using Cross-Sectional Information in Bayesian Estimation of Security Betas", *Journal of Finance*, 28 (December 1973), 1233–1239.

3 A Multi-index Risk Model of the Japanese Stock Market

Edwin J. Elton and Martin J. Gruber

I Introduction

The two largest stock exchanges in the world are the Tokyo and the New York Stock Exchange. The Tokyo Stock Exchange is now larger in the aggregate market value of listed companies than the New York Stock Exchange. Despite the size and importance of the Japanese market, there is a paucity of research on Japanese security markets compared to the enormous amount of research on U.S. securities markets.

One of the major current areas of research in U.S. markets is estimating the influences or factors which affect returns.[1] Identifying these influences and estimating the return generating process is important for a multitude of applications such as estimating the variance covariance structure of returns, for equilibrium pricing, and for event studies. This study is of interest both because it examines a different (and important) market than that examined in previous studies and because it uses methodology which has not previously been employed. To the best of our knowledge, this is the first examination of the number of factors affecting Japanese security prices.

Our methodology differs from past methodology in two ways. First, we employ a new set of statistical techniques to examine the hypothesized return generating structure across samples at a point in time. This alllows us to determine whether the structure is a common structure or unique to a particular sample. Second, we examine the reasonableness of our estimated return generating process by examining how useful it is for decision making in a forecast mode. There is a number of alternative ways that a return generating process can be estimated; there are arguments for and against each. One test that any estimated model ought to meet is that its use leads to better decisions.

The paper is divided into 6 sections. In the second section, we examine how many factors are in the return generating process for Japanese securities and discuss the estimation of these factors. In the third section, we compare the performance of our multifactor return generating process to the single index model as a model for describing security returns. In the fourth section, we examine how well our return generating model performs, compared to a single index model, for decision making purposes. In the fifth section, we examine how well the return generating process which was determined on statistical grounds can be explained in terms of economic variables.

While the analysis in sections 2 through 4 develops and tests a risk structure for Japanese stock prices, the fifth section begins the exploration of a new topic. For many modeling purposes, e.g., the creation of index funds, all that is needed is a model which describes the pattern of returns and which is reasonably robust over time. However, it is useful if the statistically derived indices are associated with economic influences. This is true for it raises our confidence that the indices we have found are not due to chance and it may lead eventually to the development of a forecasting model based on macro variables. In the fifth section of this paper we present some evidence that the indices we have developed in the earlier sections are in fact associated with economic variables. While the analysis is preliminary at this stage it suggests that further research in this area might be fruitful. In the fifth section we return to the indices developed in earlier sections and perform standard A.P.T. tests to examine how many factors are priced in the sense that greater sensitivity to these factors leads to differential average return.

II Identifying the Factors

The first step we use to estimate the return generating process involves factor analyzing the historical time series of returns. The advantages and disadvantages of using factor analysis to identify the influences which are present in the return generating process are well documented in the literature of financial economics.[2] One key aspect of the controversy over the use of factor analysis is the problem of identifying the number of factors which are significant in explaining the covariance structure of security returns.[3] A large part of the problem stems from our inability to factor analyze large numbers of securities. Two methods have been introduced to deal with this problem. The first involves performing factor analysis on subsets or groups of securities. This multi-sample approach was introduced by Roll and Ross (1980). The second is the portfolio approach introduced by Chen (1983).

In the group or multi-sample approach, securities are divided into samples and maximum-likelihood factor analysis is used to extract factors from each sample.[4] The difficulty with this approach is that the factors extracted in each sample need not be extracted in the same order or even with the same sign. How then can one determine whether one has extracted the same factors or different factors (unique to each group) as one goes from group to group? While this is a problem, its solution represents an opportunity to improve our identification of the return generating process when we use the grouping technique. By analyzing the factors produced from different groups and identifying those influences which are common across two or more groups we can differentiate between unique and general factors.

Chen's portfolio approach rests on examining the return behavior of portfolios of securities rather than individual issues. There are two disadvantages to this approach. First, no matter how large the sample used to form portfolios, one can not tell whether one has measured factors unique to that sample or general factors common to all securities. Second, the results obtained by this methodology are very sensitive to the portfolio formation technique employed.

There are two previous papers, Cho (1984) and Brown and Weinstein (1983), which sought as we shall do to identify the common factors across groups. Cho (1984) used inter-battery factor analysis, a technique which looks directly at the inter-group correlation matrix to produce estimates of the number of factors. This technique allows the estimation of the number of common factors present for any particular significance level. The results reported by Cho (1984) show that the number of factors found:

(1) is very sensitive to the significance level selected.

(2) depends on the members of the sample. The number of factors found across 21 samples varied from three to nine.

A related approach was used by Brown and Weinstein. They divided a group into two subgroups and performed factor analysis on each subgroup and on the overall group. They examined differences in the unexplained sum of squares between the overall group and the total of the two subgroups. Since the unexplained sum of squares is unaffected by an orthogonal transformation of any factor structure, Brown and Weinstein could compare the residual sum of squares from the subgroups with the residual sum of squares from the overall group with the same number of factors extracted. If the factors from one group are merely an orthogonal transformation of the factors from a second group, the residual sum of squares should not be statistically different.

Our major tests are very much in the spirit of the Cho and Brown and Weinstein papers. We initially divided our 393 stock sample into 4 samples each containing either 98 or 99 stocks.[5] We then perform maximum-likelihood factor analysis within each of the four samples. While we examine some standard estimating techniques to determine the number of factors within a sample, our primary tool to determine the number of factors was to test whether the factors extracted from any sample are linear transformations of the factors extracted from other samples. We used canonical correlation to perform these tests.

The remainder of this section is divided into three parts: In the first, we briefly describe our overall sample. In the second we discuss the method used and the empirical results in determining the number of factors. In the third, we discuss the determination of which factor solution we use as the return generating process.

2.1 *Sample Selection*

Our sample is the 400 stocks comprising the NRI 400 stock index. We were interested in the NRI 400 stock index because it is one of the most widely used indexes in Japan. In addition, the 400 stocks in the index constitute 70.9 percent of the total capitalization of the first section of the Tokyo stock exchange and 62.9 percent of the total Tokyo stock exchange. The value of the NRI 400 was 266,092 billion yen and 1,905 billion dollars as of April 1987.

We had 180 months of price and dividend data on the stocks making up the NRI Index: from April 1971 through March 1986. Because of missing data we had to delete 7 of the 400 stocks. The remaining 393 stocks were broken into 4 samples with the first three samples containing 98 stocks and the fourth, 99 stocks. The four subsamples were formed both because of the limitations of the maximum-likelihood factor analysis program employed and because of the advantages of testing factor structures across different samples. It is to this topic that we now turn.

2.2 *How Many Factors?*

Tests of the appropriate number of factors to include in the return generating process can be separated into those which look at one group at a time and those which take advantage of the fact that solutions for more than one group have been obtained. While we shall emphasize the latter because, as explained below, it consider the commonality of the factors selected, we shall briefly examine the standard single group tests.

2.2.1 *Single Group Tests*

To obtain an initial idea of how many factors might be present in the return generating process, ten factor solutions (using maximum-likelihood factor analysis) were performed on each of our four samples. That is, for each sample a maximum-likelihood solution involving first one factor, then two factors, then three factors, and continuing through ten factors was found. There are three commonly used techniques, in the literature on factor analysis, which are employed to decide on the correct number of factors needed to explain the covariance matrix. These are chi-square [Lawley and Maxwell (1971)], Akaike's information criteria (1974), and Schwartz's Baysian criteria [Schwartz (1978)]. Of these three criteria, Schwartz's is the most conservative in estimating the number of factors which are significant. The Chi-square test and Akaike's information criteria tend to include factors which, while statistically significant, have little economic importance. When we use either of the latter two tests the results show that there are at least 10 factors present, for each sample, in the return generating process. We did not test for the optimum number since we had not performed factor solutions involving the extraction of more than ten factors and since our alternative tests and previous attempts by others to identify the return generation processes on other samples of securities indicate the presence of fewer than ten factors.[6]

When we employ Schwartz's Baysian Criteria we get a much more parsimonious description of the return generating process. Schwartz's criteria produces a statistic which reaches its minimum at the 'correct' number of factors extracted. The value of Schwartz's statistic for each group for alternative numbers of factors 1 through 10 is shown in fig. 3.1. Schwartz's criteria identified three factors as significant in the return generating process for sample 1, and four factors for samples 2, 3, and 4.

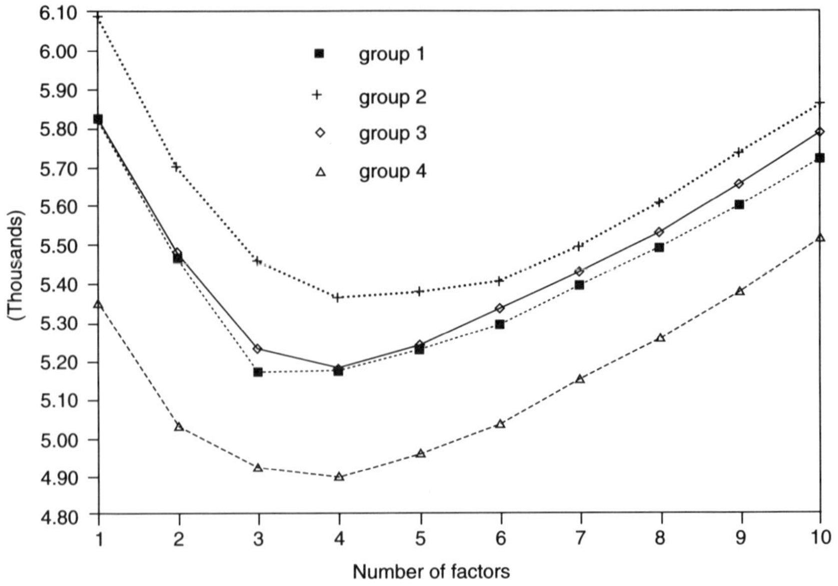

Figure 3.1
Schwartz's Bayesian criterion

The conclusion from examining the number of factors present in the return generating process of each sample separately is somewhat ambiguous. It rests on the choice of the test employed to determine significance. The answer would seem to be either four or ten or more. The next step is to use information from more than one group to decide on the number of factors.

2.2.2 *Multiple Group Tests*

The intent of our analysis is to estimate a return generating process that describes the return on all stocks which are like the stocks in the NRI 400 Index. When we examine any one of our four samples as we add more factors to the solution, we increase the probability that the added factors are idiosyncratic to the stocks in that sample or subset of those stocks rather than factors which explain the covariance structure of returns among large groups of securities. If, in fact, our factor solution from a sample has measured general influences, then the solution from a second group should capture the same general influences. However, we cannot simply compare the first factor from a sample with the first factor from

Table 3.1
Canonical R. ith canonical R^2 from the i factor solution.

i	R^2
1	0.929
2	0.799
3	0.664
4	0.589
5	0.211
6	0.043
7	0.028

another sample and the second with the second, etc. Factor solutions are not unique up to a linear transformation. Therefore, the first factor from one sample may be the second factor from a second sample or even a linear combination of the first, second, third and fourth factors from the second sample. While there are some attributes of maximum-likelihood factor analysis which will tend to extract factors in a parallel manner and to some extent lessen this problem, it does not eliminate the problem.[7] There is a method for correcting this problem.

What we would like to do for an n factor solution is to find that linear combination of the n factors from one sample that is most highly correlated with the best linear combination of the n factors from a second sample. After removing this correlation we would like to find the second linear combination of the n factors from the first sample which is most highly correlated with the linear combination of the n factors from the second sample. We would like to do this n times. This is exactly what canonical correlation does. By finding best fit linear combinations it removes the problem of the factors from one sample being linear transformations of the factors from a second sample. If, in fact, one has estimated too many factors—e.g. n instead of $n - k$—then the $n - k + 1$ canonical variates (linear combination of the n factors) from one sample should be uncorrelated with the $n - k + 1$ canonical variate from a second sample.

In table 3.1 we present the average (across four samples) squared canonical correlation for the first canonical variate out of the one factor solution, the second canonical variate out of the two factor solution, proceeding through the seventh canonical variate out of the seven factor solution. From examining these results it appears likely that the correct solution is

Table 3.2
An example of a factor pattern: correlation of factor between samples 1 and 2.[a]

	F1	F2	F3	F4	F5
1. Four factors:					
Sample 1					
F1	0.974	–	–	–	
F2	–	0.895	–	–	
F3	–	–	0.904	–	
F4	–	–	–	0.690	
2. Five factors:					
Sample 2					
F1	0.973	–	–	–	–
F2	–	0.863	–	0.220	–
F3	–	–	0.901	–	–
F4	–	–	–	–	0.721
F5	–	0.174	−0.185	–	–

a. '–' = less than 0.1.

either four or five factors. The association of the fourth linear combination from a four factor solution is almost 60% while for the fifth linear combination from a five factor solution it is just above 20% and for the sixth linear combination of the six factor solution it is less than 5%.

The evidence so far would seem to support a four factor solution with the fifth factor worth considering. While we have argued that canonical correlation is the correct way to determine whether factor structures from one group are the same as those from a second group it is worthwhile taking a look at the simple correlation pattern between factors. This will allow us to see the type of orthogonal transformation that can take place. Table 3.2 presents the simple correlation between the factors extracted from samples 1 and 2 for the four factor and five factor solution. Note that in the four factor solution, the only correlations above 0.10 occur for the first factor from sample 1 with the first factor from the second sample, the second with the second, etc. When we go to the five factor solution the clear pattern fractures. In addition to the correlation pattern being much less clear, some factors from one group do not seem to be associated at all with factors from the other group. For example, factor 5 from sample 1 and factor 4 from sample 2 have only minimal correlation with any of the factors arrived at from the other group. Once again we see support for the four factor solution.

Table 3.3
Average R^2 across 20 size portfolios with alternative factor solutions.

	2 factors	3 factors	4 factors	5 factors	6 factors
Sample 1	0.686	0.713	0.771	0.772	0.772
Sample 2	0.663	0.700	0.763	0.777	0.779
Sample 3	0.673	0.681	0.764	0.768	0.769
Sample 4	0.678	0.731	0.763	0.770	0.775

2.2.3 *Correlation Test*

As a final check on the decision to use a four factor model, we examined the association between solutions involving alternative numbers of factors and returns over time. We could have examined this for individual stocks or for the market as a whole but instead decided to employ a portfolio approach. The portfolio approach is not only useful for estimating time series association; it will allow us to obtain better estimates of sensitivities and will be useful later in this paper in examining cross-sectional relationships. Because we wished to form portfolios for cross-sectional testing as well as time series analysis we wished to have portfolios which would have differences in average return. An instrumental variable was needed for return. Because of the documentation of the size effect in the Japanese market (as well as the U.S. market) size was chosen as the instrumental variable.[8] The 393 stocks in our sample were divided into 20 portfolios based on size.

These portfolios were formed every month and the returns computed over the next month. For each portfolio the returns were regressed against the two, three, four, five and six factor solutions from each of our samples. The average R^2 for each of the four solutions (one from each sample) over the 20 groups are shown in table 3.3 and plotted in fig. 3.2. The additional explanatory power from increasing the number of factors beyond 4 is very small in absolute terms and relative to the contribution of the first four factors. This reinforces the earlier evidence that four factors are adequate to define the return generating process for large stocks in the Tokyo Stock Exchange.

2.3 *Which Four Factor Solution?*

After having decided to employ a four factor model, we still have a problem to solve. We have four different four factor models, one derived

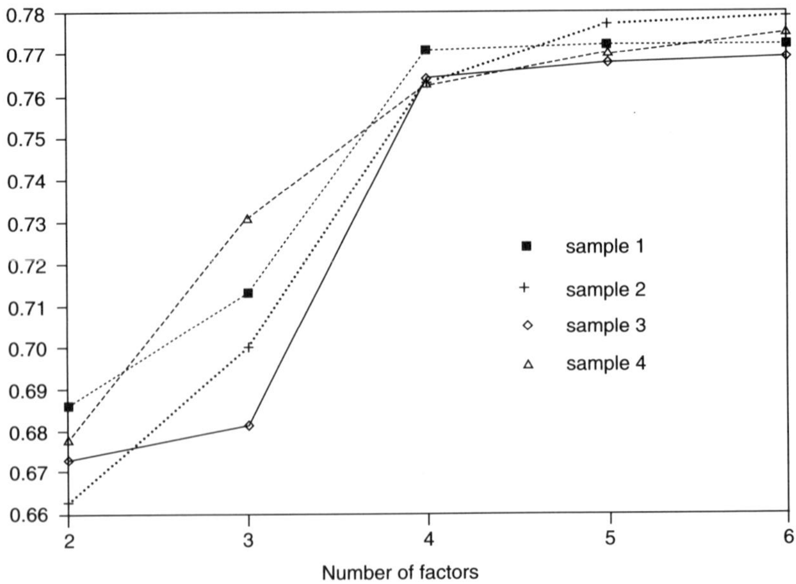

Figure 3.2
R^2 of factors with 20 portfolios

from each of our four samples. One must be selected as the basis for the remainder of our tests. This is not as important a decision as it may at first seem. We know from the results of our canonical correlation tests that each of the sets of four factors (actually linear transformations of the four factors) are very highly correlated with each other. We have previously presented evidence that the four factors are capturing the same fundamental influences in the return generating process and hence it should not make such difference which of the four factor solutions we use.

Nevertheless, we have to make a choice of one solution (or sample) to use for the remainder of this study. To make this choice we performed two types of tests. The first looked at the R^2 of each of our sample four factor solutions with two different return series. The second examined the residual correlation of returns after the correlation with the four indices had been removed.

2.3.1 *Correlation Tests*

Table 3.4 presents for each of the four factor solutions (one from each sample) both the correlation with a value weighted index of the first sec-

Table 3.4
R^2 with four factor solutions.

	From sample 1	From sample 2	From sample 3	From sample 4
TSE first section	0.925	0.902	0.928	0.912
Average with 20 size portfolios from Nomura 400	0.771	0.763	0.764	0.763

tion of the Tokyo Stock Exchange and the average correlation with the twenty portfolios formed from the NRI 400. The results are very similar across the four samples. It appears that it makes little difference which of the samples (factor solutions) we pursue, though those based on samples 1 and 3 appear to do slightly better.

2.3.2 *Residual Correlation Test*

If we have correctly identified the return generating process then residuals from our model should be unrelated. One way to choose among the alternative candidates is to look at the model which produces the smallest average residual correlation. Once again the 20 portfolios formed from the NRI 400 were used to perform the test. For each portfolio, the residuals from the four factor model were computed at each moment in time. The correlations between all pairwise combinations of residuals were computed. Since we had twenty portfolios, we had 190 correlation coefficients. Since we had four estimates of the factor structures we had four different estimates of each of the 190 correlation coefficients. We can examine the ordering of the ability of each factor solution to produce residual correlations close to zero. Table 3.5 presents this ordering of factor solutions from best to worst. While few of the entries are statistically significant, the ordering of the sample factor solutions is similar to that found earlier, with the factor solution from sample one being the best and that from sample three only slightly inferior. Based on these tests we will use the four factor solutions from sample 1 as the model of the return generating process through the remainder of this paper.

2.4 *Summary on the Choice of a Factor Structure*

Up to this point we have investigated the estimation of the return generating process. Based on single group tests and canonical correlation

Table 3.5
Differences in the absolute value of the correlation coefficient.[a]

	Column value minus row value			
	1	3	2	4
1		−0.0051	−0.0081	−0.0161
		(0.0047)	(0.0050)	(0.0039)
2			−0.0029	−0.0110
			(0.0056)	(0.0054)
3				−0.0081
				(0.0042)

a. The numbers not in parentheses represent the absolute value of the correlations from the sample shown in the left-hand column, minus the absolute value of the residual correlation from the sample shown at the top of the table. Thus, a negative number indicates the sample on the left performed better (produced lower residual correlation). These are mean differences and the number shown in parentheses are the standard deviations of the mean.

tests which look for common influences across groups, we have concluded that there are four factors present in the return generating process for large Japanese stocks. We have shown that while these factors can be estimated from any of our samples, sample 1 is certainly no worse than the other samples and so will be used four future testing. We will now turn to an examination of both the explanatory power of the four factor model and the stability of the sensitivity to factors over time.

III Model Explanatory Power and Factor Sensitivity Stationarity

Having determined that returns are related to four factors and having produced a particular four factor solution, the next step is to examine how much of the total return is explained by these four factors and to compare this to the amount explained by the more conventional single index model.

To examine this, we utilized the 20 groups ranked by size discussed in the previous section. Grouping will of course increase the amount explained by any model. At the same time it creates a manageable set of data that can allow not only an examination of average explanatory power but an examination of explanatory power across sets of stocks.

Table 3.6 shows the sensitivities and adjusted R^2 when the returns on each of the 20 portfolios are regressed against the four factors for the 15 year period April 1971 to March 1986. Across the 20 portfolios the aver-

Table 3.6
Sensitivities and explanatory power for the four-factor model.[a]

	Beta coefficients				
	F1	F2	F3	F4	Adj. R^2
1	0.0428	0.0092	−0.0088	−0.0199	0.8168
2	0.0442	0.0048	−0.0048	−0.0203	0.8201
3	0.0427	0.0034	−0.0067	−0.0158	0.8580
4	0.0417	−0.0003*	−0.0060	−0.0137	0.8239
5	0.0421	0.0041	−0.0001*	−0.0121	0.7516
6	0.0396	0.0022*	−0.0030*	−0.0066	0.7689
7	0.0388	0.0077	0.0034*	−0.0028*	0.7504
8	0.0380	0.0078	0.0013*	0.0013*	0.7767
9	0.0417	0.0059	0.0011*	0.0010*	0.8130
10	0.0356	0.0025*	0.0020*	0.0001*	0.7266
11	0.0375	0.0023*	0.0071	0.0051	0.7732
12	0.0384	−0.0007*	0.0101	0.0053	0.7642
13	0.0347	−0.0037	0.0104	0.0084	0.7479
14	0.0374	−0.0029*	0.0084	0.0134	0.8112
15	0.0368	−0.0037	0.0100	0.0138	0.7605
16	0.0384	−0.0059	0.0188	0.0168	0.8086
17	0.0330	−0.0087	0.0134	0.0179	0.7395
18	0.0385	−0.0004*	0.0152	0.0151	0.7371
19	0.0364	−0.0022*	0.0163	0.0194	0.6995
20	0.0364	−0.0065	0.0171	0.0230	0.6626
Average:					0.7765

a. Asterisks denote insignificance at the 5% level.

age adjusted R^2 is 78%. Of the 80 different sensitivity estimates all but 18 are significant at the 5% level.

As a standard of comparison we utilized the single index model. This involved regressing returns on the 20 portfolios against the NRI 400 Index. The NRI 400 Index is a value weighted index. It is made up of the same 400 stocks we are analyzing. Thus, the relationship between the 20 portfolios and the index is likely to be higher than if we had chosen another market index. Table 3.7 shows the results.[9] As one might expect given the construction of the index, the R^2 declines which size. However, the extent of the decline is dramatic. The adjusted R^2 is less than 50% for

Table 3.7
Sensitivity and explanatory power for 1 index model.

	Beta coefficient	Adj R^2	Alpha	Avg. return
1	1.1373	0.9065	−0.0018	0.0117
2	1.1289	0.8790	−0.0030	0.0104
3	1.0283	0.8700	0.0000	0.0122
4	0.9610	0.8180	−0.0002	0.0112
5	0.9570	0.7649	0.0030	0.0144
6	0.8697	0.7525	0.0007	0.0110
7	0.7877	0.6675	0.0022	0.0115
8	0.7942	0.6693	0.0038	0.0132
9	0.8130	0.6904	0.0000	0.0096
10	0.7067	0.5650	0.0069	0.0153
11	0.7037	0.5610	0.0037	0.0121
12	0.7097	0.5081	0.0036	0.0120
13	0.6232	0.4174	0.0098	0.0172
14	0.6203	0.4022	0.0058	0.0132
15	0.6307	0.3663	0.0073	0.0147
16	0.6137	0.3365	0.0106	0.0179
17	0.4815	0.2137	0.0124	0.0181
18	0.6001	0.2916	0.0109	0.0180
19	0.5349	0.2083	0.0135	0.0199
20	0.4841	0.1439	0.0203	0.0260
Average			0.5516	

the last eight portfolios and less than 15% for the portfolio of smallest stocks.

The explanatory power of the single index model is much less than that of the four factor model. The average R^2 is 55% compared to 78% for the four factor model. Thus, the four factor model explains considerably more of the time series of security returns.

Examining the composition of the first factor shows that it resembles an equally weighted market index. Thus it is interesting to examine the explanatory power of this factor relative to the NRI 400. Table 3.8 shows the comparison. The average R^2 is 67% which is higher than the average R^2 for the single index model using the NRI 400. The explanatory power declines slightly as the size of the firm declines. However, the decline is

Table 3.8
Explanatory power of regression of returns of 20 portfolios on return of NRI 400 and factor 1.[a]

	Adjusted R^2	
	NRI 400	F1
1	0.9065	0.6447
2	0.8790	0.6839
3	0.8700	0.7502
4	0.8180	0.7429
5	0.7649	0.6995
6	0.7525	0.7488
7	0.6675	0.7190
8	0.6693	0.7488
9	0.6904	0.7996
10	0.5050	0.7256
11	0.5610	0.7376
12	0.5081	0.7098
13	0.4174	0.6564
14	0.4022	0.6998
15	0.3663	0.6363
16	0.3365	0.6358
17	0.2137	0.5033
18	0.2916	0.5796
19	0.2083	0.4900
20	0.1439	0.4220
Average	0.5516	0.6667

a. Time period: April 1972–March 1986 (NRI 400), April 1971–March 1986 (factor 1).

nowhere near as pronounced as the decline when using the NRI 400 as the market factor. Thus, the first factor has a much more uniform explanatory power than does using the NRI 400 as the index.

Comparing the explanatory power of the first factor in the four factor model with all four factors shows that the added three factors explain a significant proportion of the variability of returns.

The sensitivity of portfolio returns to the NRI 400 Index (beta) also declines with size. This is not at all expected. Beta is usually considered a measure of risk. For U.S. data the beta coefficient increases as size decreases. Thus smaller firms are viewed as having greater risk. For Japanese data the reverse is true. The smaller firms have much lower betas than the large firms. Some caution is in order. The firms in the sample are all fairly large. There are 1100 firms in the first section of the Tokyo stock exchange. The NRI 400 includes 400 companies selected from among the largest firms on the Tokyo Stock Exchange. Thus the relationship between size and beta is found in the larger firms of the first section of the Tokyo Stock Exchange. The second result that is evident from table 3.7 is that return is strongly related to size. Examining the last column of table 3.7 shows a difference between the return on the small and large firms of over one percent per month. Furthermore, the relationship is almost monotonic.

The reduction in beta as size decreases as well as an increase in average return means that the smaller firms provide a higher return as well as lower beta. If beta is a risk measure, this evidence strongly favors the purchase of small stocks. Alternatively, this could be viewed as evidence that beta is not a sufficient metric for risk. The relationship between return and size is also evident in the four factor model. For example, the sensitivities shown to factor four are ranked by size. A similar pattern, although less pronounced, is seen in factors 2 and 3. Thus, part of what the four factor model is picking up relative to the one factor model is a size effect. In summary, the four factor model does a much better job of explaining the time series pattern of return than does the single index model. Most of the advantage comes from explaining return on stocks of companies below the average size of companies included in the NRI 400.

Another interesting question is the stability of the sensitivity of return to the factors. We will examine the stability of the sensitivities for factor 4. We concentrate on factor 4 because it generally has the least stable sensitivity of our four factors. Table 3.9 shows the sensitivity coefficients for factor 4 for the 15 year period and three non-overlapping five year periods. While not identical, clearly the sensitivities have the same pattern across the 20 groups. The correlation between the sensitivities between the years 1971–1976 and 1976–1981 is 0.97. The correlation between the years 1976–1981 and 1981–1986 is 0.95. The average absolute difference in sensitivity between 1971–1976 and 1976–1981 was 0.0024 when the average absolute value of the sensitivity in 1971–1976 was 0.0105. Thus on average, the change was less than 23%. Likewise, the average absolute difference in sensitivity between 1976–1981 and 1981–1986 was 0.0039, with an average absolute value of the sensitivity in 1976–1981 of 0.0139. Thus, the average change was bout 28%. Thus the sensitivity measures between non-overlapping periods are very stable for factor 4. The stability is even more pronounced for other factors.

Table 3.9
Sensitivity to factor 4.[a]

Portfolio	71/04–86/03	81/04–86/03	76/04–81/03	71/04–76/03
1	−0.0199	−0.0261	−0.0196	−0.0155
2	−0.0203	−0.0219	−0.0193	−0.0164
3	−0.0158	−0.0180	−0.0162	−0.0135
4	−0.0137	−0.0173	−0.0109	−0.0127
5	−0.0121	−0.0068*	−0.0107	−0.0162
6	−0.0066	−0.0018*	−0.0073	−0.0074
7	−0.0028*	0.0040*	−0.0048*	−0.0045*
8	0.0013*	0.0042*	−0.0009*	0.0031*
9	0.0010*	−0.0006*	0.0018*	0.0002*
10	0.0001*	0.0031*	0.0005*	−0.0008*
11	0.0051	0.0055*	0.0057*	0.0043*
12	0.0053	0.0073	0.0069	0.0037*
13	0.0084	0.0126	0.0049*	0.0060
14	0.0134	0.0084	0.0156	0.0140
15	0.0138	0.0180	0.0172	0.0083
16	0.0168	0.0125	0.0164	0.0177
17	0.0179	0.0187	0.0133	0.0155
18	0.0151	0.0133	0.0134	0.0132
19	0.0194	0.0230	0.0165	0.0153
20	0.0230	0.0238	0.0234	0.0216

a. Asterisks denote insignificance at 5% level.

In this section we have shown that a four factor model explains returns better than a one factor model. In addition, we have examined the stability of the sensitivities and have shown them to be very stable over time.

IV Index Tracking

In the prior section we showed that the four factor model explained a significantly greater percentage of return variability than did the market (one factor) model. Some increase in explanatory power is not surprising given the greater number of factors. However, the four factor model consistently has a high explanatory power across all portfolios, where the explanatory power for the one factor model deteriorates badly with size. A much more powerful test would be to make comparisons in a forecast mode. One method of doing this is analyzed in this section.

The test we will perform involves index matching. First, based on each model a portfolio of a small number of stocks that most clearly matches the return pattern of a pre-selected index is formed. In the case of the market model, we construct a portfolio with the same sensitivity (beta) as the index in question with minimum residual risk, and with (approximately) a fixed number of securities. In the case of the four factor model, we construct a portfolio that has the same sensitivity as the index on each of the four factors, with minimum residual risk and with (approximately) a fixed number of securities. The second step in this test is to examine the ability of these portfolios to match the index over a period of time subsequent to when they are formed.

The index matching test is a joint test of a number of hypotheses. One aspect affecting performance is whether there are one or four factors in the market. Even if there are four factors, the one factor model could still perform better if the historically estimated sensitivities for the four factor model were poor forecasts of future sensitivities, while the historical sensitivity for the single index model was a good predictor of future sensitivities. Finally, we might not be able to distinguish differences in the performance of our two models even if the four factor model was a superior description of reality, if the sensitivity of the market to these four factors was very stable over time. In this case, matching market betas is equivalent to matching factor sensitivities. Thus, our tests are joint tests of the model, stability of the sensitivities and the stability of the relationship of the market to the factors.

The index we selected to match was the Nikkei 225. We attempted to match the index over the five years from January 1, 1981 to December 31, 1986. The first step was estimating sensitivities for each security. Sensitivities had to be estimated for both the market model and the four factor model. Sensitivities were estimated on a quarterly basis for each model. For the market model we simply ran a regression of the return on each of the 393 stocks in our study versus the Tokyo Stock Exchange Index at the beginning of each quarter using the previous five years of data. For the four factor model a factor analysis was run at the beginning of each quarter using the prior eleven years of return data to determine the composition of the factors. Then, at the beginning of each quarter we ran a regression over the same period of returns on the 393 securities which comprise our samples versus return on the four factors. The regression coefficients were the sensitivities or betas used in the next step. In order to study the ability of our four factor model or the market model to produce portfolios which matched a particular index (e.g., the Nikkei 225) the sensitivity of that index was measured by regressing it against both the Tokyo Stock Exchange Index for the market model or the four indices for the four factor model.

Once the sensitivities were determined, we calculated the composition of the portfolio intended to match the index. Matching portfolios were determined for portfolios of about 25, 50 and 100 securities.

For example, for the market model and 25 securities, the following quadratic programming problem was solved:

$$\text{minimize} \sum_i X_i^2 \sigma_{\varepsilon_i}^2$$

subject to

$$\sum X_i \beta_i = \beta_p \text{ (sensitivity matching)}, \tag{1}$$

$$0 \leqslant X_i \leqslant 0.04 \text{ (no 'short sales' and 'upper bond')}, \tag{2}$$

where

X_i is the proportion in security i,

β_i is the sensitivity of a security to the market,

β_p is the sensitivity of the Nikkei 225 to the market,

$\sigma_{\varepsilon_i}^2$ is the residual risk from the market model.

The first constraint causes a matching of sensitivities. For the one factor model this causes the beta on the matching portfolio to be the same as the beta on the Nikkei 225.

For the four factor model the first constraint presented above is replaced by a constraint that requires that the beta (sensitivity) be matched on each of the four factors. We wanted to have the same number of securities in the portfolio whether we matched using the one factor model or the four factor model. This guarantees that relative performance is unaffected by differences in the size of the portfolios. The constraint on the maximum invested in a security guarantees that there will be roughly the same number of securities in the two portfolios. In subsequent tables we will examine alternative values of the constraint on maximum investment. We shall use upper limits of 0.04, 0.02, and 0.01 and refer to the portfolios as

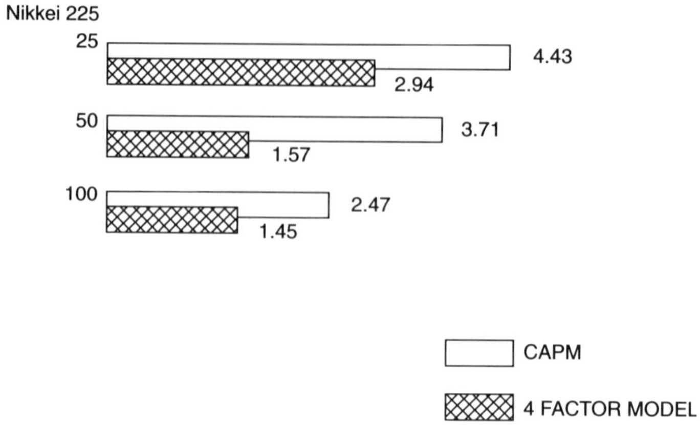

Figure 3.3
Comparison of single and 4-factor model (difference in return)

having 25, 50 or 100 securities. In actual practice, a number of the portfolios had slightly more securities than the number shown.

The same procedure was repeated every quarter, or 20 times over the five year period.

Having determined the portfolio composition at the beginning of each quarter, we than calculated the return on the Nikkei 225 adjusted for dividends each month as well as the return on the matching portfolio using the market model and the matching portfolio using the four factor model.[10] To examine which model matches the adjusted Nikkei 225 more closely, we calculated the monthly difference in return between the index and the matching portfolio and squared it. We than computed the average squared difference between the index and the two matching portfolios (fig. 3.3). Results for portfolios of size 25, 50 and 100 are presented. We also performed one further test. Since financial stocks are thinly traded, we excluded financial stocks from those which could be held in the matching portfolio. Since financial stocks are believed to move together, this tests the ability to match when a segment of the market is excluded. We tested this for a fifty stock portfolio.

In all four tests the matching portfolios formed using four factors outperformed the matching portfolios using one factor. Using the four factor model cut the average squared forecasting error in some cases by more than 1/2. This test involves forecasting the model and parameters. Thus the difference in number of factors during the fit period does not bias the results. The ability of the four factor model to allow the construction of a portfolio that better tracks a second portfolio is powerful evidence that the four factor model better describes reality.[11]

V Relationship of Factors to Economic Variables

In earlier sections, we constructed and presented evidence on the existence of four factors in the return generating process for Japanese securities. It would be convenient in predicting and understanding these factors if they were associated with economic variables. There is a difficulty with this approach. Since the four factors are not unique to a linear transformation, there are, of course, an infinite number of four factor models that would serve equally well. Thus, which factor is associated with which economic variable or set of economic variables is arbitrary.

Any information contained in the current level of economic variables should be incorporated in security prices. What should affect security returns is an unanticipated change in the level of the variables. We were unable to obtain expectational data on the variables we used. Thus we were forced to compromise. As our unanticipated change we used the continuously compounded change in the level of the variable. This definition of unanticipated change implicitly assumes that investors predicted zero change in the economic index. This is not dissimilar to the approach taken by others. A more complicated procedure would involve detailed research to determine a forecasting technique for each variable and would involve extensive research projects by themselves. Error in our determination of the forecast model should result in our finding less association than truly exists.

Table 3.10 lists the economic variables that we used. These variables can be classified as measures of inflation rates, interest rates, foreign trade, petroleum prices, economic conditions and U.S. interest rates and inflation.

As discussed earlier, there is a large number of alternative four factor models that are identical in their ability to explain returns. Thus it would be very arbitrary to simply relate any single factor to the economic variables. Rather, what we did was calculate the canonical correlation between the four factors and the economic variables. The cumulative correlation for the four canonical variables is 29.6% in the 15 year period from April 1971 to March 1986, and 63.9% in the five year period from April 1984 to March 1986. Thus, the statistically determined factors do have a strong relationship to the economic variables.

Table 3.10

(1) Inflation rate:
Consumer price index
Wholsesale price index
Yen/dollar rate (US dollar central rate)
Export price index (YEN base)
Import price index (YEN base)
Nikkei commodity price index
Expected inflation rate
(2) Interest rate:
Call rate
10 yr. gov't bond yield
Difference in rates between short and long term interest
Difference in short term interests between Japan and USA
(3) Foreign trade:
Exports quantum index
Imports quantum index
Crude oil import quantity
(4) Petroleum prices:
Crude oil import price
(5) Economic conditions:
Workers' households disposable income
Production index
Inventory index
Value of public contracts
Number of corporate bankruptcies
Index of business outlook about small enterprises
Retail trade index (seasonally adjusted)
Forecast industrial production rate
(6) U.S. interest rate and inflation:
Consumer price index of USA
3-month TB rate
Treasurites securities yields (20 years, avg.)

While the work in this brief section is preliminary in nature it does indicate that economic factors have an influence on the risk structure of security returns. These results suggest that continuing work in this area should prove promising.

VI Cross-Sectional Tests

In this section of the paper we examine the relationship of average returns to the factor sensitivities. This is considered a standard APT type test. Factors are generally divided into two types of factors, so-called priced factors and unpriced factors. Priced factors are factors that not only explain the time series of returns but also have their sensitivities related to average returns. Unpriced factors are factors that affect the time series of returns but whose sensitivities are not related to average return.

Both types of factors are important in trying to explain the time series of returns. However, for explaining expected return only price factors are important.

The examination of priced and unpriced factors was determined in a procedure similar to Roll and Ross (1980). At the beginning of each year a regression was run using data from the prior five years. The regression related return on our 20 portfolios to the return on the four factors. After estimating the sensitivities from the time series regression, a cross-sectional regression was run in each of the next 12 months. The regression has the form:

$$\text{return on portfolio} \quad i = \lambda_0 + \sum_{j=1}^{4} \lambda_i \beta_{ij},$$

where

β_{ij} are the sensitivities estimated from the five year time series regression,

λ_j are estimated from the regression.

The λ_j were estimated for each of the 12 months. At the end of the year (beginning of the next) a new five year time series regression was run to estimate sensitivities. These sensitivities are then used in the next year, and so forth. Since we had 15 years of data and need five years to estimate the time series regression, we have ten years of monthly λ_js or a total of 120.

Table 3.11 shows the results. The average for each λ_j is the average value over the 120 months. The T-values are calculated by using the 120

Table 3.11
Values of lambda

	Average	S.D.	T-Value	$\#\|T\| > 1^*$	$\#\|T\| > 2^*$
Lambda 1	0.098	1.214	0.884	51/120	17/120
Lambda 2	−0.063	0.934	−0.738	62/120	22/120
Lambda 3	0.005	0.873	0.062	54/120	21/120
Lambda 4	0.193	1.127	1.880	69/120	33/120

observations on λ_j to obtain a standard deviation of the mean and this is used to calculate T. The last two columns report one more measure of significance. For each of the 120 cross sectional regressions we obtain a T value. The last two columns show how often the absolute value of the T is greater than 1 or 2.

By any normal measures of significance only factor four is priced. Thus, factors 1, 2 and 3 affect return but the investor does not earn excess return by having a portfolio whose returns are sensitive to these factors. Since these factors are important in affecting the risk of a large portfolio but not the return, the investor should make the sensitivity to these factors for the portfolio as close to zero as possible.

VII Conclusion

In this paper we have estimated the return generating process for large stocks on the Tokyo Stock Exchange. We have found that four factors are sufficient to describe the return generating process. In determining if four factors were sufficient, a new methodology for identifying the factors which make up the return generating process was described and applied. In addition, we have found that the impact of these factors on returns are reasonably stable over time and that at least in one application (replicating the performance of stock indices) the factors have meaningful forecasting ability. Next we showed that the factors are highly correlated with changes in a set of economic variables. Finally we examined the ability of the factors to explain cross-sectional differences in return.

Notes

This paper owes much to our collaboration with the quantitative analysis team of the Nomura Securities group (MERRIT 21). In particular, our research would have been almost impossible without the efforts by two individuals, Mr. Y. Akeda and Mr. Y. Kato of the Nomura Research Institute.

1. See Roll and Ross (1980), Brown and Weinstein (1982), and Dhrymes, Friend and Gultekin (1984).

2. See Roll and Ross (1980), Brown and Weinstein (1983), Dhrymes, Friend and Gultekin (1984), and Gibbons (1981).

3. This problem is separable from but also associated with determining the number of factors which are priced.

4. Cho, Elton and Gruber (1984) have demonstrated that maximum-likelihood factor analysis is robust in identifying the correct number of factors under reasonable sets of assumptions.

5. Our sample was the NRI 400. Seven stocks were discarded because of data problems.

6. See for example, Roll and Ross (1980) and Gibbons (1981).

7. See Ross and Roll (1980) and Dhrymes, Friend and Gultekin (1984) for a debate on this issue.

8. For evidence on the Japanese market see Nakamura and Terada (1984).

9. That the four factor model has a higher explanatory power than a single factor market model in the fit period is to be expected. The size of the difference is, however, different than for U.S. studies as is the deterioration with size. In the next section, we will analyse explanatory power in forecasting.

10. Dividends average about 1% per annum. Dividend payments were implicitly reinvested in the portfolio at the proportions existing at the time the stock went ex-divided.

11. As we discussed earlier, this is a joint test. However, it is not very plausible that the four factor model is more stable than the one factor model. Its superior performance is likely to be because of the presence of multiple factors rather than greater stability of sensitivities.

References

Akaike, H., 1974, A new look at the statistical identification model, *IEEE Transactions on Automatic Control*, 716–723.

Brown, Steve and Mark Weinstein, 1983, A new approach to testing asset pricing models: The bilinear paradigm, *Journal of Finance* 38, 711–743.

Chen, Nai-Fu, 1983, Some empirical tests of the theory of arbitrage pricing, *Journal of Finance* 38, no. 5, 1393–1414.

Cho, D. Chinhyung, 1984, On testing the arbitrage pricing theory: Inter-battery factor analysis, *Journal of Finance* 19, no. 1, 1–10.

Cho, D. Chinhyung, Edwin Elton and Martin Gruber, 1984, On the robustness of the Roll and Ross arbitrage pricing theory, *Journal of Financial and Qualitative Analysis* 19, no. 1, 1–10.

Dhrymes, Phoebus, Irwin Friend and N. Bulent Gultekin, 1984, A critical re-examination of the empirical evidence on the arbitrage pricing theory, *Journal of Finance* 39, no. 2, 323–346.

Elton, Edwin and Martin Gruber, 1987, *Modern portfolio theory and investment analysis* (Wiley, New York) 3rd ed.

Gibbons, Mike, 1981, Empirical examination of the return generating process of the arbitrage pricing theory, Working paper (Stanford University, Stanford, CA).

Hamao, Yasushi, 1988, An empirical examination of the arbitrage pricing theory: Using Japanese data, *Japan and the World Economy* 1, 45–61.

Lawley, D. N. and A. E. Maxwell, 1971, *Factor analysis as a statistical method* (Macmillan, New York).

Nakamura, Takeo and Noboru Terada, 1984, The size effect and seasonality in Japanese stock returns, Paper presented at the Institute for Quantitative Research in Finance.

Roll, Richard and Steve Ross, 1980, An empirical investigation of the arbitrage pricing theory, *Journal of Finance* 35, no. 5, 1073–1103.

Schwartz, G., 1978, Estimating the dimension of a model, *Annals of Statistics* 6, 461–464.

4

Do Investors Care About Sentiment?

Edwin J. Elton, Martin J. Gruber, and Jeffrey A. Busse

Lee, Shleifer and Thaler (1991) (LS&T) claim they have uncovered a new influence (factor), small investor sentiment that affects the risk of common stocks.[1] Furthermore, they believe that this factor is especially important in explaining the return pattern of closed-end funds and small stocks. They claim that firms with high sensitivity to this factor must earn an extra return as compensation for this extra risk (market price of risk positive). Finally they argue that this factor can be measured by the change in the discount on closed-end funds.

Determining which factors explain the return of individual securities is one of the key issues in investment research. Which of these factors are priced is the fundamental issue of asset pricing theory. Thus their claims, if correct, make an important contribution to our understanding of how capital markets function.

In this paper we explore whether investor sentiment (as measured by the change in the discount on closed-end funds) is an important factor in the return-generating process for common stocks and whether one set of firms closed-end funds with greater sensitivity to this factor offer, and can be expected to offer, a higher expected return. Our results do not support any of the contentions of LS&T. We first explore the importance of sentiment on the return-generating process (RGP). Initially we show that the discount on closed-end funds does not enter the RGP more frequently than a set of indexes constructed in an analogous manner from a set of firms not subject to small investor sentiment (large institutionally-held industrial firms). In fact, the frequency with which the discount for closed-end funds enters the return-generating process is not much different from what would be expected by chance. Second, we show that if the indexes are measured as industry return indexes rather than discounts, they enter the return-generating process more frequently. Industry return indexes are used as a reference because industry return indexes are not considered systematic factors. Third, when we examine the pattern of sensitivity to the change in the discount of closed funds across size categories using the same two-factor model employed by LS&T, we get a pattern like theirs. However, using a more general multi-factor model, this pattern disappears. Finally, we relate the sentiment index to a set of empirically derived factors. We show that the empirically derived factors are not affected by sentiment.

When we examine expected returns we find results consistent with the results obtained by an examination of the return-generating process. We show that closed-end funds do not have higher average return than would be expected given their sensitivities to a multi-index model. Thus, there is no evidence that firms with higher sensitivity to the change in discount on closed ends give a higher return.

The paper is divided into three sections. In the first section we discuss the return-generating process, the sample data, and index construction. In the second section we present evidence on whether sentiment affects the return-generating process. In the third and last section we provide evidence on whether sentiment risk is priced.

I The Return-Generating Process, Data, Samples and Index Construction

In this section we discuss the return-generating process (RGP), the data, the samples we employ, and the construction of the investor sentiment index.

A The Return-Generating Process

In order to measure the importance of adding sentiment to the RGP we need to specify a base RGP that doesn't include sentiment. We used two different base RGPs. First, because LS&T use a one-index model as a base to which they added sentiment, we employed a similar one-index model. The one-index model is

$$R_{it} = \alpha_i + \beta_{ij} R_{jt} + e_{it}$$

where

1. R_{it} is the return in month t of a security or portfolio i in excess return form.

2. R_{jt} is the return on index j in period t in excess return form.[2]

3. β_{ij} is the sensitivity of stock or portfolio i to index j.
4. e_{it} is the residual of stock or portfolio i in period t.
5. α_i is the non-systematic mean return for stock or portfolio i.

We do not believe that a one-index model is an appropriate RGP, but rather we rely on recent literature that finds evidence for a four-index or at most a five-index model.[3] The multi-index return-generating process can be represented as

$$R_{it} = \alpha_i + \Sigma_j \beta_{ij} R_{jt} + e_{it}$$

We employ a four-index form of the model developed and tested in Elton, Gruber and Blake (1996a) and (1996b). The indexes we employ are the excess return on the S&P 500, an index that represents the return on a portfolio of small (low capitalization) stocks minus the return on a portfolio of large capitalization stocks, an index that represents the return on a portfolio of "growth" stocks minus the return on a portfolio of "value" stocks, and an index of the excess return on a portfolio of bonds.[4]

B Data

Data came from six sources. All security returns, including market returns on closed-end funds, are from the monthly CRSP tape. Index returns for the S&P index and the value weighted CRSP index, and returns on size deciles, were also from CRSP. The small minus large index and value growth indexes were from Prudential Bache. The bond index is from Shearson-Lehman. Finally, open-end mutual fund data was provided by MICROPAL.

Net asset value came from two sources: for closed-end funds it was provided to us by Lipper; for industrial companies it was taken from the Compustat tapes.

C Samples

To text the return-generating process we used three samples of individual security returns and three samples of portfolio returns. The first individual security return sample was made up of the 586 NYSE stocks that had continuous return history from January 1969 to December 1994. To guard against a concern that this sample is not representative of the full population, we also constructed a sample of all stocks listed on CRSP that had a minimum of three years of history between January 1980 and December

1994. This sample had 4,967 firms. Closed-end funds and utility stocks were excluded from the two stock samples. The final sample of individual security returns consisted of the 99 utility stocks which had a complete history of data from January 1969 to December 1994. We used this sample because LS&T argued that utility stocks have low institutional ownership and were therefore subject to sentiment.

The three portfolio samples consisted of two sets of passive and one set of active portfolios. The first set of passive portfolios were the CRSP size deciles. These were selected because of their use by LS&T and the more general use of size portfolios in testing return-generating process. The second set of passive portfolios were 28 industry return indexes. These indexes were constructed by sorting our 586 industrial firms into groups by two-digit SIC code. Then, for all industries with more than five members, a value-weighted return index was constructed.[5] The active portfolio was a sample of 267 mutual funds that had data from January 1979 to January 1993 and listed common stock investment as their investment objective.

These portfolios are especially interesting because mutual funds have an incentive to offer funds that span the set of important indexes. If sentiment is an index that investors care about, then the mutual fund industry should offer an array of funds with different loadings on this factor. If they did not, then a mutual fund would gain a large inflow of funds if they offered differential sensitivity to it, and other funds would likely follow suit. Thus, examining mutual fund returns is a useful way of examining which factors are important.

D Index Construction

Since our sample period does not coincide with that of LS&T, it was necessary to reconstruct their sentiment indexes. We followed their procedure in index construction almost exactly. The indexes are value-weighted. The discount is the net asset value minus the stock price over the net asset value times 100. When the monthly change in the discount was calculated, we maintained a common number of firms at the start and end of the month. Thus, if a firm would have entered our index during the month of January, it was not used in calculating the change in discount for January but was in February. The primary change we made from the LS&T procedure was to exclude from the index funds in their first six months of their existence.[6] We did this because of evidence that during this period the discount on closed-end funds is affected by arbitrage and price stabilizing actions of investment bankers and behaves differently from the discount of other closed-end funds. We calculated two measures of the discount on closed-end funds, one for stock funds and one for bond funds. Both are interesting to study. The discount on equity closed-end funds is the primary measure used by LS&T. It has the disadvantage that "sentiment" can affect both market value and net asset value. Thus LS&T went to some lengths to try to argue that the equity closed-end funds held large stocks whose price was determined by institutions not subject to "sentiment." Bond funds do not have these problems. Bond markets are dominated by institutional traders. Furthermore, arbitrages are fairly easily undertaken and the possibility of price discrepancies is constantly monitored. Thus, it is hard to argue that individual bonds are subject to "sentiment." The discount on closed-end bond funds is thus a purer measure of what the equity market will pay for a set of assets whose value is unaffected by "sentiment." Our indexes contained many more funds than those constructed by LS&T for there were more funds in existence during the more recent period of our study. Over period we had a maximum of 32 stock closed-end funds and 38 bond closed-end funds. Since LS&T used an equity sentiment index, we will emphasize the results for this index.

Later we will compare the performance of these closed-end fund indexes to a set of indexes that were constructed in an analogous manner but using data for industrial firms. We selected the four industries with the largest number of firms in our sample, where industries were determined by two-digit SIC code. For these industries we ranked firms by market capitalization. We then selected from each industry the twenty largest firms that had over 50% institutional ownership. If "sentiment" is related to irrational behavior of small investors, then these firms should be unaffected by sentiment. Since for industrial firms net asset value (i.e., book value) is only available quarterly, these indexes are computed quarterly.

Finally, we constructed a set of return indexes. These indexes were value-weighted and comprised the same firms that we used in constructing the discounts. For comparison purposes, all indexes that could be computed monthly were also computed on a quarterly basis.

II Does Sentiment Affect the Return-Generating Process?

Modern asset pricing theory proves that for sensitivity to a factor to be priced it is necessary for the factor to be a systematic influence. Identifying systematic influences is a complex process. The return on any industry portfolio will enter the return-generating process for some securities. In fact, the return on most random portfolios of securities would also enter the return-generating process for some set of securities. Thus, to see if sentiment as measured by the change in the discount on closed-end funds (called ΔD-EF for equity funds or ΔD-BF for bond funds) is systematic it is necessary to compare its importance in the return-generating process to some factors most investigators would not believe are priced. Industry return indexes are a natural candidate. Industry return indexes will surely enter the return-generating process for most firms in the industry they were constructed from and likely for many firms in closely related industries. One test we will use for examining the importance of sentiment in the return-generating process is to see how often it is significant in time series estimates of this process relative to a set of industry return indexes computed for both the closed-end fund sample and other industries.

Before we compare the significance of ΔD-EF or ΔD-BF with the significance of industry return indexes, it is useful as an intermediate step to compare the significance of the change in discount on closed-end funds with the significance of the change in discount for a set of industry indexes constructed in such a way that sentiment is unlikely to play a role. As discussed earlier, the comparison group is the change in discount on a value weighted portfolio of 20 large firms, which exhibited high institutional ownership, drawn from each of four industries.[7] Sentiment is supposed to affect small firms with low institutional ownership. Because of large firm size and high institutional ownership, these industry indexes should not be affected by a sentiment index.

A *The Significance of Sentiment*

As stated earlier, we used several samples of individual securities and portfolios to judge the importance of factors in the return-generating process. Tables 4.1 and 4.2 show number of times that a factor is significant at the 5% level for each of the six candidates for a factor in the return-generating process. The candidates examined are the change in discount on equity funds, the change in discount on bond funds and the change in discount for each of the four industry samples. Table 4.1 presents the results for individual securities, while Table 4.2 presents the results for portfolios of securities. In both Tables 4.1 and 4.2, Panel A shows the results for the two-index model (the S&P plus one of the six ΔD's) while Panel B shows the results for the five-index model (the S&P, small minus large, value minus growth, a bond index plus one of

Table 4.1
Number of times individual security sensitivities are significant at the 5% level

	Discounts				Returns			
	A. 2 index model		B. 5 index model		C. 2 index model		D. 5 index model	
	585 industrial stock sample	99 utility stock sample	585 industrial stock sample	99 utility stock sample	585 industrial stock sample	99 utility stock sample	585 industrial stock sample	99 utility stock sample
Closed end stock funds	35	0	48	2	58	1	55	3
Closed end bond funds	53	36	74	34	71	73	82	30
Transportation	155	4	69	3	255	5	103	6
Industrial machinery	85	3	63	0	202	37	63	2
Electronics	103	5	67	4	172	49	100	25
Chemicals	90	4	99	25	87	9	70	6

The table shows the number of times the individual security sensitivities are significant at the 5% level in regressions of the excess returns of the securities against various models. The indices in the 2 index model are the excess return on the S&P500 index plus the index shown. The 5 Index model contains the excess return on the S&P500 index, the difference in return between a small cap portfolio and a large cap portfolio based on Prudential-Bache indices, the difference in return between a high growth portfolio and a value portfolio based on Prudential-Bache indices, the excess return on the Shearson Lehman Government Corporate bond index, and the index shown. The models in panels A and B contain ΔD, which represents the change in the value weighted discount index, where the index is given by the difference between the book value and the market value divided by the book value for the 4 industries and the difference between the net asset value and market value divided by the net asset value for the closed end funds. The models in panels C and D contain value weighted Industry returns. Returns and discount changes are of a quarterly frequency. The sample period is from 1980 through 1994.

Table 4.2
Number of times portfolio sensitivities are significant at the 5% level

	Discounts						Returns					
	A. 2 index model			B. 5 index model			C. 2 index model			D. 5 index model		
	267 mutual funds	10 size portfolios	28 SIC portfolios	267 mutual funds	10 size portfolios	28 SIC portfolios	267 mutual funds	10 size portfolios	28 SIC portfolios	267 mutual funds	10 size portfolios	28 SIC portfolios
Closed end stock funds	15	0	2	24	0	4	35	9	3	20	0	3
Closed end bond funds	45	4	1	43	1	4	75	2	4	41	0	4
Transportation	100	10	18	40	0	6	133	10	19	52	1	11
Industrial machinery	33	2	9	30	1	3	144	10	21	51	4	9
Electronics	31	3	12	27	0	8	47	9	16	40	1	8
Chemicals	35	3	5	45	4	8	64	3	9	28	3	6

The table shows the number of times the portfolio sensitivities are significant at the 5% level in regressions of the excess returns of the portfolios against various models. The indices in the 2 index model are the excess return on the S&P500 index plus the index shown. The 5 Index model contains the excess return on the S&P500 index, the difference in return between a small cap portfolio and a large cap portfolio based on Prudential-Bache indices, the difference in return between a high growth portfolio and a value portfolio based on Prudential-Bache indices, the excess return on the Shearson Lehman Government Corporate bond index, and the index shown. The models in panels A and B contain ΔD, which represents the change in the value weighted discount index, where the index is given by the difference between the book value and the market value divided by the book value for the 4 industries and the difference between the net asset value and market value divided by the net asset value for the closed end funds. The models in panels C and D contain value weighted industry returns. Returns and discount changes are of a quarterly frequency. The sample period is from 1980 through 1994.

the six ΔD's). Panels C and D parallel Panels A and B except that the indexes measuring change in discounts have been replaced with return indexes.[8]

Consider first the results for individual securities shown in Panel A of Table 4.1. For individual security returns, ΔD-EF is important in fewer cases than any other ΔD's. In fact, the 35 significant betas for the sample of 586 industrial firms is five more than would be expected by chance, and the zero for utilities is five less than would be expected by chance. All other ΔD's come in more often than ΔD-EF. Part of this is likely to arise because these indexes are better proxies for other variables omitted from the return-generating process. For the stock sample ΔD-BF enters the return-generating process more often than ΔD-EF but still enters the return-generating process less frequently than the industrial indexes. For the utility sample it enters the return-generating process much more frequently. LS&T excluded all bond funds from the results they reported for their sentiment index. However, as discussed earlier, ΔD-BF could be viewed as a sentiment index.

Panel B shows the results when the ΔD's are added to four-index base model. This model has been shown to work about as well as any return-generating process in other studies.[9] ΔD-EF is significant a few more times with the five-index model but is still not significant much more than one would expect by chance across the two stock samples. Furthermore, with one exception, once again all the other ΔD's are significant more often than ΔD-EF. If we were to select another index in the return-generating process it would be one of the other ΔD's. Note also that in Panels A and B the change in the discount on equity funds is significant a smaller percentage of the time for utility stocks than it is for industrial stocks. This is exactly the opposite of the conjecture of LS&T. Once again, ΔD-BF is significant more often than ΔD-EF. In all samples it enters the return-generating process about as often as the change in industry discounts.

The results for portfolios (Panels A and B of Table 4.2) are similar. When the two-index model is used (Panel A), ΔD-EF enters the return-generating process about the number of times we would expect by chance and less than the number of times the other ΔD's enter except for ΔD-BF for the 28 industry portfolios. When the five-index model is used, ΔD-EF is significant less times than the other ΔD's with two exceptions in one sample.

When the five-index model is examined, many of the ΔD's are significant slightly more than would be expected by chance. However, they enter much less often than other indexes enter when the five-index model is estimated. For the mutual fund sample, the S&P index enters significantly 265 times, the small minus large 155 times, the value growth 148 times, and the bond index 107 times. This is much larger than the number of times any of the ΔD's are significant. For the size and SIC groups the index with the least significance from the base four-index model is significant about the same number of times as the most significant ΔD, but which of the indexes is least significant varies across samples.

The question remains as to whether the ΔD's are measuring a fundamental influence (sentiment) or are simply acting as a proxy for either industry return or omitted variables. The ΔD's are of course correlated with industry returns (given the way ΔD is constructed, the correlation is negative). For the industry sample the book values will change very slowly over time. Thus ΔD will be primarily affected by the change in market value. This is reflected in the correlation of the value-weighted return indexes and the ΔD. For the four industrial ΔD's these correlations are −.54, −.53, −.77 and −.41 respectively. Likewise the book value for the bond closed-end funds will change less than the market value and fairly independently of the market value. Thus one would expect a high correlation between industry return of the bond closed-end funds and ΔD and the simple correlation is −.52. Since equity market movements affect both the market and book value for equity mutual funds, we would expect a lower correlation for this sample and returns, and this is what we observe (−.38). However, the question still remains whether even the limited significance of ΔD in the return-generating process is primarily due to the effect of industry returns on the ΔD's. To test this, we construct a value-weighted industry return index for each of our four industries.

The results are shown in Panels C and D of Tables 4.1 and 4.2 for the two- and five-index models. First, compare the results for the two-index ΔD model and the two-index return model (Panels A and C). In all but one case the industry return index is significant more often than the ΔD term. This is true whether the sample is individual security returns or a portfolio of returns. Now compare the five-index models. Once again, whether the sample is individual securities or portfolios, the return index in general has more significant coefficients than did the ΔD's. The evidence in total supports the notion that it is industry return indexes that explain security or portfolio returns and even the limited significance of the ΔD's is primarily because they are a proxy for a return index.

However, whether one looks at ΔD's or industry returns, the number of times they are significant does not support the presence of a systematic risk that is priced in the market.

B Does Another Variable Proxy for Sentiment?

Others have argued that ΔD-EF might be important but have its presence masked because it is correlated with a variable which is accepted as systematic and included in the return-generating process.

For example, ΔD-EF might be an important reason why size or growth minus value enter the return-generating process. To test this we regressed ΔD-EF against the base four model. The adjusted R^2 was negative. Thus it is not an explanation for size or growth minus value. When we regressed ΔD-BF against the four-index model, the adjusted R^2 was .24. The significant coefficient was associated with the growth minus value index. As discussed elsewhere, the growth minus value index is highly related to a market book index. ΔD is also a market book index for a particular industry. Thus its relationship to an aggregate market book index is hardly surprising or meaningful.[10]

C Sentiment and Size

One of the major ways to judge the contribution of a set of indexes to the return-generating process is to use portfolios formed on the basis of size as the unit of observation in time series tests. Size portfolios have been used as the unit of observation by Fama and French (1992) and Gibbons, Ross and Shanken (1989), among others, and play a key role in the testing of sentiment by LS&T. Thus it is worthwhile to examine this sample in more detail.

As discussed earlier, we used as our ten size portfolios the CRSP size deciles ordered from smallest to largest formed from NYSE stocks. Also, to better allow comparison with the LS&T results, in this section we follow their procedure and use Value Weighted New York Stock Exchange index (VWNY) as the market index rather than the S&P index used in other parts of this study.[11]

In Tables 4.3, 4.4 and 4.5 we present the results for the period October 1979 through December 1994. Panel A of Table 4.3 shows the results of a regression of the return for each decile on the change in the discount of closed-end equity funds (ΔD-EF) and the VWNY index (a two-factor RGP). The first column is the beta on the ΔD-EF, the second column is the *t* value, and the third column is the R^2. These results are comparable to Table VII of LS&T, although they report results for the period 1975–1985. Note that the R^2's are close to those found by LS&T. The pattern of regression coefficients are also suggestive of the LS&T results. The

Table 4.3
Regression results of CRSP market capitalization deciles against index models and the change in the industry value weighted discount

	A. Closed end stock funds						B. Transportation					
	2 index			5 index			2 index			5 index		
Decile	Beta(ΔD-EF)	t-stat	R-sq	Beta(ΔD-EF)	t-stat	R-sq	Beta(ΔD-TR)	t-stat	R-sq	Beta(ΔD-TR)	t-stat	R-sq
1	−0.110	−0.292	0.564	0.185	1.000	0.905	−0.200	−3.300	0.656	−0.014	−0.440	0.908
2	−0.177	−0.697	0.706	0.020	0.170	0.946	−0.132	−3.750	0.759	0.001	0.030	0.948
3	−0.141	−0.707	0.795	0.018	0.170	0.951	−0.076	−2.570	0.807	0.033	1.860	0.952
4	−0.018	−0.100	0.843	0.110	1.300	0.967	−0.075	−2.950	0.857	0.017	1.130	0.963
5	−0.035	−0.222	0.855	0.097	1.310	0.971	−0.063	−2.850	0.871	0.017	1.390	0.971
6	−0.092	−0.644	0.876	0.010	0.940	0.972	−0.068	−3.370	0.891	0.004	0.350	0.970
7	−0.003	−0.028	0.905	0.088	1.300	0.972	−0.067	−4.280	0.926	−0.017	−1.480	0.971
8	−0.108	−1.037	0.924	−0.035	−0.460	0.967	−0.046	−3.050	0.930	−0.007	−0.570	0.967
9	−0.034	−0.496	0.964	0.015	0.270	0.977	−0.025	−2.540	0.967	−0.010	−1.020	0.978
10	0.028	0.541	0.973	−0.014	−0.510	0.993	−0.022	2.920	0.973	−0.002	−0.419	0.992

The table shows results from regressions of returns of the CRSP market capitalization deciles against the 2 index and 5 index models. The 2 index model is the excess return on the S&P500 index and the change in the industry value weighted discount. The 5 index model is the excess return on the S&P500 index, the difference in return between a small cap portfolio and a large cap portfolio based on Prudential-Bache indices, the difference in return between a high growth portfolio and a value portfolio based on Prudential-Bache indices, the excess return on the Shearson Lehman Government Corporate bond index, and the change in the industry value weighted discount. Beta(ΔD-EF) is the beta on the change in the closed-end equity funds value weighted discount. Beta(ΔD-TR) is the beta on the change in the transportation industry value weighted discount. Returns and discount changes are of a quarterly frequency. The sample period is from 1980 through 1994.

Table 4.4
Regression results of CRSP market capitalization deciles against index models and the change in the industry return

	A. Closed end stock funds						B. Transportation					
	2 index			5 index			2 index			5 index		
Decile	Beta(return)	t-stat	R-sq	Beta(return)	t-stat	R-sq	Beta(return)	t-stat	R-sq	Beta(return)	t-stat	R-sq
1	0.250	0.767	0.566	−0.217	−1.340	0.904	0.600	4.720	0.685	−0.028	−0.310	0.908
2	0.920	1.820	0.718	0.073	0.730	0.946	0.469	5.720	0.806	0.057	1.030	0.947
3	0.291	1.700	0.801	0.039	0.440	0.950	0.363	5.430	0.855	0.054	1.060	0.950
4	0.234	1.540	0.844	−0.005	−0.060	0.962	0.303	5.130	0.886	0.022	0.520	0.962
5	0.199	1.510	0.860	−0.011	−0.170	0.970	0.276	5.450	0.901	0.038	1.050	0.970
6	0.246	2.050	0.882	0.057	0.930	0.972	0.260	5.620	0.915	0.043	1.250	0.971
7	0.155	1.540	0.907	0.007	0.110	0.970	0.224	6.160	0.941	0.075	2.370	0.973
8	0.194	2.200	0.926	0.070	1.110	0.966	0.123	3.210	0.931	−0.016	−0.470	0.967
9	0.078	1.320	0.964	0.014	0.290	0.977	0.057	2.230	0.966	0.000	−0.010	0.977
10	−0.092	−2.110	0.974	−0.023	−0.930	0.992	−0.089	−5.120	0.979	−0.019	−1.380	0.992

The table shows results from regressions of returns of the CRSP market capitalization deciles against the 2 index and 5 index models. The 2 index model is the excess return on the S&P500 index and the change in the industry value weighted return. The 5 index model is the excess return on the S&P500 index, the difference in return between a small cap portfolio and a large cap portfolio based on Prudential-Bache indices, the difference in return between a high growth portfolio and a value portfolio based on Prudential-Bache indices, the excess return on the Shearson Lehman Government Corporate bond index, and the change in the industry value weighted return. Beta(return) is the beta on the change in the industry value weighted return. Returns are of a quarterly frequency. The sample period is from 1980 through 1994.

smallest stocks have negative weights; the largest decile stocks positive weights. Like LS&T, we find the regression coefficient in general increase as we examine larger firms. In fact, the rank correlation between deciles and the regression coefficients on ΔD-EF is .71. As in the latter period studied by LS&T, none of the regression coefficients on ΔD-EF from any of the 10 size portfolios are statistically different from zero. LS&T interpret these results as indicating that there is a sentiment index and that different size firms have different sensitivity to it.

In Table 4.3 we also report analogous results for the five-index regression. The goodness of fit (particularly for the small stocks) is much better than in the case of the two-index model. Note that the relationship between the regression coefficient on ΔD-EF and the size deciles is actually reversed. Large companies tend to have negative loadings and small companies positive loadings (the Spearman rank correlation is −.71).

The pattern of coefficients that LS&T argued supported sentiment as an influence is reversed when a more realistic return-generating process is used. This occurs even though the correlation of ΔD-EF with a size variable, or in fact any of the variables in the return-generating process, is quite low.

Examining the betas on sentiment in the two-index model, LS&D speculate that the index ΔD-EF is a proxy for a systematic sentiment index that affects small stocks and large stocks differently. The index supposedly works because of the individual ownership of small stocks and of closed end mutual funds. An alternative explanation is that ΔD-EF is simply a proxy for other relationships which are part of a more realistic RGP. If this is true, there should be nothing special about the variable ΔD-EF but the variable ΔD constructed for any industry not affected by sentiment could also proxy for the omitted variables. We first examined ΔD computed for stocks in the transportation industry. Recall that the index was constructed from large stocks with high institutional ownership so that it should be unrelated to investor sentiment if it exists. The results are shown in Panel B of Table 4.3. Note first that in a two-index model the results parallel, and in fact better fit the LS&T sentiment story, than the results using ΔD-EF. The R^2 are higher (better fit), the pattern is stronger, from minus to plus, as we go to larger stocks, all of the coefficients are statistically different from zero, and the rank correlation between the sensitivity to ΔD-TR and size decile is higher (.96). There is nothing unique about ΔD-EF; in fact, looking at the influence of ΔD for an industry gives stronger results. When we look at the role of ΔD-TR in a five-index model we again see results directly analogous to what we saw with

Table 4.5
Spearman rank correlation between decile and regression coefficient

	A. Industry VWD		B. Industry return	
	2 index	5 index	2 index	5 index
Transportation equipment	0.960	−0.280	−1.000	−0.212
Industrial machinery	0.850	−0.080	−0.975	−0.733
Electronics	0.790	0.100	−0.987	−0.188
Chemicals	−0.850	−0.300	−0.685	−0.018
Equity sentiment	0.710	−0.710	−0.915	−0.006
Bond sentiment	0.880	−0.400	−0.248	−0.188

The table shows the Spearman rank correlation coefficient between the rank of the CRSP market capitalization decile and the coefficient on either the change in the industry value weighted discount or the coefficient on the industry return. The coefficients are computed from a regression of the excess returns of the CRSP decile against the 2 index and 5 index models and the change in the industry value weighted discount or the industry return. The indices in the 2 index model are the excess return on the S&P500 index and the indicated index. The 5 index model contains the excess return on the S&P500 index, the difference in return between a small cap portfolio and a large cap portfolio based on Prudential-Bache indices, the difference in return between a high growth portfolio and a value portfolio based on Prudential-Bache indices, the excess return on the Shearson Lehman Government Corporate bond index, and the indicated index. Returns and discount changes are of a quarterly frequency. The sample period is from 1980 through 1994.

ΔD-EF. The explanatory power of the model goes way up. None of the regression coefficients on ΔD-TR are statistically different from zero, and the relationship between deciles and the coefficient of ΔD-TR becomes negative (Spearman rank correlation of −.28) and is not significant.

Once again the ΔD variable appears to be acting as a proxy for omitted influences and the effect of this variable seems to disappear when a more robust model of the return-generating process is used.

In Table 4.5 we present the rank correlation between size and the change in the discount for other industries and for a closed-end bond fund sentiment index. Except for chemicals, the results are all analogous to those found for ΔD-EF. Chemicals show the opposite sign for the change in discounts computed for other industries.

As discussed earlier, ΔD may simply be proxying for return. If ΔD-EF is simply a noisy measure of industry return, then we should get similar but stronger results if we replace the change in discount for any industry with the index of return for that industry. We do this in Table 4.4. The entries in these Panels directly parallel the entries in Panel A and B for Table 4.3. Note the sign of the relationship is reversed since ΔD moves in the opposite direction of returns. (The two measures are highly negatively correlated as discussed earlier.)

When we examine the results for the two-index RGP in Panel A of Table 4.4, we find the reversal of signs for the largest stocks, higher t values than in Panel A of Table 4.3 (although only two are significant) and higher R^2. When a two-index model is used, the return for closed-end equity funds better explains returns than the change in the discount for these funds. When we examine the five-index model we find much better explanatory power than in the two-index case. We also find that the significance of the industry return index has markedly decreased. In the two-index case the Spearman rank correlation between size and the regression coefficient on industry return is −.915, while in the five-index case it is −.006. Using return indexes produces the same type of results we found for the change in discount, but the results are even stronger.

When we examine an index of the return on transportation stocks we get analogous results. In the two-index case the return on the transportation index explains the return in deciles better than the return on closed ends funds and the pattern of coefficients is more pronounced than when the change in the discount is used. When the five-index model is used, all of the return indexes and all of the change in discount indexes work poorly.

In summary, when a two-index model is employed we get a strong pattern in the beta on the second index using either the change in the discount or return. However, few of the coefficients are significant. Using data from equity or bond mutual funds works no better, and in fact is inferior to using data from a transportation index. There is nothing special about the index constructed from closed-end equity funds. When a five-index model is employed, we see that the change in discount and the return indexes no longer show strong pattern across size deciles found with the two-index models.

D Sentiment and Empirically Derived Factors

In the earlier section we used as a return-generating process four prespecified factors. An alternative way to specify the return-generating process is to empirically derive factors. We used as our empirical derived model the factors described in Connor and Korajczyk (1986).[12] These factors are derived from the variance covariance matrix using principal components analysis. Table 4.6 shows the simple correlation of the equity sentiment index with the first five empirically derived factors. The largest

Table 4.6
Correlation matrix of change in sentiment indices and five stock market factors

	Factor 1	Factor 2	Factor 3	Factor 4	Factor 5
C.E. sentiment	−0.02	−0.05	0.02	−0.01	0.06
Transportation	−0.55	0.28	−0.42	0.20	0.14
Industrial machinery	−0.60	−0.26	0.02	0.13	0.21
Electronics	−0.79	−0.01	−0.24	0.29	0.36
Chemicals	−0.64	−0.53	−0.05	0.46	0.28

The table shows the correlations between changes in the closed-end fund value weighted discount or changes in the four industry value weighted discounts and five stock market factors. The data is of a quarterly frequency. The sample period is from June 1980 through December 1992. The factors are those developed by Connor and Korajczyk (1986).

value is .06 with factor 5. Each of the factors has a higher correlation with each of the industry indexes than it has with the equity sentiment index.

We regressed each factor against the four-index base model with and without equity sentiment. For all five factors except the first the adjusted R^2 was lowered when sentiment was included in the regression (for the first factor it was unchanged). For each factor the F test associated with adding a sentiment index to the base model finds the sentiment index result in no improvement at the 5% level. Thus equity sentiment does not appear to be related to empirically derived factors.

The fact that equity sentiment is not related to empirically derived factors is powerful evidence that sentiment is not in the RGP. The concern with empirical factors has always been that one can have too many factors. Since one is unsure what they represent a factor can occur and not have any economic significance. However, is it hard to understand how a factor which is supposed to have economic significance like sentiment could possibly enter the return-generating process and yet not be related to empirical factors.

One argument that has been put forth is that closed-end mutual funds sell at a price below net asset value because they must offer a higher rate of return since they are riskier and this risk is unrelated to other fundamental characteristics determining return. In the next section we examine this conjecture.

III Discounts on Closed End Funds and Expected Returns

Over our sample period the return earned on stock closed-end funds exceeded the return earned on their net asset value. (This latter number is the return that would have been earned by investors if the fund was an open-end fund.) The extra return was primarily due to a decrease in the average discount from about 20% to 10% during the period. However, examining raw return ignores differences in the systematic risk of the funds. When we employ the four-index model to adjust for systematic risk, we find that risk-adjusted return (α) for closed-end stock funds is $-.174\%$ per month, while for closed-end bond funds it averages -0.161% per month.

If in constructing this model we had ignored a systematic source of risk that impacted fund returns (for example, sentiment), then the risk-adjusted return ignoring this factor should be positive, not negative. This holds because the investor would receive an extra return to compensate for the omitted risk.[13] If sentiment risk was a systemic factor impacting holders of closed-end funds, then including a sentiment index should cause the risk-adjusted return to decrease. In fact, including ΔD-EF for stock and ΔD-BF for bond funds causes the risk-adjusted returns (α) for each type of fund to increase, not decrease.[14] Looking at risk-adjusted returns provides no evidence that sentiment risk impacts expected returns in a manner consistent with sentiment risk being a source of risk to fund holders.

The analysis just discussed depends somewhat on the period selected. Another way to analyze the issue is to see if, given the characteristics of closed-end funds, one should expect an extra return due to sentiment risk. As we show below, the return to investors on closed-end funds is not only a function of the return on net asset value, but also a function of both the discount and change in the discount. In order to examine the effect of a discount, we must first relate the return on the shares of a closed-end fund to the return on net asset value. Then we can examine the excess return and risk of investor return and NAV return to see if closed end funds can offer an extra return to investors as compensation for sentiment. We discuss the difference, first assuming that the risk of investor return and NAV return is the same. We then show that the actual differences in risk between NAV return and market return make it even more likely that sentiment risk is not priced.

As shown below, the return on the shares in a closed-end fund can be related to the return on the underlying assets.

Define

1. R_I as the return to an investor in a closed-end fund
2. R_{disc} as the return (or rate of change) on the discount
3. R_{NAV} as the return on the net asset value

4. P_t as price at time t
5. D_t as the dividend at time t
6. N_t as net asset value at time t
7. d_t as the discount at time t

The return to the investor and the return on the NAV from time zero to one, and the return on the discount are given respectively by

$$R_I = \frac{P_1 + D_1 - P_0}{P_0}$$

$$R_{\mathrm{NAV}} = \frac{N_1 + D_1 - N_0}{N_0}$$

$$d_1 = \frac{N_1 - P_1}{N_1}$$

From these definitions it follows that investor return is related to the return on the NAV as follows:

$$(1 + R_I) = (1 + R_{\mathrm{NAV}})\left(\frac{1 - d_1}{1 - d_0}\right) + \frac{D_1 d_1}{P_0}$$

While the discount will vary from year to year, the expected value of a change in the discount must be zero. If it were to be negative (positive) an investor would have to expect the price of the fund to grow (decline) continuously relative to the net asset value of the firm until the price was much larger (smaller) than net asset value. Taking the expected value of both sides and setting the expected value of the change in the discount to zero, we have

$$E(R_I) = E(R_{\mathrm{nav}}) - \frac{D_1 d_1}{P_0}$$

From this equation we see that if the price of the fund is below the net asset value of the fund (the fund sells as a discount) then the expected return to investors exceeds the expected return on fund assets. This occurs because the discount allows the dividend stream to be purchased at a lower price.

Before we examine the implications of this equation for the effect of sentiment risk on risk-adjusted returns (α), we have to state some general properties we would expect to find for the α's on closed-end funds.

The shares of closed-end funds are traded assets. With a properly defined asset pricing model, the average alpha on traded assets should be zero. Of course, for any period the average alpha may be above or below zero. If sentiment risk were priced, ignoring it should result in obtaining a larger, and in fact positive, alpha for closed-end funds. The issue to be discussed is whether given the expected return relationship defined above we should reasonably expect a positive or negative alpha on investor returns if alphas are measured ignoring sentiment risk. If we should expect a negative alpha, it would be inconsistent with sentiment risk and would suggest the negative alpha we found empirically in the previous section was not due to our having selected an abnormal period.

We first discuss this under the assumption that the sensitivities (risks) of the market return and NAV return are the same. Shortly we will explore the impact of differences in sensitivities. When sensitivities are the same, the only difference in expected alphas on NAV and market return comes about because of the discount. The alphas on NAV returns in the period discussed earlier were negative. But this is a general result not restricted to this period of time, as there is ample evidence that open-end funds have negative alphas post-expenses. Thus the negative alpha on NAV returns is reasonable, and is consistent with a large body of evidence.[15]

Furthermore, the size of the NAV alpha we found is similar in magnitude to the alpha found on open-end funds. The issue is whether the discount is likely to be sufficient to make the expected market alpha positive as it would have to be if sentiment risk affected the return and alpha of closed-end funds.

The discount in our sample period is about 12% for equity funds on average and 3% for bond funds. Of greater importance, these numbers are consistent with the discounts found over long time periods. For an expected return of 10.6% for stock and a 5.1% expected bond return (numbers roughly consistent with Ibbotson (1997)), the $E(r_{mkt})$ would be expected to exceed $E(r_{\mathrm{NAV}})$ by 1.3% for stock funds and .10% for bond funds.[16] The possible increase in alpha due to the discount is smaller in magnitude than the annualized negative alphas on NAV returns found for both open and closed-end funds. Therefore, even under these extreme assumptions we would not expect to observe positive alphas on investor return as required by the sentiment story.[17]

The empirical evidence shows that the sensitivities for market return are different than for NAV return, unlike the assumption made above.

Table 4.7
Closed end sample four index regression results

	α	$\beta_{S\&P}$	β_{S_m-Lg}	β_{Gr-Vl}	β_D	R^2
Stock funds						
Investor	−0.1740	0.758	0.505	−0.119	0.384	0.52
NAV	−0.1894	0.752	0.371	0.168	0.147	0.76
Bond funds						
Investor	−0.1611	0.191	0.172	−0.411	0.934	0.34
NAV	−0.0299	0.053	0.069	−0.062	0.979	0.77

The table shows average values from regressions of excess returns of the closed-end stock and bond samples against the excess return on the S&P500 index, the difference in return between a small cap portfolio and a large cap portfolio based on Prudential-Bache indices, the difference in return between a high growth portfolio and a value portfolio based on Prudential-Bache indices, and the excess return on the Shearson Lehman Government Corporate bond index. The stock sample consists of 32 funds. The bond sample consists of 38 funds. Returns are of a monthly frequency. The sample period is from 1980 through 1994.

They are different in a direction that lowers the alpha on market return and thus makes the pricing of a sentiment index even more unlikely. We will now discuss the fact that there is a logical reason why this should be true.

In Table 4.7 we report the average sensitivities (betas) associated with investor return and NAV return from our four-index model. For stock funds the sensitivity of the NAV return and investor return to the S&P index are virtually the same. However, the sensitivity varies on each of the other indexes. We believe that the direction of the difference in each of these indexes is consistent with the relationship between sensitivities and firm characteristics found in general and that the direction of the differences found in our sample period is extremely plausible.

The investor return has a much higher sensitivity (beta) to the small minus large return variable than does the NAV return. To analyze this we examined whether the beta on the small-large return index was related to the size of firms. We first divided the 586 stocks in our common stock sample into 20 groups, with the first group containing the $1/20^{th}$ of the stocks with the smallest total equity capitalization and the 20th group the $1/20^{th}$ of the stocks with the largest capitalization. The return on each group was calculated using an equally weighted portfolio of the stocks within the group. Time series data was then used to regress the return on each group against our four-index model. The beta on the small-large variable was then regressed (in cross section) on the natural logarithm of the average capitalization of the firms in each group. The results were as follows:

$$\beta_{S-L} = 1.856 - .191\ln(size) \qquad R^2 = .954$$

There is obviously a very strong relationship between the sensitivity to the small minus large index and the size of the companies involved. Companies which are smaller in size have a larger beta in our model.

Examining the NAV beta for the small minus large index shows that the assets on closed-end equity funds have a beta equal to the largest 20% of industrial firms in our sample. This is consistent with the argument made by LS&T that closed-end funds hold relatively large firms. The closed-end stock funds are well below average in size (total capitalization), and in fact would rank in the lowest 40%, in size, of our sample of industrial firms. Thus the closed-end stock funds are smaller in size than the companies they hold. The difference in size, combined with the negative sign on size, explains why investor returns have a larger beta then NAV returns. The same relationship holds for closed-end bond funds, but it is even more pronounced (bound funds are smaller and NAV returns act more like large firms).

The relationship of the sensitivity of the growth-value variable is also plausible, given the characteristics of funds. We repeated the process we employed to discover th relationship between the small minus large beta and size to discover the relationship between the growth minus value beta and the ratio of market-to-book. We formed twenty portfolios by ranking the 586 stocks on their market-to-book ratio for each portfolio, and then regressed the growth minus value beta for each portfolio from our four-index model against the ln of the market-to-book ratio. The results were as follows:

$$\beta_{G-V} = -.255 + .370\ln\,(market/book) \qquad R^2 = .89$$

These is strong evidence that firms which have higher market-to-book ratios have larger betas with respect to our growth minus value return index.

The sensitivity to the growth minus value beta computed on NAV would imply an average market-to-book ratio on the assets of closed-end equity funds of 1.35. The market-to-book ratio on closed-end equity funds is .90. Thus the closed-end equity funds have a smaller market-to-book ratio than the assets they hold. Given the relationship just described, this would imply that the sensitivity on the growth-value index should be smaller for investor returns than NAV returns. In fact, this is what we find (see Table 4.7). Similar results hold for closed-end bond funds.

The final sensitivity to examine is the sensitivity to the bond factor. We related this sensitivity to dividend yield. We once again used the same procedure as in the previous two cases. Our 586-stock sample was divided into 20 portfolios based on dividend yield (the dividend-to-price ratio). Then the sensitivity of each portfolio to the bond variable was regressed (cross sectionally) against the average dividend yield for each portfolio. The results were

$$\beta_{\text{bond}} = -.255 + 3.434\ (\mathit{Dividend/Price}) \qquad R^2 = .297$$

While this relationship is weaker than those found for the size and growth betas, it is still significant at the 1% level.

To maintain the tax advantage afforded to mutual funds, closed-end funds must pay out 95% of their income from dividends and capital gains received each year. This results in larger dividend yields for closed-end funds than the stocks or bonds they hold and thus gives them more bond-like characteristics and a higher beta with our bond variable.

The three sensitivities that are different on investor return than NAV return for closed-end stock funds are consistent with the difference between the characteristics of the closed-end stock funds and the characteristics of the assets they hold. Thus the negative alpha on market returns cannot be explained by unreasonable betas. The question remains: can we go further and make definitive statements about the riskiness of the investor return and NAV return? The relative smallness of the closed-end funds and the empirical evidence supporting a positive premium required for small size would imply that the investor return is riskier than NAV return and investors require a higher expected return on shares than on NAV. The growth minus value beta for investor returns being closer to value and the evidence that value stocks must offer a higher return is again consistent with the investor return being riskier. The closed-end stock funds also have higher sensitivity to the bond index. The evidence here is also for a positive market price. Thus the characteristics of closed-end stock funds suggest that the investor return is riskier than the NAV return.

The results for closed-end bond funds are even clearer. For bond funds the beta on bonds is about the same for investor return as NAV return. However, the sensitivity to the S&P return is much higher for investor return than NAV return. This is to be expected since the equity is traded.

Since higher sensitivity to the S&P requires a higher return, the difference in required return for investors relative to NAV is likely to be even higher for bond funds. However, the small discount means this difference in risk will not be compensated for and the alpha is negative, unlike what would be required for a sentiment story.

Let us summarize what we have learned in this section. NAV alphas are negative. This is consistent with the findings on open-end mutual funds. Since closed-end funds have prices and returns freely determined in the open market, if we have identified the correct return-generating process they should have alphas equal to zero. If sentiment risk is important, and if we leave it out, closed-end funds should have positive alphas. They do sell at discounts. They do offer higher average investor return than average NAV return. However, after the adjustment for our four sources of systematic risk, the α on investor return is less than the alpha on NAV return. Furthermore, examining the pattern of betas on investor return compared to NAV return shows that a non-positive alpha is to be expected. The evidence is clear that the alpha from a four-index model is negative and these results are inconsistent with the existence of a priced sentiment index.

Conclusion

In this article we explore whether sentiment could reasonable be expected to be a factor affecting expected return. Modern asset pricing theory require that only sensitivity to systematic factors in the return-generating process be priced. We first explore whether sentiment was a factor in the return-generating process. We showed that a sentiment index computed from closed-end funds enters the return-generating process no more often than indexes computed in the same way from large firms which have high institutional ownership in other industries. We next showed that sentiment indexes enter the return-generating process less often than industry indexes. Since industry return indexes are not considered priced indexes, this makes it less likely that sentiment indexes are priced. In doing all of this analysis we employed both a two-index model similar to that of the LS&T, and five-index model which also included a size and growth variable. The presence of these additional variables in general changed the relationship of sentiment indexes and industry return indexes in the return-generating process.

As another test of the role of sentiment indexes in the return-generating process, we examined whether sentiment was related to empirically derived factors. We used the Connor and Korajczyk factors. The simple correlation of the sentiment indexes derived from closed-end funds was less than .03 for any of five factors found by Connor and Korajczyk. Sentiment is not related to any of the systematic factors derived from the variance-covariance matrix of security returns.

We examined whether the index is priced. For traded assets the alpha from a properly defined asset pricing model should be zero. If we leave out sentiment, and sentiment is important in the asset pricing model, then the alphas should be positive. We show that the alpha investors receive has historically been negative. Furthermore, examining the risk to investors relative to the risk on NAV indicates that the negative alpha is to be expected. The discount on closed-end funds is insufficient to provide a positive alpha, and there is no evidence supporting sentiment as part of the return-generating process or asset pricing model.

Notes

1. Also see Chen, Kan and Miller (1993a, 1993b) and Chopra, Lee, Shleifer and Thaler (1993a, 1993b).

2. When the index is the difference in return of two portfolios, the risk-free rate cancels out.

3. See Elton, Gruber and Blake (1996a) (1996b), Fama and French, (1993), Connor and Korajczyk (1986).

4. Empirical tests of this model versus alternative models are contained in Elton, Gruber and Blake (1997). In interpreting some of the results presented in this paper, it might help the reader to recognize that the growth-value index is highly correlated with the market-to-book ratio Fama and French (1993), among others, have employed in their research.

5. Industry return has also been used in tests of RGP, e.g., Gibbons, Ross, and Shanken (1989).

6. There is one other change. LS&T used weekly data on discounts to approximate monthly data. Then they used discounts on the Friday closest to month-end to calculate the month-end discount. This was necessary because their data on net asset value came from the *Wall Street Journal* which only reports it as of Friday. We used Lipper data on net asset value in order to be able to compute the discount at the end of the month.

7. The sample was the 20 largest firms from each industry which had over 50% institutional ownership.

8. We checked to see whether using monthly rather than quarterly data affected the number of times ΔD-EF and ΔD-BF were significant. The results were essentially the same. We also repeated the analysis excluding the firms in the industries for which we constructed industry indexes. Again, the results were essentially unchanged.

9. See Fama and French (1993) and Elton, Gruber, and Blake (1996a, 1996b, and 1997).

10. This section and the one that follows tend to support the arguments made by Chen, Kan, and Miller (1993), that the small firm effect and the equity premiums payable are in fact two separate and distinct phenomena.

11. All tables were also constructed with the S&P Index substituted for the NYSE, and both the results and conclusions are virtually identical.

12. We thank Bob Korajczyk for supplying us with the factors. The data ends in December, 1992, which is slightly shorter than our sample period in the rest of the study.

13. This assumes that the sensitivities are positive, which they are, and that the market price of risk is positive for sentiment which is the argument of LS&T.

14. The α on stock funds increases from $-.1740\%$ to $-.161\%$, while for bond funds it goes from $-.161\%$ to $+.0012\%$.

15. One could argue that closed-end funds should have different α's than open-end. These are arguments that would lead to larger or smaller alphas on closed-end funds relative to open-end funds. One argument of why it should by larger is that closed-end funds do not have to worry about redemptions and therefore hold cash (the use of futures eliminates this problem). An argument for smaller alpha is that closed-end funds do not have the market discipline of inflows and outflows due to performance and therefore are less performance-oriented.

16. These numbers are computed by using equation (1).

17. Although we are assuming in this section that the betas on the investor's return are the same as on NAV, if they are set by the betas on the NAV the discount would impact them. Inserting any asset pricing model for $E(r_{NAV})$ in equation (1) shows that betas and alphas should be adjusted by the same percentage. Since the alpha on NAV is negative, under the assumptions just discussed the alpha on investor return would be even more negative.

References

Chen, Nai-fu, Raymond Kan, and Merton H. Miller, 1993b, A rejoinder, *Journal of Finance* 48, 795–800.

Chen, Nai-fu, Raymond Kan, and Merton H. Miller, 1993a, Yes, discounts on closed-end funds are a sentiment index, *Journal of Finance* 48, 801–808.

Chopra, Navin, Charles M. C. Lee, Andrei Shleifer, and Richard H. Thaler, 1993a. Yes, discounts on closed-end funds are a sentiment index, *Journal of Finance* 48, 801–808.

Chopra, Navin, Charles M. C. Lee, Andrei Shleifer, and Richard H. Thaler, 1993b. Summing up, *Journal fo Finance* 48, 811–812.

Connor, Gregory and Robert Korajczyk, 1986. Performance Measurement with the Arbitrage Pricing Theory: A New Framework of Analysis. *Journal of Financial Economics* 15, 373–394.

Elton, Edwin J., Martin J. Gruber, and Christopher R. Blake, 1996a. The persistence of risk-adjusted mutual fund performance, *Journal of Business* 69, 133–157.

Elton, Edwin J., Martin J. Gruber, and Christopher R. Blake, 1996b. Survivorship bias and mutual fund performance, *Review of Financial Studies* 9, 1097–1120.

Elton, Edwin J., Martin J. Gruber, and Christopher R. Blake, 1997. Common factors in mutual fund returns, Working paper, New York University.

Fama, Eugene F. and Kenneth R. French, 1992, The cross-section of expected stock returns, *Journal of Finance*, 47, 427–466.

Fama, Eugene F. and Kenneth R. French, 1993, Common risk factors in the returns on bonds and stocks, *Journal of Financial Economics* 33, 3–53.

Gibbons, Michael R., Stephen A. Ross, and Jay Shanken, 1989, A test of the efficiency of a given portfolio, *Econometrica* 57, 1121–1152.

Ibbotson Associates, 1989, Stocks, bonds, bills, and inflation yearbook.

Lee, Charles M. C., Andrei Shleifer, and Richard H. Thaler, 1991, Investor Sentiment and the Closed End Fund Puzzle. *Journal of Finance* 46, 75–109.

Valuation

5 Valuation and Asset Selection Under Alternative Investment Opportunities

Edwin J. Elton and Martin J. Gruber

Valuation models have received wide usage in finance and economics. They have been used to derive propositions in corporate finance, test hypothesis in investments and corporate finance, and are currently finding application in regulatory proceedings. Almost all of the applications have used either the constant investment opportunities model or the standard growth model.[1] The purpose of this paper is to review the assumptions about the investment opportunities schedule underlying these models, to examine reasonable alternative assumptions, to derive closed form solutions to these alternatives, and to investigate the implications of these closed form solutions for the optimum investment behavior of the firm. So as not to obscure the basic issues, we will restrict ourselves to considering an all equity internally financed firm.[2]

I Assumptions about Investment Schedules

Valuation models employed in the finance and economic literature can be conveniently divided into two types. The first type assumes that the investment schedule is exogenously determined, while the second assumes that management's initial investment decision affects future investment opportunities. The constant investment opportunities model of Solomon (8), where investment is the same dollar amount in each period, will be shown to be an example of the first type. As shown later, the standard growth model associated with J. B. Williams (9), M. Gordon (3) and Gordon and Shapiro (2), where growth is assumed to be equal to the product of the firm's retention rate and rate of return on investment, is an example of the second type. In this section we will examine various assumptions about investment opportunities for models of both types. In subsequent sections we will analyze the valuation models implied by the various assumptions concerning the time path of investment opportunities.

A Exogenously Determined Time Dependency

The simplest assumption concerning the time path of investment opportunities is that the growth rate in the total amount of investment that is available at any rate of return is constant over time.[3] If we let

1. $g_I(t)$ = the rate of growth at time t in the total amount of investment opportunities available at any average rate of return,

2. c_0, c_1 = constants,

3. $I(t)$ = the total investment available at time t given the initial level of investment is $I(0)$.

then

$$g_I(t)_t = c_0 \tag{m-1}$$

Let us now consider an investment opportunities schedule (IOS) and its movement over time. The investment opportunities schedule is a plot of rate of return versus the amount of investment which is available at that rate of return.[4] Since more investments should be available at lower rates of return, this schedule should normally be negatively sloped as in Figure 5.1.[5] The arrows in Figure 5.1 indicate the time path of the investment

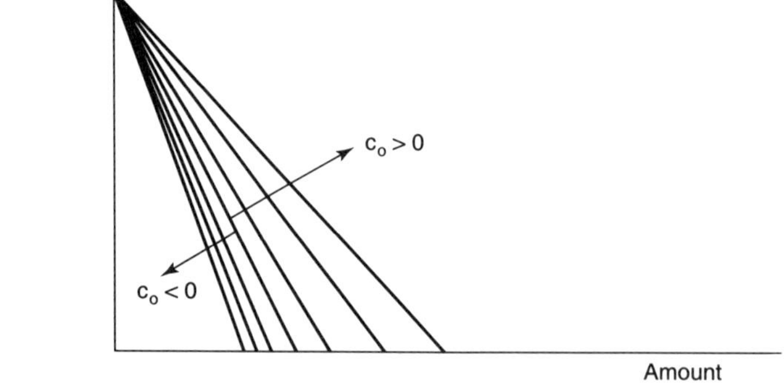

Figure 5.1
Investment opportunities schedule for m-1

opportunities schedule over time, given alternative assumptions about the sign of c_0. Notice that in Figure 5.1 for positive growth, successive IOS curves are further apart over time (while for negative growth, they grow closer together.)[6] This occurs because with positive constant growth rates, the absolute change in investments increases as the level of investment increases over time.[7]

Model m-1 is consistent with much of the theoretical and empirical work that has been done on the investment function. For example, if investment is a linear function of either the size of the firm (as measured by assets) or a linear function of the past level of investments, m-1 is the appropriate growth model.[8] We will now show this for each case.

Let

$A(t) =$ assets at time t

$\dot{A}(t), \dot{I}(t) =$ the derivative of the variable with respect to time.

Then if investment $I(t)$ is a linear fraction of assets, we have

$$I(t) = c_1 + c_0 A(t) \tag{1}$$

Taking the derivative of (1) with respect to time

$$\dot{I}(t) = c_0 \dot{A}(t)$$

By definition

$$I(t) = \dot{A}(t)$$

Therefore

$$\dot{I}(t) = c_0 I(t)$$

or

$$g_I(t) = \frac{\dot{I}(t)}{I(t)} = c_0$$

which is (m-1). (m-1) would also result from a situation where investment in t depended upon the past level of investments.

$$I(t+1) = I(t) + \dot{I}(t) = c_1 I(t)$$

rearranging

$$\frac{\dot{I}(t)}{I(t)} = c_1 - 1 = c_0$$

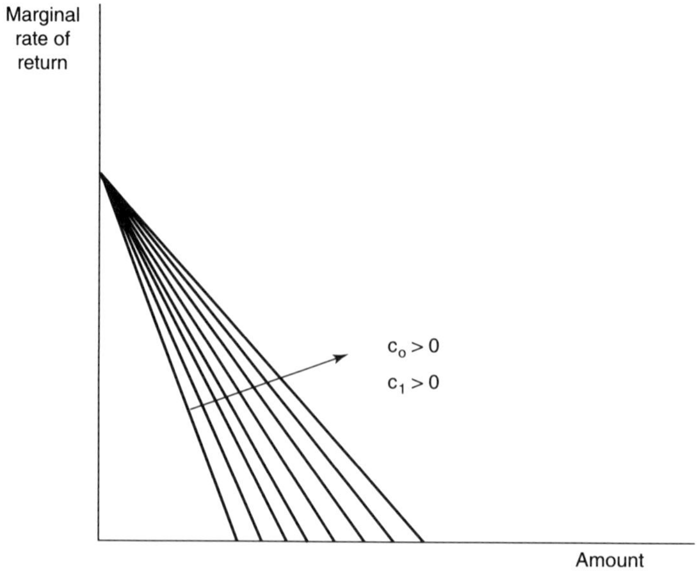

Figure 5.2
Investment opportunities schedule for m-2

which is once again m-1. m-1 also, of course, encompasses the constant investment opportunities model of Solomon. The constant investment opportunities model is obtained by setting c_0 equal to zero in m-1. This results in an investment opportunities schedule which is unchanged over time.

An alternative model to m-1 is a model where the dollar amount of shift in the IOS is a constant through time. This pattern of change results from a model like

$$g_I(t) = \frac{c_1}{c_0 + c_1 t} \qquad \text{(m-2)}$$

Figure 5.2 represents the investment opportunities schedule underlying m-2. As shown is Figure 5.2, the investment schedule shifts to the right over time. The dollar amount of shift in any period is c_0/c_1 and is a constant.[9] Model m-2 represents the situation where the increase in investment opportunities are independent of the size of the firm. The empirical evidence of Hymer and Pashigian (4) would be supportive of such an assumption. The assumptions underlying m-2 are also consistent with the econometric studies supporting production functions with constant return to scale.

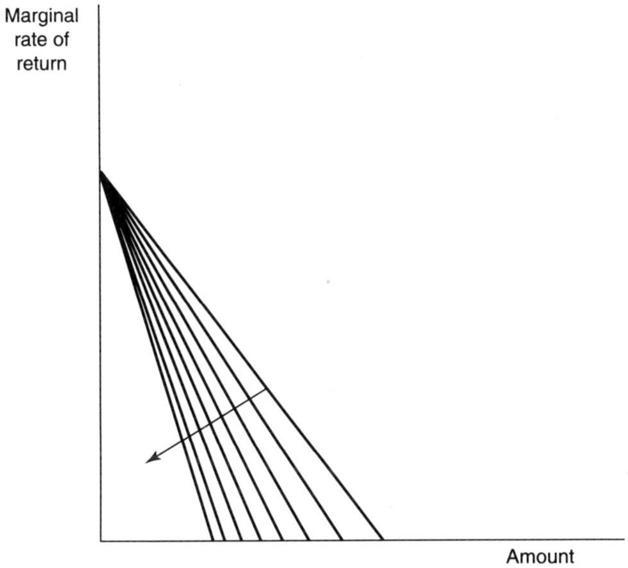

Figure 5.3
Investment opportunities schedule for m-3 when $\frac{c_1}{c_0} < c_2$ and $c_2 > 0$

m-1 and m-2 capture many of the potential time paths of new investment. Another possible pattern would be for investment opportunities to become smaller over time, though at first they might grow. Patterns that involve an eventual deteriation in investment opportunities can be represented by

$$g_I(t) = \frac{c_1}{c_0 + c_1 t} - c_2 \qquad \text{(m-3)}$$

If we assume that $c_1/c_0 < c_2$ and $c_2 > 0$ we get a series of IOS's like those depicted in Figure 5.3.

This pattern could represent the situation where the firm had access to special opportunities yielding more than the cost of funds, but competitive forces errode these opportunities over time.

If, $c_1/c_0 > c_2$ and $c_2 > 0$, then the IOS would at first shift to the right, but at a slower and slower rate over time and would eventually shift to the left asymptotically approaching zero. This could represent a firm that was expected to face extraordinary inovative opportunities in the near future, but would again be subject to competitive forces over time.

An examination of model (m-3) shows that it is the general case of all specific models discussed to this point. Thus, later derivations will be restricted to (m-3) and the implications of other models will be obtained by setting the appropriate constants equal to zero.[10]

Before leaving this section one other issue should be discussed. The valuation models derived from investment models such as those just discussed, assume that investment yields constant returns over an infinite life. With this assumption, new investment is investment after adjusting for any replacement investment (which is already valued through the assumption of infinite life). Thus, a leftward shift in net investment opportunities is consistant with rightward shift in the total investment schedule (net new investment plus replacement investment). Furthermore, modest rightward shifts in the net investment schedule imply large rightward shifts in total new investments. Thus, with reasonable entry into markets, investment schedules that shift leftwards probably are the more realistic assumption.

B *Managerially Determined Time Dependency*

By far the most frequently analyzed growth models in finance assume that management's initial investment affects the investment opportunities in subsequent periods. For example, the standard growth model is

$$g_I(t) = \frac{I(0)}{E(0)}r = \frac{I(t)}{E(t)}r \qquad \text{(m-4)}$$

where $E(0)$ = earnings at time 0

$E(0)$ = investment at time 0

r = average rate of return which is a function of $I(0)$

In this model, the ratio of investment to earnings (the retention rate) is assumed constant at each moment of time. Taking the derivative of model (m-4) with respect to $I(0)$, we have

$$\frac{\partial g_I(t)}{\partial I(0)} = \frac{1}{E(0)}\frac{\partial rI(0)}{\partial I(0)}$$

$rI(0)$ is total revenues from the investment. Since the total revenues from investment increases as we add more investments, the derivative is positive and growth is an increasing function of the level of investment. Firm investment increases as r is lowered, so that the IOS schedule shifts by a larger and larger amount over time as r is lowered.

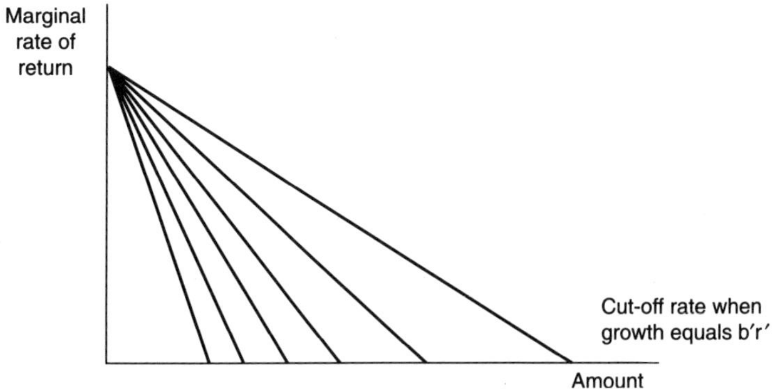

Figure 5.4a
Investment opportunities schedule for m-4

Put another way. If the firm invests an extra dollar (selects a lower r), the extra dollar of investment is assumed to make extra investment opportunities available next period at all rates of return.[11] This type of externality, where the selection of an investment now shifts the IOS schedules for all rates of return in all future periods is typical of models assuming managerially determined time dependencies.

The previous discussion can be illustrated with a diagram. Figure 5.4a shows the investment opportunities schedule if the firm selected retention rate b' and the associate rate of return r'. Figure 5.4b shows the investment schedule if the firm selects retention rate b'' along with its associated rate of return r''.

Any of the models discussed earlier can have this property added to it. For example

$$g_I(t) = c_0 + c_1 r \quad c_1 < 0 \tag{m-5}$$

is identical to m-1 except that the distance between subsequent investment opportunity schedules increases as r becomes larger. In the subsequent section we will also analyze

$$g_I(t) = \frac{c_1}{c_0 r + c_1 t} - c_2 \tag{m-6}$$

$$g_I(t) = \frac{c_1}{\frac{c_0}{r} + c_1 t} - c_2 \tag{m-7}$$

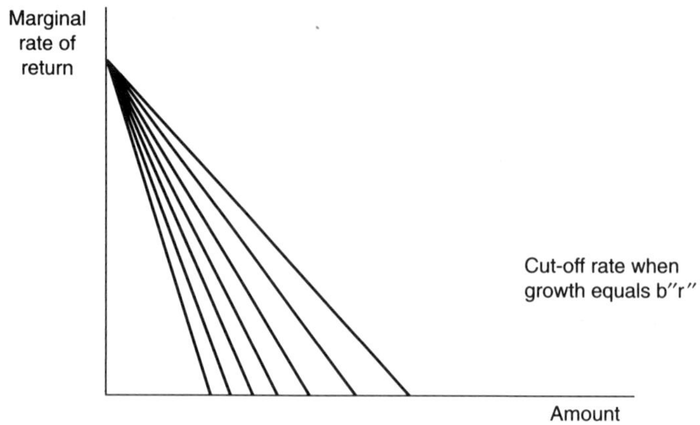

Figure 5.4b
Investment opportunities schedule for m-4

II The Implications of Alternative Assumption about Investment Opportunities for Firm Valuation and Asset Selection

In the first section of this paper we have discussed alternative scenerios about how the investment schedule facing the firm might change over time. Each of these alternatives can find some support in the economic literature. Furthermore, we have seen that all of these scenerios can be represented by a small set of growth models. In this section of the paper we shall take these growth models and explore their implications for firm valuation and asset selection. This section has two parts. In the first we will examine those models where the investment schedule exhibits a time dependency which is independent of management decisions. In the second we will explore those models where the change in the investment schedule is a function of management decisions as well as time.

A Exogenously Determined Time Dependency

In Section I we saw that the general model (m-3) could be used to represent a large number of alternative patterns for investment opportunities depending on the values of c_0, c_1, and c_2. The valuation model which equation (m-3) leads to as derived in Appendix A is

$$V(0) = \frac{E(0)}{k} + \frac{I(0)(r-k)}{k(k+c_2)} + \frac{I(0)(r-k)}{k(k+c_2)^2}\frac{c_1}{c_0} \qquad \text{(V-3)}$$

where $V(0)$ = the market value of an all equity firm at time zero
$E(0)$ = Earnings at time zero
$I(0)$ = Investment at time zero
k = Stockholder's required return for a firm of a given risk[12]
r = the average rate of return earned on investment $I(0)$ all other terms as before.

The value of the firm is equal to the capitalized value of expected earnings in the absence of investment, plus a premium related to the firm's ability to find investments with an average yield, above the stockholders' required return. This premium is determined by the firm's optimum initial investment decision and the growth rate in the investment schedule which the firm faces. Thus, the higher c_1 and the lower c_0 and c_2 the higher the value of the firm.

If c_2 equals zero (model m-2), then the value of the firm is

$$V(0) = \frac{E(0)}{k} + \frac{I(0)(r-k)}{k^2} + \frac{c_1}{c_0}\frac{I(0)(r-k)}{k^3} \qquad \text{(V-2)}$$

The value of the premium that results from the ability to invest funds above stockholders required return is easy to see from this model. The second term is the present value of investing an amount of funds $I(0)$ at a rate r in each year from now to infinity. The third term is the capitalized value of the extra funds that can be invested at r because of the growth in the investment schedule over time.

Before leaving this section it is interesting to examine the model when c_1 and c_2 both equal zero. In this case

$$V(0) = \frac{E(0)}{k} + \frac{I(0)(r-k)}{k^2}$$

This is the well known model for valuation given "constant investment opportunities." Thus, equation (V-3) represents the general valuation model for most cases of exogenously determined time dependency which might be of interest.

The optimum investment behavior given exogenously determined time dependency can be determined by taking the derivative of equation V-3, setting it equal to zero, and rearranging terms. As shown in Appendix A, this yields

$$r + I(0)\frac{\partial r}{\partial I(0)} = k$$

The term on the left is simply the marginal return on investment. Thus, one necessary condition for the value of the firm to be maximized is that the marginal return on investment is equal to k the stockholder's required return. This implies that the firm should take all investments with a yield higher than k.

B Managerially Determined Time Dependency

In Section I we examined several models which incorporated both the time dependency of changes in the investment schedule and the dependency of these changes on management's decisions. In this section we shall examine the valuation and optimum investment decisions that are implied by growth equations (m-5), (m-6), and (m-7), as well as the standard growth model which is a special case of (m-5) referred to as (m-4).

1. Model (m-5)—The simple linear relationship.

In Appendix B we show that if $g_I(t) = c_0 + c_1 r$ then the value of the firm is equal to

$$V(0) = \frac{E(0)}{k} + \frac{I(0)(r-k)}{k(k - c_0 - c_1 r)} \tag{V-5}$$

Once again, the value of the firm is seen to be equal to the capitalized value of expected earnings in the absence of investment plus a premium which is related to the firm's ability to find investments which yield more than the stockholder's required return.

The optimum cut-off rate for new investment implied by this valuation model can be found by differentiating it with respect to $I(0)$ and setting the derivative equal to zero. This yields

$$r + I(0)\frac{\partial r}{\partial I(0)} = k - \frac{c_1 I(0)\dfrac{\partial r}{\partial I(0)}(r-k)}{k - c_0 - c_1 r} \tag{2}$$

It is easy to derive those conditions under which the optimum cut-off rate for new investment is equal to k. For equation (2) to equal k the last term on the right-hand side must equal zero. This can occur only if $r = k$. Thus a necessary condition for $r + I(0)\partial r/\partial I(0) = k$ is that the marginal return on investment equals the average return on investment. Since this is in general not true, since $\partial r/\partial I(0) < 0$ and since for the firm to have finite value $k - c_0 - c_1 r > 0$, equation (2) implies that the cut-off point for new investment is above the stockholder's required return. This might, at first, seem surprising, but, upon consideration of equation (m-5), the reasons for it become apparent. The investment function under study assumes certain externalities to a present investment. Specifically as shown in Section 1, the less investment taken now, the larger r and the higher the growth rate in the entire investment schedule over time.[13]

The most widely used growth model in the financial literature is a special form of equation (V-5). In this form, which we have refered to as "the standard growth model," $c_0 = 0$ and $c_1 = I(0)/E(0) = I(t)/E(t)$ substituting these expressions into equation (V-5) yields[14]

$$V(0) = \frac{E(0) - I(0)}{k - \dfrac{I(0)}{E(0)} r} \tag{3}$$

The optimal cut-off rate implied by the standard growth model can be found by differentiating this equation with respect to $I(0)$ and setting the derivative equal to zero.

$$\frac{\partial V(0)}{\partial I(0)} = -\frac{1}{k - \dfrac{I(0)}{E(0)} r} + \frac{E(0) - I(0)}{\left(k - \dfrac{I(0)}{E(0)} r\right)^2} \left(\frac{r}{E(0)} + \frac{I(0)}{E(0)} \frac{\partial r}{\partial I(0)}\right)$$

or rearranging

$$r + I(0)\frac{\partial r}{\partial I(0)} = \frac{k - \dfrac{I(0)}{E(0)} r}{1 - \dfrac{I(0)}{E(0)}}$$

But from equation (3)

$$r + I(0)\frac{\partial r}{\partial I(0)} = \frac{E(0)}{V(0)} \tag{4}$$

The derivation of the valuation models for these two growth models is directly parallel to that presented in Appendix A. The reader can see by analogy with model (m-3) that the two valuation models are

$$V = \frac{E(0)}{k} + \frac{I(0)(r - k)}{k(k + c_2)} + \frac{I(0)\dfrac{c_1}{c_0 r}(r - k)}{k(k + c_2)^2} \tag{V-6}$$

and

$$V = \frac{E(0)}{k} + \frac{I(0)(r-k)}{k(k+c_2)} + \frac{I(0)\frac{c_1 r}{c_0}(r-k)}{k(k+c_2)^2} \tag{V-7}$$

These closed form relations are almost identical to equation (V-6). The only difference is that the third term is either divided by, or multiplied by r. However, this slight modification of the third term makes an important difference in the optimal cut-off rate for new investment.

Taking the derivation of equation (V-6) with respect to $I(0)$ setting it equal to zero, and solving for the marginal cut-off rate for new investment, we find

$$r + I(0)\frac{\partial r}{\partial I(0)} = k - \frac{\frac{c_1}{c_0}\left(\frac{k}{r} - 1\right)^2}{k + c_2 + \frac{k}{r^2}\frac{c_1}{c_0}}$$

Unless no investment opportunities exist, with a yield above the stockholder's required return, the firm should have a cut-off rate for new investment below k. The reason for this is easy to see from the growth model, equation (m-6). This model makes the assumption that future investment opportunities will be higher as more investment is accepted today. Present investments have an externality in the sense that they are assumed to produce future investment opportunities. Thus, the rate of return demanded on present investments is below the cost of financing these investments.

The marginal cut-off rate for new investments derived from equation (m-7) is

$$r + I(0)\frac{\partial r}{\partial I(0)} = k + \frac{\frac{c_1}{c_0}(r-k)^2}{k + c_2 + \frac{c_1}{c_0}(2r-k)}$$

In this case, as long as $r = k$ the cut-off rate is above the stockholder's required return. The reason for this is that the growth model used to derive this expression makes the assumption that taking more investment now leads to a decrease in future investment opportunities.

III Conclusion

In this paper, we have studied growth models which allow for a wide variety of assumptions about the time path of the investment schedule facing the firm. One set of models allowed alternative patterns of change to be only a function of time. The second set of models allowed the pattern of investment opportunities to vary, not only with time, but also with management decisions on initial investment. Models were studied which allowed present investments to either increase or decrease future investment opportunities. Closed form valuation models were derived and the implications of these valuation models for the appropriate cut-off rate for new investment was investigated for all these growth models. It is interesting to note that when managerially determined time dependencies were introduced, the optimum cut-off point for new investment could be above or below the rate of return required by stockholders, depending on the type of dependency introduced.

Appendix A

Derivation of Generalized Time Dependency

The growth in investment is

$$g_I(t) = \frac{\dot{I}}{I} = \frac{\frac{dI}{dt}}{I} = \frac{c_1}{c_0 + c_1 t} - c_2 \tag{A-1}$$

Multiplying both sides by dt we have

$$\frac{dI}{I} = \frac{c_{1dt}}{c_0 + c_1 t} - c_2 dt$$

Integrating each side and letting k equal the constant of integration yields

$$\ln I = \ln(c_0 + c_1 t) - c_2 t + k$$

rearranging

$$I(t) = (c_0 + c_1 t)e^{-c_2 t}e^k$$

Setting $t = 0$

$$I(0) = c_0 e^k$$

Thus

$$I(t) = \frac{I(0)^t}{c_0}(c_0 + c_1 t)e^{-c_2 t} \tag{A-2}$$

Given an initial marginal efficiency of capital schedule (at time zero) the marginal efficiency of investment schedule at time t can be found by solving equation (A-2) for all possible levels of $I(0)$.

Since r is constant, we have[16]

$$E(t) = E(0) + \int_0^t \dot{E}(t) = E(0) + \int_0^t rI(t) \tag{A-3}$$

Substituting for $I(t)$ and integrating yields

$$E(t) = E(0) - \frac{rI(0)}{c_2} e^{-c_2 t} - \frac{rI(0)c_1}{c_0 c_2^2}(c_2 t + 1)e^{-c_2 t} + \frac{rI(0)}{c_2} + \frac{rI(0)c_1}{c_0 c_2^2} \tag{A-4}$$

The initial value of the firm is

$$V(0) = \int_0^\infty [E(t) - I(t)]e^{-kt} \tag{A-5}$$

Substituting for $E(t)$ and $I(t)$ and integrating yields

$$V(0) = \frac{E(0)}{k} + \frac{I(0)(r-k)}{k(k+c_2)} + \frac{I(0)\frac{c_1}{c_0}(r-k)}{k(k+c_2)^2} \tag{A-6}$$

To solve for the cut-off rate which maximizes the value of the firm, differentiate equation (A-6) with respect to $I(0)$

$$\frac{\partial V(0)}{\partial I(0)} = \frac{r-k}{k(k+c_2)} + \frac{I(0)\frac{\partial r}{\partial I(0)}}{k(k+c_2)} + \frac{\frac{c_1}{c_0}(r-k)}{k(k+c_2)^2} + \frac{\frac{c_1}{c_0}I(0)\frac{\partial r}{\partial I(0)}}{k(k+c_2)^2} \tag{A-7}$$

Setting the derivative equal to zero and rearranging, yields

$$r + I(0)\frac{\partial r}{\partial I(0)} = k \tag{A-8}$$

Appendix B

Derivation of the Value of the Firm and the Optimum Investment Behavior with Managerially Determined Time Dependency

1. Model I

$$g_I(t) = \frac{\dot{I}}{I} = \frac{\frac{dI}{dt}}{I} = c_0 + c_1 r \tag{B-1}$$

Multiply both sides by dt yields

$$\frac{dI}{I} = (c_0 + c_1 r)\,dt$$

In order to solve this differential equation we must specify a starting condition $I(0)$. This equation is a linear differential equation if $I(0)$ uniquely determines a constant r at all moments in time. We will now show that this is true.

For any particular value of $I(t)$

$$\frac{\dot{I}(t)}{I(t)} = (c_0 + c_1 r(t)) \tag{B-2}$$

where $r(t)$ is uniquely determined by $I(t)$

$$\dot{I}(t) = (c_0 + c_1 r(t))I(t)$$

and

$$I(t+1) = I(t) + \dot{I} = (1 + c_0 + c_1 r(t))I(t) = bI(t) \tag{B-3}$$

where b is equal to $(1 + c_0 + c_1 r(t))$

If

1. $a(r')$ = the amount of investment yielding rate r' at time t
2. r_c = the cutoff rate for new investment assumed constant over time.

$$r(t) = \frac{\int_{r_c}^{\infty} sa(s)\,ds}{\int_{r_c}^{\infty} a(s)\,ds}$$

$$r(t+1) = \frac{\int_{r_c}^{\infty} bsa(s)\,ds}{\int_{r_c}^{\infty} ba(s)\,ds} = r(t)$$

Recognizing that the level of investment in $t+1$ is given by equation (B-3) and that at time $t+1$, $r(t)$ and thus b is a constant

$$r(t+1) = \frac{\displaystyle\int_{r_c}^{\infty} r' \frac{bdI(r')}{dr'}\,dr'}{\displaystyle\int_{r_c}^{\infty} \frac{bdI(r')}{dr'}\,dr'} = r(t)$$

Thus $r(t)$ is a constant over time, and is equal to $r(0)$ and thus is uniquely determined by the initial level of investment taken $I(0)$. Throughout this paper we have used r to refer to the average rates of return on new investment. The reader should keep in mind that as above it is a function of $I(0)$.

Once we have rewritten equation (B-2) as

$$\frac{dI}{I} = [c_0 + c_1 r]\, dt$$

we see that for any given value of $I(0)$ we have a linear differential equation with the following solution

$$I(t) = I(0)e^{(c_0+c_1 r)t}$$

Substituting equation (B-2) and $\dot{E} = rI$ into equation (A-3)

$$V(0) = \frac{E(0)}{k} + I(0)\left[\frac{1}{c_0 + c_1 r - k} - r\left(\frac{1}{k(c_0 + c_1 r)} + \frac{1}{(c_0 + c_1 r)(c_0 + c_1 r - k)}\right)\right]$$

$$= \frac{E(0)}{k} + \frac{I(0)(r-k)}{k(k - c_0 - c_1 r)} \tag{B-4}$$

Taking the derivative of equation (B-4) and setting it equal to zero and solving, yields

$$r + I(0)\frac{\partial r}{\partial I(0)} = k - \frac{c_1 I(0)\dfrac{\partial r}{\partial I(0)}(r-k)}{k - c_0 - c_1 r} \tag{B-5}$$

Notes

1. The constant investment opportunities model is described in Solomon (8). The standard growth model is described in J. B. Williams (9), Gordon (3) and Gordon and Shapiro (2).

2. The derivations in this paper are based on a firm which uses internal financing. However, in the absence of taxes and transaction costs, all of the valuation models and optimum investment criteria are equally valid for a firm employing new equity. The proof of this follows directly from Miller and Modigliani (6). In addition all derivations will assume that new investment opportunities are in the same risk class as the companies' past investments.

3. The implication of this growth model for the valuation of public utilities has been investigated by the authors (along with Zvi Lieber) in [1]. All of the growth models in this paper could be stated in terms of I rather than $g_I = \dot{I}/I$. For Example model (1) would be $\dot{I} = c_0 I$. Closed form valuation models can be derived with this modification.

4. This should not be confused with the marginal efficiency of capital schedule which is a plot of the total investment available at *or above* a rate of return against the rate of return.

5. We have drawn the investment opportunities schedule as a negatively sloped linear function. This has been done to simplify the diagram. Neither linearity nor negativity is a necessary assumption of any of the proofs which follow.

6. The time path of the IOS can be seen by integrating model m-1 to yield

$I(t) = I(0)e^{c_0 t}$

and examining the implication of this for marginal investment. It is important to note that these schedules refer to new investment not total investment which also includes investment necessary to maintain existing assets. A negatively shifting net investment schedule is of course consistent with a positively shifting total investment schedule. This point is amplified later in the text.

7. We are making the normal assumption that the cutoff rate for new investments is constant over time.

8. See Singh & Whittington |7| for some evidence on this relationship.

9. This can be seen by integrating m-2 to yield $I(t) = I(0)(1 + (c_1/c_0)t)$. If c_0 or c_1 are negative, then no solution exists for $I(t)$. Thus the curve cannot shift to the left.

10. The implication of (m-3) for investment is presented in Appendix A.

11. Some authors in an attempt to eliminate this dependency use a constant c for growth, rather than br. They also frequently assume that earnings and investment grow at the same rate. It can easily be shown that this implies $c = br$.

12. This term is sometimes called the firm's cost of capital. Since the cut-off rate on new investment is also called the cost of capital, and since, for some models analyzed in this paper, the cut-off rate is not equal to the stockholder's required return, we will avoid the term "cost of capital" altogether.

13. If the cash flow from a project were defined to include the reduction in future opportunities that resulted from taking the project (the externalities) then the appropriate cut-off rate would be k.

14. This is easily recognized as the standard growth model when we recognize that $I(0)/E(0)$ is the fraction of earnings retained b and $E(0)–I(0)$ is the initial dividend so

$$V(0) = \frac{D(0)}{k - br}.$$

16. The proof that r is constant is trivial and follows from the cut-off rate being constant. An explicit proof for a more difficult model is presented in Appendix B.

References

1. Elton, Edwin J., Gruber, Martin J. and Lieber, Zvi, "Valuation, Optimal Investment and Financing for the Firm Subject to Regulation", *Journal of Finance*, May 1975.

2. Gordon, Myron and Shaprio, E., "Capital Equipment Analysis: The Required Rate of Profit", *Management Science*, Vol. 3, October, 1956, pp. 102–110.

3. ———. *The Investment Financing and Valuation of the Corporation*, (Homewood, Illinois: Richard D. Irwin), 1962.

4. Hymer, S., and Pashigian, P., "Firm Size and Rate of Growth", *Journal of Political Economy*, Vol. 7, No. 6, (December, 1962), pp. 556–69.

5. Miller, Merton, "Discussion", *Journal of Finance*, Vol. 18, (May, 1963), pp. 313–316.

6. ——— and Modigliani, Franco, "Dividend Policy, Growth and the Valuation of Shares", *Journal of Business*, XXXIV (October, 1961).

7. Singh, A., and Whittington, C., *Growth, Profitability, and Valuation* (C.U.P., Cambridge, 1968).

8. Solomon, Ezra, *The Theory of Financial Management*, (New York: Columbia University Press), 1963.

9. Williams, J. B., *The Theory of Investment Value*, 1936.

II Solving for Optimal Portfolios

In this section we derive simple rules for solving for optimal portfolios. The first four chapters present various aspects of our simple rules research; the fifth uses simple rules to analyze an important problem in portfolio theory. The basic idea behind simple rules is as follows: The future variance/covariance matrix of security returns is best estimated by imposing a structure on how securities move together, the simplest structure being a single-index model. If we impose a structure on how securities move together, then the variance/covariance matrix of security returns can be explicitly inverted. This inversion generates a closed-form solution to the portfolio problem and a set of simple rules for forming optimal portfolios. Simple rules are ranking devices and cut-off rates that, when followed, produce optimum portfolios. These simple rules are not an approximation but rather, under the assumptions about the variance/covariance matrix, produce the exact solution that would be found by solving for the optimum using quadratic programming.

When we first devised these rules, one of their important uses was to calculate efficient frontiers. A number of firms used them for that purpose. The availability of modern computing power and portfolio programs has made this use less important. Simple rules, however, also provide an understanding of why securities enter the optimum portfolio and this continues to be of key importance. When a firm selects projects, it ranks them and decide on where to cut. Simple rules show that in putting together an optimum portfolio, one should rank securities and then determine a cutoff rate. These simple rules show you exactly how to do it. What makes a security desirable and high ranking is clear-cut. For example, if the single-index model is used to estimate the variance/covariance matrix of security returns, then it is optimum to determine a securities desirability by its excess return (expected return minus riskless rate) divided by beta. Since there is a fair amount of uncertainty in estimating these quantities, simple rules allow the manager to see which securities are near the cutoff and which require additional analysis that might change the decision about inclusion. A third use for simple rules is to provide a framework where important issues such as the effect of estimation error, transactions costs, and more complicated margin rules can be explored. The first chapter in this section is the original simple-rules article. In it we derive the ranking device and cutoff rates when the return-generating process is the single-index model or all pairwise correlations between securities is a constant. In the second chapter, we show how acting as if there is a riskless rate (even when one does not exist) allows the determination of the full efficient frontier. The third chapter is an example of the type of analysis that results when we assume a more complicated structure of how securities move together.[1]

When we wrote the fourth chapter, we thought it would have wide application. Fama had theorized that security price returns were best characterized as having a non-normal stable distribution. If this was true, there was no technique for determining efficient portfolios. We showed that simple rules could be devised to overcome this problem. In ensuing years, researchers investigating portfolio optimization have been content to concentrate their analysis on mean and variance, and have paid little or no attention to portfolio analysis when returns are non-normal stable.

The last chapter is an application of simple rules to solve an important problem. Much of the information supplied to portfolio managers is in the form of discrete rankings such as buy, hold, and sell. This article shows how this information can be employed to construct optimal portfolios.

The simple-rules literature has gone in two directions since our original article. First, there have been studies that have discussed the effects of speeding up the ranking and selection process by calculating the cut-off rate of securities and eliminating those that are below the cut-off rate. Second, some analysts use simple rules to analyze important problems. For example, Brown and Chen have analyzed the effect of estimating error using simple rules, and Alexander has examined the impact of more realistic margin rules using them.[2]

Notes

1. For another example see Edwin J. Elton and Martin J. Gruber, *Simple Criteria for Optimal Portfolio Selection: The Multi-Index Case in Portfolio Management 25 Years After,* (Amsterdam: Elsevier, 1979).

2. Brown, Stephen, and Chen, Son-Nan "Estimation Risk and Simple Rules for Optimal Portfolio Selection"; *Journal of Finance* 38, no. 4 (1983): 1087–1094; and Alexander, Gordon J., "Short Selling and Efficient Sets," *Journal of Finance* 48, no. 4 (1983): 1497–1506.

6 Simple Criteria for Optimal Portfolio Selection

Edwin J. Elton, Martin J. Gruber, and Manfred W. Padberg

Modern portfolio theory dates from Markowitz's [9, 10] pioneering article published in 1952 and subsequent book. Markowitz's suggestions were intended to be practical and implementable. It is ironic that the primary outgrowth has been normative and theoretical and that modern portfolio theory has rarely been implemented.

There are three major reasons why portfolio theory has not been implemented. These are:

1. the difficulty in estimating the type of input data necessary (particularly correlation matrices);
2. the time and cost necessary to generate efficient portfolios (solve a quadratic programming problem); and
3. the difficulty of educating portfolio managers to relate to risk return tradeoffs expressed in terms of covariances as well as returns and standard deviations.

There have been two approaches in the literature to solving the first of these problems. One has been to use a single index model to generate variance-covariance structures. The second is to assume a simple structure for the variance-covariance matrix. In particular the assumption that all pairwise correlations are the same has been shown to do an excellent job of forecasting future correlation structures.[1] In this paper we shall employ these two approaches, which were formulated to solve the first problem, in a manner which should go a long way towards eliminating the second and third problem.

Specifically, we will show that if one is willing to accept the existence of a risk free asset and is willing to either (1) assume that the single index model adequately describes the variance-covariance structure or (2) assume that a good estimate of all pairwise correlation coefficients is a single number, then a simple decision criterion (which does not involve mathematical programming) can be used to reach an optimal solution to the portfolio problem. Furthermore, this simple decision criterion has an intuitive interpretation and its basis is easily understood. This simple method not only allows one to determine which securities are included in an optimal portfolio but also how much to invest in each. Furthermore, the technique allows the definition of a cut-off rate defined solely in terms of the characteristics of the individual security, such that the impact on the optimal portfolio of the introduction of any new security into the manager's decision set can quickly and easily be seen. Finally, the technique makes clear to the manager what characteristics of a security are desirable.[2]

This paper is divided into two sections corresponding to the two approximations to the variance-covariance structure. In the first section we assume that the only source of joint movement of two securities comes about because of a common response to market movements. In the second section we will derive a simple numerical solution technique when the correlation coefficient between all pairs of securities can be assumed to be the same. Throughout, we will assume the existence of a riskless asset. This implies that the separation theorem holds and that the investor should maximize the ratio of excess return on a portfolio divided by the standard deviation of the portfolio. Also, throughout the paper we will make the blanket assumption that there is at least one security in the set of all investment opportunities whose expected return is strictly greater than the return on the riskless asset. In each section we will consider both the case where short sales are allowed and the case where they are forbidden.

I The Single Index Model and the Construction of Optimal Portfolios

In this section we shall assume that the standard single index model is an accurate description of reality. That is

1. $R_i = \alpha_i + \beta_i I + \varepsilon_i$
2. $I = A_{N+1} + \varepsilon_{N+1}$
3. $E(\varepsilon_{N+1}\varepsilon_i) = 0, i = 1, \ldots, N$
4. $E(\varepsilon_i\varepsilon_j) = 0, i = 1, \ldots, N; j = 1, \ldots, N; i \neq j$

where R_i = the return on security i (a random variable)

I = a market index (a random variable)

β_i = a measure of the responsiveness of security i to changes in the market index

α_i = the return on security i that is independent of changes in the market index

ε_i = a variable with a mean of zero and variance $\sigma_{\varepsilon_i}^2$

σ_m^2 = the variance of the market index

The last two equations characterize the approximation of the standard single index model to the variance-covariance structure. The assumption implied by these equations is that the only joint movement between securities comes about because of a common response to a market index.

We shall show that under these assumptions one can solve for optimal portfolios with simple decision criteria without resorting to mathematical programming. The methods we shall derive for finding optimal portfolios are more accurate than the linear programming approximations which have been put forth and in fact reach the same solution to the portfolio problem as the exact quadratic programming method.[3] In addition they are so simple that once the β for each stock has been derived the optimal portfolio can be found, without the use of a computer, in a few minutes time.

We shall study two cases involving different degrees of complexity. In the first case we shall assume that short selling is allowed while in the second case we shall not allow short selling. In both these cases lending and borrowing can take place at the riskless rate of interest.

1 *Optimum Portfolios with Short Selling*

In this section we shall derive the expression for that portfolio which has the highest excess return to standard deviation (θ) when short selling is allowed.

We shall first find an unconstrained vector of the relative weights for each security so that the θ for the portfolio is maximized. Then we shall scale these weights to insure that we are fully invested.

In addition to the symbols already defined

Let R_f = the riskless lending-borrowing rate

X_i = the relative weights we place on each security ($X_i > 0$ for a long position, $X_i < 0$ for a short position)

R_p = return on the portfolio (a random variable)

σ_p = the standard deviation of the return on the portfolio

Then the problem is given the assumption of the single index model to find a set of X_i's to maximize

$$\theta = \frac{\bar{R}_p - R_f}{\sigma_p} \tag{1}$$

where the bar over a variable denotes its expected value.

Now[4]

$$\bar{R}_p - R_f = \sum_{i=1}^{N} X_i(\bar{R}_i - R_f)$$

and

$$\sigma_p^2 = E\left(\sum_{i=1}^{N} X_i R_i - \sum_{i=1}^{N} X_i \bar{R}_i\right)^2$$

Employing the single index assumptions outlined above[5]

$$\sigma_p = \left[\sum_{i=1}^{N} X_i^2 \beta_i^2 \sigma_m^2 + \sum_{i=1}^{N} \sum_{\substack{j=1 \\ j \neq i}}^{N} X_i X_j \beta_i \beta_j \sigma_m^2 + \sum_{i=1}^{N} X_i^2 \sigma_{\varepsilon_i}^2\right]^{1/2}$$

Then

$$\theta = \frac{\sum_{i=1}^{N} X_i(\bar{R}_i - R_f)}{\left[\sum_{i=1}^{N} X_i^2 \beta_i^2 \sigma_m^2 + \sum_{i=1}^{N} \sum_{\substack{j=1 \\ j \neq i}}^{N} X_i X_j \beta_i \beta_j \sigma_m^2 + \sum_{i=1}^{N} X_i^2 \sigma_{\varepsilon_i}^2\right]^{1/2}}$$

Note that θ is homogeneous of degree zero. Thus maximizing θ without the constraint on the sum of the X_i's yields the same optimum as maximizing θ with the constraint.

To find that set of X_i's which maximize θ we take the derivative of θ with respect to each X_i and set it equal to zero.[6]

$$\frac{d\theta}{dX_i} = (\bar{R}_i - R_f) - \frac{\sum_{i=1}^{N} X_i(\bar{R}_i - R_f)}{\sigma_p^2}\left[x_i \beta_i^2 \sigma_m^2 + \beta_i \sum_{\substack{j=1 \\ j \neq i}}^{N} x_j \beta_j \sigma_m^2 + X_i \sigma_{\varepsilon_i}^2\right] = 0$$

for $i = 1, 2, \ldots, N$

Defining $Z_i = (\bar{R}_p - R_f/\sigma_p^2)X_i$ and solving this expression for any Z_i yields[7]

$$Z_i = \frac{\bar{R}_i - R_f}{\sigma_{\varepsilon_i}^2} - \frac{\beta_i \sigma_m^2 \sum_{j=1}^{N} Z_j \beta_j}{\sigma_{\varepsilon_i}^2} \tag{2}$$

Multiplying both sides of the equation by β_i

$$Z_i \beta_i = \frac{\bar{R}_i - R_f}{\sigma_{\varepsilon_i}^2} \beta_i - \frac{\beta_i^2 \sigma_m^2 \sum_{j=1}^{N} Z_j \beta_j}{\sigma_{\varepsilon_i}^2}$$

Adding together the N equations of this form yields

$$\sum_{j=1}^{N} Z_j \beta_j = \sum_{j=1}^{N} \left[\frac{\bar{R}_j - R_f}{\sigma_{\varepsilon_j}^2} \beta_j \right] - \sigma_m^2 \sum_{j=1}^{N} Z_j \beta_j \left[\sum_{j=1}^{N} \frac{\beta_j^2}{\sigma_{\varepsilon_i}^2} \right]$$

or

$$\sum_{j=1}^{N} Z_j \beta_j = \frac{\sum_{j=1}^{N} \left[\frac{\bar{R}_j - R_f}{\sigma_{\varepsilon_j}^2} \beta_j \right]}{1 + \sigma_m^2 \sum_{j=1}^{N} \frac{\beta_j^2}{\sigma_{\varepsilon_j}^2}} \tag{3}$$

Substituting equation (3) into equation (2) yields

$$Z_i = \frac{\bar{R}_j - R_f}{\sigma_{\varepsilon_i}^2} - \left[\sigma_m^2 \frac{\sum_{j=1}^{N} \left[\frac{\bar{R}_j - R_f}{\sigma_{\varepsilon_j}^2} \beta_j \right]}{1 + \sigma_m^2 \sum_{j=1}^{N} \frac{\beta_j^2}{\sigma_{\varepsilon_j}^2}} \right] \frac{\beta_i}{\sigma_{\varepsilon_i}^2}$$

Note that the term in brackets depends only on the population of the stocks being considered and is independent of the composition of the optimal portfolio. This term can be calculated before the search for the optimal portfolio begins. Let us call this term C_0. Then

$$Z_i = \frac{\bar{R}_i - R_f}{\sigma_{\varepsilon_i}^2} - C_0 \frac{\beta_i}{\sigma_{\varepsilon_i}^2} = \frac{\beta_i}{\sigma_{\varepsilon_i}^2} \left[\frac{\bar{R}_i - R_f}{\beta_i} - C_0 \right]$$

Table 6.1

Security no.	Mean return	Beta	Residual risk	Stan. dev.
1	12	$20/\sqrt{8}$	50	10
2	10	$2\sqrt{8}$	32	8
3	8	$\sqrt{8}$	8	4
4	6	$\frac{1}{2}\sqrt{8}$	2	2

The value of Z_i for all stocks can easily be calculated. Having done so we must scale the Z_i so that we have invested 100% of our funds.[8] That is we must insure that

$$\sum_{j=1}^{N} |Z_j| = 1.$$

Thus the fraction of our portfolio which we should invest in any stock (X_i^0) is equal to[9]

$$X_i^0 = \frac{\dfrac{(\bar{R}_i - R_f) - C_0\beta_i}{\sigma_{\varepsilon_i}^2}}{\displaystyle\sum_{j=1}^{N} \left| \frac{(\bar{R}_j - R_f) - C_0\beta_j}{\sigma_{\varepsilon_i}^2} \right|} \tag{4}$$

The advantage of a formula like (4) is that it can easily be calculated and an optimal portfolio arrived at for any population of stocks.

Let us illustrate this with an example. Consider the four securities whose characteristics are shown in Table 6.1. Further assume that $R_f = 2$ and $\sigma_m^2 = 1$. Then

$$\sum_{j=1}^{N} \frac{\beta_j^2}{\sigma_{\varepsilon_j}^2} = 4$$

and

$$\sum_{j=1}^{N} (\bar{R}_j - R_f)\beta_j/\sigma_{\varepsilon_j}^2 = [(10/50)(20/\sqrt{8}) + (8/32)(2\sqrt{8})$$

$$+ (6/8)\sqrt{8} + (4/2)(1/2)(\sqrt{8})] = 22/\sqrt{8}.$$

Thus we have

$$Z_1 = \frac{10}{50} - \frac{20}{\sqrt{8}50}\left(\frac{22}{5\sqrt{8}}\right) = \frac{10 - 11}{50} = -\frac{1}{50}$$

$$Z_2 = \frac{8}{32} - \frac{2\sqrt{8}}{32}\left(\frac{22}{5\sqrt{8}}\right) = \frac{40 - 44}{32.5} = -\frac{1}{40}$$

$$Z_3 = \frac{6}{8} - \frac{\sqrt{8}}{8}\left(\frac{22}{5\sqrt{8}}\right) = \frac{30 - 22}{8.5} = \frac{1}{5}$$

$$Z_4 = \frac{4}{2} - \frac{\sqrt{8}}{4}\left(\frac{22}{5\sqrt{8}}\right) = \frac{40 - 22}{20} = \frac{9}{10}$$

$$\sum_{i=1}^{4} |Z_i| = 229/200$$

Thus

$$X_1^0 = -4/299 \qquad X_2^0 = -5/229 \qquad X_3^0 = 40/229 \qquad X_4^0 = 180/229$$

2 *Optimal Portfolios When Short Sales Are Not Allowed*

If we restrict management prerogatives by disallowing short sales we must modify the solution presented in the last section. In particular, if short selling is disallowed then we must introduce the constraints that all $X_i \geqslant 0$. This requires employing the Kuhn-Tucker conditions. Since the variance-covariance matrix is positive definite the Kuhn-Tucker conditions are both necessary and sufficient for an optimum. (See Appendix C.) The equivalent of equation (2) using the Kuhn-Tucker conditions is[10]

$$Z_i = \frac{\bar{R}_i - R_f}{\sigma_{\varepsilon_i}^2} - \frac{\beta_i}{\sigma_{\varepsilon_i}^2}\sigma_m^2 \sum_{j=1}^{N} \beta_j Z_j + \mu_i \tag{5}$$

where

$$Z_i \geqslant 0, \mu_i \geqslant 0, \quad \text{and} \quad \mu_i Z_i = 0 \qquad \text{for all } i.$$

Now let us assume for a moment that we can find all stocks which would be in an optimal portfolio (call the set of such stocks k) and arrange these stocks as $i = 1, 2, \ldots, k$. For the sub-population of stocks that make up the optimal portfolio

$$Z_i = \frac{\bar{R}_i - R_f}{\sigma_{\varepsilon_i}^2} - \frac{\beta_i}{\sigma_{\varepsilon_i}^2}\sigma_m^2 \sum_{j=1}^{k} Z_j \beta_j \qquad \text{and} \qquad \mu_i = 0$$

Multiplying both sides by β_i summing over all stocks in k and rearranging yields

$$\sum_{j=1}^{k} Z_j\beta_j = \frac{\sum_{j=1}^{k}\left[\frac{\bar{R}_j - R_f}{\sigma_{\varepsilon_j}^2}\beta_j\right]}{1 + \sigma_m^2 \sum_{j=1}^{k} \frac{\beta_j^2}{\sigma_{\varepsilon_j}^2}} \tag{6}$$

Notice since the set k contains all stocks with positive Z_i's

$$\sum_{j=1}^{N} Z_j\beta_j = \sum_{j=1}^{k} Z_j\beta_j \tag{7}$$

and let

$$\phi_k = \sigma_m^2 \frac{\sum_{j=1}^{k} \frac{\bar{R}_j - R_f}{\sigma_{\varepsilon_j}^2}\beta_j}{1 + \sigma_m^2 \sum_{j=1}^{k} \frac{\beta_j^2}{\sigma_{\varepsilon_j}^2}} \tag{8}$$

Using (8) we obtain after substitution and rearranging from equation (5) the following expression for Z_i:

$$Z_i = \frac{\beta_i}{\sigma_{\varepsilon_i}^2}\left[\frac{\bar{R}_i - R_f}{\beta_i} - \phi_k\right] + \mu_i \tag{9}$$

Since $\mu_i \geqslant 0$, including μ_i can only increase the value of Z_i. Thus if Z_i is positive with $\mu_i = 0$, the inclusion of μ_i can never make it zero. Hence if Z_i is positive when $\mu_i = 0$ the security should be included. If $Z_i < 0$ when $\mu_i = 0$ positive values of μ_i can increase Z_i. However, since the product of μ_i and Z_i must equal zero, positive values of μ_i imply $Z_i = 0$. Hence any security with $Z_i < 0$ when $\mu_i = 0$ must be rejected.

In order to determine if a security should be included it is necessary to deal with three types of securities; those with positive β_i, those with negative β_i, and those with $\beta_i = 0$. Let us start by assuming that all securities have positive β_i's.

Then we show in Appendix A that if a security with a particular $(\bar{R}_i - R_f)/\beta_i$ is included in the optimal portfolio all securities with higher values of $(\bar{R}_i - R_f)/\beta_i$ must be included in the optimal portfolio. This holds because with $\beta_i > 0$ the sign of Z_i depends on the sign of the term in the brackets. The term in the brackets is $(\bar{R}_i - R_f)/\beta_i$ minus a constant. Thus if a stock with a particular $(\bar{R}_i - R_f)/\beta_i$ has a positive Z_i all stocks with higher excess return to β ratios will also have a positive Z_i. Thus all we have to do to find the securities included in the optimal portfolio is rank from 1 to N all securities by $(\bar{R}_i - R_f)/\beta_i$. Then compute a value for equation (8) as if the set k only contained the first security. This will always be positive. Next we calculate equation (8) setting $i = 2$ and letting the set k contain the first two securities. We proceed for $i = 3, 4, \ldots$ until Z_i computed from equation (9) with $\mu_i = 0$ turns negative. If it turns negative for the $j + 1$st security then the set k contains the first j securities $(i = j)$. Appendix B presents a proof that once Z_i from equation (9) turns negative it can never be made positive for any security not in the set k by adding more securities to the portfolio. Hence we have found a simple and fast way to define all securities in the set k. Once these securities are found the Z_i value for all securities in the set can be found simply by calculating the Z_i for each security from equation (9) recognizing that the μ_i for each of these securities equals zero.

The fraction of our funds which should be placed in each security can be found by recognizing that the sum of the fractions must equal 1 or by dividing the Z_i found for each security in the set k by the sum of the Z_i for the set k. Once again, a simple and very quick procedure has been found for designing an optimal portfolio.

Let us illustrate this with an example. Consider the numbers shown in Table 6.1. Ranking by excess return to β shows that the securities in decreasing order of desirability are 4, 3, 2, 1. The term in the brackets for security 4 is[11]

$$\left[\frac{4}{\frac{1}{2}\sqrt{8}} - \left(\frac{4 \cdot \frac{1}{2}\sqrt{8}}{2}\right)\left(\frac{1}{1 + 2/2}\right)\right] > 0$$

The term in the brackets for security 3 when the portfolio consists of 3 and 4 is

$$\left[\frac{6}{\sqrt{8}} - \left(\frac{4 \cdot \frac{1}{2}\sqrt{8}}{2} + \frac{6 \cdot \sqrt{8}}{8}\right)\left(\frac{1}{1 + 2}\right)\right] > 0$$

The term in the brackets for security 2 when the portfolio consists of 2, 3 and 4 is

$$\left[\frac{8}{2\sqrt{8}} - \left(\frac{4 \cdot \frac{1}{2}\sqrt{8}}{2} + \frac{6 \cdot \sqrt{8}}{8} + \frac{8 \cdot 2\sqrt{8}}{32}\right)\left(\frac{1}{1+3)}\right)\right] < 0$$

Thus the optimum portfolio consists of a portfolio of security 3 and 4 with the weights of[12]

$$X_3^0 = Z_3 = \frac{\sqrt{8}}{8}\left[\frac{6}{\sqrt{8}} - \left(\frac{14\sqrt{8}}{8}\right)\left(\frac{1}{3}\right)\right] = \frac{1}{6}$$

$$X_4^0 = Z_4 = \frac{\frac{1}{2}\sqrt{8}}{2}\left[\frac{8}{\sqrt{8}} - \left(\frac{14\sqrt{8}}{8}\right)\left(\frac{1}{3}\right)\right] = \frac{5}{6}$$

We have not as yet dealt with the case of securities with negative β's. If all securities had negative β's an argument and set of proofs analogous to that described above would hold except that stocks would be ranked in ascending order by $(\bar{R}_i - R_f)/\beta_i$.

If stocks with both negative and positive β's are present then one should follow the procedure outlined above to see which of the positive β stocks should be included in the portfolio. When no more positive β stocks are included, stocks with negative β's should be tried (starting with the one with the smallest $(\bar{R}_i - R_f)/\beta_i$ until no more enter. If any negative β stocks enter, it must decrease the size of the term in brackets in (8) and so the highest excess return to positive β stocks previously rejected should be checked to see if it now enters. If more positive β stocks enter, then the negative β stock list should be checked and the procedure repeated iteratively until no more stocks enter. In actual practice this iterative procedure will converge almost instantaneously because of the very small number of stocks with negative β's.

The last problem left to deal with is the problem of stocks with zero β. From equation (9) if any stocks exist with zero β then they should be included in the optimal portfolio if their expected return exceeds the riskless rate of interest. Hence when the first positive stocks (and all other stocks) are checked to see if they belong in the optimal portfolio, all zero β stocks with an expected return above the riskless rate should be included in the portfolio since they do not alter the value of ϕ_k given by (8).

Before leaving this section, it is worthwhile considering the implications of our model for the revision of portfolios when a new stock is introduced into the population of stocks under consideration. The present framework drastically simplifies the revision problem.

Let us take the case of a new stock with a positive β. If the excess return to β ratio for the new stock is below the excess return to β ratio of the highest numbered stock excluded from the portfolio (that is the excluded stock with the highest excess return to β ratio), then the new stock will not enter our optimum portfolio. If the new stock has an excess return to β ratio above the stock with the lowest excess return to β ratio which was previously included in the portfolio, it will enter. Furthermore, stocks previously in the portfolio with low excess return to β ratios will have to be rechecked using equations (8) and (9) to see if they remain. Finally, if the stock has an excess return to β ratio between the lowest in the portfolio and the highest not in the portfolio, equation (9) will have to be used to see if it enters or not. If it enters, all stocks which were previously in the portfolio remain in the portfolio. Negative β stocks can be handled in an analogous manner.

II Constant Correlation Coefficients and the Construction of Optimal Portfolios

In this section, we will assume that all pairwise correlation coefficients are equal. While this probably does not represent the true pattern one finds in the economy, it is very difficult to obtain a better estimate. Elsewhere [1] we have shown that this assumption produces better estimates of future correlation coefficients than do historical correlation coefficients or those produced from the single index approximation discussed in section one. In fact, the assumption of a constant correlation coefficient produced forecasts which were about as accurate as any of nine techniques we tried. As discussed earlier, the optimum portfolio is that which maximizes the ratio of excess return on the portfolio to its standard deviation of returns. Letting

1. σ_{ij} = covariance between security i and security j
2. σ_i^2 = the variance of security i
3. ρ = the correlation coefficient between any two securities
4. all other terms as before

then excess returns on a N security portfolio is

$$\bar{R}_p - R_f = \sum_{i=1}^{N} X_i(\bar{R}_i - R_f)$$

and the standard deviation is

$$\sigma_p = \left[\sum_{i=1}^{N} X_i^2 \sigma_i^2 + \sum_{i=1}^{N} \sum_{\substack{j=1 \\ j \neq 1}}^{N} X_i X_j \sigma_{ij} \right]^{1/2}$$

A Optimal Policies When Short Sales Are Allowed

If we allow short sales then we maximize $\theta = (\bar{R}_p - R_f)/\sigma_p$ without restricting the sign of X_i. The first order conditions necessary for a maximum were presented by Lintner [4] and are;

$$Z_i \sigma_i^2 + \sum_{\substack{j=1 \\ j \neq i}}^{N} Z_j \sigma_{ij} = \bar{R}_i - R_f \qquad i = 1, \ldots, N$$

where

$$Z_i = X_i(\bar{R}_p - R_f)/\sigma_p^2$$

This is equal to

$$Z_i \sigma_i^2 (1 - \rho) + \rho \sigma_i \sum_{j=1}^{N} Z_j \sigma_j = \bar{R}_i - R_f$$

Solving for Z_i yields[13]

$$Z_i = \frac{\bar{R}_i - R_f}{\sigma_i^2 (1 - \rho)} - \frac{\rho}{1 - \rho} \frac{1}{\sigma_i} \sum_{j=1}^{N} Z_j \sigma_j \tag{10}$$

The term $\sum_{j=1}^{N} Z_j \sigma_j$ can be eliminated by multiplying through by σ_i and summing

$$\sum_{j=1}^{N} Z_j \sigma_j = \sum_{j=1}^{N} \frac{\bar{R}_j - R_f}{\sigma_j (1 - \rho)} - \frac{\rho}{1 - \rho} N \sum_{j=1}^{N} Z_j \sigma_j$$

Solving for $\sum_{j=1}^{N} Z_j \sigma_j$ yields

$$\sum_{j=1}^{N} Z_j \sigma_j = \frac{1}{1 - \rho + N\rho} \sum_{j=1}^{N} \frac{\bar{R}_j - R_f}{\sigma_j}$$

Substituting this into equation (10) yields

$$Z_i = \frac{(\bar{R}_i - R_f)}{\sigma_i^2(1-\rho)} - \frac{\rho}{1-\rho}\frac{1}{1-\rho+N\rho}\frac{1}{\sigma_i}\sum_{j=1}^{N}\frac{\bar{R}_j - R_f}{\sigma_j} \tag{11}$$

Thus the amount to invest in each security is

$$X_i^0 = \frac{Z_i}{\sum_{j=1}^{N}|Z_j|}$$

$$= \frac{1}{\sum_{j=1}^{N}|Z_j|}\frac{1}{\sigma_i}\frac{1}{1-\rho}\left[\frac{\bar{R}_i - R_f}{\sigma_i} - \frac{\rho}{1-\rho+N\rho}\sum_{j=1}^{N}\frac{\bar{R}_j - R_f}{\sigma_j}\right] \tag{12}$$

This equation can be used to determine whether a stock is sold short or purchased long and the amount invested in each stock. Several conclusions can be drawn. First, the above is an extremely simple equation. For even a medium sized portfolio X_i could be determined from the estimates quickly using only a pencil and paper. Second, if a stock with a particular excess return to standard deviation is purchased long all stocks with higher ratios are also purchased long. This is true since the terms in the bracket of equation (12) determines the sign of X_i and the second term is the same constant for all securities. The contrary is of course also true if a security with a particular excess return to standard deviation ratio is purchased short all securities with a smaller ratio are also purchased short. This can be illustrated with a simple example. Consider the example shown in Table 6.1. Calculating excess returns to standard deviation and other useful quantities yield the numbers shown in Table 6.2.

With a correlation coefficient assumed to be .5 we have from equation (11)

Table 6.2

Security	$\bar{R}_i - R_f$	$1/\sigma_i$	$(\bar{R}_i - R_f)/\sigma_i$
1	10	1/10	1
2	8	1/8	1
3	6	1/4	1.5
4	4	1/2	2.0
			5.5

$$Z_1 = \frac{1}{1-.5}\frac{1}{10}\left[1 - \frac{.5}{1-.5+2}(5.5)\right] = 2(1/10)[1-1.1] = -2/100$$

$$Z_2 = 2(1/8)[1-1.1] = -1/40$$

$$Z_3 = 2(1/4)[1.5-1.1] = 1/5$$

$$Z_4 = 2(1/2)[2-1.1] = .9$$

Scaling the above so that the sum of the absolute values equals 1.0 yields the same results as shown in Section I.

B Optimal Policies When Short Sales Are Not Allowed

If short selling is not allowed then we have to rely on the Kuhn-Tucker conditions. As detailed in Appendix C they are both necessary and sufficient. The Kuhn-Tucker conditions which maximize θ are

1. $\bar{R}_i - R_f - Z_i\sigma_i^2 - \sum_{\substack{j=1 \\ j \neq i}}^{N} Z_j\sigma_{ij} + \mu_i = 0$
2. $Z_i \geqslant 0 \quad \mu_i \geqslant 0$
3. $Z_i \cdot \mu_i = 0$

Solving for Z_i we have

$$Z_i = \frac{\bar{R}_i - R_f}{\sigma_i^2(1-\rho)} - \frac{1}{\sigma_i}\frac{\rho}{1-\rho}\sum_{j=1}^{N} Z_j\sigma_j + \frac{\mu_i}{\sigma_i^2(1-\rho)}$$

Without loss of generality, we can assume that the first k securities are included. For an excluded security, $Z_i = 0$ so that the summation in the equation can be written as summing to k rather than N. For an included security, μ_i is zero. Thus for these securities

$$Z_i = \frac{\bar{R}_i - R_f}{\sigma_i^2(1-\rho)} - \frac{1}{\sigma_i}\frac{\rho}{1-\rho}\sum_{j=1}^{k} Z_j\sigma_j$$

Multiplying both sides by σ_i and summing allows us to solve for $\sum_{j=1}^{k} Z_j\sigma_j$.

$$\sum_{j=1}^{k} Z_j\sigma_j = \sum_{j=1}^{k} \frac{\bar{R}_j - R_f}{\sigma_j}\frac{1}{1-\rho+k\rho}$$

Substituting this expression into the equation for Z_i given the above yields

$$Z_i = \frac{\bar{R}_i - R_f}{\sigma_i^2(1-\rho)} - \frac{1}{\sigma_i}\frac{\rho}{1-\rho}\frac{1}{1-\rho+k\rho}\sum_{j=1}^{k}\frac{\bar{R}_j - R_f}{\sigma_j} + \frac{\mu_i}{\sigma_i^2(1-\rho)} \tag{13}$$

The term containing the μ_i can only increase Z_i. Hence if Z_i is positive with μ_i zero a positive value of μ_i cannot make $Z_i = 0$. Thus any security with positive Z_i when $\mu_i = 0$ must be included. Correspondingly, any security with negative Z_i when $\mu_i = 0$ must be excluded.

Rearranging the above for included securities yields

$$Z_i = \frac{1}{1-\rho}\frac{1}{\sigma_i}\left[\frac{\bar{R}_i - R_f}{\sigma_i} - \frac{\rho}{1-\rho+k\rho}\sum_{j=1}^{k}\frac{\bar{R}_j - R_f}{\sigma_j}\right]$$

The sign of Z_i depends on the terms in the brackets. Since the last term in the brackets is a constant for any k if a security with a particular rate $(\bar{R}_i - R_f)/\sigma_i$ has a positive Z_i, then all securities with a higher ratio must also be included. It can be shown in a manner analogous to Appendix B that if a stock has a negative Z_i all lower ranking stocks will also have a negative Z_i if they are added. These two characteristics can be used to determine decision rules for solving the portfolio problem. Rank stocks in decreasing order of excess return to standard deviation, add securities until the term in the brackets becomes negative. Once the term in the brackets is negative for the security added last, it will be negative for any additional securities that are added.

The optimum amount to invest in each security is given by the above divided by the sum of the Z_i. Thus

$$X_i^0 = \frac{Z_i}{\sum_{i=1}^{k} Z_i}$$

Let us illustrate this with an example. Consider the example shown in Table 6.1 with $\rho = .5$ and the intermediate calculations shown in Table 6.2. The ranking of the securities in decreasing order of desirability is 4, 3, 2, 1. Including only 4 the expression in the brackets is[14]

$$\left[2 - \frac{.5}{1 - .5 + .5}2\right] > 0$$

Including 3 and 4 the expression in the brackets for security 3 is

$$\left[1.5 - \frac{.5}{1 - .5 + 1} 3.5\right] > 0$$

Including 2, 3 and 4 the expression in the brackets becomes

$$\left[1 - \frac{.5}{1 - .5 + 1.5} 4.5\right] < 0$$

Thus 3 and 4 are included. The amount of each is

$$X_4^0 = 2 \cdot \frac{1}{2} \left[2 - \frac{.5}{1 - .5 + 1} 3.5\right] = 5/6$$

$$X_3^0 = 2 \cdot \frac{1}{4} \left[1.5 - \frac{.5}{1 - .5 + 1} 3.5\right] = 1/6$$

These are the same as the proportions calculated in Section One.

Before closing this section a couple of observations are in order. First, if a new stock is under consideration it will be included if its excess return to standard deviation ratio exceeds that of the lowest ranking stock included in the portfolio, and will be excluded if its excess return to standard deviation ratio is below that of the highest ranking excluded stock.[15] This makes very explicit the characteristics that will make a stock enter and means that the proportions in the optimum portfolio will only have to be recalculated occasionally. Second, the introduction of a new stock is unlikely to cause a radical change in the stocks included in the optimal portfolio. At most, the entry of a new stock should cause a marginal change in the optimal excess return to standard deviation cutoff rate. Thus, using the old cutoff rate as a starting point in determining the new cutoff rate should lead to a quick solution to the problem.

III Conclusion

In this paper we have developed decision rules that allow one to reach optimal solutions to realistic portfolio problems without ever solving a mathematical programming problem. Furthermore, the characteristics of the stock that make it desirable are readily understood and calculated. In a forthcoming paper, we will show that similar (but more complex) results can be reached when we introduce multiple indices and more complicated correlation structures.

Appendix A

Proof that if any stock with a positive β belongs in an optimal portfolio, all stocks with positive β's which have a higher ratio of excess return to β belong in that portfolio.

Given that an optimal portfolio exists containing some set of securities k, then by equation (9) it follows from $\mu_i = 0$ and $Z_i > 0$ that

$$\frac{\bar{R}_i - R_f}{\beta_i} > \phi_k,$$

if stock i is contained in the portfolio. Consequently, for any stock j with

$$\frac{\bar{R}_j - R_f}{\beta_j} > \frac{\bar{R}_i - R_f}{\beta_j}$$

it follows that the expression for Z_j given by (9) is positive with $\mu_j = 0$. Consequently, by the Kuhn-Tucker conditions (5), stock j belongs to the optimal portfolio.

Appendix B

Proof that if any stock with a positive β is not in an optimal portfolio no stock with a lower excess return to β ratio and a positive β can be in the optimal portfolio.

Given that an optimal portfolio exists containing some set of securities k, then by equation (9) it follows from $Z_i = 0$ and $\mu_i \geqslant 0$ that

$$\frac{\bar{R}_i - R_f}{\beta_i} \leqslant \phi_k$$

if stock i is not contained in the portfolio. Consequently, for any stock j with

$$\frac{\bar{R}_j - R_f}{\beta_j} < \frac{\bar{R}_i - R_f}{\beta_i}$$

it follows that the expression for Z_j given by (9) is non-positive with $\mu_j = 0$. Consequently, by the Kuhn-Tucker conditions (5), stock j does not belong to the optimal portfolio.

Appendix C

In order to prove that the methods employed in the paper yield optima in both the cases where short sales are allowed and disallowed, respectively, we need to show that the function θ is pseudo-concave on the domain of positivity of θ. More precisely, let $\Gamma = \{X \in \mathbf{R}^n \mid \sum_{i=1}^{N}(\bar{R}_i - R_f)X_i > 0\}$. By our blanket assumption mentioned in the introduction, it follows that Γ is nonempty and furthermore, that Γ is an open convex subset of $\mathbf{R}^n$. To prove that $\theta = \theta(X)$ is pseudo-concave on Γ we have to show (see Mangasarian [7, p. 141]) that for every $\bar{X} \in \Gamma$ and all $X \in \Gamma$ such that $\nabla\theta(\bar{X})(X - \bar{X}) \leqslant 0$ it follows that $\theta(X) \leqslant \theta(\bar{X})$, where $\nabla\theta(\bar{X})$ is the gradient of θ evaluated at $\bar{X}$. Since $\bar{X} \in \Gamma$, it follows that $\bar{X} \neq 0$ and consequently, by the positive-definiteness of the variance-covariance matrix, that the numerator of θ does not vanish. Denoting by Q the variance-covariance matrix and by R the vector with components $\bar{R}_i - R_f$, $i = 1, \ldots, N$, we can write $\theta(X) = (RX)(XQX)^{-1/2}$. Consequently, $\nabla\theta(\bar{X})(X - \bar{X}) = (RX)(\bar{X}Q\bar{X})^{-1/2} - (R\bar{X})(\bar{X}Q\bar{X})^{-3/2}(\bar{X}QX)$. From the Cauchy-Schwartz inequality (see Mangasarian [7, p. 7], it follows that $\bar{X}QX \leqslant (\bar{X}Q\bar{X})^{1/2}(XQX)^{1/2}$ and hence that $\theta(X)$ is pseudo-concave. (For an alternative proof of the pseudo-concavity of $\theta(X)$ see also Mangasarian [7, p. 148, Problem 6.1].) Having established the pseudo-concavity of $\theta(X)$, it now follows from Theorem 9.3.3 of Mangasarian [7, p. 141] that in the case where short-sales are allowed the calculations of Sections I.1 and II.1 produce an optimum. Similarly, from Theorem 10.1.2 of [7] sufficiency of the Kuhn-Tucker conditions ensues, when short-sales are disallowed. Since the constraints of our optimization problem are linear, it follows from our blanket assumption mentioned in the introduction, that Slater's constraint qualification [7, p. 155] is satisfied and hence by Theorem 10.2.7 [7, p. 156], necessity of the Kuhn-Tucker conditions follows.

Notes

1. See Elton and Gruber [1].

2. The results contained in this paper have been announced previously (without proofs) in [3].

3. Sharpe [11] presents a linear programming approximation to the quadratic programming problem.

4. X_i can be negative for short sales. We are following Lintner's [6] suggestion in treating short sales. That is the short seller pays any dividends which accrue to the person who lends him the stock and gets a capital gain (or loss) which is the negative of any price appreciation.

In addition the short seller is assumed to receive interest at the riskless rate on both the money loaned to the owner of the borrowed stock and the money placed in escrow when the short sale is made. See Lintner [6] for a full discussion of these assumptions.

5. The expected return is unchanged when the single index model is employed.

6. Since the denominator appearing in θ is defined with respect to a positive-definite quadratic form, θ is continuously differentiable everywhere except for the point X with all coordinates $X_i = 0$ for $i = 1, \ldots, N$. It is not difficult, however, to verify that θ is bounded by zero. For $X \neq 0$, it follows from the Cauchy-Schwartz inequality that θ is bounded from above and that the maximum is unique up to a multiplicative factor. Consequently, the calculation outlined above produces a maximum. See Appendix C and Lintner [6]. Note furthermore, that the maximum value of θ and thus the transformation of X to Z below involves a positive factor. This follows since the standard deviation and excess return of the optimal portfolio are both positive since otherwise the investor holds the riskless asset.

7. A complication could occur if residual risk is zero. If only one security (i) has a zero residual risk then equation (2) is

$$\sigma_m^2 \sum_{j=1}^{N} \beta_j X_j = (\bar{R}_i - R_f)/\beta_i.$$

If more than one security has zero residual risk then a riskless portfolio can be found since $\sigma_p^2 = (X_1^2\beta_1^2\sigma_m^2 + X_2^2\beta_2^2\sigma_m^2 + 2X_1X_2\beta_1\beta_2\sigma_m^2) = (X_1\beta_1 + X_2\beta_2)^2\sigma_m^2$. This equals zero if $X_1\beta_1 = -X_2\beta_2$. This riskless portfolio is an alternative to the riskless asset. The analysis proceeds after any adjustments in R_f. In practice one would not expect zero residual risk.

8. We take the absolute values because of the possibility of short sales as explained above. Short sales involve an outlay equal to the price of the stocks involved.

9. Treynor and Black [14] have constructed a model for the first of the four cases dealt with in this paper, namely the single index representation of the variance-covariance matrix under the short sales case. However, our results for this case differ from theirs. The differences arise because Treynor and Black [14] assume both that the single index model holds and that a market security exists which while defined as the weighted sum of individual securities has zero residual risk. Fama [4] has shown that these two assumptions are inconsistent and can't be made simultaneously.

10. A complication could occur if residual risk were zero. In this case $\sum_{i=1}^{k} \beta_i Z_i$ equals the maximum $(\bar{R}_i - R_f)/\beta_i$ with zero residual risk. The rest of the analysis follows. It should be noted that the Kuhn-Tucker multipliers μ_i appearing in (5) as well as elsewhere in this paper are the usual multipliers up to multiplication by the constant σ_p for the optimal portfolio.

11. Inspection shows that the first security is always included. Thus this step is not necessary.

12. By chance the Z_i add to one.

13. Any security with $\sigma_i^2 = 0$ is a riskless asset. The one with the highest return is the preferred one and R_f is the return on this security. Hence at this step $\sigma_i^2 > 0$.

14. Inspection shows that the highest ranking security is always included so that this step could have been skipped.

15. If its excess return to standard deviation ratio falls between these two limits, equation (13) will have to be used to see if the stock should be included or excluded.

References

1. Edwin J. Elton and Martin J. Gruber. "Estimating the Dependence Structure of Share Prices—Implications for Portfolio Selection," *Journal of Finance*, Vol. XXVII, No. 5 (December 1973), pp. 1203–33.

2. ———. *Finance As A Dynamic Process* (Prentice Hall, Englewood Cliffs, New Jersey, 1975).

3. Edwin J. Elton, Martin J. Grober and Manfred W. Padberg. "Portfolio Selection—The Exploitation of Special Structures," *Bulletin of ORSA*, Vol. 22, Supplement 1 (Spring 1974), p. B-88 (abstract).

4. Eugene F. Fama. "Risk Return and Equilibrium: Some Clarifying Comments," *Journal of Finance*, Vol. 23 (March 1968), pp. 29–40.

5. Henry Latane and Donald Tuttle. "Criteria for Portfolio Building," *Journal of Finance*, Vol. XXII, No. 3 (September 1967), pp. 359–74.

6. John Lintner. "The Valuation of Risk Assets on the Selection of Risky Investments in Stock Portfolios and Capital Budgets," *The Review of Economics and Statistics* (February 1965), pp. 13–37.

7. Olvi Mangarsarian. *Nonlinear Programming* (McGraw-Hill, New York 1969).

8. James Mao. "Essentials for Portfolio Diversification Strategy," *Journal of Finance* (December 1970).

9. Harry Markowitz. *Portfolio Selection* (John T. Wiley & Sons, Inc., New York 1959).

10. ———. "Portfolio Selection," *Journal of Finance* (March 1952), pp. 77–91.

11. William Sharpe. "A Linear Programming Algorithm for Mutual Fund Portfolio Selection," *Management Science* (March 1967), pp. 499–510.

12. ———. "A linear Programming Approximation for the General Portfolio Selection Problem," *Journal of Financial and Quantitative Analysis* (December 1971), pp. 1263–76.

13. ———. "Simple Strategies for Portfolio Diversification: Comment," *Journal of Finance*, Vol. XXVII, No. 1, pp. 127–29.

14. Jack L. Treynor and Fischer Black. "How to Use Security Analysis to Improve Portfolio Selection," *Journal of Business* Vol. 46 pp. 66–86.

7

Simple Criteria for Optimal Portfolio Selection: Tracing out the Efficient Frontier

Edwin J. Elton, Martin J. Gruber, and Manfred W. Padberg

In a series of papers [1], [2], [3], and [4], we have shown that under alternative sets of assumptions about the form of the variance covariance structure of common stock returns, simple ranking devices can be used to determine optimal portfolios. These simple ranking devices have two advantages. First, the characteristics of a stock that make it desirable are unique to an individual stock and easily understood by portfolio managers. Secondly, the optimum portfolio is easy to determine and can normally be found with pencil and paper or at worst a hand calculator.

In each of these papers, we assumed the existence of a risk free asset and hence a unique optimum portfolio. This was not necessary. The purpose of this paper is to show how this assumption can be relaxed and our simple technique used to generate the full efficient frontier. In particular, we will show how the simple techniques described in the above papers can be used to find all corner portfolios. Since portfolios intermediate to corner portfolios are linear combinations of corner portfolios, this technique allows the construction of the full efficient frontier. In this paper, we will demonstrate how to find the efficient frontier for two cases: the single index model and a model assuming the correlation coefficient between all stocks is identical. We will examine both the case where short selling is allowed and the case where it is disallowed. The extension of the procedure described here to all of the other models described in [1], [2], [3] and [4] follows directly.

I The Single Index Model and the Construction of Optimal Portfolios

In this section we shall assume that the standard single index model is an adequate description of reality. That is

1. $R_i = \alpha_i + \beta_i I + \varepsilon_i$

2. $I = \alpha_{N+1} + \varepsilon_{N+1}$

3. $E(\varepsilon_{N+1}\varepsilon_i) = 0 \qquad i = 1, \ldots, N$

4. $E(\varepsilon_i \varepsilon_j) = 0 \qquad i = 1, \ldots, N$

$j = 1, \ldots, N$

$i \neq j$

where R_i = the return on security i (a random variable)

I = a market index (a random variable)

β_i = a measure of the responsiveness of security i to changes in the market index

α_i = the return on security i that is independent of changes in the market index

ε_i = a variable with a mean of zero and variance $\sigma^2_{\varepsilon_i}$

σ^2_m = the variance of the market index

The last two equations characterize the approximation of the standard single index model to the covariance structure. The assumption implied by these equations is that the only joint movement between securities comes about because of a common response to a market index.

A Short Sales Allowed

In (1), we showed that under the assumption of the single index model, one can solve the optimal portfolios with simple decision criteria without resorting to mathematical programming. In particular, we showed that if short sales were allowed, the optimal amount to invest in each security (X_i^0) is[1]

$$X_i^0 = \frac{Z_i}{\sum_{j=1}^{n} |Z_i|} \tag{1}$$

where Z_i is defined by

$$Z_i = \frac{\beta_i}{\sigma^2_{\varepsilon_i}} \left[\frac{\bar{R}_i - R_f}{\beta_i} - \phi_N \right] \tag{2}$$

and ϕ_N is defined by

$$\phi_N = \sigma_m^2 \frac{\sum_{j=1}^{N}\left[\frac{\bar{R}_j - R_f}{\sigma_{\varepsilon_j}^2}\beta_j\right]}{1+\sigma_m^2\sum_{j=1}^{N}\frac{\beta_j^2}{\sigma_{\varepsilon_j}^2}} \tag{3}$$

These equations allow one to solve for the composition of the optimal portfolio given the ability of the investor to borrow and lend unlimited amounts of funds at that riskless rate. If such borrowing and lending is disallowed, the concept of a riskless rate can still stand as an artifact to trace out the entire efficient frontier. The efficient frontier can be traced out by solving (1), (2), and (3) for a sequence of arbitrarily selected R_f. For example, R_f could start at zero and vary by .1 to maximum $\bar{R}_i$.[2]

If instead one wished to trace out corner portfolios a different procedure is needed. To understand the procedure first note that the sign of Z_i depends on the term in the brackets in equation (2). Note also that the term ϕ_N in the brackets of equation (2) is a constant independent of i. Hence for positive β_i if $(\bar{R}_i - R_f)/\beta_i$ is greater than the constant the security is purchased long; if it is less, it is sold short; and if it is equal, it is neither purchased nor sold short.[3] It is this latter condition which determines a corner portfolio. For any security, this can occur only once. This holds because $(\bar{R}_i - R_f)/\beta_i$ is a linear function of R_f. Likewise, the second term in the brackets is also linear in R_f. Two linear functions will have at most one intersection in the range of interest.

Therefore, to determine the corner portfolios:

1. For each security i, solve equation (2) for the value of R_f which makes Z_i and hence X_i^0 zero. Each distinct value of R_f greater than the lower bound will be uniquely associated with one corner portfolio.
2. For each value of R_f defined in Step 1, we use equations (1), (2), and (3) to determine the value of all X_i^0 in that corner portfolio.
3. Solve for the return and risk for each corner portfolio determined in Step 2.

Portfolios with $\bar{R}_p$ between corner portfolios can be determined in the usual way.[4]

B *Optimal Portfolios when Short Sales are Not Allowed*

When short sales are not allowed, Kuhn-Tucker conditions are required to determine an optimum. In (1), we showed that if unlimited lending and borrowing can take place at the rate R_f, the optimum amount to invest in security i is

$$X_i^0 = \frac{Z_i}{\sum_{j \in k} Z_j} \qquad \text{for all } Z_i > 0 \tag{4}$$

where

(A) k is the set of securities in the optimal portfolio.

$$\text{(B)}\ Z_i = \frac{\beta_i}{\sigma_{\varepsilon_i}^2}\left[\frac{\bar{R}_i - R_f}{\beta_i} - \phi_k\right] \tag{5}$$

$$\text{(C)}\ \phi_k = \sigma_m^2 \frac{\sum_{j \in k} \frac{\bar{R}_j - R_f}{\sigma_{\varepsilon_j}^2}\beta_j}{1 + \sigma_m^2 \sum_{j \in k} \frac{\beta_j^2}{\sigma_{\varepsilon_j}^2}} \tag{6}$$

Before addressing ourselves to the problem of tracing the entire efficient frontier, it is useful to review the ranking procedure that permits one to determine an optimal portfolio for a particular riskless rate R_f. Suppose first that all β_j are positive. Then all we have to do to arrive at an optimal portfolio is to rank from 1 to N all securities by $(\bar{R}_i - R_f)/\beta_i$ (highest to lowest). Then compute a value for equation (6) as if the set k only contained the first security. Next we calculate Z_i from equation (5) setting $i = 2$. If $Z_2 \leqslant 0$, we stop. The optimal portfolio contains only the first security. Otherwise we compute ϕ_k from (6) letting the set k contain the first two securities. We proceed for $i = 3, 4, \ldots$ until Z_i computed from equation (5) turns negative. If it turns negative for the $j + 1^{\text{st}}$ security then the set k contains the first j securities. Since the set k arrived at this way satisfied the Kuhn-Tucker conditions, we have found a simple and fast way to define all securities in the set k. Once these securities are found the X_i^0 value for all securities in the set can be found simply by calculating the Z_i for each security from equation (5), dividing each Z_i by the sum of the Z_i over the set k. Note that from equation (5) the desirability of any security and the amount we invest in it will be uniquely related to its excess return to β ratio. Negative or zero betas can easily be handled by the methods discussed in (1).

If lending and borrowing at a riskless rate is disallowed, the general shape of the efficient frontier can be traced out by repeating the above analysis for alternative values of R_f. However, the task is simplified by finding all "corner" portfolios along the efficient frontier.

In order to determine critical values of the riskless rate R_f which determine a different set k of securities to be included in an optimal portfolio, we write $R_f = R_f^0 + \lambda$, where R_f^0 is a riskless rate for which we have previously determined an optimal portfolio. We are then interested in R_f for values of $\lambda \geqslant 0$. We observe that using (6), relation (5) can be rewritten for Z_i as follows:

$$Z_i(\lambda) = \alpha_i - \Psi_i \lambda \tag{7}$$

α_i is given by $\alpha_i = Z_i(0) - \mu_i$

where μ is the Kuhn-Tucker multiplier which has a value equal to 0 when Z_i from equation (5) is zero and a value of $-Z_i$ when Z_i calculated from equation (5) is negative.

$$\Psi_i \text{ is given by } \Psi_i = \frac{1}{\sigma_{\varepsilon_i}^2} - \beta_i \frac{\sigma_m^2}{\sigma_{\varepsilon_i}^2} \left[\frac{\sum_{j \in k} \frac{\beta_j}{\sigma_{\varepsilon_j}^2}}{1 + \sigma_m^2 \sum_{j \in k} \beta_j^2 / \sigma_{\varepsilon_j}^2} \right] \tag{8}$$

In particular, $Z_i(\lambda)$ is a linear function of λ. Consequently, if for $R_f = R_f^0$ the optimal portfolio contains security i at a positive level Z_i, then security i will remain in an optimal portfolio with $R_f = R_f^0 + \lambda$ for a sufficiently small positive change λ provided that $\Psi_i \leqslant 0$. If, however, $\Psi_i > 0$, then security i is a candidate for leaving the optimal portfolio when a small positive change in λ is considered. More precisely, letting K^+ denote the set of securities that are in the optimal portfolio at strictly positive level, we are interested in security j having $(\alpha_j/\Psi_j) = \min\{(\alpha_i/\Psi_i) \mid \Psi_i > 0, i \in K^+\}$, since it is the first candidate to leave the optimal portfolio. Similarly, letting K^- denote the set of securities having $\mu_i > 0$, i.e. for which $Z_i = (\beta_i/\sigma_{\varepsilon_i}^2)[(\bar{R}_i - R_f)/\beta_i - \phi_k] < 0$ the first security to enter the optimal portfolio is given by the security e for which $(\alpha_e/\Psi_e) = \min\{(\alpha_i/\Psi_i) \mid \Psi_i < 0, i \in K^-\}$. Consequently, if $\Psi_j > \Psi_e$, security e will enter the optimal portfolio prior to security j leaving the optimal portfolio, whereas if $\Psi_j < \Psi_e$ security j will leave the optimal portfolio before e is considered for inclusion. So far we have not yet discussed securities for which $Z_i = 0$, which can be included in the optimal portfolio at zero level. Let us call the set of these securities K^0. Obviously, if Ψ_i as defined by (8) are all positive or zero for securities in K^0, one will not include any one of these securities in the optimal portfolio. However if $\Psi_i < 0$, some of these securities should enter the optimal portfolio. Prior to determining the next corner portfolio, one has to establish which securities in K^0 should enter the optimal portfolio at zero level. Once this is done, we can then determine the next critical value $\lambda' = \min\{(\alpha_j/\Psi_j), (\alpha_e/\Psi_e)\}$ where now Ψ_j and Ψ_e are calculated with respect to the possibly enlarged optimal portfolio.

The preceding readily defines a procedure for tracing out the entire efficent frontier. Starting with minimum R_f determine the optimal portfolio by the ranking procedure outlined above.[5] Classify all securities as "belonging" to the optimal portfolio or "not belonging" to the optimal portfolio including those for which formula (5) results in $Z_i = 0$. (In Appendix A we describe a procedure for carrying out this classification). Determine λ' and repeat.

Finally, the proportions in the optimal portfolio are calculated at every critical value of λ in the usual way, whereas optimal portfolios for "in between" values of λ are obtained by simple linear interpolation, i.e. as convex combinations of the respective corner portfolios.

II Constant Correlation Coefficients and the Construction of Optimal Portfolios

In this section, we will assume that all pairwise correlation coefficients are equal. While this probably does not represent the true pattern one finds in the economy it is very difficult to obtain a better estimate. Elsewhere [5] we have shown that this assumption produces better estimates of future correlation coefficients than do historical correlation coefficients or those produced from the single index approximation discussed in section one. In fact the assumption of a constant correlation coefficient produced forecasts which were about as accurate as any of nine techniques tried in (5).

The derivation of the equations representing the optimal portfolio to hold with riskless borrowing and lending is given in (1). If short sales are allowed, the procedures outlined in Section IA of this paper are optimum if Z_i is defined as:

$$Z_i = \frac{1}{(1-\rho)\sigma_i}\left[\frac{\bar{R}_i - R_f}{\sigma_i} - \phi'_N\right]$$

where ρ = the correlation coefficient between the returns on any two stocks

$\sigma_i =$ the standard deviation of the return on stock i

$$\phi'_N = \frac{\rho}{1-\rho+N\rho}\sum_{j=1}^{N}\frac{\bar{R}_j - R_f}{\sigma_j}$$

If short sales are disallowed, the procedures outlined in Section IB of this paper are optimum if Z_i is given by

$$Z_i = \frac{1}{(1-\rho)\sigma_i}\left[\frac{\bar{R}_i - R_f}{\sigma_i} - \phi'_k\right]$$

where

$$\phi'_k = \frac{\rho}{1-\rho+N\rho}\sum_{j\in k}\frac{\bar{R}_j - R_f}{\sigma_j}$$

and Ψ_i is given by

$$\Psi_i = \frac{1}{\sigma_i(1-\rho)}\left[\frac{1}{\sigma_i} - \frac{\rho}{1-\rho+k\rho}\sum_{j\in k}\frac{1}{\sigma_j}\right].$$

With these changes, the procedures follow directly from those outlined earlier.

III Conclusion

In this paper, we have shown how the simple procedures constructed, under the assumption of unlimited lending and borrowing at the riskless rate, can be extended to trace out the full efficient frontier.

Appendix

Consider the set K^0 for which $Z_i = 0$ in equation (5). It is easy to show that these can be included or excluded at the R_f being considered since they do not effect ϕ_k. For any security in set K^0 it must be true that $(\bar{R}_i - R_f)/\beta_i$ is the same constant. Consider an increase in R_f by an amount δ. Then these can be ranked by $(\bar{R}_i - R_f - \delta)/\beta_i = (\bar{R}_i - R_f)/\beta_i - (\delta/\beta_i)$. Since $(\bar{R}_i - R_f)/\beta_i$ is the same they can be ranked by $(-\delta/\beta_i)$.

It follows that positive beta securities should be ranked in descending order of β_i and negative beta stocks in ascending order. Any remaining ties must be identical securities and the one(s) with the largest $\sigma_{\varepsilon_i}^2$ can be excluded.

If $\Psi_i < 0$ for a security, it should be in the included set since an increase in λ would cause it to have a positive Z_i. Thus securities in set K^0 should be added to the included set k in decreasing order of β_i for positive Beta and ascending order for negative Beta until $\Psi_i \geqslant 0$ for the next security to be added. Furthermore an examination of Ψ_i shows that only either positive Beta securities or negative Beta securities would be added depending on the sign of $\sum_{i=1}^{k}(\beta_i/\sigma_{\varepsilon_i}^2)$.

Notes

1. X_i can be negative for short sales. We are following Lintner's [6] suggestion in treating short sales. That is the short seller pays any dividends which accrue to the person who lends him the stock and gets a capital gain (or loss) which is the negative of any price appreciation. In addition the short seller is assumed to received interest at the riskless rate on both the money loaned to the owner of the borrowed stock and the money placed in escrow when the short sale is made. See Lintner [6] for a full discussion of these assumptions. Readers who believe that $\sum_{i=1}^{N} x_i = 1$ in the case of short sales can make this substitution in equation (1) and the solution still holds.

2. Throughout the analysis of the efficient frontier one must deal with the problem of establishing the lowest point on the frontier which is of interest. Since most analysis is performed in nominal terms and since the investor is always free to hold cash the lowest point on the efficient frontier of interest will usually be that associated with a lending rate of zero. However nothing in the analysis restricts the user from defining lower regions on the efficient (stock) frontier by considering values of R_f below zero. In fact in the limit R_f can be examined as it approaches infinity.
3. The opposite set of statements can be made for negative β.
4. One desires corner portfolios since intermediate portfolios can be determined by calculating portfolios consisting of adjacent corner portfolios. This is also true when the R_f's are arbitrarily selected if adjacent portfolios differ by at most one security. Readers who believe $\sum_{i=1}^{N} x_i = 1$ in the case of short sales can trace out the full efficient frontier by determining and two arbitrary portfolios.
5. Zero is normally the lowest lending rate of interest since cash can be held. The analysis does not assume that funds can be borrowed at this rate since the efficient portfolio at all higher rates will be traced out. If the analysis is being conducted in real terms an appropriate lower level must be selected.

References

1. Edwin J. Elton, Martin J. Gruber, and Manfred W. Padberg. "Simple Criteria for Optimal Portfolio Selection," *Journal of Finance*, (December 1976), pp. 1341–1357.

2. ———, ———, and ———. "Simple Criteria for Optimal Portfolio Selection with Upper Bound Constraints," *Operations Research*, (November–December 1978).

3. ———, ———, and ———. "Simple Criteria for Optimal Portfolio Selection—The Multi-Group Case," *Journal of Financial and Quantitative Analysis*, (March 1979), pp. 329–345.

4. ———, ———, and ———. "Simple Criteria for Optimal Portfolio Selection—The Multi-Index Case," in Elton, Edwin J., and Gruber, Martin J., *Portfolio Theory: Twenty-five Years Later* (Amsterdam, North Holland), 1979.

5. Edwin J. Elton and Martin J. Gruber. "Estimating the Dependence Structure of Share Prices —Implications for Portfolio Selection," *Journal of Finance*, Volume 27, Number 5 (December 1973), pp. 1203–1233.

6. John Lintner. "The Valuation of Risk Assets on the Selection of Risky Investments in Stock Portfolios and Capital Budgets," *The Review of Economics and Statistics* (February 1965), pp. 13–37.

8

Simple Rules for Optimal Portfolio Selection: The Multi-Group Case

Edwin J. Elton, Martin J. Gruber, and Manfred W. Padberg

The inception of modern portfolio theory dates from Markowitz's pioneering article [7] and subsequent book [8]. Yet despite the early development of a full theory of portfolio management, this theory has rarely been implemented. One problem arises from the difficulty in generating inputs to the general portfolio model. Index models and simple structures for correlation relationships, which go a long way towards solving this problem, have been developed. Yet the time and cost of solving actual portfolio problems (involving the solution of a quadratic programming problem) and more importantly the difficulty of educating portfolio managers to relate to risk return trade-offs in terms of covariances has virtually brought the application of portfolio theory to a halt.

In an earlier paper [3] we showed that if one is willing to accept the existence of a risk-free asset and is willing to either:

1) assume that the single index model adequately describes the variance-covariance structure; or

2) assume that a single number is a good estimate of all pair-wise correlation coefficients[1]

then a simple decision rule (which does not involve an iterative algorithm) can be derived for the selection of optimal portfolios. Furthermore, this simple decision rule does not involve covariances or correlations and is formulated in terms to which the portfolio manager should be able to relate.

The purpose of this paper is to extend the development of simple decision rules to cases where more complex models are used to represent the correlation structure between stocks. Two cases will be examined. One is a multi-group model, which assumes that the correlation coefficients between any firm in one group and all other firms are identical for members of the same group. This was selected since we have shown in an earlier study that this technique provided useful forecasts of future correlation structures. These forecasts were judged useful in two ways. They led to more accurate estimates of actual future correlation coefficients than the single index model, multiple index models, the use of an overall average correlation coefficient, and historic pairwise correlations. Second, they led to the selection of portfolios which proved more efficient (in future periods) than the above mentioned techniques. Hence decision rules for portfolio selection when the multi-group model is used will be examined in this paper.

The second case that will be explored is one in which a particular multi-index model is used to represent the correlation structure between securities. Multi-index models have gained attention because of their ability to account for more of the covariance structure than single index models. While there are many forms of multi-index models, the one we have chosen to explore is the diagonal form first presented in Cohen and Pogue [1].

This paper is divided into two sections according to the two models of estimating the covariance structure between securities described above.

I Multiple Group Models

In [4] the authors presented a simplified structure for the correlation matrix which did an excellent job of forecasting future correlation matrices and led to the selection of efficient portfolios. The structure rested on the assumption that the correlation matrix could be partitioned into submatrices where all correlation coefficients within a submatrix are the same but the value of the correlation coefficient might differ between the submatrices. For example, if there were two industries in our sample—chemicals and steels—then this assumption implies that the correlation coefficient between all steels is the same constant (ρ_{ss}); that the correlation coefficient between all chemicals is the same (ρ_{cc}) but potentially different from the correlation coefficient for steels; and that the correlation coefficient between a steel firm and a chemical firm is still a third constant (ρ_{cs}).[2] This is illustrated in Figure 8.1. In this section, we will derive simple decision rules for the construction of optimal portfolios when the correlation structure between securities is described by this multi-group model. Once again we will separate the case where short selling is allowed from the case where short selling is forbidden.

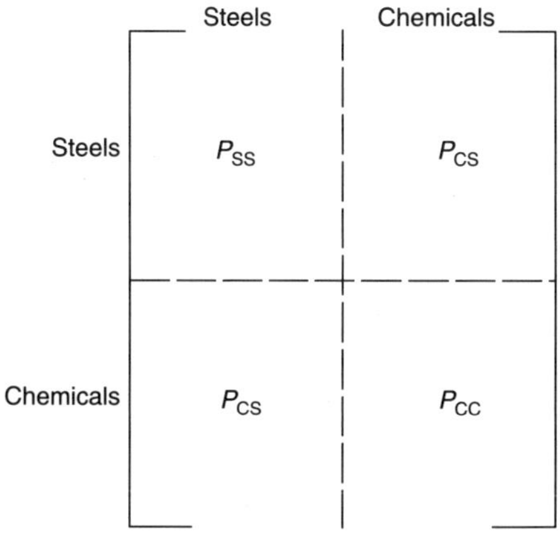

Figure 8.1

A Short Selling Allowed

Let us define:

1. ρ_{kk} = the correlation coefficient between members of group k
2. ρ_{kt} = the correlation coefficient between members of group k and t
3. σ_i = the standard deviation of security i
4. σ_{ij} = the covariance between security i and security j
5. $\bar{R}_i$ = the expected return on security i
6. R_f = the risk-free rate of interest
7. $\bar{R}_p$ = the expected rate of return on the optimal portfolio
8. σ_p = the standard deviation of the optimal portfolio
9. N_k = the number of securities in group k
10. X_k = the set of stocks in group k
11. P = the number of groups
12. M_i = the fraction of funds invested in security i

If we allow short sales and assume the existence of a riskless asset, then the appropriate objective function is to maximize θ the excess return on the portfolio divided by the standard deviation of the portfolio.[3] The first order conditions necessary for a maximum are presented by Lintner [6].[4] They are

$$Z_i\sigma_i^2 + \sum_{\substack{j=1 \\ j \neq 1}}^{N} Z_j\sigma_{ij} = \bar{R}_i - R_f \qquad i = 1, \ldots, N \tag{1}$$

where $Z_i = M_i(\bar{R}_p - R_f)/\sigma_p^2$.

For a security i, which is a member of group k, equation (1) can be written as

$$Z_i\sigma_i^2(1 - \rho_{kk}) + \sigma_i \sum_{g=1}^{p} \rho_{kg}\phi_g = \bar{R}_i - R_f \tag{2}$$

where we have set $\phi_g = \sum_{j \in X_g} \sigma_j g_j$. Solving for Z_i yields

$$Z_i = \frac{1}{\sigma_i(1 - \rho_{kk})}\left[\frac{\bar{R}_i - R_f}{\sigma_i} - \sum_{g=1}^{p} \rho_{kg}\phi_g\right] \tag{3}$$

The above would be a solution if we can express the quantities ϕ_g in terms of the other variables in equation (3). This can be accomplished by multiplying each equation (3) (one of each value of g) by σ_i and summing over all members of a particular group. Rearranging the resulting expressions yields one equation for each group as follows:

$$(1 - \rho_{kk})\phi_k + N_k \sum_{g=1}^{p} \rho_{kg}\phi_g = \sum_{j \in X_k} \frac{\bar{R}_j - R_f}{\sigma_j} \tag{4}$$

where the index k assumes all values $1, 2, \ldots, p$. After dividing each equation (4) by the factor $(1 - \rho_{kk})$, this system of equations can be written in matrix notation as $A\,\underset{\sim}{\phi} = C$ where A is a matrix of size $p \times p$ with elements

$$a_{kg} = \begin{cases} N_k\rho_{kg}/(1 - \rho_{kk}) & \text{if } k \neq g \\ 1 + N_k\rho_{kk}/(1 - \rho_{kk}) & \text{if } k = g \end{cases}$$

and where $\underset{\sim}{\phi}$ is the vector with p components $\phi_g g = 1, \ldots, p$, and C is the vector with p components $\sum_{j \in X_g}(\bar{R}_j - R_f)/[\sigma_j(1 - \rho_{gg})]$ for $g = 1, \ldots, p$. The solution to the system of equations (4) can thus be found by inverting the $p \times p$ matrix A. And using equation (3) we can thus determine the solution in terms of the variables Z_i.[5] Note that equation (3) is of the form

$$Z_i = \frac{1}{\sigma_i(1 - \rho_{kk})}\left[\frac{\bar{R}_i - R_f}{\sigma_i} - \psi_k\right] \tag{5}$$

where the constant ψ_k has the same value for all members of group k. The value of ψ_k is determined solely by the characteristics of the population of stocks under consideration. Since it does not depend on the composition of the optimal portfolio, its value can be computed before the analysis of the optimal portfolio is begun. Then it is a trivial task to calculate Z_i for all securities. In fact it can easily be done with pencil and paper in a few minutes.[6] Note how easy it is to determine if any stock should be held long or sold short. If the excess return to standard deviation for any security is larger than its group constant, it should be bought; if it is smaller, it should be sold short.

The optimum amount to invest in each security M_i^0 can be found quite easily by scaling the Z_i's so that the sum of their absolute values adds to one

$$M_i^0 = \frac{Z_i}{N_1 + N_2 \sum_{j=1} + \cdots + N_P |Z_j|}.$$

This completes our discussion of multiple group selection with short sales. It remains to examine the case of no short sales.

b Short Sales Not Allowed

If short sales are not allowed, we have to make use of the Kuhn-Tucker conditions. In (3) we prove that they are both necessary and sufficient. The Kuhn-Tucker conditions for the problem of maximizing θ can be written as follows:

$$(\bar{R}_i - R_f) - Z_i\sigma_i^2 - \sum_{\substack{j=1 \\ j\neq i}}^{N} Z_j\sigma_{ij} + u_i = 0 \tag{6}$$

$$Z_i \geqslant 0 \qquad u_i \geqslant 0 \tag{7}$$

$$Z_i u_i = 0 \tag{8}$$

In this section we will use X_k' to denote the *total* set of securities in group K (formerly denoted by X_k). X_k will then refer to the *subset* of group X_k' which is in the optimal portfolio. As will become clear shortly, this change in notation allows us to use the equations of Section A for the case of no short sales. Solving for Z_i for members of group k yields

$$Z_i = \frac{\bar{R}_i - R_f}{\sigma_i^2(1-\rho_{kk})} - \frac{1}{\sigma_i}\sum_{g=1}^{p}\frac{\rho_{kg}}{1-\rho_{kk}}\phi_g + \frac{u_i}{\sigma_i(1-\rho_{kk})} \tag{9}$$

where we have again abbreviated

$$\phi_g = \sum_{j\in X_g'} \sigma_j Z_j \quad \text{for } g = 1, \ldots, p.$$

First note that $Z_i = 0$ for any security that is not in the optimal portfolio. Consequently, $\phi_g = \sum_{j\in X_g} \sigma_j Z_j$ for $g = 1, \ldots, p$, i.e., the summations can be taken over all members of the subset X_g rather than over the set X_g'. Secondly, from the complementarity conditions (8), u_i is zero for all securities in the optimal portfolio. There two observations together imply that the system of equations (4) can again be used to solve for the quantities ϕ_g, for $g = 1, \ldots, p$. Substituting the solutions into equation (9) yields equation (5) with the additional term

$$\frac{u_i}{\sigma_i(1-\rho_{kk})} \quad \text{or} \quad Z_i = \frac{1}{\sigma_i(1-\rho_{kk})}\left[\frac{\bar{R}_i - R_f}{\sigma_i} - \psi_k\right] + \frac{u_i}{\sigma_i(1-\rho_{kk})}.$$

The term containing the u_i can only increase Z_i. Hence if Z_i is positive with u_i equal to zero, a positive u_i cannot make $Z_i = 0$. Thus any security with positive Z_i when $u_i = 0$ must be included. Correspondingly, any security with negative Z_i when $u_i = 0$ must be excluded. It thus follows from the Kuhn-Tucker conditions, that within each group k the following properties hold: If a security with a particular value $(\bar{R}_i - R_f)/\sigma_i$ has a positive Z_i, then all securities with a higher excess-return-to-standard-deviation ratio also produce a positive Z_i. Similarly, if a stock produces a negative Z_i, all lower ranking stocks will also have a negative Z_i. Consequently, *within each group of securities there is a group-specific security i such that all securities having a larger ratio* $(\bar{R}_j - R_f)/\sigma_j$ *will be in the optimal portfolio, whereas all securities having a lower ratio will not be in the optimal portfolio.* In order to determine an optimal portfolio, all that remains to be done is to find the cutoff rate in each group. The following seems to us to be an efficient method, since the number of different groups considered will typically be small.

1. Rank all stocks in each group by decreasing excess return to standard deviation. Go to 2.

2. Determine an optimal portfolio for stocks from group 1 only and mark group 1 as being checked. Compute the quantities ψ_k for $k = 1, \ldots, p$. Go to 3.

3. If for the top ranking securities in the unchecked groups the term in the brackets in equation (5) is zero or negative or if there are no more unchecked groups, stop. Otherwise, pick any one of the unchecked groups, for which the expression (5) is positive, say group q, and go to 4.

4. Determine an optimal portfolio among the stocks from the groups already checked and the current group q in such a fashion that whenever a new stock from group q is included, optimality for the checked groups is reestablished immediately. (This can be accomplished by a modification of any "backtracking" scheme.) Once an optimal solution for all checked groups is attained including group 1, mark group q as being checked and go to 3.

The procedure determines the cut-off rates and the values for Z_i. The optimal amount to invest in each security is determined by dividing each Z_i by the sum of the Z_i's. The crucial step in the procedure is, of course, the reoptimization called for in step 4 whenever one considers a new stock in the current group q for inclusion in the "current" optimal portfolio. The backtracking procedure must make use of the fact that all of the currently considered stocks in group q remain in the portfolio while adjustments (addition/deletions) are made only in groups already checked. In Appendix A we state formulas for adding/dropping securities in a particular group and we will illustrate the procedure next by means of a numerical example.

Example 1 Suppose that we have two different groups with eight and seven securities, respectively. The excess returns to standard deviation for each security in each group are given by the data in Table 8.1. Furthermore, let $\rho_{11} = 1/2$, $\rho_{12} = 1/3$, and $\rho_{22} = 2/5$. Starting with group 1, we find that securities 1, 2, and 3 constitute an optimal portfolio if one considers group 1 only. Using formula (A-1) of Appendix A, we find that $\psi_1 = 6$ and $\psi_2 = 4$.

Furthermore, the auxiliary quantities for the recalculation of the ψ_g are given by (A-2) and we obtain $a_{11} = \frac{1}{8}$, $a_{12} = \frac{1}{12}$, and $a_{22} = \frac{7}{30}$. We proceed now with group 2 and find that security 1 of group 2 must be included

Table 8.1

Group 1	10	7	7	6	4	3	3	2
Group 2	8	4.5	4	4	3	2	1	×

since $8 - 4 > 0$. Computing the new ψ_g by (A-1) we find $\psi_1 = 6\frac{8}{35}$ and $\psi_2 = 4\frac{16}{25}$. Thus the optimum portfolio consists of the first three securities in group 1 and the first security of group 2.

II The Diagonal Form of the Multi-Index Model

Cohen and Pogue [1] have presented a multi-index model that leads to a diagonal form for the covariance structure between securities. The assumptions underlying the model are that each stock is linearly related to one group index and that each group index is linearly related to a market index. This model can be represented as

$$R_i = \alpha_i + \beta_i J_j + \varepsilon_i$$

$$J_j = \gamma_j + b_j I_m + C_j$$

$$I_m = a + d$$

$$E(\varepsilon_i \varepsilon_k) = 0 \qquad i = 1, \ldots, N \qquad k = 1, \ldots, N \qquad i \neq k$$

$$E(C_j C_\ell) = 0 \qquad j = 1, \ldots, P \qquad \ell = 1, \ldots, P \qquad j \neq \ell$$

$$E(\varepsilon_i C_j) = 0 \qquad i = 1, \ldots, N \qquad j = 1, \ldots, P$$

$$E(\varepsilon_i d) = 0 \qquad i = 1, \ldots, N$$

$$E(C_j d) = 0 \qquad j = 1, \ldots, P$$

where

1. R_i = the return on security i which is in group j (a random variable)
2. J_j = the return on the index for group j
3. I_m = the market index
4. β_i = a measure of the responsiveness of security i to changes in the group index J_j
5. α_i = the return on security i that is independent of the group index
6. ε_i = a variable with mean of zero and variance $\sigma_{\varepsilon_i}^2$ which measures the variance of security i not associated with changes in the group (or market) index
7. b_j = a measure of the responsiveness of index j to changes in the market index
8. γ_j = the return on index j that is independent of the market index

9. C_j = a variable with a mean of zero and a variance of σ_j^2 which measures the variance of group j not associated with changes in the market index

10. σ_m^2 = the variance of the market index

11. a = the mean return of the market

12. d = a variable with a mean of zero and variance equal to σ_m^2

13. P = the number of group (indices) which are appropriate

These equations make clear the approximations of the diagonal form of the multi-index model to the variance covariance structure. While each stock is linearly related to one group index and all group indices are linearly related to the market, the residuals from any of these relationships are assumed to be uncorrelated.

In this section we shall develop simple decision rules for portfolio composition when this diagonal form of the multi-index model is assumed to be a reasonable way to forecast future correlation coefficients. We shall separate the case where short selling is permitted from the case where it is not allowed.

A Short Selling Allowed

If short selling is allowed, and the existence of a riskless asset is assumed, then the portfolio manager's task is to find the portfolio that has the largest excess return to risk. We can employ the general equation (1) originally presented by Lintner to solve this problem.

For a security i which is affected by group index k, equation (1) can be written as

$$Z_i\sigma_{\varepsilon_i}^2 + \beta_i \sum_{g=1}^{p} d_{gk}\phi_g = \bar{R}_i - R_f \tag{10}$$

where

1. $d_{gk} = b_k b_g \sigma_m^2 \qquad \text{for } g \neq k$

2. $d_{kk} = b_k^2 \sigma_m^2 + \sigma_k^2 \qquad \text{for } g = k$

3. $\phi_g = \sum_{j \in X_g} \beta_j Z_j$

solving for Z_i yields

$$Z_i = \frac{\beta_i}{\sigma^2_{\varepsilon_i}}\left[\frac{\bar{R}_i - R_f}{\beta_i} - \sum_{g=1}^{p} d_{gk}\phi_g\right]. \tag{11}$$

The above would be a solution if we can express the quantities ϕ_g in terms of known parameters. This can be accomplished by multiplying each equation (11) by β_j and summing over all members of the group. Performing this summation and rearranging yields the following equation for each group:

$$\phi_k + \sum_{j\in X_k} \frac{\beta_j^2}{\sigma^2_{\varepsilon_i}} \sum_{g=1}^{p} d_{gk}\phi_g = \sum_{j\in X_k} \frac{(\bar{R}_j - R_f)\beta_j}{\sigma^2_{\varepsilon_j}}. \tag{12}$$

This system can be written in matrix notation $A\,\underset{\sim}{\phi} = C$ where A is a $p \times p$ matrix with elements

$$a_{kg} = \begin{cases} \sum_{j\in X_g} \dfrac{\beta_j^2}{\sigma^2_{\varepsilon_j}} d_{gk} & \text{if } k \neq g \\[2ex] 1 + \sum_{j\in X_k} \dfrac{\beta_j^2}{\sigma^2_{\varepsilon_j}} d_{kk} & \text{if } k = g \end{cases}$$

and where $\underset{\sim}{\phi}$ is the vector with p components ϕ_g $g = 1, \ldots, p$ and C is a vector of $\underset{\sim}{p}$ components $\sum_{j\in X_g}((\bar{R}_j - R_f)/\sigma^2_{\varepsilon_j})\beta_j$ for $g = 1, \ldots, p$. Once again, the solution to this system is found by inverting the matrix.[7]

Note that equation (11) has the form

$$Z_i = \frac{\beta_i}{\sigma^2_{\varepsilon_i}}\left[\frac{\bar{R}_i - R_f}{\beta_i} - \psi_k\right] \tag{13}$$

where ψ_k has the same value for all members of group k. This produces a set of arguments about selection and which securities are sold long or short, analogous to those presented in Section I except that the conclusions and arguments are reversed when β is negative.

B *Short Sales Not Allowed*

If short sales are not allowed, we have to make use of the Kuhn-Tucker conditions. The general form of the Kuhn-Tucker conditions necessary to maximize θ have already been presented in equations (6), (7), and (8). We shall now apply them to the diagonal form of the multiple index model when there are P groups. Once again a change in notation allows us to utilize the equations derived in the previous section. Let X_k' denote the securities in set k and let X_k denote the set of included securities in set k. This change in notation allows us to use the equations for the case of no short sales presented in Section IIA. Solving for Z_i for members of group k yields

$$Z_i = \frac{\beta_i}{\sigma_{\varepsilon_i}^2}\left[\frac{\bar{R}_i - R_f}{\beta_i} - \sum_{g=1}^{p} d_{gk}\phi_g\right] + \frac{u_i}{\sigma_{\varepsilon_i}^2} \tag{14}$$

where the d_{gk} are defined as before and

$$\phi_g = \sum_{j \in X_g'} \beta_j Z_j.$$

Note that $Z_i = 0$ for any portfolio which is not in the optimal portfolio. Hence, $\phi_g = \sum_{j \in X_g'} \beta_j Z_j = \sum_{j \in X_g} \beta_j Z_j$; the summation can be taken over all members of the set X_g rather than over the set X_g'. Also note that from the complementary conditions, $u_i = 0$ for all securities in the optimal portfolio. From these two conditions the system of equations (10) can again be used to solve for the quantities ϕ_g, $g = 1, \ldots, p$. Substituting the solutions into (14) yields equation (13) with the additional term $(u_i/\sigma_{\varepsilon_i}^2)$ or

$$Z_i = \frac{\beta_i}{\sigma_{\varepsilon_i}^2}\left[\frac{\bar{R}_i - R_f}{\beta_i} - \psi_k\right] + \frac{u_i}{\sigma_{\varepsilon_i}^2}. \tag{15}$$

The term containing u_i can only increase Z_i. As pointed out in Section I, since $u_i > 0$ when $Z_i = 0$ and $u_i = 0$ when $Z_i > 0$, any security with positive Z_i when $u_i = 0$ must be included and any security with negative Z_i when $u_i = 0$ must be excluded. Hence equation (1) describes the optimal portfolio in the following manner: any security which has a positive value of Z_i should be included in the optimal portfolio; any security which has a negative value of Z_i should be excluded.

It follows from the above discussion and from the discussion in Section IB that within each group of securities there is a specific cut-off point such that

1. all securities with a positive β_i and a value of $(\bar{R}_i - R_f)/\beta_i$ greater than the cut-off point are included
2. all securities with a positive β_i and a value of $(\bar{R}_i - R_f)/\beta_i$ less than the cut-off point are excluded
3. all securities with a negative β_i and a value of $(\bar{R}_i - R_f)/\beta_i$ less than the cut-off point are included

4. all securities with a negative β_i and a value of $(\bar{R}_i - R_f)/\beta_i$ greater than the cut-off point are excluded.

To define an optimal portfolio all that remains is to find the cut-off point for each group. A procedure directly analogous to that outlined in Section IB can be used, remembering that it is necessary to check both positive and negative Beta stocks for inclusion or exclusion at all steps.

One the search procedure has been completed and all securities with positive Z_i's are found, the fraction of funds to place in each security is

$$M_i^0 = \frac{Z_i}{\sum_{j \in X_1,\ldots,X_p} Z_i}.$$

Once *again* the problem of considering a new security for inclusion in the optimal portfolio becomes rather simple. The above procedure will lead to a set of cut-off points for $(\bar{R}_i - R_f)/\beta_i$ for both positive and negative β securities for each group. These cut-off points allow us to determine quickly the effect on the optimal portfolio of a new security. For example if a new security for group k with a positive β is considered, then

1. if its $(\bar{R}_i - R_f)/\beta_i$ is less than ψ_k, it can safely be discarded, or
2. if its $(\bar{R}_i - R_f)/\beta_i$ is more than $\psi_{k'}$, then it must be included and the optimum recalculated.

Even if new calculations are needed, the amount of computation needed is very small.

III Conclusion

In this paper we have developed decision rules that allow one to reach optimum solutions to portfolio problems without resorting to any complicated nonlinear programming algorithms. Furthermore, the characteristics of a stock that make it desirable are readily understood and calculated. Since the assumptions necessary to apply the simplified computational procedure discussed in this paper have been shown elsewhere [4] to be the preferred method of obtaining inputs to portfolio problems, the procedure discussed in this paper should find extensive application in the future.

Appendix A

In this appendix we state the formulas that are necessary to update the quantities ψ_k for $k = 1, \ldots, p$ of Section I when additions/deletions of securities from a particular group k of stocks are considered. To derive the formulas, the reader should note that one has to invert the matrix equation $\underset{\sim}{A}\ \phi = C$ of Section I. However, this can be done explicitly for the number of groups being considered or implicitly if the procedure discussed earlier is followed. If the procedure discussed earlier is followed, ψ_k is updated continuously. Specifically, let us suppose that we wish to determine the *new* quantities ψ_k of equation (5) when a subset $\Delta_k \subseteq X_k'$ of securities in group k is added. Denote by ψ_k^{new} the resulting quantities for $k = 1, \ldots, p$ whereas ψ_k denote the "current" values [the initial conditions are $\psi_g = 0$ for $g = 1, \ldots, p$]. Then

$$\psi_g^{new} = \psi_g + a_{gk}(\psi_k^{new} - \psi_k)/a_{kk}$$

$$\psi_k^{new} = \left\{(1 - \rho_{kk})\psi_k + a_{kk} \sum_{h \in \Delta_k} (\bar{R}_h - R_f)\Big/\sigma_h\right\}\Big/[1 - \rho_{kk} + n_k a_{kk}] \tag{A-1}$$

where $n_k = |\Delta_k|$ denotes the number of securities added in group k and the a_{gk} are defined *recursively* as follows: Initially, let $a_{gj} = \rho_{gj}$ for all $g = 1, \ldots, p$ and $j = 1, \ldots, p$. After the subset $\Delta_k \subseteq X_k'$ of n_k securities in group k has been added, the *new* quantities a_{gj}, denoted by a_{gj}^{new}, are computed as follows:

$$a_{gj}^{new} = a_{gj} - [n_k a_{gk} a_{kj}]/[1 - \rho_{kk} + n_k a_{kk}] \tag{A-2}$$

where indices g and j assume (independently) all values $1, 2, \ldots, p$, whereas the index k, of course, designates the group in which we have added the securities. Note that the initial a_{gj} are symmetric since $\rho_{gj} = \rho_{jg}$ and that by the transformation (A-2) symmetry is preserved, which implies that only the upper diagonal part must be calculated.

Suppose next that we want to *drop* a subset $\Delta_k \subseteq X_k'$ of securities from a portfolio. Again, let $n_k = |\Delta_k|$ denote the number of such securities. The new quantities ψ_g and a_{gj} are computed as follows:

$$\psi_g^{new} = \psi_g + a_{gk}(\psi_k^{new} - \psi_k)/a_{kk}.$$

$$\psi_k^{new} = \left\{(1 - \rho_{kk})\psi_k - a_{kk} \sum_{h \in \Delta_k} (\bar{R}_h - R_f)\Big/\sigma_h\right\}\Big/[1 - \rho_{kk} - n_k a_{kk}] \tag{A-3}$$

and the new quantities a_{gj}, denoted a_{gj}^{new}, are computed as follows:

$$a_{gj}^{new} = a_{gj} + (n_k a_{gk} a_{kj})/(1 - \rho_{kk} - n_k a_{kk}). \tag{A-4}$$

In order to rederive formulas (A-1) through (A-4), the reader should note that the matrix A to be inverted when a subset of securities $\Delta_k \leqslant X_k'$ is added or dropped changes as follows: $A^{new} = A + u - v$ here u is a column vector satisfying $u_i = 0$ for $i \neq k$, $i = 1, \ldots, p$ $u_k = \pm u_k/(1 - \rho_{kk})$ and v is a row vector with elements $v_i = \rho_{ki}$ for $1 = 1, \ldots, p$. The inverse of A^{new} can be calculated by the formula:

$$[A + u - v]^{-1} = A^{-1} - [1/(1 + vA^{-1}u)](A^{-1}u)(vA^{-1}).$$

Observing that in the matrix equation of section I $A \underset{\sim}{\phi} = C$ the right-hand vector C changes in its kth component by $\pm\sum_{h\in\Delta_k}(\bar{R}_h - R_f)/\sigma_h$, all the formulas of this appendix follow.

Appendix B

In this appendix, we state the formulas that are necessary to update the quantities ψ_k for $k = 1, \ldots, p$ in Section II, when additions/deletions of securities from a particular group k of stocks are considered. They are derived in the same fashion as in Appendix A and can be stated as follows: Initially, let $\psi_k = 0$ for $k = 1, \ldots, p$ and let $a_{gk} = b_g b_k \sigma_m^2$ for $g \neq k$ and $a_{kk} = \sigma_k^2 + b_k^2 \sigma_m^2$ for $k = 1, \ldots, p$. When a subset $\Delta_k \leqslant X_k'$ of securities in a particular group k is added, the new quantities ψ_g are obtained by

$$\psi_g^{new} = \psi_g + (a_{gk}/a_{kk})(\psi_k^{new} - \psi_k)$$

$$\psi_k^{new} = \left\{\psi_k + a_{kk}\sum_{h\in\Delta_k}\beta_h(\bar{R}_h - R_f)\Big/\sigma_{\varepsilon_h}^2\right\}\Big/\left[1 + \sum_{h\in\Delta_k}\frac{\beta_b^2}{\sigma_{\varepsilon_h}^2}a_{kk}\right]. \tag{B-1}$$

The auxiliary quantities a_{gj} are updated as follows:

$$a_{gj}^{new} = a_{gj} - \left[\left(\sum_{h\in\Delta_k}\frac{\beta_h^2}{\sigma_{\varepsilon_h}^2}\right)a_{gk}a_{kj}\right]\Big/\left[1 + \left(\sum_{h\in\Delta_k}\frac{\beta_b^2}{\sigma_{\varepsilon_h}^2}\right)a_{kk}\right] \tag{B-2}$$

where the indices g and j assume all values $1, 2, \ldots, p$. Note that again, due to symmetry, one needs to compute only the upper diagonal part of the coefficients. Similarly, if a subset of securities $\Delta_k \leqslant X_k'$ of group k is dropped, the quantities ψ_g must be recalculated as follows:

$$\psi_g^{new} = \psi_g + (a_{gk}/a_{kk})(\psi_k^{ne} - \psi_k)$$

$$\psi_k^{new} = \left\{\psi_k - a_{kk}\sum_{h\in\Delta_k}\beta_h(\bar{R}_h - R_f)/\sigma_{\varepsilon_h}^2\right\}\Big/\left[1 + \sum_{h\in\Delta_k}\frac{\beta_h^2}{\sigma_{\varepsilon_h}^2}a_{kk}\right] \tag{B-3}$$

The auxiliary quantities a_{gj} are recalculated as follows:

$$a_{gj}^{new} = a_{gj} + \left[\left(\sum_{h \in \Delta_k} \frac{\beta_h^2}{\sigma_{\varepsilon_h}^2}\right) a_{gk} a_{kj}\right] \Big/ \left[1 + \sum_{h \in \Delta_k} \frac{\beta_h^2}{\sigma_{\varepsilon_h}^2}\right) a_{kk}\right]. \qquad \text{(B-4)}$$

Notes

1. For evidence on the ability of a single number to represent correlation structures, see Elton and Gruber [4].

2. Grouping was performed in two ways: along traditional industry lines and by using a varimax rotation of factor loadings of historic rate of return data. See Elton and Gruber [4] for a more detailed discussion of the methodology and results.

3. We are following Lintner's [6] suggestion in treating short sales. That is, the short seller pays any dividends which accrue to the person who lends him the stock and gets a capital gain (or loss) which is the negative of any price appreciation. In addition the short seller is assumed to receive interest at the riskless rate on both the money loaned to the owner of the borrowed stock and the money placed in escrow when the short sale is made. See Lintner [6] for a full discussion of these assumptions.

4. See Lintner [6] for a proof that this is the correct objective function.

5. Note that no matter how many securities are considered the matrix to be inverted depends only on the number p of different group considered. Since the number p will typically be small compared with the total number of securities involved, the computation is significantly simplified. Note also that the matrix need only be inverted once to solve for all cases involving a specific number of groups. For example, a specific solution to the matrix inversion can be performed for the four group case and this solution used on any problem involving four groups.

6. It is interesting to note that the implementation of the multi-group case is no more difficult than the implementation of the single group case when short selling is allowed. See Elton, Gruber and Padberg [3] for a discussion of the single group case.

7. This can be done in general notation rather than being problem specific.

References

[1] Cohen, Kalman J., and Gerald Pogue. "An Empirical Evaluation of Alternative Portfolio Models." *Journal of Business*, Vol. 40, No. 1 (April 1967), pp. 166–193.

[2] Elton, Edwin J., and Martin J. Gruber. *Finance As a Dynamic Process*. Englewood Cliffs, N.J.: Prentice-Hall, 1975.

[3] Elton, Edwin J., Martin J. Gruber, and Manfred W. Padberg. "Optimal Portfolio Selection Via Simple Decision Rules." Forthcoming, *Journal of Finance* (December 1977).

[4] Elton, Edwin J., and Martin J. Gruber. "Estimating the Dependence Structure of Share Prices—Implications for Portfolio Selection." *Journal of Finance*, Vol. 27, No. 5 (December 1973), pp. 1203–1233.

[5] Latane, Henry, and Donald Tuttle. "Criteria for Portfolio Building." *Journal of Finance*, Vol. 22, No. 3 (September 1967), pp. 359–374.

[6] Lintner, John. "The Valuation of Risk Assets in the Selection of Risky Investments in Stock Portfolios and Capital Budgets." *The Review of Economics and Statistics* (February 1965), pp. 13–37.

[7] Markowitz, Harry. "Portfolio Selection." *The Journal of Finance* (March 1952), pp. 77–91.

[8] ———. *Portfolio Selection.* New York: John Wiley and Sons, Inc., 1959.

[9] Sharpe, William. "A Linear Programming Algorithm for Mutual Fund Portfolio Selection." *Management Science* (March 1967), pp. 499–510.

[10] ———. "A Linear Programming Approximation for the General Portfolio Selection Problem." *Journal of Financial and Quantitative Analysis* (December 1971), pp. 1263–1276.

9 Simple Rules for Optimal Portfolio Selection in Stable Paretian Markets

Vijay S. Bawa, Edwin J. Elton, and Martin J. Gruber

I Introduction

It is well known that when the joint probability distribution of security returns is multivariate normal, optimal portfolios for all risk-averse investors lie on the Markowitz-Tobin mean, variance admissible frontier. The optimal portfolio can be obtained by matrix inversion (see, for example, Lintner [10] or Merton [12]) if short sales are permitted; otherwise, mathematical programming algorithms are needed to solve the underlying parametric quadratic programming problem. Sharpe [16] has shown that if the security returns are generated by a single-index model and if residuals are uncorrelated, then the underlying optimization problem is simplified with significant computational savings. In a series of recent papers, Elton, Gruber and Padberg [3, 4, 5, 6, 7] have shown that under the assumption of the Sharpe single-index model, as well as for several other models that generate special covariance structures, optimal portfolios can be constructed by simple rules that do not involve using quadratic programming techniques. Furthermore, these rules lead to a unique ranking of securities such that the desirability of any security for inclusion in a portfolio can be judged before the portfolio composition itself is obtained. This provides an intuitive explanation to the practioner as to why (and how much of) a security should be included in a portfolio.

It is also known (see, for example, Bawa [1], Fama [8, 9], Press [13, 14] and Samuelson [15] that when the joint probability distribution of security returns follow a multivariate stable distribution with characteristic exponent α, $0 < \alpha \leqslant 2$, portfolio returns follow a univariate stable distribution with the same characteristic exponent α. In addition, the distributions of portfolio returns belong to a two parameter (location, scale) family of distributions for (1) Symmetric nonnormal multivariate stable distributions as defined by Press [13, 14], (2) A linear dependence structure with nonnormal multivariate stable distributions as defined by Fama [8, 9] or Samuelson [15] for the symmetric case and Bawa [2] for the asymmetric case.[1] For these distributions, mean is the appropriate return measure while scale parameter (also referred to as dispersion parameter in the literature) is the appropriate risk measure. Thus for an arbitrary value of α, $1 < \alpha \leqslant 2$, optimal portfolios can be obtained using mathematical programming techniques (see, for example, Ziemba [16]) that are very similar, though not identical to the ones employed for the case of normal distributions.[2] The scale parameter of the portfolio replaces the standard deviation used in the case of normal distribution and the underlying optimization problem being solved is a parametric convex programming problem, instead of a parametric quadratic programming problem.

In this paper we show that optimal portfolios can be obtained by simple procedures for multivariate stable distributions with arbitrary α, $1 < \alpha \leqslant 2$, under several specific models of the dependence structure including a single-index model. Our assumptions are analogous to those in Elton, Gruber, and Padberg [3] and the simple procedures are analogous to, though slightly more complex than those developed in [3] for mean variance portfolio problems. Of particular interest is the fact that there is an optimal way to rank securities for inclusion in the optimal portfolio for arbitrary α, $1 < \alpha \leqslant 2$ that is analogous to that which was proved optimal for the mean variance case [3]. Our results provide simple decision rules to solve the portfolio problems posed in Fama [8], the single-index model case in Samuelson [15] and Bawa [2], and for special dependence structure cases in Press [3, 14]. They also provide an intuitive explanation to the practioner as to why (and how much of) a security should be included in the optimal portfolio and constitute an important step in actual implementation of portfolio theory.

In the paper, we will only consider assumptions analogous to those made in [3], that is (i) no short sales are allowed, (ii) a riskless asset exists and one can borrow and lend any amount of the riskless asset and (iii) the joint probability distribution of security returns is multivariate stable with characteristic exponent α, $1 < \alpha \leqslant 2$, defined either by a single-index model or the special case of Press's [13, 14] model with constant coscale factor (analogue of constant correlation for normal distributions). Since most institutions are either prevented by law from short selling or choose not to do so, this is a particularly relevant case. In Sections 2 and 3 we consider the case of a single index model generating security returns and Press's model with constant coscale factor respectively and show that all the results obtained in [3] carry over. Note that in going from the normal distribution to the nonnormal stable family, the solution to the underlying optimization involves algebraic equations of order $(\alpha - 1)$ (where α is the characteristic exponent, $1 < \alpha \leqslant 2$) rather than linear (i.e., when $\alpha = 2$) equations. Thus all of the results obtained in [4]–[7] carry over from normal distributions to the entire family of stable distributions except for appropriate notational changes and associated higher degree of algebraic complexity and manipulations in deriving the results. For example, those who may be bothered by the assumption of a riskless asset can consider it a mathematical artifact and can use the results of this paper to solve for the full admissible frontier by varying the riskless rate (see Elton, Gruber, and Padberg [4]).

II Optimal Portfolios for Single Index Model

We let R_i denote the random return on security i, $i = 1, 2, \ldots, n$. We assume that R, with $R' = (R_1, R_2, \ldots, R_n)$, has a multivariate stable distribution with characteristic exponent α, $1 < \alpha \leqslant 2$ and constant skewness index for each security. We further assume that the comovement of security returns is given by the following single index model:

$$R_i = \alpha_i + \beta_i I + \varepsilon_i \qquad i = 1, 2, \ldots, n \tag{1}$$

where $(\varepsilon_1, \varepsilon_2, \ldots, \varepsilon_n, I)$ are assumed to be independent random variables with univariate stable distributions with common characteristic exponent α and a common skewness index. In addition, we let

$\mu_m = E(I)$

S_m = scale parameter of the market index I

β_i = a measure of responsiveness of security i to changes in the market index.

α_i = return on security i that is independent of changes in the market index.

ε_i = a random variable with mean zero and scale parameter S_i.

The assumption implied by the index model is that the only joint movement between securities comes because of a common response to a market index.

If we let X_i denote the fractional amount invested in security i, $i = 1, 2, \ldots, n$, let R_X denote the return on portfolio X, and define $\bar{R}_i \equiv E(R_i)$, then with no short selling,

$$\bar{R}_X \equiv E(R_X) = \sum_1^n X_i \bar{R}_i \tag{2}$$

and[3,4]

$S_X \equiv$ scale parameter of portfolio X,

$$S_X = \left\{ \sum_1^n X_i^a S_i^a + S_m^a \left(\sum_1^n \beta_i X_i \right)^\alpha \right\}^{1/\alpha} \tag{3}$$

If we let R_F denote the return on a riskless asset, then it follows from the well known separation result (see, for example, Fama [9], Ziemba [17] for a proof for symmetric stable distributions and Bawa [2] for asymmetric stable distributions) that all risk-averse investors will allocate the wealth between the riskless asset and a mutual fund of risky assets. The composition of this mutual fund is obtained via the solution to the following optimization problem:

$$\max \theta = \frac{\bar{R}_X - R_F}{S_X} \tag{I}$$

subject to

$$\sum_1^n X_i = 1$$

$$X_i \geqslant 0 \qquad \text{for } i = 1, \ldots, n$$

We note that θ is homogeneous of degree zero and the optimal solution to (I) can be obtained by first maximizing θ subject to only the nonnegativity constraints and then scaling the optimal solution. Substituting for $\bar{R}_X$ and S_X from (2) and (3), we note that the Kuhn-Tucker conditions for the optimal solution subject to only nonnegativity constraints are:[5]

$$(\bar{R}_i - R_F)S_X^{-1} - (\bar{R}_X - R_F).$$

$$\left(S_i^\alpha X_i^{\alpha-1} + S_m^\alpha \left(\sum_{j=1}^n X_j \beta_j \right)^{\alpha-1} \beta_i \right) S_X^{-\alpha-1} + \mu_i = 0 \quad i = 1, 2, \ldots, n \tag{4}$$

$$X_i, \mu_i \geqslant 0 \quad i = 1, 2, \ldots, n \tag{5}$$

$$X_i \mu_i = 0 \quad i = 1, 2, \ldots, n \tag{6}$$

Multiplying through equation (4) by S_X, defining $Z_j = X_j[(\bar{R}_X - R_F)^{1/(\alpha-1)} S_X^{-(\alpha/(\alpha-1))}]$ and redefining $\mu_i = \mu_i S_X S_i^{-\alpha}$ and rearranging equation (4) yields:

$$Z_i^{\alpha-1} = \frac{(\bar{R}_i - R_F)}{S_i^\alpha} - \frac{S_m^\alpha}{S_i^\alpha}\left(\sum_{j=1}^n Z_j\beta_j\right)^{\alpha-1}\beta_i + \mu_i$$

or

$$Z_i^{\alpha-1} = \frac{\beta_i}{S_i^\alpha}\left(\frac{\bar{R}_i - R_F}{\beta_i} - \phi_\kappa\right) + \mu_i, \tag{7}$$

where

$$\phi_\kappa = S_m^\alpha\left(\sum_{j=1}^n Z_j\beta_j\right)^{\alpha-1}. \tag{8}$$

Equation (7) is identical in form to those found in Elton, Gruber and Padberg [3] and all of the conclusions discussed there follow immediately. First if $\beta_i > 0$ a security can only be included in the optimum portfolio if the term in parentheses is positive. As discussed in footnote 4 we feel $\beta_i > 0$ is the only empirically relevant case. Thus β_i/S_i^α is positive. If $Z_i > 0$ then $\mu_i = 0$. Thus for Z_i to be greater than zero the term in the parentheses must be positive.

Secondly, securities can be ranked by their excess mean return to Beta ratios with the optimum portfolio consisting of the top ranked securities. Assume security a is in the optimum portfolio. Then security b if it has a higher excess return to Beta ratio must have a larger value for the term in the brackets. Since by assumption the term in the brackets was positive for security a, it must be positive for security b which has a higher excess return to Beta ratio. Thus the excess return to Beta ratio is a natural ranking device and the highest ranked securities are included in the optimum portfolio when returns are non-normal stable. This is identical to the conclusion reached in [3] when mean and variance are the appropriate characteristics of portfolios.

Let set κ be the set of securities included in the optimum portfolio. Since $Z_j = 0$ for securities not in set κ we have $\sum_{j=1}^n Z_j\beta_j = \sum_{j\in\kappa} Z_j\beta_j$ and equation (8) becomes $\phi_\kappa = S_m^\alpha(\sum_{j\in\kappa} Z_j\beta_j)^{\alpha-1}$. Also we have for elements of the set κ, $\mu_j = 0$. Thus for elements in set κ, we have

$$Z_i^{\alpha-1} = \frac{\beta_i}{S_i^\alpha}\left(\frac{\bar{R}_i - R_F}{\beta_i} - \phi_\kappa\right). \tag{9}$$

Taking the $(\alpha - 1)$ root of both sides of (9) and substituting in for ϕ_κ, we obtain

$$Z_i = \left(\frac{(\bar{R}_i - R_F)}{S_i^\alpha} - \frac{S_m^\alpha}{S_i^\alpha}\beta_i\left(\sum_{j\in\kappa} Z_j\beta_j\right)^{\alpha-1}\right)^{1/(\alpha-1)}.$$

Multiplying by β_j and summing both sides over set κ yields

$$\sum_{j\in\kappa} Z_j\beta_j = \sum_{j\in\kappa}\left(\frac{(\bar{R}_j - R_F)\beta_j^{\alpha-1}}{S_j^{\alpha}} - \frac{S_m^{\alpha}}{S_i^{\alpha}}\beta_j^{\alpha}\left(\sum_{j\in\kappa} Z_j\beta_j\right)^{\alpha-1}\right)^{1/(\alpha-1)},$$

or

$$1 = \sum_{j\in\kappa}\left(\frac{(\bar{R}_j - R_F)\beta_j^{\alpha-1}}{S_j^{\alpha}}\cdot\frac{1}{(\sum_{j\in\kappa} Z_j\beta_j)^{\alpha-1}} - \frac{S_m^{\alpha}\beta_j^{\alpha}}{S_j^{\alpha}}\right)^{1/(\alpha-1)}.$$

This equation has the form

$$1 = \sum_{j\in\kappa}\left(\frac{D_j}{\phi_\kappa} - F_j\right)^{1/(\alpha-1)} \tag{10}$$

where D_j is always positive. While the solution to this equation for ϕ_κ initially appears difficult the nature of the problem vastly simplifies the task. From equation (9) we set that if securities are ranked by excess return to Beta and security j is the lowest ranked security included in the portfolio

$$\frac{\bar{R}_j - R_F}{\beta_j} > \phi_\kappa \geqslant \frac{\bar{R}_{j+1} - R_F}{\beta_{j+1}}$$

In addition at the optimum, equation (10) must be satisfied. Notice that for equation (10) to be satisfied when j is the last security included in the portfolio the RHS of equation (10) must be greater than or equal to one for $\phi_\kappa = (\bar{R}_{j+1} - R_F)/(\beta_{j+1})$. This is true for the RHS of (10) decreases monotonically with increases in ϕ_κ. This property together with the fact that the RHS of (10) increases any time a security is added to a portfolio for a given ϕ_κ can be used to find the composition of the optimal portfolio.

Thus the optimal set of securities to include can be found by the following straightforward sequential procedure: initially define set κ as containing the first security and let $\phi_\kappa = (\bar{R}_2 - R_F)/\beta_2$. If the RHS of (10) is less than one it cannot equal one anywhere in the range $(\bar{R}_1 - R_F)/\beta_1 \geqslant \phi_\kappa \geqslant (\bar{R}_2 - R_F)/\beta_2$. Next define set κ as including the first two securities and set $\phi_\kappa = (\bar{R}_3 - R_F)/\beta_3$. If the RHS of (10) is less than one follow the same procedure with respect to security 3. Continue until with the first j securities in the included set (κ) and $\phi_\kappa = (\bar{R}_{j+1} - R_F)/\beta_{j+1}$ the RHS of equation (10) is greater than one. The optimum set will then include the first j securities.

To complete the construction of the optimal portfolio the value of ϕ_κ must be determined. Equation (10) must be solved for ϕ_κ. The solution is facilitated by knowledge that when j securities are included in the optimal portfolio, ϕ_κ must be smaller than $(\bar{R}_j - R_F)/\beta_j$ and larger than or equal to $(\bar{R}_{j+1} - R_F)/\beta_{j+1}$. Once ϕ_κ is determined the value of Z_i can be determined for all securities with $(\bar{R}_j - R_F)/\beta_j$ greater than ϕ_κ from equation (9). Finally the optimal proportion to invest in each security can be found by scaling the Z_j, i.e., $X_j = Z_j / \sum_{j \in \kappa} Z_j$.

III Optimal Portfolios for Constant Coscale Factor Model

In this section we employ the notation of the last section, and assume that R has a multivariate stable distribution as defined by Press [13, 14]. We further assume the special case of constant coscale factor, i.e., (see [13], [14] for details) if we let $\sum = (S_{ij})$ denote the scale-coscale matrix, then $S_{ij} = \rho S_i S_j$ for $i \neq j$ and $S_{ii} = S_i^2$. More importantly, for a portfolio X,

$$\bar{R}_X \equiv E(R_X) = \sum_{i=1}^{n} X_i E(R_i) = \sum_{i=1}^{n} X_i \bar{R}_i \tag{11}$$

and

$$S_X^\alpha = \frac{1}{2}\left(X' \sum X\right)^{\alpha/2} = \frac{1}{2}\left(\sum_{i=1}^{n} X_i^2 S_i^2 + 2\rho \sum_{i=1}^{n-1} \sum_{j=i+1}^{n} X_i X_j S_i S_j\right)^{\alpha/2} \tag{12}$$

Except for the mean and scale parameter of a portfolio X now given by (11) and (12) respectively, the optimal portfolio is obtained as in Section 2. Thus separation results hold in this case as well and the optimal 'mutual fund' of risky assets is obtained as the optimal solution to the optimization problem (I) with $\bar{R}_X$ and S_X now defined by (11) and (12) respectively. Furthermore, analysis in [3] for normal distributions (i.e., $\alpha = 2$) carries over exactly in this case without modifications and will not be repeated here. We recall that the simple sequential procedure described in Section 2 to obtain the optimal portfolio holds in this case as well with $(\bar{R}_i - R_F)/\beta_i$ in the last section replaced by $(\bar{R}_i - R_F)S_i$.

IV Conclusions

In this paper, we have shown that the construction of optimal portfolios can be vastly simplified by using simple ranking procedures when returns follow a stable distribution and the dependence structure has any of several standard forms. This ranking procedure simplifies the computations necessary to determine an optimum portfolio. In addition it clarifies the characteristics of the security that make its inclusion in an optimum portfolio desirable. The significance of our results for the nonnormal stable distributions increases when one notes that no other algorithm is known to exist that efficiently obtains the admissible portfolios.

Notes

1. It should be noted that the asymmetric stable distributions defined in Bawa [2] are generalizations of symmetric stable distributions in [8], [9] and [15], with the skewness parameter β assumed to an arbitrary constant, $-1 \leqslant \beta \leqslant 1$, across security returns. $\beta = 0$ corresponds to symmetric distributions.

2. It is known that diversification is preferred by all risk-averse investors only for $1 < \alpha \leqslant 2$. For $\alpha \leqslant 1$, specialization is the preferred strategy. As in [8], [9] and [15], we assume that $1 < \alpha \leqslant 2$.

3. Note that for symmetric distributions, (3) has been derived in Fama [8, 9] and Samuelson [15]. For asymmetric distributions with constant skewness index, Bawa [2] has shown that the same result holds.

4. We assume $\beta_i > 0$. This is the only empirically relevant case.

5. Kuhn-Tucker conditions are necessary and sufficient for the optimization problem at hand if one can show that θ is a pseudo concave function of X (Margasarian, O. L. [11; p. 145] shows concavity is not needed—only pseudo concavity is required). It is shown in Margasarian [11; p. 198] that if $\theta = \phi/\psi$ and ϕ is linear and positive and ψ is convex and $\psi > 0$, then θ is pseudo concave. $\psi \equiv S$ the scale parameter which is positive for all X and convex. $\phi \equiv \bar{R}_X - R_F$. For equilibrium $E(R_i) > R_F$; hence $\bar{R}_X > R_F$ for all $X \geqslant 0$. Thus Kuhn-Tucker conditions are necessary and sufficient.

References

1. V. S. Bawa. "Optimal Rules for Ordering Uncertain Prospects." *Journal of Financial Economics*, Vol. 2 (1975).

2. ———. "On Optimal Portfolio Selection Rules" (forthcoming).

3. Edwin J. Elton, Martin J. Gruber, and Manfred W. Padberg. "Simple Criteria for Optimal Portfolio Selection." *Journal of Finance*, Vol. 31 (1976).

4. ———. "Simple Criteria for Optimal Portfolio Selection: Tracing the Efficient Frontier." *Journal of Finance*, Vol. 33 (June, 1978).

5. ———. "Simple Criteria for Optimal Portfolio Selection; The Multi Group Case." *Journal of Financial and Quantitative Analysis*, Vol. 12 (September, 1977).

6. ———. "Simple Criteria for Optimal Portfolio Selection with Upper Bound Constraints." *Operations Research*, Vol. 25 (November–December, 1977).

7. ———. "Simple Criteria for Optimal Portfolio Selecton: Multi-Index Case," in Elton, Edwin J., and Gruber, Martin J., *Portfolio Theory: Twenty-five Years Later* (Amsterdam, North Holland), 1979.

8. Eugene Fama. "Portfolio Analysis in a Stable Paretian Market." *Management Science*, Vol. 11 (1965).

9. ———. "Risk, Return, and Equilibrium." *Journal of Political Economy*, Vol. 78 (1971).

10. John Lintner. "The Valuation of Risk Assets and The Selection of Risky Investments in Stock Portfolios and Capital Budgets." *Review of Economics and Statistics*, Vol. 47 (February, 1965).

11. O. L. Mangasarian. *Nonlinear Programming*, (New York: McGraw Hill, 1969).

12. R. C. Merton. "An Analytic Derivaton of Efficient Frontier." *Journal of Financial and Quantitative Analysis*, Vol. 7 (1972).

13. S. J. Press. "Multivariate Stable Distributions." *Journal of Multivariate Analysis*, Vol. 2 (1972).

14. ———. *Applied Multivariate Analysis* (New York: Holt Reinhart and Winston, 1972).

15. P. A. Samuelson. "Efficient Portfolio Selection for Pareto-Levy Investments." *Journal of Financial and Quantitative Analysis*, Vol. 2 (1967).

16. W. F. Sharpe. "A Simplified Model for Portfolio Analysis." *Management Science*, Vol. 9 (1965).

17. W. T. Ziemba. "Choosing Investment Portfolios When The Returns have Stable Distributions." *Mathematical Programming in Theory and Practice*, Edited by Hammer, P. L. and Zoutendijk, G., North Holland (1974).

10

Portfolio Analysis with Partial Information: The Case of Grouped Data

Edwin J. Elton and Martin J. Gruber

Almost all of the literature in finance analyzing the selection of optimum portfolios assumes that the agent making the decision has a full set of estimates of the expected return for each security and the variance covariance matrix between securities. In actual practice most decision makers simply receive a list of stocks with a ranking on each stock (usually from one to five) and perhaps some partial risk information. If stocks are ranked (grouped) from 1 to 5, stocks ranked in group 1 are best buys, stocks ranked 2 are buys, 3 are holds, 4 are sells and 5 are definite sells. The importance of grouped data can be seen from a survey of 40 financial institutions undertaken by the authors. Eighty percent of the institutions stated that the data the brokerage community and/or their analysts supplied to the portfolio managers were in the form of grouped data. The problem is made even more complex by the variety of criteria used in the grouping. Of the institutions using grouped data, 50% used data grouped on expected return, 30% on risk adjusted return, 10% on expected deviations from a CAPM model, and 10% responded they did not even know the basis of the ranking.

The purpose of this paper is to determine what we can learn from portfolio theory about optimum decisions if all the investor knows is the grouping of stocks plus *at best* the average characteristics of the stocks in a group. This analysis is important because these are the data most investors utilize to make their portfolio decisions. We are not acting as apologists for making decisions based on grouped data; we are merely recognizing that this is done and attempting to determine what theory can add to the decision process given that it is done. In particular we will be concerned with three problems.

1. Under what conditions is it optimal to select all of the members of one group before selecting members of a second group?

2. What are the proportions to invest in each of the securities of a selected group and when are they equal?
3. How much should be invested in each of the groups that are selected?

In §1 we will assume that stocks are grouped on the basis of expected return. In §2 we assume grouping on risk adjusted return. In §3 we assume grouping on deviations from a CAPM. The user of the grouping is assumed to have information about the group characteristics but not to know the value for each stock or the value of the criteria on which grouping is performed.

I Grouping by Expected Return

We will start by assuming that stocks are grouped from highest to lowest solely on the basis of expected return. Since expected return is probably the most commonly used criterion for grouping we assume the investor acts as if the expected return is different for each group but is the same for the members of the same group.

Grouping is most useful if when one member of a group is included in an optimal portfolio, every member should be included, and if when one member is excluded, every member must be excluded. We will analyze this situation throughout the paper, both in this section and in later sections. In order to study the optimality of including or excluding groups in their entirety some structure must be imposed on the covariances among securities.[1] The most general assumption is that the investor has no information on variances or covariances and therefore assumes they are the same for all stocks in all groups. In succeeding parts of this section we will assume that the investor has estimates of the variance for the typical stock in a group but cannot differentiate between the variance of stocks in the same group, and finally that the investor has estimates of the beta, and residual risk for the typical stock in a group.

A Constant Variances and Covariances

If the portfolio manager is only supplied a grouping of stocks all securities in a group must be treated as if they have the same expected return and the same risk. When securities in a group are treated as being identical, if one is included in a optimal portfolio then they are all included. Furthermore, since they have the same characteristics, they are included in equal amounts. Thus, without loss of generality we can assume that the first group is included in its entirety and that each security is held in the same proportion. Next we ask whether group 2 should be included. To analyze this let:

1. $\bar{R}_i$ be the expected return of a security in group i. This is assumed to be estimated for each group and to be estimated to be the same for all members of the same group.
2. N_i be the number of securities in group i.
3. P be the subscript used to indicate a portfolio.
4. σ_{kl} be the covariance between securities. This is assumed to be identical for all pairs of securities.
5. σ_k^2 be the variance of security k. This is assumed to be the same for all securities.
6. R_F be the riskless rate of interest.
7. X_i be the fraction of the total funds invested in a stock in group i.

With riskless lending and borrowing, the appropriate objective is to maximize the slope of a line tangent to the efficient frontier and passing through the riskless interest rate.[2] Denoting this slope as θ, the investor's problem may be expressed as:

$$\text{Maximize} \quad \theta = \frac{\bar{R}_p - R_F}{\sigma_p} \tag{1}$$

Subject to:

1. $\Sigma X_i = 1$,
2. $X_i \geqslant 0$.

The expected return on a portfolio of group 1 and 2 is:

$$\bar{R}_p = N_1 X_1 \bar{R}_1 + N_2 X_2 \bar{R}_2 \tag{2}$$

recognizing that $N_1 X_1 + N_2 X_2 = 1$, the variance of the portfolio can be written as:

$$\sigma_p^2 = (N_1 X_1^2 + N_2 X_2^2)(\sigma_k^2 - \sigma_{kl}) + \sigma_{kl}. \tag{3}$$

Substitution (3) and (2) into (1) yields:

$$\theta = \frac{N_1 X_1(\bar{R}_1 - R_F) + N_2 X_2(\bar{R}_2 - R_F)}{[(N_1 X_1^2 + N_2 X_2^2)(\sigma_k^2 - \sigma_{kl}) + \sigma_{kl}]^{1/2}}.$$

If short sales are forbidden, then at the optimum $d\theta/dX_i + \mu_i$ must be equal to zero where μ_i is the Kuhn Tucker multiplier. This multiplier has a value of zero when X_i is positive and has a positive value when X_i is zero. Since group one is included, $\mu_1 = 0$. Setting $d\theta/dX_1 = 0$ and solving for X_i yields:

$$X_1 = \frac{1}{\lambda}\frac{[(\bar{R}_1 - R_F)]}{[\sigma_k^2 - \sigma_{kl}]}, \tag{4}$$

where λ is the ratio of excess return to variance on the portfolio which would be selected by an investor.

Taking the derivative of θ with respect to X_2 yields:

$$\frac{d\theta}{dX_2} = (\bar{R}_2 - R_F) - \lambda X_2(\sigma_k^2 - \sigma_{kl}) + \mu_2'$$

where μ_2' is μ_2 times a positive constant. Average variances are considerably larger than average covariances. Thus, $(\sigma_k^2 - \sigma_{kl})$ should in general be positive. Likewise, for risk averse investors, λ must be positive. Given these conditions and the fact μ_2' is zero or positive, if the expected return on the stock in group 2 is greater than the riskless rate, X_2 must be positive for the derivative to be zero. Thus, as long as expected return is greater that the riskless rate of interest, group 2 should be included in entirety. Setting $d\theta/dX_2$ equal to zero results in an expression analogous to equation (4).

Recognizing that $1/\lambda(\sigma_k^2 - \sigma_{kl})$ is a constant for all securities, setting μ_i to zero for included securities and taking the ratio of X_1 to X_2 yields:

$$\frac{X_1}{X_2} = \frac{(\bar{R}_1 - R_F)}{(\bar{R}_2 - R_F)}. \tag{5}$$

Thus, the fraction of funds invested in securities of group 1 compared to group 2 is directly proportional to the excess returns of the two groups.

Using similar analysis it can be shown that the same conclusions hold when a third, fourth, or fifth group is considered. Thus, if groups are formed on expected return and the investor is unwilling to differentiate between securities on the basis of risk:

1. groups are selected or rejected in entirety.
2. any group where the expected return is greater than the riskless rate is included in entirety.

3. it is optimal to invest equal amounts in each of the securities of any particular group.

4. the proportion to invest in securities of a group is directly related to the excess return of the group.

Having discussed portfolio selection when securities are grouped by expected return but are not differentiated between on the basis of risk, it is useful to analyze selection when assumptions concerning risk are made. The easiest assumption to analyze is the assumption of constant covariance.

B Constant Covariances and Different Variances

Assume investors have no information about covariance and therefore assume that they are all the same. Suppose, however, that investors recognize that the variances of stocks in one group may differ from variances of stocks in any other group. The variance of all stocks within any one group are assumed to be the same. What can be said about security selection and the optimality of selecting a group in its entirety? Equation (3) still represents the variance on the portfolio if we designate the variances of groups 1 and 2 by different symbols. Exactly parallel to the analysis of the prior section we obtain that for $d\theta/dX_1$ to equal zero and for X_1 to be positive

$$X_1 = \frac{1}{\lambda}\frac{(\bar{R}_1 - R_F)}{(\sigma_1^2 - \sigma_{kl})} \tag{6}$$

where σ_1^2 is the variance of the typical stock in group one. Likewise

$$X_2 = \frac{1}{\lambda}\frac{(\bar{R}_2 - R_F)}{(\sigma_2^2 - \sigma_{kl})}. \tag{7}$$

The variances in the above expression are average security variances. In general these are about 6 times as large as average covariances.[3] Thus it is reasonable to assume that $\sigma_i^2 - \sigma_{kl}$ is positive. Once again a group should be included in its entirety as long as the expected return on the securities in the group is greater than the riskless rate of interest.

The fraction of wealth to be invested in a stock in group 1 compared to a stock in group 2 is found by dividing equation (6) by equation (7) or

$$\frac{X_1}{X_2} = \frac{\dfrac{(\bar{R}_1 - R_F)}{(\sigma_1^2 - \sigma_{kl})}}{\dfrac{(\bar{R}_2 - R_F)}{(\sigma_2^2 - \sigma_{kl})}}. \tag{8}$$

Similar expressions are obtainable when 3 or more groups enter the optimum.[4] With the assumption of constant covariance condition (1)–(3) remain identical to those presented for the previous case but condition (4) changes and becomes:

(4) The proportion to invest in securities of a group depends on the excess returns in a group and the variance of securities in a group and the average covariance.

C Constant Correlation Model

We will continue the assumption made in §1.B above except that the correlation rather than the covariance between all securities will be assumed to be the same.

With this assumption the security selection can be done using the simple rules developed by Elton, Gruber and Padberg (1976). As Elton, Gruber and Padberg have shown, the amount to invest in security i is proportional to Z_i where

$$Z_i = \frac{1}{(1-\rho)\sigma_i}\left[\frac{\bar{R}_i - R_F}{\sigma_i} - C\right] \quad \text{and} \quad C = \frac{\rho}{1-\rho+N_k\rho}\sum_{j\in k}\frac{\bar{R}_j - R_F}{\sigma_j},$$

where

1. Z_i is λX_i and is proportional to the amount invested.
2. ρ is the correlation coefficient.
3. σ_i is the standard deviation of security i.
4. k is the set of included stocks.
5. N_k is the number of stocks in the set k.
6. other terms as before.

$\bar{R}_i$ and σ_i for all securities from a group are assumed to be the same. Therefore, from the equation above, if one security from a group is included (positive Z_i) all securities from that group will have positive Z_i's and will be included.

As shown by Elton, Gruber and Padberg, the selection rule involved ranking securities by excess return to standard deviation. Given the assumption above, all securities in a group are equally desirable and thus the groups should be ranked by excess return to standard deviation. If groups are formed solely on the basis of return then it is possible that the second or third group has a higher excess return to standard deviation and thus should enter before the first group enters. For a group to be selected in its entirety generally requires an assumption of a constant standard deviation for all members of a group. This is a more restrictive assumption than if the grouping was initially done on a risk adjusted basis. In a subsequent section we will examine the use of grouping on a risk adjusted basis. We will assert here a result which we demonstrate in this later section. It is extremely unlikely that more than one group will enter the optimal portfolio.

In summary, assuming a constant correlation and the same standard deviation of each security in a group.

1. only one group is likely to be selected.
2. the group selected is the group with the highest ratio of excess return to standard deviation, which may not be group 1.
3. all securities within the group are held in equal amounts.

For the final case in §1 assume that investors believe that groups are formed on the basis of expected return. However, assume that the investor is also supplied information on the average beta and residual risk for each group. Then results exactly parallel to the case just discussed follow. The only difference is that groups are selected on the basis of excess return to beta rather than standard deviation.

II Risk Adjusted Expected Returns

The first question to ask is why employ risk adjusted returns where expected returns are not generated by an equilibrium model. There are two connected reasons. Any model of equilibrium returns imposes a set of very strong assumptions on the capital market. Recent literature has cast doubt on the appropriate equilibrium model to use. Second the use of any portfolio selection model assumes that stocks which are out of equilibrium can be identified. Thus any equilibrium model holds at best as a first approximation.

In this section we shall assume that the investor is supplied information on group membership and that the grouping is done on the basis of one of two ranking criteria. The first is excess return to standard deviation and the second is excess return to Beta.

A *Ranking by Excess Return to Standard Deviation*

The concept of ranking stocks by excess return to standard deviation was suggested in the literature many years ago. For example, Latané and Tuttle

(1967) suggested this was an appropriate way to rank stocks as far back as 1967. The measure has further intuitive appeal from Sharpe's use of excess return to standard deviation as a measure of portfolio performance. More recently, Elton, Gruber and Padberg (1976) have proved that this is the optimal way to rank stocks if one makes the assumption of a constant correlation between stocks. This assumption gains support from empirical work by Elton and Gruber (1973), and Elton, Gruber and Urich (1978) in which the assumption of constant correlation is shown to lead to better forecasts of covariances and the selection of better portfolios than single and multiple index models.

In this section we shall assume that stocks are divided into five groups on the basis of excess return to standard deviation and that the correlation between any two stocks is equal to a single number denoted by ρ.

The simple rule of Elton, Gruber and Padberg is once again appropriate and

$$Z_i = \frac{1}{(1-\rho)\sigma_i}\left[\frac{\bar{R}_i - R_F}{\sigma_i} - C\right] \quad \text{and} \quad C = \frac{\rho}{1-\rho+N_k\rho}\sum_{j \in k}\frac{\bar{R}_j - R_F}{\sigma_j}.$$

Furthermore, the optimum fraction of the portfolio to put in any stock is equal to Z_i divided by the sum of Z_i's.

It is easy to show that it is optimum for at least one security to enter as long as a stock has an expected return greater than the riskless rate. Thus at least group 1 should be held. Define E_i as $(\bar{R}_i - R_F)/\sigma_i$. Then the condition for group 2 to enter is that E_2 is greater than C or

$$E_2 > \frac{\rho}{1-\rho+N_1\rho}(N_1E_1) > 0.$$

Rearranging and simplifying

$$\frac{E_1}{E_2} < \frac{(1-\rho)+N_1\rho}{N_1\rho}. \tag{9}$$

Thus if one stock from group 2 is held all stocks from group 2 should be held.

From the formula we cannot make definitive statements about whether stocks from group 2 should be purchased. Purchase depends on the excess return to standard deviation, the number of stocks in group 1, and the correlation coefficient.

To get an idea of the likely magnitude that the ratio of E_1 to E_2 would have to take on for group 2 to enter we examine equation (9) for values of

ρ of 0.25 and 0.5 and values of N_1 of 10, 50 and 100. Given empirical results on correlation coefficients and the results of our survey of managers these represent reasonable values. The ratio of E_1 to E_2 would have to be less than the numbers shown in the table for group 2 to enter.

	N_1		
ρ	10	50	100
0.25	1.30	1.06	1.03
0.50	1.10	1.02	1.01

Since the average firm in our sample places 50 stocks in group 1 and since the typical ratio of excess return to risk for group 1 to that of group 2 is considerably above 6/100 of 1 percent it seems highly unlikely that stocks from a second ranked group will be included in the optimal portfolio.[5] Furthermore, it can easily be shown that stocks in group 1 should not be held in equal proportions. Employing equation (8) and assuming that only group 1 is held, we find

$$\frac{Z_1}{\sum Z_i} = \frac{\dfrac{1}{\sigma_i}}{\sum_{j=1}^{N_1} \dfrac{1}{\sigma_j}}$$

or the fraction of funds which should be placed in each stock is inversely related to the standard deviation of the return on each stock.

In summary

1. it is likely that only group 1 is held.
2. stocks in a group should be held in amounts inversely proportional to their standard deviation.

B Ranking by Excess Return to Beta

The concept of dividing stocks into groups by excess return to Beta also has support in the financial literature. It has been suggested as an ad hoc ranking device, it is the Treynor measure of portfolio performance, and it has been shown by Elton, Gruber and Padberg (1976) to be the optimal way to rank stocks if the structure of returns are best described by the single index model.

In this case as Elton, Gruber and Padberg have shown

$$Z_i = \frac{\beta_i}{\sigma_{ei}^2}\left[\frac{\overline{R}_i - R_F}{\beta_i} - C\right] \qquad \text{where}$$

$$C = \frac{\sigma_m^2 \sum_{j\in k}\left(\dfrac{\overline{R}_j - R_F}{\sigma_{ej}^2}\beta_j\right)}{1 + \sigma_m^2 \sum_{j\in k}\beta_j^2/\sigma_{ej}^2} \qquad \text{where}$$

1. β_i is a measure of the sensitivity of stock i to return on the market.
2. σ_m^2 is the variance of the market.
3. σ_{ej}^2 is the residual risk.

Let $(\overline{R}_i - R_F)/\beta_i$ for group 1 be denoted by E_1.

It is easy to see from this equation that if the ratio of excess return to beta is positive for group 1, then all positive beta stocks from group 1 will be held in the optimal portfolio. This is true regardless of the level of beta (as long as it is positive) and residual risk on each stock.

Beta and residual risk do affect the fraction of the portfolio that should be held in each stock. The optimum fraction of funds to be placed in each stock is

$$\frac{Z_i}{\sum_j Z_j} = \frac{\beta_i/\sigma_{ej}^2}{\sum \beta_j/\sigma_{ej}^2}.$$

Thus the proportion to place in each stock is directly related to a security's Beta and inversely related to is residual risk.

The decision criteria for when an investor should hold a second group is more complex than in the previous case. Solving for this criteria in a manner parallel to the constant correlation case yields

$$\frac{E_1}{E_2} < 1 + \frac{1}{\sigma_m^2 \sum_{j=1}^{N_1} \beta_j^2/\sigma_{ej}^2}.$$

$\beta_j^2\sigma_m^2$ is the market related variance and σ_{ej}^2 is the residual variance. For individual stocks, market related variance averages a third of total variance. With this approximation the inequality becomes

$$\frac{E_1}{E_2} < 1 + \frac{2}{N_1}.$$

For reasonable size N_1, its unlikely that group 2 enters.

In summary

1. If a group enters, it enters in entirety.
2. It is likely only one group enters.
3. Included stocks are held in unequal proportions. The proportion which should be invested in any stock in a group is directly related to its Beta and inversely related to its residual risk.

III Ranking by Deviations from the Security Market Line

In this section of the paper we assume that securities are grouped by employing data on how far they lie above or below a security market line. In recent years, a number of institutions have prepared forecasts of expected return and Beta for the stocks which they follow. These stocks are then plotted in expected return Beta space and a forecasted security market line is fitted to the data, usually via regression analysis or by fitting it through R_F and a forecasted $\bar{R}_m$. The distance each security lies from the line (α_i) is then computed. Securities are grouped on the basis of their α_i.

A *Grouping by Alpha*

We will initially assume that the grouped data is the only data that is used in the decision making process. This is equivalent to assuming that the Beta, the variance and the covariance between all securities are the same. In fact, we have already analyzed this case in §1. If the Beta for all securities is the same then $\bar{R}_i - R_F = \alpha_i + \beta_i(\bar{R}_m - R_F)$. A ranking of grouping on $\bar{R}_i$ is identical to a ranking or grouping on α_i. The entire analysis of §1 of this paper follows and the conclusions arc identical to those presented in that section.

B *Grouping by Alpha with Information about Beta*

Some firms which provide grouped data report a beta for each group. Decisions are to be made in terms of the groups constructed on the basis of alpha but with a forecasted beta reported for each group. The assumption is that the alpha and the beta are the same for the members of the same group. Residual risk is assumed to be the same for all stocks and we assume zero covariance between residuals.

Under these assumptions, the first order conditions become

$$\bar{R}_i - R_F = \beta_i \sigma_m^2 \sum_{j=1}^{N+1} Z_j \beta_j + Z_i \sigma_e^2 - \mu_i \qquad \text{where} \tag{10}$$

σ_e^2 = the residual risk of security i assumed constant for all securities.

Note that the equation includes all securities including the market security, the $N+1$ security. The market portfolio can contain securities the firm does not follow and hence it is more than the sum of the securities under study. Assuming that α_i is the deviation from the standard CAPM we have

$$\alpha_i = \bar{R}_i - [R_F + \beta_i(\bar{R}_m - R_F)].$$

Substituting for $\bar{R}_i$ in equation (10). Recognizing that equation (10) holds for the market, and that μ_i is zero for included securities and rearranging yields:[6]

$$Z_i = \frac{\beta_i}{\sigma_e^2}\left[\frac{\alpha_i}{\beta_i} - \mu_m\right]. \tag{11}$$

The results differ according to whether an investor finds it optimal to place some funds in the market portfolio. If this investment is optimal we obtain:

$$Z_i = \alpha_i/\sigma_e^2.$$

A unique ranking for stocks exists in terms of α_i. Grouping on these criteria becomes appropriate. All groups with positive α_i should be accepted in entirety. Equal funds should be placed in all stocks in the same group. If more than one group has positive alphas then the fraction held in the securities of each group is directly proportional to their alphas; for example, if group 1 and group 2 have positive alphas $Z_1/Z_2 = \alpha_1/\alpha_2$.

The same simple conclusions do not hold if the market portfolio is not held. From equation (11) stocks should be ranked and grouped in terms of α_i/β_i not in terms of α_i. Thus it could be optimum for group 2 to enter before group 1 enters.

IV Summary

In this paper we have begun the study of a problem which, while important, has been neglected in the literature. Most portfolio managers and individuals are supplied data in the form of discrete rankings rather than in the form of expected returns, standard deviations and covariances as assumed in portfolio theory. Given this data how can an investor make optimal portfolio decisions? We have explored a number of rules. For example, if the grouping is based on expected return and no additional information is used,

1. Groups are selected or rejected in entirety.
2. Any group with an expected return greater than the risk free rate is selected in entirety.
3. Equal amounts are invested in each security.
4. The proportion to invest in each security is related to the excess return of a group.

Different rules result from different beliefs concerning the criteria used to form the groups. In this paper we have derived appropriate rules for alternative sets of grouping criteria that are used in the financial community.[7]

Notes

1. For example, assume perfect negative correlation between two securities, one in a high ranked group and one in a low ranked group. There is a zero risk combination of these two securities and if return on this riskless combination is greater than the riskless rate, then both securities should be included in a portfolio. If the other securities in the lower ranked group are not negatively correlated with securities in the higher ranked group, and their return is sufficiently low, they should not be held.

2. See Elton and Gruber (1987) for a general discussion of this criteria.

3. See Elton and Gruber (1973) for evidence on this.

4. Note a lower ranked group may have more invested in it than a high ranked group.

5. Some firms depending on the value of E_1, E_2 and N_1 may hold more than one group. This analysis can be used to gain insight into the decision of how to form groups. Institutions tend to use one of two types of criteria for grouping. They either set targets in terms of relative rates of return for the groups or limit the fraction of stocks which should be allowed to enter each group. We can think of criteria on relative performance as a specification of the size of E_1/E_2 and limits on the proportion of stocks in group 1 as a specification of N_1 (since the size of the population of stocks analyzed is known).

These two criteria are not independent. Changes in N_1 will affect E_1/E_2. As more stocks are added to group 1 we would expect E_1/E_2 to go down. The analysis in the text gives more guidance to setting either N_1 or E_1/E_2. Many firms use group 1 as their recommended list. For these firms, it is useful to understand the effect of N_1 and E_1/E_2 on the optimality of the policy.

6. If the residuals are correlated the optimum equation becomes:

$$Z_i = \frac{1}{\sigma_e^2 - \sigma_{e_{ij}}}\left[\alpha_i - \frac{\sum_{i\in S}\alpha_i}{\sigma_e^2 + (N-1)\sigma_{e_{ij}}}\right] - \mu_m\left(\beta_i - \frac{\sum_{j\in S}\beta_j}{\sigma_e^2 + (N-1)\sigma_{e_{ij}}}\right).$$

From this equation it is easy to see that if one member of a group enters, all members of the group enter. There are two subcases which should be examined. The first and simpler case is where it is optimum for the investor to place some of his or her funds in the market portfolio. In this case μ_m is equal to zero and the above equation reduces to

$$Z_i = \frac{1}{\sigma_e^2 - \sigma_{e_{ij}}}\left[\alpha_i - \frac{\sum_{i\in S}\alpha_i}{\sigma_e^2 + (N-1)\sigma_{e_{ij}}}\right].$$

In this case α_i is the optimum criteria on which to form groups. Group 1 with the biggest α_i will always be the most desirable group to hold followed by group 2, etc. All stocks in a group will be held in the same proportion.

If the market is not held, the results become more complex. From the first equation above the group with the highest α_i is not necessarily the most desirable group. To see this just imagine that group 1 has a bigger alpha but a much larger beta than group 2.

7. We would like to thank the Institute for Quantitative Research in Finance for financial support for this project.

References

Elton, Edwin J., and Martin J. Gruber, *Modern Portfolio Theory and Investment Analysis*, John Wiley and Sons, New York, 1987.

——— and ———, "Estimating the Dependence Structure of Share Prices—Implications for Portfolio Selection," *J. Finance*, 8 (December 1973), 1203–1232.

———, ——— and Manfred Padberg, "Simple Criteria for Optimal Portfolio Selection," *J. Finance*, 11 (December 1976), 1341–1357.

———, ——— and Tom Urich, "Are Betas Best?" *J. Finance*, 23 (December 1978), 1375–1383.

Latané, H. and D. Tuttle, "Criteria for Portfolio Building," *J. Finance*, (September 1967), 359–373.

Sharpe, William, "Mutual Fund Performance," *J. Business*, 39, 1 (January 1966).

Treynor, J., "How to Rate Management of Investment Funds," *Harvard Business Rev.*, 43, 1 (January/February 1965), 63–75.

III Other Objective Functions

In this section, we explore portfolio analysis that goes beyond examining an efficient frontier in single-period, mean-variance space. The section has two parts; the first is concerned with single-period analysis and the second is concerned with multiperiod analysis.

In the first part we have included four articles that explore our interest in analyzing the portfolio for structures different from the standard representation of the problem. The first two chapters examine the portfolio problems when price relatives (one plus return) are log-normally distributed. By employing the central limit theorem and recognizing that the price relative over a longer interval is a product of price relatives computed over shorter intervals, one can argue that at least at longer intervals the log of price relatives should have a stable distribution. A log-normal distribution for price relatives is the simplest of these stable distributions. Empirical evidence exists that supports this assumption for returns. The first two chapters solve for the optimum portfolio for two different problem formulations. Hakansson and Latanne have argued for maximizing the geometric mean of a portfolio as a reasonable objective for an investor interested in long-term performance. In the first chapter we show algorithmically how a portfolio could be constructed with that objective if the log of price relatives is normally distributed.

In the second chapter we derive an efficient set theorem and show how to find the efficient frontier when the space of relevance is log investment relatives and standard deviation of the log of investment relatives.

The third chapter deals with a different class of problems, one that considers liabilities as well as assets. For financial intermediaries, the investment problem can best be described as meeting a stream of liabilities at minimum cost or, alternatively, as maximizing net worth. We analyze this problem in a mean-variance framework where the manager has a choice of a cash-flow-matched portfolio, a duration-matched portfolio, portfolios that match factors in the return-generating process, and a special portfolio of above equilibrium return assets. We show that if all assets are in equilibrium, you cash-flow match. If some assets are out of equilibrium and the manager requires immunization, then a combination of cash-flow matching and duration matching is appropriate. Finally, in the more general case, all four portfolios discussed enter into some efficient combination. For this case we solve for the optimum combination of portfolios and the composition of each portfolio.

In the last chapter we consider the portfolio problem when returns are not normal but a linear return-generating process is the appropriate description of how returns on a security are generated. We prove that the optimum solution involves a combination of factor-matching portfolios and a special portfolio. We show how each of these portfolios is constructed and create an equilibrium pricing model.

In the second part of this section we present some of our research on multiperiod models in finance. The first chapter lays out the framework of analysis used in the latter articles. This article was one of the first applications of dynamic programming in finance and reviews some of the major areas of application. It led ultimately to our book *Finance as a Dynamic Process.*

In the second essay we examine the theoretical optimality of two multiperiod decision criteria. The first is to maximize the utility of multiperiod returns. The second is maximizing the geometric mean return. In both cases, we assume that the goal of portfolio managers is to maximize the expected utility of investors' wealth at some terminal date. In the essay we describe the conditions that under which the decision criteria are optimal and when they fail.

The third chapter explores the applicability of single-period analysis when the investor attempts to maximize the expected utility of lifetime consumption. The results for both separable and nonseparable utility functions are derived. We derive conditions when the single-period analysis is directly appropriate and when the single-period analysis must be modified, and how it needs to be modified.

Single-period Analysis

11

On the Maximization of the Geometric Mean with Log-Normal Return Distribution

Edwin J. Elton and Martin J. Gruber

One criterion for portfolio selection which has received a great deal of attention in the economic literature is the maximization of the geometric mean return (see Samuelson [22], Hakansson [11], Latane [15], and Latane and Tuttle [14]).[1] While this criterion has been advocated by a number of researchers, these same researchers have pointed out that no procedure currently exists for finding that portfolio which maximizes the geometric mean.[2]

The purpose of this paper is to prove the optimality of a procedure which can be used to construct that portfolio of assets which has the highest possible geometric mean return when the returns on portfolios of securities are lognormally distributed.[3] This case is of special interest because of the large body of theoretical and empirical literature which suggests that rates of return are in fact lognormally distributed.[4]

In the first section of this paper, we will discuss circumstances under which the geometric mean is the appropriate decision criterion. In the second section of this paper, we shall show that if returns are lognormally distributed, the portfolio with the highest geometric mean must lie on the efficient frontier in (arithmetic) mean variance space. This not only is important for computational considerations, it also has implications for economic theory.[5] For example, it means that Markowitz-Tobin mean variance analysis is relevant for an investor maximizing the geometric mean, and much of the efficient market literature which depends on investors being on the efficient frontier is relevant. Finally, in the third section, we will show that the portfolio on the efficient frontier which has the highest geometric mean return can be readily defined in terms of the slope of the efficient frontier.

I Conditions for the Optimality of the Geometric Mean

The maximization of geometric mean return has been justified as a criteria for portfolio selection in two ways. First because it can lead to the selection of portfolios with the highest expected utility of terminal wealth, if utility functions are of the log form and second because it leads to the selection of portfolios with intuitively appealing characteristics. We shall examine each of these justifications in turn.

In order to examine the relationship between the geometric mean and the expected utility of terminal wealth we must define some terms.

Let

1. $W_T' =$ the invester's wealth as of a horizon year T, a stochastic variablé,
2. $W_t =$ the investor's initial wealth,
3. $R_{it} =$ a random variable equal to one plus return, (t is a period index and i denotes a particular return),
4. $P_{it} =$ the probability of R_{it} occurring.

Investor's terminal, wealth is equal to $W_T = W_t(R_{it} \cdot R_{it+1} \cdots R_{iT-1}$. If the investor's utility function is of the log form then the utility of terminal wealth is given by

$$\ln W_T = \ln W_t + \ln R_{it} + \ln R_{it+1} + \cdots + \ln R_{iT-1}$$

and the expected utility of terminal wealth is given by

$$E[\ln W_T] = \ln W_t + E[\ln R_{it}] + E[\ln R_{it+1}] + \cdots + E[\ln R_{iT}]_{-1}$$

or

$$E(\ln W_T) = \ln W_t + \sum_i \ln R_{it}^{P_{it}} + \sum_i \ln R_{it+1}^{P_{it+1}} + \cdots + \sum_i \ln R_{iT-1}^{P_{iT-1}}. \tag{1}$$

Since utility functions are unique up to a linear transform we can subtract $\ln W_t$ (a constant) from both sides of the equation and state that the portfolio which maximizes

$$E(\ln(W_T/W_t)) = \sum_i \ln R_{it}^{P_{it}} + \sum_i \ln R_{it+1}^{P_{it+1}} + \cdots + \sum_i \ln R_{iT-1}^{P_{iT-1}}$$

maximizes the expected utility of terminal wealth.

The formula for the single period geometric mean is $\prod_i R_{it}^{P_{it}}$. The single period geometric mean criteria calls for us to select a portfolio in each period (j) so as to maximize this expression. But from expression (1) the expected utility of investor wealth is maximized if

$$\sum_{j=t}^{T-1} \sum_{i} \ln R_{ij}^{P_{ij}} \tag{2}$$

is maximized. If new portfolios can be selected each period, this is equivalent to maximizing $\sum_i \ln R_{ij}^{P_{ij}}$ for all j between t and T.

We can take the antilog of this expression without affecting the maximum, since the antilog is a monotonic transform. Thus, an equivalent criteria is Maximize $\prod_i R_{ij}^{P_{ij}}$ or simply maximize the geometric mean return in every period.[6]

The use of the geometric mean as a decision criteria has also been defended because it produces a series of decisions with intuitively appealing characteristics. To see this let X' = the growth rate (assuming continuous compounding) in capital over the investor's horizon. Then by definition

$$W_T' = W_t \exp(X') \tag{6}$$

or

$$X' = \ln(W_T'/w_t). \tag{7}$$

We saw earlier that the one period geometric mean maximizes the expected value of (7). Thus for a multi-period horizon selecting that portfolio with maximum geometric mean each period, produces the maximum expected growth rate in wealth. Furthermore, as the number of periods over which this decision rule is applied becomes very large, the probability approaches one that the growth rate in wealth produced by the geometric mean decision rule will be higher than the growth rate produced by any other strategy. Several authors have asserted that since maximizing the long term growth rate in wealth should be almost a universal goal, the geometric mean is often (if not always) a proper decision rule for selecting portfolios.[7]

II Maximizing the Geometric Mean and Mean-Variance Efficiency

As discussed earlier, there is substantial empirical evidence supporting an assumption that one plus the return is log normally distributed. Let R_i be one plus return, a variable which is log normally distributed and let:

1. μ be the mean of R_i,
2. σ be the standard deviation of R_i,

3. m be the mean of $\log R_i$,
4. s be the standard deviation of $\log R_i$.

It is well known that there exists a one-to-one mapping between a m, s^2 pair and the corresponding moments of R_i:[8]

$$\mu = \exp(m + \tfrac{1}{2}s^2) \tag{8}$$

$$\sigma^2 = \exp(m + \tfrac{1}{2}s^2)^2[(\exp s^2) - 1]. \tag{9}$$

Utilizing equations (8) and (9) to solve for m in terms of σ and μ yields:

$$m = \ln \mu - \tfrac{1}{2}\ln[(\sigma^2/\mu^2) + 1] \tag{10}$$

Maximizing m, the mean log return is equivalent to maximizing the geometric mean return since, as shown in §1:

(a) when the geometric mean is the appropriate decision criterion, it is sufficient to find that portfolio which maximizes the geometric mean of one period returns even in the context of a multi-period portfolio problem;

(b) the geometric mean is defined as $\prod_i R_i^{P_i}$;

(c) taking the log of the geometric mean does not affect the ranking of portfolios since the log function is a monotonic transformation;

(d) the log of the geometric mean is $\sum_i P_i \ln R_i$ which is the mean log return.

To show that the portfolio that maximizes m is mean-variance efficient, we must show that (for a constant μ), m is increased as σ is decreased and (for a constant σ), m is increased as μ is increased or:

$$\frac{\partial m}{\partial \mu} > 0, \qquad \frac{\partial m}{\partial \sigma} < 0.$$

Utilizing equation (10) we have:

$$\frac{\partial m}{\partial \mu} = \frac{2\sigma^2 + \mu^2}{\mu(\sigma^2 + \mu^2)} \frac{+}{+} = + \qquad \textit{and} \qquad \frac{\partial m}{\partial \sigma} = \frac{-\sigma}{\sigma^2 + \mu^2} = \frac{-}{+} = -$$

where μ is the mean of R_i a lognormally distributed variable. Since μ is the price relative or one plus the rate of return from holding a portfolio, and since the return from a portfolio can never be less than minus one hundred per cent, μ cannot be negative. The variance and standard deviation are of course also positive and thus the derivatives have the appropriate signs. In short, if returns are lognormally distributed, the portfolio that maximizes the geometric mean lies on the efficient frontier in (arithmetic) mean return standard deviation space.[9]

III The Portfolio that Maximizes the Geometric Mean

Having proved that the portfolio with the highest geometric mean is on the efficient frontier, we shall now identify that point on the frontier which provides the highest geometric mean. Letting $\sigma = f(\mu)$ and taking the derivative of equation (10) with respect to μ to obtain the condition for a maximum yields:

$$f'(\mu) = \frac{2f(\mu)}{\mu} + \frac{\mu}{f(\mu)}. \tag{11}$$

Substituting σ for $f(\mu)$, $\partial\sigma/\partial\mu$ for $f'(\mu)$ and rearranging yields

$$\frac{\partial\mu}{\partial\sigma} = \frac{\sigma\mu}{2\sigma^2 + \mu^2} \tag{12}$$

as a condition for an optimum.

The efficient frontier is concave from below.[10] Therefore, the left hand side of (12) $\partial\mu/\partial\sigma$ is monotonically decreasing. The right hand side of (12) $\sigma\mu/(2\sigma^2 + \mu^2)$ first increases and then decreases.[11] This implies that (12) can hold for up to two portfolios. If both portfolios exist, then a comparison between them in terms of the original equation (10) is necessary. If (12) never holds, then one of the end points (minimum variance or maximum return) is optimum.[12]

IV Conclusion

In this paper we have presented a method for determining that portfolio which has the largest geometric mean return when price relatives are lognormally distributed. The determination of this portfolio has major implications for economic theory. Hakansson [11], has shown that in general, maximizing the geometric mean will lead to the selection of portfolios which are not on the efficient frontier in (arithmetic) mean variance space. This implies that Markowitz-Tobin type analysis is not only irrelevant, but misleading for an investor who either (1) has a logarithmic utility function and is facing a single or multi-period portfolio selection problem, or (2) wants to maximize the expected long run growth rate of wealth. Since most tests of efficient markets, evaluation of mutual funds, and descriptive models of investor behavior depend on mean variance efficiency, this is disturbing.

We have shown that when price relatives are log normally distributed, the portfolio which maximizes the geometric mean lies on the efficient frontier in (arithmetic) mean variance space. Thus single period Markowitz-Tobin analysis is consistent with certain types of multi-period problems and with problems involving the maximization of long run growth.

Notes

1. Throughout this paper returns are used to refer to investment relatives (one plus the return). The geometric mean has been advocated by [2], [11], [15], and [16].

2. For example see [11].

3. Empirical evidence that the investment relatives are lognormally distributed for portfolios is provided by Hodges [13]. Kendall [14], Moore [19] and Osborne [21] provide further evidence by their examination of the distribution of price changes of indices. These latter authors have also provided evidence that investment relatives for securities are lognormally distributed. One set of theoretical conditions under which lognormally distributed portfolio returns are consistent with lognormally distributed security returns have been set forth by Merton [18].

4. A disagreement exists today about whether returns are in fact lognormally distributed [14], [19], [21] or follow a stable Paretain distribution [10], [17]. While the resolution of this debate is beyond the scope of this paper, there is sufficient evidence to suggest that deviations from the lognormal distribution are nonexistent or of such a small order of magnitude to make the lognormal case worth further study.

5. It is possible that this problem could be solved more efficiently as a nonlinear programming problem. This could only be determined by direct tests. Two cautions are in order. First, promising techniques such as the gradient method do not reach an optimum in a finite number of steps where our procedure guarantees an optimum in a finite number of iterations. Second, our experience with problems of 80 constraints is that we could produce the full efficient frontier in 2 minutes on a 360-50. If we modify the program for just this problem, time could be somewhat reduced. While no direct comparison is possible, results for nonlinear techniques as reported by Colville [3] would not suggest a computational saving. Actually a combination of an initial solution produced by gradient techniques as a starting solution to a quadratic programming algorithm might be most efficient.

6. An alternative of the geometric mean criterion is to select that portfolio which has the highest expected geometric mean over the multiperiod time horizon under consideration. The conditions under which this leads to the same selection criterion as maximizing a log utility function are derived in Elton and Gruber [4].

7. This line of reasoning has been followed by Latane and Tuttle [15], Latane [16], and Hakansson [11]. The reader should be careful to note that counterarguments have been offered by some authors, e.g., Samuelson [21].

8. In standard portfolio analysis, μ and σ^2 refer to the mean and variance of returns. Here of course they refer to the mean and variance of 1 plus the returns. See [1] for a derivation of (1) and (2).

9. Hakansson [11] has proved that in general the portfolio which has the largest geometric mean is not necessarily mean variance efficient. While this is true in general as just demonstrated in the text, it is not true when returns are lognormally distributed.

10. Proofs that the efficient frontier is concave in arithmetic mean-variance space are numerous and do not depend on the distribution of returns. Rather they depend on the assumption of less than perfect correlation between assets.

11. Implicitly differentiating $\sigma\mu/(2\sigma^2+\mu^2)$ yields $1-(\sigma^2/\mu^2)-2(\sigma^4/\mu^4)$ which can be positive or negative depending upon whether σ/μ is less than or greater than $(1/2)^{1/2}$.

12. With unlimited borrowing at the riskless rate of interest, the end point can be an infinitely levered portfolio.

References

1. Aitchison, John and Brown, James A. C., *The Lognormal Distribution with Special Reference to its Use in Economics*; (Cambridge University), 1957.

2. Broiman, Leo, "Optimal Gambling Systems for Favorable Games," Fourth Berkeley Symposium on Mathematical Statistics and Probability, (Berkeley, University of California Press, 1961).

3. Colville, A. R., "A Comparative Study of Nonlinear Programming Codes," (Kuhn, editor), *Proceedings of the Princeton Symposium on Mathematical Programming*, (Princeton University Press; Princeton, New Jersey), 1970.

4. Elton, Edwin J. and Gruber, Martin J., "On the Optimality of Some Multi-period Portfolio Selection Criteria," Forthcoming in *Journal of Business*.

5. ——— and ———, "Estimating the Dependence structure of Share Prices—Implications for Portfolio Selection," Vol. 28, No. 5 (Dec. 1973), pp. 1203–1232. *Journal of Finance*.

6. ——— and ———, "Portfolio Theory When Investment Relatives are Lognormally Distributed," Forthcoming in *Journal of Finance*.

7. ——— and ———, "The Multi-period Portfolio Problem—Implications for the Optimality of Single Period Decision Rules," Forthcoming in *Oxford Economic Papers*.

8. Fama, Eugene F., and Miller, Merton H., *The Theory of Finance*, (Holt, Rinehart and Winston), 1972.

9. ———, "Portfolio Analysis in a Stable Paretain Market," *Management Science*, Vol. 11, No. 3, (1965), pp. 404–419.

10. ———, "The Behavior of Stock Princes," *Journal of Business*, Vol. 38, No. 1, (1965).

11. Hakansson, Nils H., "Capital Growth and the Mean-Variance Approach to Portfolio Selection," *Journal of Financial and Quantitative Analysis*, Vol. VI, No. 1, (1971), pp. 517–558.

12. ———, "An Induced Theory of the Firm Under Risk: The Pure Mutual Fund," *Journal of Financial and Quantitative Analysis*, (June, 1970).

13. Hodges, Stewart, "On Operational Model for Portfolio Selection," Ph.D. Thesis, University of London, 1972.

14. Kendall, M. G., "The Analysis of Economic Time Series," *Journal of the Royal Statistical Society*, (Ser. A) XCVI, (1953), pp. 11–25.

15. Latane, Henry and Tuttle, Donald, *Security Analysis and Portfolio Management*, (The Ronald Press), 1970.

16. Latane, Henry, "Criteria for Choice Among Risky Ventures," *Journal of Political Economy*, (April 1959).

17. Mandelbrot, Benoit, "The Variation of Certain Speculative Prices," *Journal of Business*, Vol. 36, No. 4, (1963), pp. 394–419.

18. Merton, Robert, "Optimal Consumption and Portfolio Rules in a Continuous Time Model," *Journal of Economic Theory*, Vol. 3, No. 4, (December 1971), pp. 373–413.

19. Moore, Arnold, "A Statistical Analysis of Common Stock Prices," unpublished doctoral dissertation (Graduate School of Business, University of Chicago, 1962).

20. Mossin, Jan, "Optimal Multi-period Portfolio Policies," *Journal of Business*, Vol. 41, (April 1968), pp. 215–219.

21. Osborne, M. F. M., "Brownian Motion in the Stock Market," Operations Research, Vol. VII, (1959), pp. 145–173.

22. Samuelson, Paul, "Lifetime Portfolio Selection by Dynamic Stochastic Programming," *Review of Economics and Statistics*, Vol. LI, (August, 1969), pp. 139–146.

12

Portfolio Theory When Investment Relatives Are Log-Normally Distributed

Edwin J. Elton and Martin J. Gruber

Portfolio theory as first presented by Markowitz [10] and Tobin [16] has been shown to be correct under either of two assumptions:[1]

(1) returns are normally distributed.

(2) the investor's utility function is quadratic.

The assumption of a quadratic utility function has been questioned by a number of authors because of its implications of decreasing absolute risk aversion.[2] On the other hand, the assumption of normally distributed returns has been questioned because return distributions must be bounded from below and because empirical evidence suggests that returns are not normally distributed.[3] The current controversy over the probability distribution of returns revolves around whether one plus return is log-normally distributed or follows a stable paretian distribution.[4] Under either of these assumptions, combined with the unrealistic implications of the quadratic utility function standard portfolio theory is inapplicable.[5]

However, if investment relatives are distributed either lognormally or distributed according to a stable paretian distribution, then portfolio theory can be reformulated. Fama [4] [5] has gone a long way towards a reformulation under the assumption of stable paretian distributions. In this paper, we propose to reformulate portfolio theory under the assumption that investment relatives are lognormally distributed. This reformulation is extremely important given both the multitude of areas within economics where portfolio models have found applications and the increasing acceptance of the log-normality of price relatives in the economic literature.

This paper is divided into three sections. The first derives an efficient set theorem (analogous to the original Markowitz theorem) when portfolios are located in log space. The second section provides an algorithm for calculating such an efficient frontier. Finally, the last section proves

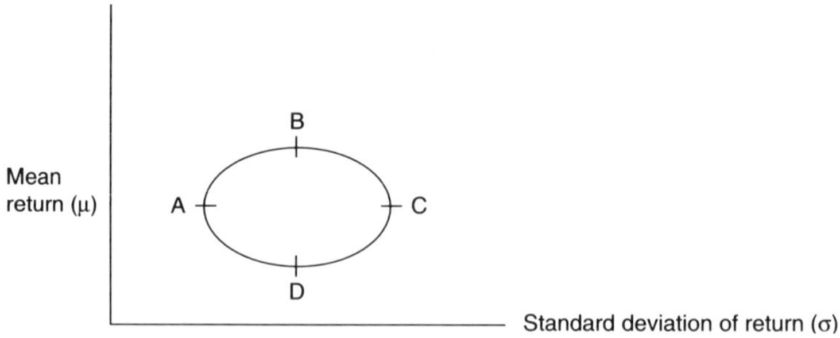

Figure 12.1

that if utility functions exhibit decreasing marginal utility of wealth, then utility curves are convex from below in log space.

I The Efficient Set Theorem

The infinite set of possible portfolios is represented diagrammatically in Figure 12.1. Tobin [16] has shown that if returns are normally distributed and investors exhibit positive marginal utility of wealth, the only portfolios which could possibly maximize the one period utility of wealth lie on the upper left hand border AB.[6] This subset of portfolios is characterized by portfolios that:

1. Maximize expected return for any level of standard deviation of return.
2. Minimize standard deviation of return for any level of expected return.

These characteristics are called the efficient set theorem.

As discussed above, theory and empirical evidence suggest that investment relatives are more likely to be lognormally distributed than normally distributed. Consequently, an efficient set theorem, when investment relatives are lognormally distributed, is highly desirable.[7] In this section we will prove that when investment relatives are lognormally distributed, there is an analogous efficient set theorem which can be derived in mean log investment relative (m), standard deviation of log investment relative (s) space. In order to derive this efficient set theorem, it is only necessary to assume that utility functions exhibit positive marginal utility of wealth. With this assumption, it can be shown that the optimum portfolio lies on the boundary of all portfolios examined in mean log investment relative, standard deviation of log investment relative space. Or that (see Figure 12.2) there is always a portfolio somewhere on the curve A' B' C' D' which is preferred to an interior point. In this section, we shall first prove that

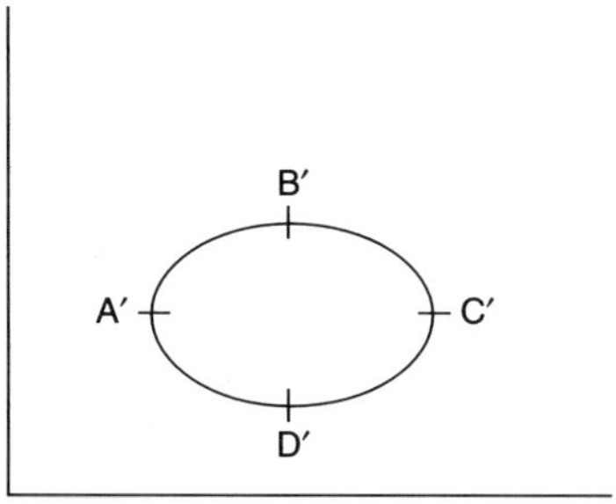

Figure 12.2

some boundary point always maximizes expected utility and then we shall determine that portion of the boundary curve A B C D which dominates all other portfolios.

If the investment relative is lognormally distributed, m is the mean of log r and s is the standard deviation of log r, then $z = (\log r - m)/s$ is normally distributed with mean of zero and standard deviation of one. The frequency function of z is well known and stationary in z, $f(z)$ space.[8]

In other words, if we standardize the log of a lognormal variable by subtracting m and dividing by s, the standardized variable z has a known distribution that is only dependent on the value of the standardized variable itself. Having derived a standardized variate, it is now possible to prove an efficient set theorem. Let:

1. $U(w_1)$ represent a one period utility function for terminal wealth.
2. $E[\ ]$ be the expected value operator.
3. w_t be wealth at t.

Since r is one plus the return on the investment portfolio, w_1 can be written as $w_0 r$.

If we let $z = (\log r - m)/s$, then $\log r = m + sz$ and w_1 is equal to[9]

$$w_1 = w_0 r = w_0 e^{m+sz}. \tag{1}$$

Expected utility of wealth can be expressed as:

$$E[U(w_1)] = \int_{-\infty}^{+\infty} U(w_0 e^{m+sz}) f(z)\, dz. \tag{2}$$

Note once again that the frequency function for the standardized variate only depends on z. Therefore, differences between the expected utilities of various portfolios are only a function of m and s, or formally $E[U(w_1)] = f(m, s)$.

Using the chain rule to take the derivative of (2) with respect to m for a fixed value of s yields

$$\frac{\partial E[U(w_1)]}{\partial m} = w_0 \int_{-\infty}^{+\infty} \frac{\partial U(w_1)}{\partial w_1} e^{m+sz} f(z)\, dz.$$

This integral is positive for all values of m: since e to any power is positive, $(\partial U(w_1))/\partial w_1$ is positive since investors are assumed to prefer more wealth to less, and $f(z)$ can only take on positive values.

A positive integral means that expected utility is maximized if m is maximized. We have completed our derivation of the analogy to the first part of the efficient set theorem, namely: maximize the expected value of the log of relative price (m) for any level of standard deviation of log price (s).

Taking the derivative of (2) with respect to s for a fixed value of m yields:

$$\frac{\partial E[U(w_1)]}{\partial s} \int_{-\infty}^{+\infty} \frac{\partial U(w_1) w_1}{\partial w_1} z f(z)\, dz. \tag{3}$$

Since $f(z)$ is symmetric about zero, (3) can be positive, negative or zero depending on whether $(\partial U(w_1)w_1)/\partial w_1$ increases, decreases or is constant as wealth changes.

Consider Figure 12.2. The derivative of expected utility with respect to m is positive; therefore, only the points on the border $A'B'C'$ can be efficient. The derivative of expected utility with respect to s has the same sign as the derivative of $(\partial U(w_1)w_1)/\partial w_1$. If the derivative of $(\partial U(w_1)w_1)/\partial w_1$ is negative, then $A'B'$ is the efficient set; if it is zero, then B' is the efficient *point*; and if it is positive, then $B'C'$ is the efficient set.[10] This completes the derivation of an efficient set theorem.

Before leaving this section it is worthwhile to examine briefly the types of utility functions for which $(\partial U(w_1)w_1)/\partial w_1$ is increasing, constant or decreasing. Taking the derivative of this expression yields:

$$\frac{\partial U(w_1)}{\partial w_1} + w_1 \frac{\partial^2 U(w_1)}{\partial^2 w_1} \gtreqless 0.$$

Rearranging yields:

$$\frac{-w_1 U''(w_1)}{U(w_1)} \lesseqgtr 1.$$

The above is the function for relative risk aversion as formulated by Pratt [15] and Arrow [2]. For utility functions which exhibit constant relative risk aversion, the relationship of the above to one is constant. If an investor has a utility function which does not exhibit constant relative risk aversion, the relative risk aversion function might pass through one. This implies that for these functions an optimum can occur on different sections of the efficient frontier depending on the investor's wealth level.

II Computing an Efficient Frontier

In the previous section we showed that utility is maximized if m is made as large as possible for any value of s. It is well known that a one-to-one mapping exists between points in m, s space, and points in μ, σ space.[11] The relationships are

$$\mu = e^{m+s^2/2}, \quad \text{and} \tag{4}$$

$$\sigma^2 = (e^{m+s^2/2})^2(e^{s^2} - 1). \tag{5}$$

The loci of points of constant s can be plotted in μ, σ space by examining the equation

$$s = \left[\ln\left(\frac{\sigma^2}{\mu^2} + 1\right)\right]^{1/2} = c \quad \text{(a constant)}$$

for different values of c. Rearranging yields

$$\mu = \frac{1}{[e^{c^2} - 1]^{1/2}}\sigma$$

which is the equation of a family of straight lines emanating from the origin in μ, σ space (see Figure 12.3). The preferred portfolio on a ray of constant s is the one that maximized m.

$$m = \log\mu - s^2/2.$$

If s is constant, then m is made as large as possible by maximizing μ. Thus, μ is maximized by moving as far from the origin as possible along a ray of constant s. Examine the ray $O\ A\ Y$. Portfolio Y dominates portfolio A and all other portfolios along the line $O\ A\ Y$, for although is has the same value of s, it has a higher value of μ and thus a higher value of m. Similarly, the efficient set in μ, σ space can be defined by examining all rays emanating from the origin, and for each ray selecting that feasible portfo-

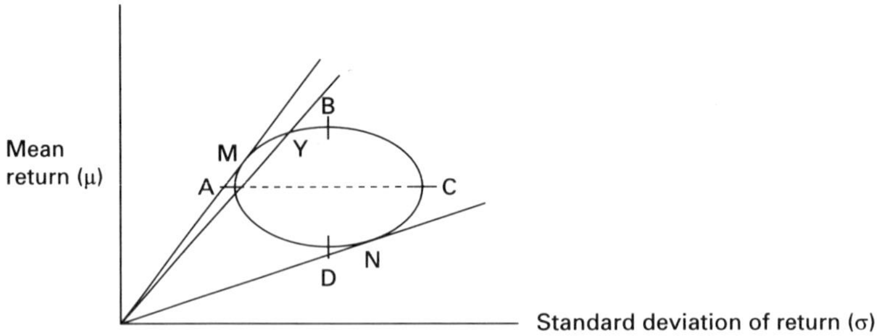

Figure 12.3

lio which lies furthest from the origin. Thus in Figure 12.3 the efficient set lies along the boundary curve $M\ B\ C\ N$. The points M and N are the two tangency points of the rays of constant s and the boundary curve of all feasible portfolios. The point M can be alternatively defined as that portfolio with the maximum attainable ratio of μ to σ. The point N can be alternatively defined as that portfolio with the lowest attainable ratio of μ to σ. The efficient set in μ, σ space has now been defined as $M\ B\ C\ N$. Note that the efficient set in μ, σ space, when returns are lognormally distributed, is considerable different from the efficient set when returns are normally distributed. The efficient set with lognormal returns may not contain some portfolios which are efficient when returns are normally distributed (the region $A\ M$) but it contains additional portfolios in the region $B\ C\ N$. Since all of the portfolios which are efficient in m, s space lie on a boundary in μ, σ space, the efficient frontier in m, s space can be constructed by first constructing the boundary in μ, σ space.

The boundary in μ, σ space can be calculated by solving three quadratic programming problems.[12]

1. Maximize $\mu - \lambda\sigma$.
2. Maximize $\mu + \lambda\sigma$.
3. Maximize $-\mu + \lambda\sigma$.

The efficient set can then be found by employing the tangency condition discussed above to delete part of the boundary.

III The Convexity of Utility Curves

In the section we will prove that if investors exhibit decreasing marginal utility of wealth, utility functions must be convex from below in expected

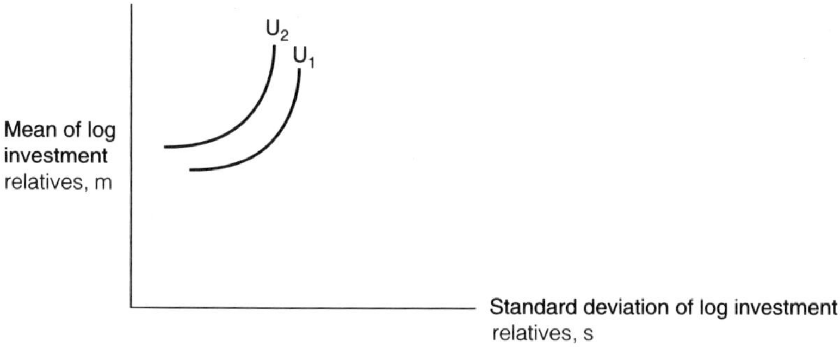

Figure 12.4

log investment relative (m), standard deviation of log investment relative (s) space.

Figure 12.4 represents a hypothetical indifference map in m, s space. While we do not as yet know that utility functions are convex from below, we do know from a previous section (see Section I), that utility increases as we move up in m, s space. For example, points along U_2 represent a higher level of utility than points along U_1.[13] Let us select two points on U_1 and call them (m, s), (m', s'). If we let $m''s''$ represent a portfolio on the line connecting $m's'$ and m, s, then the portfolio will have coordinates:

$$[m'', s''] = [xm + (1 - x)m', xs + (1 - x)s']0 < x < 1. \tag{6}$$

If the utility of this combined portfolio is greater than U_1, then utility functions are convex from below.

Let w_{1i} be a particular outcome of w_1, the terminal wealth from investing in the portfolio with an expected log investment relative and standard deviation of log investment relative given by (m, s). Then from equation (1):

$$w_{1i} = w_0 e^{m \div sz_i} \tag{7}$$

Similarly:

$$w'_{1i} = w_0 e^{m' \div s'z_i} \tag{8}$$

Define w''_{1i} as shown in equation (9)

$$\log w''_{1i} = x \log w_{1i} + (1 - x) \log w'_{1i} \tag{9}$$

As will be apparent shortly, this definition of w''_{1i} yields a point on the line connecting $m\ s$ and $m's'$. Substituting equation (7) and (8) into (9) and employing equation (6) yields:

$$w''_{1i} = w_0 e^{m'' \div s'' z_i} \tag{10}$$

This is a point on the line connecting $m\ s$ and $m's'$. Subtracting $\log w_0$ from both sides of equation (9) and noting that $(x) + (1 - x) = 1$, we have:

$$\log w''_{1i} - \log w_0 = x \log w_{1i} - x \log w_0 + (1 - x) \log w'_{1i} - (1 - x) \log w_0.$$

This simplifies to

$$\log \frac{w''_{1i}}{w_0} = x \log \frac{w_{1i}}{w_0} + (1 - x) \log \frac{w'_{1i}}{w_0}. \tag{11}$$

From the assumption that investors exhibit decreasing marginal utility of wealth employing equation (11) we know that[14]

$$U\left[\log \frac{w''_{1i}}{w_0}\right] > xU\left[\log \frac{w_{1i}}{w_0}\right] + (1 - x)U\left[\log \frac{w'_{1i}}{w_0}\right]. \tag{12}$$

Substituting equations (7), (8) and (10) into equation (12) yields

$$U(m'' + s''z_i) > xU(m + sz_i) + (1 - x)U(m' + s'z_i). \tag{13}$$

Taking the expected value of (13) cannot change the sign of the inequality since the density function of z is non-negative for all values of z. Therefore:

$$E[U(m'' + s''z)] > xE[U(m + sz)] + (1 - x)E[U(m' + s'z)]. \tag{14}$$

Since both terms on the right side of the inequality have the same utility (U_1), an average of the two terms must have the same utility U_1. Therefore,

$$E[U(m'' + s''z)] > U_1$$

or the utility curves are convex from below in m, s space.[15]

IV Conclusion

In this paper under the assumptions of lognormally distributed investment relatives and positive marginal utility of wealth, we have:

1. derived an efficient set theorem in log investment relative, standard deviation of log investment relative space.

2. presented an algorithm for determining the portfolios in this efficient set.

3. derived the surface in μ, σ space along which the optimum portfolios must lie.

4. demonstrated that utility curves in log investment relative, standard deviation of log investment relative space must be convex from below if investors exhibit decreasing utility of wealth.

Notes

The authors would like to thank Larry Ritter for helpful comments and suggestions.

1. See Feldstein [7] and Tobin [16].

2. See Pratt [15], and Mossin [13].

3. See [6].

4. One plus return is usually defined as the investment relative assuming re-investment of dividends. We shall refer to this as an investment relative throughout the rest of this paper. For a discussion of this controversy, See [6], [8], [9], [11] and [14].

5. For example, if price relatives follow a non-normal stable paretian distribution standard, deviations are not a meaningful measure of risk (variances are infinite). On the other hand, as Feldstein [7] has shown, if price relatives are lognormally distributed, then utility functions are not necessarily convex from below in arithmetic mean variance space, and a unique maximum need not exist.

6. Other assumptions can be used to derive the efficient set theorem. They involve restricting the utility function so that it is concave and increasing to the left, (e.g., Fama and Miller [4] pp. 224).

7. Empirical evidence that the investment relatives are lognormally distributed for portfolios is provided by Kendall [8], Moore [12] and Osborne [14] in their examination of the distribution of price changes of indices. These same authors have also provided evidence that investment relatives for securities are lognormally distributed. Alternative sets of theoretical conditions under which lognormally distributed portfolio returns are consistent with lognormally distributed security returns are set forth by Merton [11] and Aitchison and Brown [1] page 110.

8. This statement might at first seem contrary to Feldstein [7]. Feldstein's point is that if z were set equal to the investment relative minus its mean divided by its standard deviation $(r-\mu)/\sigma$, the distribution of z would not be the same for all lognormal distributions. But by working in log space and defining z in terms of log returns, we have defined a variable which is the same for all lognormal distributions.

9. w_1 is lognormally distributed since w_0 is a known constant and r is lognormally distributed. The product of a constant and a lognormal variate is a new variable which is lognormally distributed.

10. An algorithm for determining the composition of portfolio B is contained in Elton and Gruber [3].

11. See (1) for the derivation of this relationship.

12. We have resorted to this algorithm for constructing the efficient set since there is no algorithm (short of complete enumeration) for directly constructing the efficient set in log space. For example, substituting the $\log r_i$ for r_i and variance of $\log r_i$ for variance r_i for each security and solving the quadratic programming problem will not lead to optimum portfolios since the $\log r_i + \log r_j \neq \log(r_i + r_j)$.

13. As shown in Section I, the utility could equally well increase as we move up to the right rather than up to the left. The proof of convexity is the same in either case.

14. This statement is true since $\log w_1''/w_0$ is a weighted average of $\log w_1/w_0$ and $\log w_1'/w_0$. We know that for a utility function which involves decreasing marginal utility, the utility of a weighted average will always be greater than the weighted average of the utility of the two numbers being averaged. Note that a proof like Tobin's [16] proof holds only when all outcomes are positive in the appropriate space.

15. We should point out a seeming inconsistency between our proof and Feldstein's [6] proof that utility functions are not necessarily convex from below in mean standard deviation space when returns are lognormally distributed. The basis of Feldstein's proof is that the unit normal variate only exists in mean, standard deviation space when returns are normally distributed. But when returns are lognormally distributed, the unit normal variate does exist in mean log and standard deviation log space. Just as utility functions are convex in mean return standard deviation space when returns are normally distributed, they are convex in mean log return, standard deviation log return space when returns are lognormally distributed.

References

1. John Aitschison and James A. C. Brown. *The Lognormal Distribution with Special Reference to its Use in Economics* (Cambridge University Press), 1957.

2. K. J. Arrow. *Aspects of the Theory of Risk-Bearing* (Yrjo Jahnsson Lectures, Helsinki, The Yrjo Jahnsson Foundation), 1965.

3. Edwin J. Elton and Martin, J. Gruber. "An Algorithm for Maximizing the Geometic Mean," Unpublished manuscript, New York University.

4. Eugene E. Fama and Merton H. Miller. *The Theory of Finance* (Holt, Rinehart and Winston), 1972.

5. Eugene F. Fama. "Portfolio Analysis in a Stable Paretian Market," *Management Science*, Vol. 11, No. 3 (January 1965), pp. 404–419.

6. Eugene F. Fama. "The Behavior of Stock Prices," *Journal of Business*, Vol. 38, No. 1 (July 1965), pp. 34–105.

7. M. Feldstein. "Mean Variance Analysis in the Theory of Liquidity Preference and Portfolio Selection," *Review of Economic Studies*, 1969, pp. 5–12.

8. M. G. Kendall. "The Analysis of Economic Time Series," *Journal of the Royal Statistical Society*, (ser. A) XCVI, (1953), pp. 11–25.

9. Benoit Mandelbrot. "The Variation of Certain Speculative Prices," *Journal of Business,* Vol. 36, No. 4 (October 1963), pp. 394–419.

10. H. Markowitz. *Portfolio Selection* (John Wiley: New York, New York), 1959.

11. Robert Merton. "Optimum Consumption and Portfolio Rules in a Continuous-time Model," *Journal of Economic Theory,* Vol. 2, No. 4 (December, 1971) pp. 373–413.

12. Arnold Moore. "A Statistical Analysis of Common Stock Prices," Unpublished doctoral dissertation (Graduate School of Business, University of Chicago), 1962.

13. J. Mossin. "Optimal Multi-Period Portfolio Policies," *The Journal of Business* (April 1968), pp. 215–229.

14. M. F. M. Osborne. "Brownian Motion in the Stock Market," *Operations Research,* Vol. VII (March–April 1959), pp. 145–173.

15. J. Pratt. "Risk Aversion in the Small and in the Large," *Econometrica,* Vol. XXXII, No. 1–2 (January–April, 1964), pp. 122–136.

16. J. Tobin. "Liquidity Preference as Behavior Towards Risks," *Review of Economic Studies,* Vol. XXV, No. 67 (February 1958), pp. 65–87.

13

Optimal Investment Strategies with Investor Liabilities

Edwin J. Elton and Martin J. Gruber

I Introduction

The viewpoint taken in this paper is that of a financial intermediary which has incurred one or more liabilities, wishes to allocate funds among a set of assets, and is concerned with changes in net worth.[1] This is a significant departure from traditional analysis. Traditional analysis has largely proceeded in one of two ways. Much of investment theory and analysis is concerned only with allocation among assets and assumes this allocation can be made without consideration of liabilities.[2] Almost all of the standard references on modern portfolio theory treat the problem in this way.[3] On the other hand, the literature that incorporates liabilities in the investment decision such as the duration literature uses, as an objective function, ending wealth and ignores period by period changes in wealth.[4] We feel that the inclusion of liabilities and the focus on changes in net worth are important modifications of the prior literature. The bulk of this paper is concerned with deriving the new insights that are produced by viewing the problem in this way. For example, this framework allows us to examine in great detail the role of cash flow matching and duration matching as part of an investor's portfolio. As Nelson and Schaefer (1983) point out, while these strategies are widely used, no theory exists on why investors should utilize them.

The paper evolved from extensive observation of the behavior of a number of financial intermediaries. These intermediaries manage an enormous amount of pension assets for companies. Many intermediaries place some clients' assets in actively managed accounts, some in duration matched accounts and some in a cash flow matched account. An intermediary can simply use a quadratic program to solve for an optimum overall portfolio by treating the pension liabilities as negative assets.[5] However, most pension clients require the economic intuition behind the choice and mixture of alternative types of active and passive accounts. This paper is the first to treat analytically the choice between duration matched, cash flow matched portfolios and active portfolios. It is a rigorous attempt to answer questions as to why and when an investor should use various passive techniques versus active techniques to manage funds.[6] In addition, financial intermediaries need to know how to design commingled funds and if they are harming their clients if they do so. This paper answers these questions. The answers we obtain are in many cases quite different from current beliefs.

This paper is divided into three sections. In section 2 we explore why change in net worth is a suitable decision criterion for many investors, and present a general framework of analysis consistent with this decision criterion. In section 3 we examine the efficient frontier facing the investor who limits investments to those which have the same duration as liabilities. While this self-imposed constraint can lead to suboptimization, it is worth examining because it represents the way in which many institutions operate. Section 4, the longest section of this paper, deals with optimum bond portfolio strategies in general. In this section the appropriate role of cash flow matching and duration matching investments as part of an overall bond portfolio are examined and analytical results obtained. Cases where all assets are in equilibrium and cases where some assets are out of equilibrium are studied. In addition, general solutions and solutions where short sales are restricted are examined. Explicit solutions for optimal portfolios are derived and the implications of these solutions for investor behavior are examined. While in this paper we restrict our analysis to bonds, the framework developed and many of our conclusions would hold even with the inclusion of other types of assets.

II Framework of Analysis

Let us start by examining why one might want to view the allocation problem in terms of changes in net worth. Consider three types of financial institutions, where asset-liability planning is common: insurance companies, pension funds, and banks.

Why should insurance compaines care about period to period changes in net worth rather than net worth at one particular date in the future? First, most insurance companies hope to exist into the indefinite future and do not plan a finite termination date. While at any point in time the stream of existing liabilities may terminate, as time passes new ones are added and the institution hopes this process will continue indefinitely.

Second, for most insurance companies the period by period value of their net worth affects their ability to survive and do business. An insurance company with negative net worth is insolvent even though its investment policy might result in positive net worth subsequently. Third, regulators directly tie an insurance company's ability to engage in new business to its net worth.[7] Thus, changes in net worth are a relevant variable to focus on for an important class of intermediaries.

As a second example of an intermediary where value at the horizon is often suggested as an objective function, consider a pension fund. Once again, at any point in time the liabilities have a finite termination date, but as time passes, new liabilities are added so that for most pension funds the time horizon stretches into the indefinite future. Even pension funds for retired employees where a finite termination date is reasonable should care about changes in net worth. Current accounting standards (FAS 87) call for both assets and liabilities to be recorded at market value and define procedures so that a short fall in market value of assets relative to liabilities results in adverse events for the pension fund. More particularly, failure to have assets with market values at least equal to liabilities leads to differences flowing through to the income statment of the corporation sponsoring the pension fund and results in additional payments to the fund. Thus a focus on net worth and changes in net worth is appropriate for pension funds.

Both the literature on banking and practice of banks support awareness of change in net worth as an appropriate decision criteria for decision making. For example, Grammatikos et al. (1986) specifically use the expected value of and variance of net worth as a decision framework when analyzing issues concerning US banks' foreign currency position. In addition, the Federal Home Loan Banks Board (FHLBB, 1983) has argued for the use of duration gaps as a measure to set insurance premiums for S & Ls. The analysis in this paper is very much in the spirit of both of these themes in the banking literature in that the relationship between return and risk defined in terms of net worth and of duration as a risk measure will be explicatively studied and analytical results obtained.

The argument we have made for insurance companies, pension funds and banks should apply to most financial intermediaries and many individuals. In the rest of the paper we will focus on changes in net worth. With this framework we can now develop the analysis. Let

A = an initial sum of money which can be invested,

L = the present value of the liabilities facing a firm,

R_1 = the one period spot rate,

R_A = the rate of return on assets, a random variable,[8]

R_L = the rate of return on liabilities, a random variable,

W_0 = initial net worth,

W_1 = net worth at the end of period 1,

R_N = rate of return on net worth.

The initial net worth is the asset position minus the present value of the liabilities.[9] Note that the liabilities may be payable many period in the future. In symbols $W_0 = A - L$. The rate of return the manager earns on net worth is:[10]

$$R_N = \frac{W_1}{W_0} - 1 = \frac{A(1 + R_A) - L(1 + R_L)}{(A - L)} - 1.$$

Let us examine a riskless strategy from the investor's standpoint.

2a *Riskless Portfolio*

Assume the investor has designed a portfolio of default free assets with cash flows which exactly match the cash outflows associated with the liabilities.[11] We will assume that liabilities are priced at their market value as if they were tradable assets. Pricing at market value is consistent with regulatory intent and much of regulatory practice. It is also consistent with the way investment advisors analyze pension plans and is consistent with FAS 87 regarding the valuation of pension liabilities.[12] With this assumption, the law of one price implies that the return on these assets must match the return on the liabilities or $R_A = R_L$. Furthermore, the cost of these assets must equal the present value of the liabilities and an exact match portfolio will cost L dollars. If A is larger than L and the remainder is put in the one period pure discount bond the return on the portfolio is:

$$R_N = \frac{(A - L)(1 + R_1) + L(1 + R_A) - L(1 + R_L)}{A - L} - 1 = R_1.$$

Thus the manager is guaranteed the one period spot rate and the risk of the portfolio is zero.

In traditional analysis a one period government bill is considered the riskless investment. When liabilities are considered, the riskless strategy is no longer a single instrument but rather a portfolio of 'risky assets' plus the one period government bill.[13] The return on the riskless investment has not changed but the construction of the riskless portfolio has. In subsequent sections we will use R_F to designate the return on the riskless portfolio where $R_F = R_1$.

2b Combinations of the Riskless Portfolio and Risky Assets

It is convenient for purposes of future analysis to show that in this setting all combinations of the riskless portfolio and a risky portfolio lie along a straight line passing through the riskless rate in expected return-standard deviation space. If this statement seems familiar, it is. It is one of the basic tenets of portfolio analysis. What is different in this context is that the definition of the riskless portfolio is not 100% of assets in the one period pure discount government bill, and the return on the risky portfolio is different from and more complex than the return on the risky portfolio in standard analysis.

To show the linearity let R_Y be the return on the combination of the risky portfolio and the riskless portfolio. The return on a portfolio consisting of only investment in risky assets is:

$$R_N = \frac{A(1+R_A) - L(1+R_L)}{(A-L)} - 1 = R_A + \frac{L(R_A - R_L)}{(A-L)}. \tag{1}$$

Note the return on the portfolio depends not only on the return earned on the risky assets, it depends on the difference in return between the assets and the liabilities and the amount by which assets exceed liabilities.

If this portfolio is combined with the riskless portfolio then

$$R_Y = XR_F + (1-X)\left[R_A + \frac{L(R_A - R_L)}{(A-L)}\right],$$

where X equals the fraction of the funds invested in the riskless portfolio, which is a combination of liabilities, the one period spot rate, and the cash flow matched portfolio. Employing this equation to solve for the expected value and variance of the return on portfolio Y (arguing that R_F has zero variance and zero covariance with all other investments) and using the equations for variance to eliminate X from the equation we find:[14]

$$\bar{R}_Y = R_F - \left[\frac{\bar{R}_N - R_F}{\sigma_N}\right]\sigma_Y, \tag{2}$$

where σ indicates standard deviation.

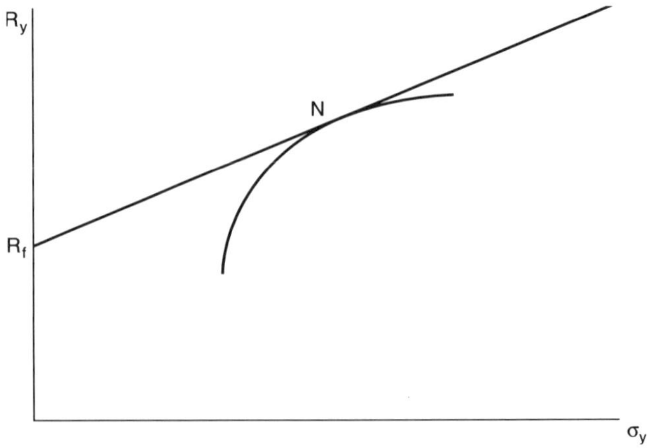

Figure 13.1

Eq. (2) is a straight line and has the same functional form as the capital market line in standard portfolio theory. What is different is the $\bar{R}_N$ and σ_N depend on both the return on assets and the return on liabilities as well as the ratio of assets to liabilities held by any investor. [See eq. (1).] In particular R_N has a standard deviation which depends on the standard deviation of the return on the assets, the return on the liabilities and the relative size of the two. Even in a world of homogeneous expectations, eq. (2) implies that alternative investors will face different efficient frontiers. If combinations of the riskless portfolio and risky portfolio lie on a straight line in expected return-standard deviation space, then the efficient frontier becomes the straight line passing through the riskless portfolio which is tangent to the efficient frontier of risky assets (see fig. 13.1). It is important to note that different investors can face different efficient frontiers not only because of heterogeneous beliefs but also (unlike traditional analysis) because of different liabilities.

It is possible that point N is optimal. However, most investors will want to combine some exact matching and one period instruments with the optimal risky portfolio. Thus, almost all investors should place some money in a cash flow matched portfolio. We will now turn to a more detailed examination of the efficient frontier of risky assets depicted in fig. 13.1. We shall first examine its composition when investments are restricted to duration matched strategies. Subsequently we will examine the more general case.

III The Efficient Frontier of Duration Matched Strategies

In this section we will examine the efficient frontier when the investor restricts the choices to immunized strategies. Although this restriction may lead to suboptimal decisions, many financial intermediaries operate under this self imposed constraint. For example, many pension funds hire insurance companies to construct a set of assets to immunize a fixed set of liabilities. In the next section we will relax this assumption and explore more general solutions. For the time being we will assume that management has decided to duration match (immunize) and to restrict themselves to holding some combinations of[15]

1. a riskless portfolio, as defined in the previous section, with return R_F,
2. a one period pure discount instruments with return R_1,
3. a portfolio of risky assets with return R_A.

By considering both the one period pure discount instrument and the riskless portfolio we allow any combination of the cash flow matched portfolio and one period pure discount instrument to be held. Thus adding a cash flow matched portfolio would be redundant. Returns are assumed to follow a one factor linear return-generating process of the form:

$$R_i = R_1 + D_i I + e_i. \tag{3}$$

To be completely general we are allowing the mean of I to be nonzero. This allows for the possibility of a term premium on bond returns. Elsewhere [Elton and Gruber (1989)] we have shown that while this type of return generating process is a very reasonable representation of returns due to shifts in the term structure as well as other sources of return, in general, a multi-index model is necessary. In this paper we will, for simplicity, use a single factor model. The generalization to a multifactor model is trivial analytically and should be obvious to the reader. Furthermore, expected returns are assumed to be given by either

$$\bar{R}_i = R_1 + D_i \bar{I}, \tag{4a}$$

or

$$\bar{R}_i = \alpha_i + R_1 + D_i \bar{I}. \tag{4b}$$

The interpretation of these equations is that the investor chooses to measure risk as a function of sensitivity to an index [e.g., duration in eq. (3)]

and that the return on assets may be [eq. (4a)] or may not be [eq. (4b)] in equilibrium as implied by arbitrage pricing theory. For example, temporary mispricing of a particular issue or issues in the bond market could cause a bond to have a positive or negative α_i in eq. (4b). Thus, the assumption underlying eqs. (3) and (4) is a one factor linear return-generating process where the investor is interested in immunizing against this source of risk and where a subset of bonds may be believed to offer a return above or below the equilibrium return.

We will assume that any mispricing occurs in assets and that liabilities will be fairly priced. We will continue to use the subscript A to stand for all assets and L for the market value (present value) of liabilities. We will also assume that at time zero $(A - L) > 0$ or that the decision maker is solvent.

Before developing the efficient frontier we need to discuss what we mean by duration matching and immunized portfolios. The return on net worth of a combination of risky assets and liabilities is:

$$R_N = \frac{AR_A - LR_L}{(A - L)}.$$

Substituting eq. (3) for R_A and R_L and rearranging we have:

$$R_N = \frac{(AR_1 - LR_1) + (AD_A - LD_L)I + Ae_A - Le_L}{(A - L)}.$$

A duration matched portfolio is a portfolio of assets and liabilities which has zero sensitivity to the factor I. This condition requires that

$$AD_A - LD_L = 0,$$

or

$$D_A = \frac{L}{A} D_L.$$

Portfolios of assets that meet this condition will be designated as duration matched or immunized portfolios. Note that immunization does not involve holding assets with an average duration equal to that of liabilities, rather the duration of liabilities must be adjusted by the ratio of liabilities to assets.

Note that combinations of duration matched portfolios and the riskless portfolio are still duration matched since each portfolio by itself is immunized. In order to clarify the subsequent analysis we shall use the term duration matched portfolio to stand for all *risky* duration matched portfolios. We now examine the combination of the riskless portfolio, the duration matched portfolio of risky assets, and the one period pure discount instrument. The following propositions hold:

PROPOSITION 1 If $\alpha_A = 0$ then the efficient frontier is a single point which represents the riskless portfolio. While investors will place some investment in the cash flow matched portfolio they will not place any funds in any other duration matched portfolio.

We will assume that a portfolio of risky assets can be constructed with any duration and that eqs. (3) and (4a) hold for each such portfolio. Employing eq. (3) along with eq. (4a) we find the return of an investment X in a portfolio of risky assets and $(1 - X)$ in the pure discount bond such that the duration on the combination equals the duration of the liabilities is:

$$R_N = \frac{A(1-X)R_1 + XA(R_1 + e_A) - L(R_1 + e_L)}{(A-L)}.$$

Expected return becomes

$$\bar{R}_N = \frac{A(1-X)R_1 + XAR_1 - LR_1}{(A-L)} = R_1 = R_F,$$

but this is identical to the expected return on the riskless portfolio. However, the risk on this portfolio is not zero. In fact, the variance of return is:

$$\mathrm{Var}(R_N) = \frac{X^2 A^2 \,\mathrm{Var}(e_A) + L^2 \,\mathrm{Var}(e_L)}{(A-L)^2},$$

where $\mathrm{Var}(e_A)$ and $\mathrm{Var}(e_L)$ are the unsystematic variance of the assets and liabilities, respectively.

Thus the investment opportunity set is a horizontal line emanating from R_F. From the efficient set theorem the only efficient portfolio is the riskless portfolio. Thus the optimum investment policy is to cash flow match the liabilities with the remainder invested in the one period government bill.

PROPOSITION 2 If $\alpha_A > 0$ the efficient frontier consists of combinations of the riskless portfolio and a portfolio of risky assets. All portfolios that include the pure discount instrument in constructing the efficient frontier of risky assets are inefficient.

An investment of X in the risky assets and $(1 - X)$ in the pure discount bond such that the combination is duration matched to the liabilities has a return of

$$R_N = \frac{A(1 - X)R_1 + XA(R_1 + \alpha_A + e_A) - L(R_1 + e_L)}{(A - L)}.$$

Note that an extra return is being earned on the assets and not on the liabilities. Thus, we are assuming that eq. (4b) holds for at least some assets and that portfolios of all durations offer the same above equilibrium returns.[16] The expected return on the combination is:

$$\bar{R}_N = R_1 + \frac{XA\alpha_A}{(A - L)},$$

while the variance of return is:

$$\sigma_N^2 = \frac{X^2 A^2 \operatorname{Var}(e_A) + L^2 \operatorname{Var}(e_L)}{(A - L)^2}.$$

We can combine this portfolio with the riskless portfolio (as shown in the prior section). These combinations lie along a straight line in expected return standard deviation space with a slope given by

$$\theta = \frac{\bar{R}_N - R_F}{\sigma_N} = \frac{\alpha_A XA}{[X^2 A^2 \operatorname{Var}(e_A) + L^2 \operatorname{Var}(e_L)]^{1/2}}.$$

The preferred portfolio is the one that maximizes this slope. Taking $d\theta/dX$ to determine the proportions to put in the portfolio offering above equilibrium returns and recalling $R_F = R_1$ we get:[17]

$$\frac{d\theta}{dX} = \frac{A\alpha_A L^2 \operatorname{Var}(e_L)}{\sigma_N^2} > 0.$$

Thus, the slope is maximized when X is made as large as possible. This implies that the investor should form the risky portfolio by short selling the one period spot rate (borrow at this rate) and use the proceeds to buy the duration matched portfolio. If short selling of the one period bond is not feasible (the more realistic situation) the investor should form the risky portfolio by placing 100% of the money in the risky duration matched portfolio. Thus, the efficient frontier consists of a straight line which represents combinations of the riskless portfolio and the duration matched portfolio. The proportion of bonds that the investor places in each depends on his or her risk return tradeoff. It is perfectly rational for an investor to choose to place a fraction of the funds in a cash flow matched portfolio (as part of the riskless portfolio) and a fraction in the more risky duration matched portfolio.

Many institutions offer both cash flow matching and duration matching portfolios to their customers. In this section we have seen that if all assets are priced in equilibrium, no investor should hold any immunized (duration matched) portfolios, except for the cash flow matched portfolio. On the other hand, if some assets are priced out of equilibrium it will almost always be advantageous to cash flow match some portion of liabilities while at the same time investing part of the funds in a portfolio which is duration matched but not cash flow matched.

We will now examine the efficient frontier when we consider non-immunized strategies.

IV Optimal Bond Portfolio Strategies in General

In this section we will expand the analysis of the efficient frontier to include additional assets and non-duration matched strategies. We will continue to assume the investor can place funds in the riskless portfolio.

4a The Portfolios Considered

We assume an investor can select an optimum portfolio by combining the riskless portfolio with three other portfolios:

1. A particular portfolio of efficiently priced assets.
2. A unique portfolio of assets with excess returns.
3. The cash flow matched portfolio.

In a separate paper [Elton and Gruber (1989)] we present a set of mutual fund theorems for alternative multi index models which can be used to show that restricting the choice to these portfolios is optimal. The economic intuition behind these results is easy to see. Our assumption concerning the return generating model means that risk is divided into diversifiable and nondiversifiable components. Since diversifiable risk is not priced, the choice among portfolios of efficiently priced assets should involve minimizing residual risk. Thus the minimum risk portfolio is in the decision set. In Appendix A we prove that the portfolio that minimizes residual risk is unique. With perfect factor replication it is the replicating portfolio. The riskless portfolio is included because it is the portfolio which allows us to eliminate the diversifiable risk associated with the investor's liabilities. The uniqueness of a portfolio of positive α assets (designated as the special portfolio) is rigorously shown in a latter section when we derive its composition. The inclusion of this portfolio in the decision set is motivated by the fact that it provides excess returns, returns which may more than compensate for the fact that it has residual risks.

The final portfolio the cash flow matched portfolio allows different amounts of the one period pure discount bond to be held since the only difference between it and the riskless portfolio is that the riskless portfolio contains some investment in the one period pure discount bond.

In the next section of the paper we will solve for the optimum composition of the risky portfolio. We shall study two cases. In the first we shall assume that the factor portfolio is perfectly correlated with the factor driving bond returns. In the second case shall assume that correlation is less than perfect and therefore the factor portfolio has residual risk.

4b The Case of a Perfectly Correlated Factor Portfolio

We will continue to assume that the investor makes an allocation decision between a risky and a riskless portfolio. To determine the composition of the risky portfolio, the investor tries to maximize the slope of the line passing through the riskless portfolio and a risky portfolio in expected return standard deviation space. Using the subscript N to denote the risky portfolio:

$$\text{Max}\,\theta = \frac{\bar{R}_N - R_F}{\sigma_N}.$$

Define

X_c = fraction of assets invested in the cash flow matching portfolio,

X_p = fraction of assets invested in the factor portfolio,

$X_s = 1 - X_c - X_p$ = fraction of assets in the special portfolio,

D_c, D_p, D_s = the duration of the cash flow, factor, and special portfolio, respectively,

L = market value of liabilities,

A = market value of assets (A is assumed greater than L at time zero).

Utilizing eqs. (4a) and (4b) and the definitions above, the expected return on a risky portfolio composed of assets invested in portfolio C, P, and S and containing liabilities L is

$$\bar{R}_N = \frac{AX_s\alpha_s + D_N\bar{I}}{(A-L)} + R_F,$$

where D_N is the duration of net worth and is given by

$$D_N = [A\{X_cD_L + X_pD_p + (1 - X_c - X_p)D_s\} - D_LL].$$

The variance of the risky portfolio is:

$$\sigma_N^2 = \frac{[D_N^2\sigma_I^2 + (X_cA - L)^2\sigma_L^2 + X_s^2A^2\sigma_s^2}{(A-L)^2},$$

where

σ_I^2 = variance of the return on the index I,

σ_L^2 = variance of the residuals (after the effect of the factor has been removed) of the cash match portfolio and the liabilities,

σ_s^2 = residual variance of the special portfolio,

σ_p^2 = residual variance of the factor portfolio.

We make the assumption in this section that the factor portfolio is perfectly correlated with the factor I, hence $\sigma_p^2 = 0$ and σ_p^2 does not appear in the variance equation. Furthermore, the residual risks of all portfolios, from the one factor model, are assumed to be uncorrelated with one another. Finally, note that the cash flow matched portfolio and the liabilities should have the same duration.

Substituting the expression for expected return and variance into θ, noting $R_F = R_1$, and substituting $1 - X_c - X_p$ for X_s yields

$$\theta = \frac{\alpha_sA(1 - X_c - X_p) + D_N\bar{I}}{[D_N^2\sigma_I^2 + (X_cA - L)^2\sigma_L^2 + (1 - X_c - X_p)^2A^2\sigma_s^2]^{1/2}}.$$

To find optimum proportions take the derivative of θ with respect to X_c and then with respect to X_p, setting each equal to zero. The derivative with respect to X_c is:

$$\frac{d\theta}{dX_c} = \frac{\bar{I}A(D_L - D_s) - \alpha_sA}{(\sigma_N^2)^{1/2}(A-L)} - \frac{(\bar{R}_N - R_F)}{(\sigma_N^2)^{3/2}(A-L)^3}[D_NA(D_L - D_s)\sigma_I^2$$
$$+ A(X_cA - L)\sigma_L^2 - A^2(1 - X_c - X_p)\sigma_s^2] = 0.$$

Substituting for R_N and σ_N^2 and simplifying yields

$$\begin{aligned}
&\bar{I}(X_cA - L)\sigma_L^2[X_p(D_s - D_p)A - D_s(A - L)] \\
&\quad + \bar{I}(1 - X_c - X_p)A\sigma_s^2[D_L(A - L) - X_p(D_L - D_p)A] \\
&\quad - \alpha_s D_N \sigma_I^2[D_L(A - L) - X_pA(D_L - D_p)] \\
&\quad - \alpha_s(X_cA - L)\sigma_L^2(A - L + X_pA) = 0. \qquad (5)
\end{aligned}$$

Similarly taking the derivative of θ with respect to X_p and simplifying yields

$$\begin{aligned}
&\bar{I}(D_p - D_s)(X_sA - L)^2\sigma_L^2 + \bar{I}A(1 - X_c - X_p)\sigma_s^2[AD_p(1 - X_c) \\
&\quad + (X_cA - L)D_L] - \alpha_s D_N \sigma_I^2[AD_p(1 - X_c) + (X_cA - L)D_L] \\
&\quad - \alpha_s(X_cA - L)^2\sigma_L^2 = 0. \qquad (6)
\end{aligned}$$

There are two solutions to these two questions. One involves imaginary values for the investment in assets and hence can be dismissed. The other solution is[18]

$$X_c = \frac{L}{A},$$

$$X_p = \frac{\bar{I}\sigma_s^2 - \alpha_s D_s \sigma_I^2}{\alpha_s \sigma_I^2(D_p - D_s) + \bar{I}\sigma_s^2} \frac{A - L}{A},$$

$$X_s = (1 - X_c - X_p) = \frac{\alpha_s D_p \sigma_I^2}{\alpha_s \sigma_I^2(D_p - D_s) + \bar{I}\sigma_s^2} \frac{A - L}{A}.$$

Several properties of the optimal solution are interesting. The most intriguing is that given assets larger in size than liabilities, the value of X_c shows that it always pays to hold a cash flow matched portfolio exactly equal in size to the liabilities. It is worth noting that since the riskless portfolio also contains a cash flow matched portfolio equal to liabilities, no matter what mixture of the risky portfolio and the riskless portfolio the investor selects, he or she will always exactly cash flow match liabilities. The intuition behind this proof is that since cash flow matching is the only way to get rid of all of the residual risk on liabilities, it pays to do so.

The remainder of the assets are invested in part in the special portfolio and in part in the factor portfolio. Let us examine the allocation of the extra assets A–L in greater detail. The fraction of these extra assets put in the special portfolio is:

$$\frac{X_s}{X_s + X_p} = \frac{\alpha_s D_p \sigma_I^2}{\alpha_s \sigma_I^2 (D_p - D_s) + \bar{I}\sigma_s^2}. \tag{7}$$

A more intuitively appealing form can be derived by expressing this relationship in terms of the average duration (D_N) of the portfolio bought with surplus funds ($A - L$). In this case D_N becomes,

$$D_N = \frac{X_s}{X_s + X_p} D_s + \frac{X_p}{X_s + X_p} D_p.$$

Substituting in the expression for X_s and X_p and simplifying and rearranging:

$$\frac{D_N}{\bar{I}\sigma_s^2} = \frac{D_p}{\alpha_s \sigma_I^2 (D_p - D_s) + \bar{I}\sigma_s^2}.$$

Substituting this into eq. (7) yields

$$\frac{X_s}{X_s + X_p} = \frac{\alpha_s D_N \sigma_I^2}{\bar{I}\sigma_s^2} = \frac{\alpha_s / \sigma_s^2}{\bar{I} D_N / D_N^2 \sigma_I^2}. \tag{8}$$

The numerator is a reward risk ratio for the special portfolio while the denominator is a reward risk ratio for an efficiently priced portfolio of duration D_N. Thus the greater the reward risk ratio for the special portfolio relative to the ratio for an efficiently priced portfolio the more is invested in the special portfolio. Up to now we have assumed that the special portfolio could be constructed without consideration of the allocation between other portfolios or the characteristics of the factor portfolio. We will now prove this.

4b1. *Composition of Special Portfolio*

In the proof we assume the previous result that an amount of assets equal to liabilities is invested in a cash flow matching portfolio. Therefore the allocation of the remaining assets can be treated as a separate portfolio problem. The slope of the tangency line connecting the riskless portfolio and the efficient frontier is

$$\theta = \frac{\sum \alpha_i X_i + D_N \bar{I}}{\left[D_N^2 \sigma_I^2 + \sum X_i^2 \sigma_i^2\right]^{1/2}},$$

where

X_k = the proportion invested in special asset k,

D_k = the duration of asset k,

$D_N = [D_p(1 - \sum X_i) + \sum X_i D_i]$,

and other terms are as before.

Taking the derivative with respect to X_k and setting it equal to zero results in

$$\alpha_k[D_N^2\sigma_I^2 + \sum X_i^2\sigma_i^2] - D_N\sigma_I^2(D_k - D_p)\sum \alpha_i X_i$$
$$- \sum \alpha_i X_i(X_k\sigma_k^2) + \bar{I}(D_k - D_p)\sum X_i^2\sigma_i^2 - D_N\bar{I}X_k\sigma_k^2 = 0.$$

Multiplying through by X_k and adding across all k results in

$$\left[D_N\sigma_I^2\sum \alpha_i X_i - \bar{I}\sum X_i^2\sigma_i^2\right] = 0.$$

Substituting this into the first order condition and simplifying yields

$$X_k = \frac{\alpha_k}{\sigma_k^2}\left[\frac{D_N^2\sigma_I^2 + \sum X_i^2\sigma_i^2}{\sum \alpha_i X_i + D_N\bar{I}}\right] = \frac{\alpha_k}{\sigma_k^2}\lambda.$$

where λ = total risk/total excess return.

Note that this is identical to the Treynor and Black (1973) result derived in another context. Since the total amount invested in the special asset is the sum of X_i, the fraction X_k represents of the alpha portfolio is given by

$$\frac{X_k}{\sum X_k} = \frac{(\alpha_k/\sigma_k^2)\lambda}{\sum(\alpha_i/\sigma_i^2)\lambda} = \frac{\alpha_k/\sigma_k^2}{\sum \alpha_i/\sigma_i^2}.$$

Thus, the composition of the special portfolio can be determined independently from the composition of the factor portfolio and depends only on characteristics of the special assets. In particular, note that characteristics of the liability structure such as its duration do not affect the composition of the special portfolio. Throughout this section, we have assumed the existence of such a portfolio. We have now shown it can be calculated and that it is unique, it is independent of the factor portfolio, and it is independent of the liability structure.

Before leaving this section we should examine one more solution. We will first delineate those conditions that cause us to short sell the factor portfolio. After defining these conditions we will derive the appropriate solution to the portfolio problem when these short sales are not allowed.

4b2. *The Optimal Solution When the Factor Portfolio Cannot Be Sold Short*

Up to now we have assumed that the factor portfolio could be sold short. The factor portfolio is sold short if $X_s/(X_s + X_p)$ is greater than one. From eq. (8) this condition is

$$\frac{\alpha_s}{\sigma_s^2} > \frac{\bar{I} D_N}{D_N^2 \sigma_I^2}.$$

The left-hand side is the reward to risk ratio of the special portfolio. The right hand side of the inequality is the reward to risk ratio of an efficiently priced portfolio of duration D_N. If this inequality holds, 100% of the free assets would be placed in the special portfolio or greater than 100% if short sales are allowed.

If the previous analysis calls for a positive amount of funds to be placed in the factor portfolio the solution is unchanged by a short sales constraint. If the solution calls for the factor portfolio to be sold short and short sales are not allowed, the solution can be obtained by setting the fraction of assets invested in the factor portfolio equal to zero and solving the restructured problem:

$$\text{Max}\,\theta = \frac{\alpha_s A(1 - X_c) + D_N \bar{I}}{[D_N^2 \sigma_I^2 + (X_c A - L)^2 \sigma_L^2 + (1 - X_c)^2 A^2 \sigma_s^2]^{1/2}},$$

where

$$D_N = A[X_c D_c + (1 - X_c) D_s].$$

The first order condition is:

$$X_c = \frac{L}{A} + \frac{A - L}{A} \frac{D_c(\bar{I}\sigma_s^2 - \alpha_s D_s \sigma_I^2)}{D_c(\bar{I}\sigma_s^2 - \alpha_s D_s \sigma_I^2) + \sigma_L^2(\bar{I} D_s + \alpha_s + \alpha_s D_L^2)}. \tag{9}$$

When the factor portfolio could be sold short, the optimum amount to invest in cash flow matching was L/A or place a sum of money exactly equal to the liabilities in the exact match portfolio. The sign of the second term determines whether more or less is invested in the cash flow match portfolio when short sales are not allowed.

Taking the second derivative of θ with respect to X_c gives

$$\frac{d^2\theta}{dX_c^2} = -D_c(\bar{I}\sigma_s^2 - \alpha_s D_s \sigma_I^2) - \sigma_L^2(\bar{I}D_s + \alpha_s + \alpha_s D_L^2).$$

For the solution for X_c to be a maximum this must be less than zero. The second derivative has the same functional form as the denominator of the fraction in eq. (9). For the second derivative to be negative, the denominator of the coefficient of A–L in eq. (9) must be positive. From eq. (7) we know that one case where we desire to sell the factor portfolio short is where $\bar{I}\sigma_s^2 - \alpha_s D_s \sigma_I^2$ is negative. This is the numerator of the coefficient of A–L in eq. (9). Thus the second term of eq. (9) is negative and we cannot get a solution to exactly cash flow match a set of funds equal to liabilities. Rather we invest more than A–L in the special portfolio and invest less than L in the cash flow matched portfolio. This is an extremely important result. Most institutions cannot or will not short sell bonds as part of their optimal portfolio. Given this constraint, it is generally optimum to still engage in some cash flow matching but to only invest a fraction of the liabilities in this manner.

4c *Optimal Investment Policy When A Factor Portfolio Has Residual Risk*

In this section we will assume that there does not exist a portfolio perfectly correlated with the factor. The assets we will consider are a cash flow match portfolio, a portfolio of efficiently priced assets with minimum residual risk at any duration level and a portfolio of inefficiently priced assets. In the last section we showed that when short sales were allowed, the cash flow matched portfolio should be held in an amount equal to the liabilities. The same conclusion holds when a zero residual risk factor portfolio does not exist. While we can formally show this, the conclusion is easy to see given the analysis in the last section. When the minimum risk portfolio has positive residual risk rather than zero risk, this portfolio is less attractive. Since the characteristics of other portfolios are held constant, making the minimum risk portfolio less attractive should not reduce the amount in the exact match portfolio. Thus, the proportion in the exact match portfolio should be at least L. For investment beyond L, the minimum risk factor portfolio dominates the exact match portfolio. Any asset in the exact match portfolio can be included in the minimum residual risk at any duration level. At any particular duration the return and systematic risk for the minimum risk portfolio and the exact match portfolio are the same. Thus, the minimum risk portfolio dominates the cash flow match portfolio for proportions in the cash flow match portfolio above L.

In the remainder of this section we will examine how to split an amount $A–L$ between the special portfolio and minimum risk factor portfolio. Once again we will maximize the slope of a line connecting the riskless portfolio (exact match plus pure discount) and the efficient frontier. We will retain the symbols used in the last section with the following exception. We will deal with the portfolio problem from the viewpoint of allocating the funds $A–L$. We will express all X_i as a fraction of this amount of funds. Therefore, $X_s + X_p = 1$. The expected return is given by

$$\bar{R}_N = \alpha_s X_s + D_N \bar{I},$$

where

$$D_N = [D_s X_s + (1 - X_s) D_p].$$

The variance requires more explanation. The systematic risk is $D_N^2 \sigma_I^2$. We believe the following is a reasonable representation of the unsystematic risk:[19]

$$\sigma_p^2 + X_s^2(\sigma_s^2 - \sigma_p^2), \quad \sigma_s^2 > \sigma_p^2.$$

This representation states that the minimum residual risk is obtained when 100% is invested in the minimum risk factor portfolio but its risk is σ_p^2 rather than zero as assumed in the previous analysis. The $(\sigma_s^2 - \sigma_p^2)$ is the incremental residual risk when some of the money is placed in the special portfolio. Given this representation, the following problem should be solved:

$$\operatorname{Max} \theta' = \frac{\alpha_s X_s + D_N \bar{I}}{[D_N^2 \sigma_I^2 + \sigma_p^2 + X_s^2(\sigma_s^2 - \sigma_p^2)]^{1/2}}.$$

The first order condition rearranged is

$$X_s = \frac{\alpha_s(\sigma_p^2 + D_p^2 \sigma_I^2) + \bar{I}\sigma_p^2(D_s - D_p)}{\bar{I}(\sigma_s^2 - \sigma_p^2)D_p - \alpha_s(D_s - D_p)D_N \sigma_I^2}.$$

Examining the second derivative shows that for this to be a maximum:

$$\frac{\alpha_s}{(\sigma_s^2 - \sigma_p^2)} < \frac{\bar{I}(D_s - D_p)}{(D_s - D_p)^2 \sigma_I^2}.$$

The left hand side is the special return per unit of incremental residual risk from holding the special assets. The right hand side is the change in systematic risk. If the above inequality does not hold, the first order condition is a maximum and X_s should be made as large as possible. Thus, for the minimum risk portfolio to be held the inequality must hold. This requires that D_s be greater than D_p. In addition, the special return to residual risk has to be sufficiently small relative to the incremental systematic return to risk. Therefore, the amount invested in the minimum risk portfolio and factor portfolio depends on systematic return and risk as well as the residual risk and extra return.

Changing the objective function to analyze the proportion to place in each special asset involves replacing X_sD_s with $\sum X_iD_i$, X_s with $\sum X_i$, and $X_s^2(\sigma_s^2 - \sigma_p^2)$ with $\sum X_i^2(\sigma_i^2 - \sigma_p^2)$. Taking the derivative of this objective function with respect to each X_k, aggregating across all X_k to simplify, results in the following expression for X_k

$$X_k = \frac{\alpha_k}{\sigma_k^2}\left(\frac{\text{Total Risk}}{\text{Total Return}}\right) + \left(\frac{D_k - D_p}{\sigma_k^2}\frac{\sigma_p^2}{D_p}\right),$$

where

$$\text{Total Risk} = D_N^2\sigma_I^2 + \sigma_p^2 + \sum X_i(\sigma_i^2 - \sigma_p^2),$$

$$\text{Total Return} = D_N\bar{I} + X_s\alpha_s.$$

Thus, the optimum proportion to invest in asset k is a function of the characteristics of the minimum risk factor portfolio. The characteristics of this portfolio needs to be known in order to determine the composition of the special portfolio. When the factor portfolio had zero residual risk, separation was possible. When the factor portfolio has positive residual risk, separation is impossible. Nevertheless, the special portfolio is unique and can be prespecified as assumed in the earlier analysis.

Conclusion

It is very common today to see insurance companies offering their pension fund customers a choice from among at least three sets of portfolios; an actively managed bond portfolio, a portfolio which matches the duration of a customer specified set of cash flows (liabilities), and a passive index fund. The question we have answered in this paper is when should a customer select one of these investments by itself or a portfolio of these investments and what is the design of the optimal portfolio.

We have shown that if a portfolio is to be fully immunized and all assets are priced in equilibrium, it never pays to put funds in an immunized portfolio which is not cash flow matched. If assets exist which offer an above equilibrium return, then in addition to placing a fraction of funds in a cash flow matched portfolio, there is an economic rationale for placing a fraction of funds in a non-cash flow matched, but duration matched portfolio.

In constructing the efficient frontier of risky assets for an investor who did not require full immunization, we considered combinations of a cash flow matched portfolio, a factor portfolio, and a special portfolio of above equilibrium return assets. We showed that there was a single combination of assets yielding equilibrium returns that was preferred and a single preferred combination of assets yielding above equilibrium returns so that our framework was general. We derived the optimal proportions in each portfolio. We showed that, whether short sales are allowed or not, it is always optimal to exact cash flow match the liabilities. Additional funds are allocated between the special assets and factor portfolio in a specified manner. When the solution calls for the factor portfolio to be sold short and short sales are forbidden the optimum investment policy consists of combinations of the exact match portfolio and the special portfolio.

While all of our analysis is general, the reader who believes that all assets are priced in equilibrium needs only set alpha to zero for the special portfolio. He will find that all proofs go through but that the fraction of assets invested in the special portfolio is zero.

Notes

1. The analysis has implications for an individual investor where the analogy to the liability stream is anticipated consumption expenditures.

2. An interesting exception to this is Liebowitz and Hendrickson (1988). They recommend a surplus framework for the portfolio problem. Part of our results regarding the riskless assets which are proved later in this paper are arrived at intuitively by Liebowitz and Hendrickson.

3. See for example, Elton and Gruber (1991). One could view multiperiod consumption investment models as an exception to this statement.

4. For example, almost all tests of immunization models use as a criteria the ability to match a pure discount instrument and examine the ending value as a way of comparing models. An exception is contained in our prior work [Elton et al. (1988)], where we examine period by period changes in net worth empirically.

5. While that solution will be mathematically equivalent to the solution presented in this paper, solving the problem by QPS will not allow the derivation of the separation properties shown in this paper or allow the user to understand the reasons for the optimum allocation. Using the results of this paper the optimum allocation can be achieved by solving a problem which is much simpler in structure than a QPS problem.

6. Nelson and Schaefer (1983, p. 65) pointed out that 'one of the deficiencies of the immunization literature is the absence of a convincing explanation of why investors should wish to immunize.' The answer of why or how much to immunize has remained unanswered until now.

7. The amount of insurance a company can write is a multiple of net worth.

8. This return includes the impact due to shifts in the term structure as well as other economic influences.

9. In the following discussion we assume that $A > L$. If assets are not equal to or larger than the liabilities not only does the investor have negative starting wealth, no riskless strategy is feasible.

10. At this point we have not restricted the form of the return distribution on assets or liabilities. These returns can originate from shifts in the term structure or any other source. Later we will specifically introduce the covariance between these returns and show how they relate to an economic index.

11. Given the large number of debt instruments available, the design of such a portfolio is always possible except in the case where liabilities occur beyond the life of the assets. The portfolio can be designed as a solution to a simple linear programming problem. See Elton and Gruber (1991).

12. Actually, under cash flow matching the discrepancy between assets and liabilities cannot occur, not only because of market forces, but also because of the manner in which actuaries function. Once cash flow matching is selected as an investment technique the actuary will use the rate on the bond portfolio as the actuarial rate in all liability calculations.

13. We refer to excess funds being placed in the one period government bill. The definition of the maturity on this bill is arbitrary, for example if regulation were to be enforced (capital adequacy examined) on a continuous basis we would use this instantaneous rate of interest as our one period riskless rate. We have purposely kept the definition of one period ambiguous for the analysis in the text follows under any definition of the appropriate measurement interval.

14. The riskless portfolio contains, in addition to the discount bond, an exact match portfolio of bonds and the liabilities. The exact match portfolio and the liabilities are obviously correlated with the liabilities in the risky portfolio and probably correlated with the assets in the risky portfolio. However, they net out of the riskless asset and the remainder is the pure discount instrument which has zero correlation with the risky portfolio.

15. Once again we emphasize that the problem could be solved as a quadratic programming problem with the liabilities included as negative assets. However, this solution is sterile insofar as yielding economic insights for the conditions under which various assets are included.

16. If we assumed there existed only one portfolio of assets with above equilibrium returns then the solution to this problem would be trivial. Enough of the one period bond would be held so that the duration of the portfolio plus the riskless bond equaled the duration of the liabilities.

17. Note that since the $A–L$ cancel in the objective function arrived at before rearranging, the problem would be unchanged if we used as an objective, dollar return on net worth rather than percent return.

18. The reader can validate this as a solution by noting that for $X_c = L/A$ the first and fourth terms of eqs. (5) and (6) are equal to zero and for either equation the other two terms reduce to the equation which is shown in the text. Examining the second derivative shows that the denominator in the expression for X_s and X_p must be positive for a maximum. If the denominator is negative the second derivative is negative, the first positive and the solution involves placing the maximum amount in the special asset.

19. There are a number of correlation patterns of residuals that would result in this representation of residual risk.

References

Elton, E. J. and M. J. Gruber, 1991, *Modern portfolio theory and investment analysis*, fourth edition (John Wiley and Sons, New York).

Elton, E. J. and M. J. Gruber, 1989, Portfolio analysis with a non-normal multi-index return generating prices, New York University's Stern School of Business, working paper.

Elton, E. J., M. J. Gruber and P. Nabar, 1988, Bond returns, immunization and the return-generating-process, in: M. Sarnat and G. Szegö, eds., *Essays in honor of Irwin Friend*, Studies in Banking and Finance (North-Holland, Amsterdam).

Federal Home Loan Banks Boards (FHLBB), 1983, Agenda for reform, A report on deposit insurance to the Congress, Washington, DC, March.

Grammatikos, T., T. Saunders and I. Swary, 1986, Returns and risks of US bank foreign currency activities, *Journal of Finance* 41 no. 3, 671–682.

Liebowitz, M. L. and R. D. Hendrickson, 1988, Portfolio optimization within a surplus framework, *Financial Analysis Journal*, March–April, 43–51.

Nelson, J. and S. Schaefer, 1983, The dynamics of the term structure and alternative portfolio immunization strategies, in: Bierwag, Kaufman and Toevs, eds., *Innovation in bond portfolio management duration analysis and immunization* (J.A.I. Press, Greenwich, CT).

Treynor, J. and F. Black, 1973, How to use security analysts to improve portfolio selection, *Journal of Business*, January, 66–68.

14

Portfolio Analysis with a Nonnormal Multi-index Return-Generating Process

Edwin J. Elton and Martin J. Gruber

I Introduction

One of the major themes in the recent literature of financial economics has been the description of returns in terms of a linear return-generating process. While there is considerable disagreement on the form of the return-generating process and even on the number of influences that should be included in it, there is general agreement that a linear return-generating process, and probably one involving more than one index, is a useful characterization of security returns. Furthermore, there seems to be increasing agreement that the components of the return-generating process are innovations in macroeconomic variables. Recent papers by Chen, Roll, and Ross (7), Hamao (18), and Burmeister et al. (4–6) help identify the type of innovations that drive returns in capital markets in both the United States and Japan. If returns are driven in whole or in part by innovations in macroeconomic variables, it is unlikely that portfolios of securities can be formed that exactly replicate the factors in the return-generating process.

The present article has two purposes. First, we analyze the investor's portfolio problem when the investor is willing to believe that security returns follow a linear return-generating process with nonreplicable factors. Second, we derive a relative pricing relationship, given that investors reach portfolio decisions as described in the first part. This article follows in the tradition of Ross (23) and Ingersoll (19). It differs from these papers assuming that factors *cannot* be replicated with traded assets. It can easily be shown that if we allow replication, our results reduce to Ross (23) or Ingersoll (19).

In addition, we follow Ingersoll in studying the case in which an investor forecasts a unique return for each stock. That is, while each stock has a return generated by one or more indexes, we allow an investor to forecast a unique component or α return. This unique return can be thought of as the expected payoff from security analysis.

We would have liked to develop a totally general solution to the problem of portfolio analysis and relative pricing under any multi-index model. However, we have had to make some assumptions. The assumptions we make are much less restrictive and the analysis is much more general than most previous analyses. We will make two utility assumptions: first, that more is preferred to less; and second, that utility functions exhibit risk aversion, in the sense that outcomes that are weakly less risky, in the Rothschild and Stiglitz (19) meaning of the term, are preferred. In addition, we shall assume that the *residuals* from the return-generating process are normally distributed. This assumption, which was first investigated by Ingersoll (19), is considerably more general than assuming that returns are normally distributed.[1] Our analysis places no restrictions on the distributions of indexes driving returns, and therefore returns themselves can follow any distribution.

The remainder of the article is divided into four sections. In section 2, we present the basic structure of the return-generating model and the portfolio problem. In section 3, we solve the optimum portfolio problem, discuss the efficient set of portfolios, and derive a "separation" theorem. In section 4, we derive relative pricing relationships for the case of heterogeneous expectations and nonreplicable indexes. We give conclusions in section 5.

II The Model Structure

This section both explicitly defines the assumptions we make about the return-generating process and formulates the structure of the portfolio problem to which this return-generating process leads.

Throughout this article, we assume that security returns are generated by a multifactor return-generating process of the following form:[2]

$$R_i = R_F + \alpha_i + \sum_{L=1}^{I} b_{iL}(R_L - R_F) + e_i, \tag{1}$$

where

1. R_i is the return on security i
2. R_F is the riskless rate of interest
3. b_{iL} is the sensitivity of stock i to index L

4. R_L is the return on index L
5. e_i is a random variable with mean zero and variance of $\sigma_{e_i^2}$
6. α_i is the unique expected return associated with stock i
7. I is the number of indexes

Some of the properties of this equation and the assumptions associated with it need to be made more explicit. With no loss of generality, we can assume that the indexes that drive returns are orthogonal to each other and that the residuals are independent of the indexes. Perhaps key to our analysis is the assumption that the investor believes there is a unique return (α_i) that he or she predicts is associated with some stocks. The potential presence of a unique α or extra return for each stock will allow us to investigate portfolio composition when investors believe stocks have a unique, nonstochastic component to expected returns and will also allow us to examine relative prices with heterogeneous expectations. Up to now we have placed no constraints on the joint distribution of the residuals. Thus, equation (1) is completely general and definitional.

The distributional assumption we make is that the residuals are distributed jointly normally. No restriction is placed on the distribution of the indexes. Thus, return distributions for individual securities and portfolios can be described by a wide variety of distributions. We will now formulate the portfolio problem with the return-generating process described above.

Consider first the parameters with which the investor must be concerned. Note for portfolio P that $\alpha_p = \Sigma X_i \alpha_i$, $b_{pL} = \Sigma X_i b_{iL}$ and $\sigma^2_{e_p} = \Sigma\Sigma X_i X_j \sigma_{ij}$, where the X's are portfolio proportions and σ_{ij} is the variance of or covariance between residuals. Since security residuals are assumed to be jointly normal, the portfolio residuals are also normal. Therefore, knowing α_i, b_{iL}, the variance of the indexes, and the variance covariance matrix of the residuals defines the return-generating function for all portfolios and the distribution of returns on these portfolios.[3] The value of these variables is all that is needed to choose among portfolios.

Next, we need to show that we wish to minimize residual variance given the expected return ($\bar{R}_p$) and all sensitivities (b_{pL}) on the portfolio. Consider two portfolio distributions with returns $Y + e_1$ and $Y + e_2$, respectively. The Y's capture all the terms in the return-generating process except the residuals. Note that the nonresidual terms are the same by assumption. Further assume that $\sigma_2^2 > \sigma_1^2$, where σ_1^2 and σ_2^2 are the variances of the mean zero residuals e_1 and e_2, respectively.

Now define a third normal variate independent of the other two. Let the mean of this variate be zero and its variance $\sigma_2^2 - \sigma_1^2$. Designate this variate as e_3. Since normals are additive, the sum of e_1 and e_3 is normal. The mean of the sum is zero, and because they are independent, the variance is σ_2^2. Thus the distribution of the sum of e_1 and e_3 has the same mean and variance as the distribution of e_2, and we can write the distribution of the portfolio returns as $(Y + e_1)$ and $(Y + e_1) + e_3$. Thus, under the assumption of normally distributed residuals for a given expected return and a given set of sensitivities (b_{iL}'s), a portfolio with a smaller variance of residuals is weakly less risky in the Rothschild and Stiglitz sense.[4] Since we assumed that utility functions exhibited Rothschild and Stiglitz risk aversion, the portfolio problem can be formulated as follows: minimize residual risk subject to constraints on expected return and the sensitivities. By varying the level of expected return and sensitivities, the efficient frontier can be traced out.

In the next section, we solve for the efficient frontier given this return-generating process, and in section 4 we derive asset-pricing relationships.

III Portfolio Analysis with Imperfect Replication

In this section of the article, we examine optimal portfolio characteristics when the indexes affecting returns cannot be exactly replicated with traded assets and investors wish to act on forecasts of unique returns. One can think of this problem as deriving optimal portfolio behavior when the indexes in the return-generating process are economic variables, as suggested by the recent literature.[5] When indexes are innovations in economic variables or nontraded assets, only by chance could we exactly replicate the indexes with traded assets. Minimum risk portfolios with sensitivity of one-on-one index and zero elsewhere are feasible to construct, but are likely to have positive residual risk.

The portfolio problem can be represented as the minimization of residual risk for all levels of each sensitivity b_{pL} and all expected possible returns. We will assume there are N risky assets and will designate the $N + 1$ asset as the riskless asset. Bars will be used to denote expected values. The problem can be formulated as follows:

Minimize

$$1/2 \sum_{i=1}^{N} \sum_{j=1}^{N} X_i X_j \sigma_{ij}$$

subject to

1. $\bar{R}_p = \sum_{i=1}^{N+1} X_i \left[\alpha_i + R_F + \sum_{L=1}^{I} b_{i_L}(\bar{R}_L - R_F) \right]$

2. $b_{pL} = \sum_{i=1}^{N} X_i b_{iL} \qquad \text{for } L = 1, \ldots, I$

3. $1 = \sum_{i=1}^{N+1} X_i$

We designate the Lagrangean as θ and the dual for each of the constraints by λ's.

The Lagrangean is

$$\theta = 1/2 \sum_{i=1}^{N} \sum_{j=1}^{N} X_i X_j \sigma_{ij} - \lambda_1 \left[\sum_{i=1}^{N+1} X_i \left\{ \alpha_i + R_F + \sum_{L=1}^{I} b_{iL}(\bar{R}_L - R_F) \right\} - \bar{R}_p \right]$$

$$- \sum_{L=1}^{I} \lambda_{L+1} \sum_{i=1}^{N} (X_i b_{iL} - b_{pL}) - \lambda_{I+2} \left(\sum_{i=1}^{N+1} X_i - 1 \right).$$

Taking derivatives with respect to the fraction of the portfolio invested in the N risky securities and the riskless security, we obtain

$$\frac{d\theta}{dX_k} = \sum_{i=1}^{N} X_i \sigma_{ik} - \lambda_1 \left[\alpha_k + R_F + \sum_{L=1}^{I} b_{kL}(\bar{R}_L - R_F) \right] - \sum_{L=1}^{I} \lambda_{L+1} b_{kL} - \lambda_{I+2}$$

$$\text{for } k = 1, \ldots, N, \qquad (2)$$

$$\frac{d\theta}{dX_{N+1}} = -\lambda_1 R_F - \lambda_{I+2}. \qquad (3)$$

Setting both equations equal to zero, employing equation (3) to eliminate λ_{I+2} from equation (2), and writing equation (2) in matrix notation where $\mathbf{b}$ is the $N \times I$ matrix of b_{kL}'s, $\mathbf{X}$ is the column vector of portfolio weights, $\boldsymbol{\sigma}$ is the variance-covariance matrix, $\boldsymbol{\lambda}$ is the column vector of duals starting with λ_2 and ending with λ_{I+1}, and $\bar{\mathbf{R}}$ is the column vector of excess expected returns,

$$\boldsymbol{\sigma}\mathbf{X} - \lambda_1 \bar{\mathbf{R}} - \mathbf{b}\boldsymbol{\lambda} = 0,$$

$$\mathbf{X} = \lambda_1 \boldsymbol{\sigma}^{-1} \bar{\mathbf{R}} - \boldsymbol{\sigma}_{-1} \mathbf{b}\boldsymbol{\lambda}. \qquad (4)$$

Notice that for each security this has the following form:

$$X_k = \gamma_{1k}\lambda_1 + \gamma_{2k}\lambda_2 + \gamma_{3k}\lambda_3 + \dots, +\gamma_{I+1,k}\lambda_{I+1} \qquad \text{for } k = 1, \dots, N. \tag{5}$$

The coefficients γ's are properties of the individual stocks under study and are unrelated to a portfolio or the set of portfolios that any investor finds optimum. The λ's take on distinctive values for any portfolios selected. Without knowing the λ's, this equation cannot be solved. However, we can use this equation to show that, for any investor, all efficient portfolios can be constructed from $I+1$ other efficient portfolios. Then we can find $I+1$ efficient portfolios that are convenient to specify, and we can trace out the efficient frontier as a combination of these portfolios. This reduces to Ross's (23) mutual fund theorem if we assume homogeneous expectations and replicable assets.

It is easy to show that identifying $I+1$ efficient portfolios allows for the specification of the full efficient frontier if these equations hold. To do this, we will show that if we know the composition of $I+1$ efficient portfolios, the composition of any other efficient portfolio can always be derived from a weighted average (portfolio) of the $I+1$ portfolios.

Let λ_i^j be the ith λ for portfolio j. Then the investment proportions for security k in portfolio j is

$$X_k^j = \sum_{i=1}^{I+1} \lambda_i^j \gamma_{ik}. \tag{6}$$

Define a set of $I+1$ arbitrary but distinct portfolios. Then portfolio p can be expressed as a linear function (weighted sum with weights W_i) of the $I+1$ portfolios if

$$X_k^p = \sum_{j=1}^{I+1} W_j X_k^j \qquad \text{for all } k. \tag{7}$$

Substituting equation (6) into equation (7)

$$X_k^p = \sum_{j=1}^{I+1} W_j \sum_{i=1}^{I+1} \lambda_i^j \gamma_{ik},$$

$$X_k^p = \sum_{i=1}^{I+1} \gamma_{ik} \left[\sum_{j=1}^{I+1} W_j \lambda_j^i \right].$$

If $\lambda_i^p = W_j \lambda_i^j$ for all i, we could express any efficient portfolio as a linear function of $I+1$ other efficient portfolios. But this is always possible, because we have $I+1$ values of λ_i^p and there are $I+1$, W_j's that we can select. Hence, any risky efficient portfolio can be expressed as a linear function of $I+1$ distinct other efficient portfolios.[6]

Any $I+1$ different combinations of efficient portfolios could be used to trace out the efficient frontier. However, it is useful to examine whether we can identify $I+1$ portfolios with special meaning.

One way to define these portfolios is in terms of portfolios that have an economic intuition behind them. One of these portfolios can be defined as the portfolio that has a beta of one on the index while having minimum residual risk. The proportions to invest in each security in these portfolios can be determined by returning to the Lagrangean function, but only insisting that the residual risk be minimized while the beta with respect to the relevant index is one.[7] For any index t, we have a Lagrangean of the form

$$L = 1/2\sum_{i=1}^{N}\sum_{j=1}^{N} X_i X_j \sigma_{ij} - \lambda_{t+1}\left(\sum_{i=1}^{N} X_i b_{it} - 1\right) - \lambda_{I+2}\left(\sum_{i=1}^{N+1} X_i - 1\right),$$

$$\frac{dL}{dX_k} = \sum_{i=1}^{N} X_i \sigma_{ik} - \lambda_{t+1} b_{it} - \lambda_{I+2} \qquad k = 1, \ldots N, \tag{8}$$

$$\frac{dL}{dX_{N+1}} = \lambda_{I+2} = 0, \tag{9}$$

where λ_{t+1} is the Lagrangean associated with the tth replicating portfolio (t varies from 1 to I). Substituting equation (9) into equation (8), expressing the results in matrix form, and solving for the vector of the portfolio weights yield $\mathbf{X} = \lambda_{t+1}\boldsymbol{\sigma}^{-1}\mathbf{b}_t$, and defining $\mathbf{Z} = \mathbf{X}/\lambda_{t+1}$ yields $\mathbf{Z} = \boldsymbol{\sigma}^{-1}\mathbf{b}_t$.

This equation is consistent with equation (4) if λ_1 and all other λ's other than λ_{t+1} are set to zero. Thus, this portfolio meets the conditions of equation (4) and is efficient. To get portfolio proportions, the Z's are scaled to add to one. The composition of these portfolios depends on the variance-covariance matrix of the residuals and the vector of b's and is easily calculated.

So far we have identified N portfolios that lie on the efficient surface in which an investor might be interested. The last portfolio can be found simply by returning to equation (4). Equation (4) is

$$\mathbf{X} = \lambda_1\boldsymbol{\sigma}^{-1}\bar{\mathbf{R}} - \boldsymbol{\sigma}^{-1}\mathbf{b}\boldsymbol{\lambda}.$$

We can write this as

$$\mathbf{X} = \lambda_1 \boldsymbol{\sigma}^{-1}(\boldsymbol{\alpha} + \mathbf{b}(\bar{\mathbf{R}}_L - R_F \mathbf{1})) - \boldsymbol{\sigma}^{-1}\mathbf{b}\boldsymbol{\lambda}.$$

Since this equation holds for all $\boldsymbol{\lambda}$ on the efficient surface, it holds at a value of $\boldsymbol{\lambda}$ such that

$$\mathbf{b}\boldsymbol{\lambda} = \mathbf{b}(\bar{\mathbf{R}}_L - R_F \mathbf{1})\lambda_1.$$

Making this substitution, the above equation becomes

$$\mathbf{X} = \lambda_1 \boldsymbol{\sigma}^{-1}\boldsymbol{\alpha}.$$

Dividing both sides by λ_1 and defining $\mathbf{Z} = \mathbf{X}/\lambda_1$,

$$\mathbf{Z} = \boldsymbol{\sigma}^{-1}\boldsymbol{\alpha}.$$

The portfolio proportions are found by scaling the Z's to add to one. Note that the composition of this portfolio is independent of the composition of any other portfolio. It can be thought of as an α portfolio. Thus, the efficient frontier can be traced out using N minimum residual risk factor approximating portfolios (not necessarily orthogonal) and one α or special portfolio, with the final portfolio being the riskless asset.

When there is imperfect factor replication, it is not internally inconsistent to assume zero covariance between residuals.[8] Under this special assumption, an even simpler solution exists. With this assumption, the α portfolio becomes

$$Z_i = \frac{\alpha_i}{\sigma_{ei}^2}, \tag{10}$$

where

1. σ_{ei}^2 is the residual risk
2. α_i is the excess return
3. Z_i is proportional to the amount invested in security i

The Z_i's are then summed to one to get security proportions. Equation (10) is of course identical to the Treynor and Black (25) solution, except that the residuals are defined with respect to a multi-index and possibly nonnormal return-generating process. Likewise, the proportions in the factor-replicating process become:

$$Z_{iL} = \frac{b_{iL}}{\sigma_{ei}^2} \qquad \text{for all } L.$$

To summarize:

1. The efficient frontier can be expressed as a combination of factor-approximating portfolios, the special portfolio, and the riskless asset (mutual fund theorem)
2. A simple formula exists for the composition of each portfolio
3. The composition of each portfolio is independent of the composition of other portfolios.

If we assume perfect factor replication, results analogous to those presented above hold. The efficient frontier is still expressible in terms of the I exact factor-replicating portfolios, the alpha portfolio, and the riskless asset. However, since the factor-replicating portfolios have zero residual risk with exact replication, combinations of efficient portfolios are linear, and the efficient frontier becomes a hyperplane.

IV Relative Pricing Relationships

Up to this point, we have derived the optimal portfolio behavior for individuals who faced a multi-index return-generating process with normally distributed residual returns but not necessarily normally distributed returns. We have described separating portfolios and analyzed the optimum composition of each. It is now possible to aggregate across individuals with heterogeneous beliefs and to describe the relative pricing relationships to which this return-generating process must lead. In this section of the article, we will analyze the case of heterogeneous beliefs with a one-index return-generating process. The multi-index case is analogous but considerably more complex. We will assume that investors have homogeneous expectations with respect to risk variables (the b_{kL}, σ_{ij} and σ_L^2) but have different beliefs about α.[9] Recall that σ_{ij} and σ_L^2 refer to residual risk from the return-generating process.

In the previous section, we showed that the efficient frontier was the locus of all combinations of a riskless asset, index-approximating portfolios, and the special portfolio. If we let the subscript p stand for a combination of these three portfolios, then we have the following for each investor:

$$\bar{R}_p = (1 - X_L - X_s)R_F + X_s\bar{R}_s + X_L\bar{R}_L, \tag{11}$$

$$b_p = X_s b_{sL} + X_L, \tag{12}$$

$$\sigma_p^2 = [X_s^2\sigma_s^2 + X_L^2\sigma_L^2 + 2X_sX_L\sigma_{Ls}], \tag{13}$$

where L is a subscript indicating the index, X_L is the fraction in the index, and other terms are as before. A set of these equations exists for each investor. For the moment we will suppress the investor notation; it will be added shortly. Solving for X_L and X_s from equations (11) and (12), eliminating these variables from equation (13), noting that

$$\alpha_p = (\bar{R}_p - R_F) - b_{pL}(\bar{R}_L - R_F)$$

and a similar expression for α_s, and simplifying yields

$$\sigma_p^2 = \left[\frac{\alpha_p^2}{\alpha_s^2}(\sigma_s^2 + b_{sL}^2\sigma_L^2 - 2b_{sL}\sigma_{Ls}) + \frac{\alpha_p}{\alpha_s}(-2b_{pL}b_{sL}\sigma_L^2 + 2b_{pL}\sigma_{Ls}) + b_{pL}^2\sigma_L^2\right].$$

This is, of course, the equation of the efficient frontier. Taking the derivative of this equation with respect to security k and utilizing the chain rule results in

$$\mathrm{Cov}(e_k e_p) = \left[\frac{\alpha_p}{\alpha_s^2}(\sigma_s^2 + b_{sL}^2\sigma_L^2 - 2b_{sL}\sigma_{Ls})\alpha_k + \frac{1}{\alpha_s}(-b_{pL}b_{sL}\sigma_L^2 + b_{pL}\sigma_{Ls})\alpha_k \right.$$
$$\left. - \frac{\alpha_p}{\alpha_s} b_{sL}\sigma_L^2 b_{kL} + \frac{\alpha_p}{\alpha_s}\sigma_{Ls}b_{kL} + b_{pL}\sigma_L^2 b_{kL}\right].$$

This derivative has to hold for every point on the efficient frontier. A convenient choice is 100% in the minimum variance replicating portfolio. At this point $p = L$, $\alpha_p = 0$, and the derivative becomes

$$\mathrm{Cov}(e_k e_L) = \frac{1}{\alpha_s}(-b_{sL}\sigma_L^2 + \sigma_{Ls})\alpha_k + b_{kL}\sigma_L^2.$$

Solving for α_k, substituting $(\bar{R}_k - R_F) - b_{kL}(\bar{R}_L - R_F)$ for α_k, and adding the subscript i to clarify that a similar equation holds for each investor, we obtain

$$\bar{R}_{ki} - R_F = b_{kL}(\bar{R}_L - R_F) + \frac{\alpha_{si}}{\sigma_{Lsi} - b_{sL}\sigma_L^2}[\mathrm{cov}(e_k e_L) - b_{kL}\sigma_L^2].$$

Note that we have added an investor subscript i to expected return for each security but not to any risk measure except those involving the special portfolio. These subscripts are necessary because, while we assume that each investor attributes the same risks to each security, the composition (and hence risk) of each investor's special portfolio will be different because of differences in expected return.

We can write this expression as

$$\bar{R}_{ki} - R_F = b_{kL}(\bar{R}_L - R_F) + H_i[\text{cov}(e_k e_L) - b_{kL}\sigma_L^2].$$

Aggregating across all investors and averaging, we find

$$\bar{R}_k^* - R_F = b_{kL}(\bar{R}_L - R_F) + H[\text{cov}(e_k e_L) - b_{kL}\sigma_L^2], \tag{14}$$

where $\bar{R}_k^*$ equals the average expectation for stock k and H is the average of H_i across all investors.

Since this equation must hold for all securities, it must hold for the market portfolio. Letting m be the market portfolio, solving for H, and substituting into equation (14) while recognizing that

$$\alpha_m = (\bar{R}_m - R_F) - b_{mL}(\bar{R}_L - R_F)$$

yields

$$\bar{R}_k^* - R_F = \alpha_m \left[\frac{\text{Cov}(e_k e_L) - b_{kL}\sigma_L^2}{\text{Cov}(e_L e_m) - b_{mL}\sigma_L^2}\right] + b_{kL}(\bar{R}_L - R_F). \tag{15}$$

But this is of the form

$$\bar{R}_k^* - R_F = \gamma_o \text{cov}(e_k e_L) + \gamma_1 b_{kL}, \tag{16}$$

which can be easily estimated.

It is interesting to note that the presence of heterogeneous expectations implies that there is a priced risk beyond sensitivity to the index (beta). To the extent that residual variance between stocks is small (or zero, which is a common assumption made in APT models), a stock's own residual variance will be a very good proxy for $\text{cov}(e_k e_L)$. This may well account for why residual variance continues to show up as a factor in equilibrium tests for CAPM and APT models.

In addition, equation (16) can be tested. Given the return-generating process, b_{kL} and $\text{Cov}(e_k e_L)$ can be estimated from a first-pass regression. Equation (16) can then be estimated from a cross-sectional regression. All such tests are obviously tests of the joint hypothesis that the return-generating process has been specified correctly and that the relative pricing relationship in equation (16) is correct. Many of the variety of tests used for standard CAPM tests could also be applied to testing equation (16).

V Conclusions

In this article, we provide the investment theory and equilibrium relationship when security returns follow a multifactor return-generating process with nonreplicable factors and heterogeneous expectations. We show that, under these assumptions, an investor's efficient frontier can be constructed as a combination of the riskless asset, a special portfolio made up of nonequilibrium securities, and one portfolio related to each index. Furthermore, the composition of each of these portfolios can be determined without reference to the others. With homogeneous estimates or risk variables, the optimal index portfolios are common across investors, while the special portfolio is unique to each investor. The special portfolio can be determined using simple analysis. We then derive the asset pricing model when investors determine their portfolios using the analysis discussed in the first section. Given the return-generating process, the heterogeneous-expectations equilibrium model we derive is expressible in terms of observable portfolios and can be tested.

Notes

We would like to thank Jon Ingersoll for helpful comments on an earlier version of this article.

1. For derivation of portfolio theory under alternative assumptions, the reader is referred to Arditti and Levy (1975), Bawa (1978), Bawa, Elton, and Gruber (1979), Elton and Gruber (1974, 1987), and Fishburn (1965).

2. For a number of multi-index models that have been proposed, the scaling of the index is arbitrary. Rescaling the R_L leads to a corresponding rescaling of the b_{iL}. Such a rescaling will not effect the composition of efficient portfolios or the composition of the portfolio the investor selects. Changing the scale of the axis of the space describing efficient portfolios will effect the location of any point on the efficient frontier. An analogy to mean variance analysis might be useful. Describing the efficient frontier in terms of variance rather than standard deviation does not effect the composition of the efficient portfolios but does affect the location of any point on the efficient frontier.

3. Ingersoll (1987) has a proof of this and suggested to us the simpler discussion used in the text.

4. For the Rothschild and Stiglitz measure, X is weakly less risky than Z if Z can be written as $X + e$ and e is a fair game. In our analysis, $X = Y + e_1$ and $Z = X + e_3$.

5. See, for example Chen, Roll, and Ross (1986).

6. The sum of the weights has not been constrained to add to one. However, we have not considered the riskless asset in our solution. Therefore, we have one more asset portfolio and one more equation. By setting the amount to invest in the riskless asset to $(1 - \Sigma W_j)$, we have satisfied the conditions.

7. We have not required that the beta on the other indexes be zero. This additional requirement does not result in an easy or intuitive solution.

8. With perfect factor replication, this is not internally consistent. See Fama (68).

9. The proofs can be extended to heterogeneity in any of the risk parameters as well as expected returns.

References

Arditti, Fred and Haim Levy, "Portfolio Efficiency Analysis in Three Moments: The Multiperiod Case," *Journal of Finance* 30 (3), 797–809 (June 1975).

Bawa, Vijay, "Safety First, Stochastic Dominance and Optimal Portfolio Choice," *Journal of Financial and Quantitative Analysis* 13 (2), 255–271 (June 1978).

Bawa, Vijay, Edwin J. Elton, and Martin J. Gruber, "Simple Rules for Optimal Portfolio Selection in a Stable Paretian Market," *Journal of Finance* 34 (2), 1041–1047 (June 1979).

Burmeister, Edwin and Marjorie McElroy, "APT and Multifactor Asset Pricing with Measured and Unobserved Factors: Theoretical and Unobserved Issues," discussion paper, Department of Economics, University of Virginia and Duke University (1989).

Burmeister, Edwin and Marjorie McElroy, "Joint Estimation of Factor Sensitivities and Risk Premia for the Arbitrage Pricing Theory," *Journal of Finance* 43 (3), 721–733 (July 1988).

Burmeister, Edwin and Kent Wall, "The Arbitrage Pricing Theory and Macroeconomic Factor Measures," *The Financial Review* 27 (1), 1–20 (February 1986).

Chen, Nai-fu, Richard Roll, and Stephen Ross, "Economic Forces and the Stock Market," *Journal of Business* 59, 383–403 (July 1986).

Elton, Edwin J. and Martin J. Gruber, "A Multi-Index Risk Model of the Japanese Stock Market," *Japan and the World Economy* 1 (1), 21–44 (1988).

Elton, Edwin J. and Martin J. Gruber, *Modern Portfolio Theory and Investment Analysis*, 3rd edition, New York: John Wiley and Sons, 1987.

Elton, Edwin J. and Martin J. Gruber, "Portfolio Theory When Investment Relatives are Lognormally Distributed," *Journal of Finance* 24, 1265 (September 1974).

Elton, Edwin J. and Martin J. Gruber, "An Algorithm for Maximizing the Geometric Mean," *Management Science*, 483–488 (December 1974).

Elton, Edwin J. and Martin J. Gruber, "Estimating the Dependence Structure of Share Prices —Implications for Portfolio Selection," *Journal of Finance* 8 (5), 1203–1232 (December 1973).

Fama, Eugene, "Risk Return and Equilibrium: Some Clarifying Comments," *Journal of Finance*, 23 (1), 29–40 (March 1968).

Fama, Eugene, "The Behavior of Stock Market Prices," *Journal of Business* 38, 34–105 (January 1965).

Farrell, James, "Analysis Covariation of Returns to Determine Homogeneous Stock Grouping," *Journal of Business* 47 (2), 186–207 (April 1974).

Fishburn, Peter, "Mean Risk Analysis with Risk Associated Below Target Returns," *American Economic Review* 67 (2), 116–126 (March 1977).

Gibbons, Michael, "Empirical Examination of the Return-Generating Process of the Arbitrage Pricing Theory," working paper, Stanford University (1989).

Hamao, Yasushi, "An Empirical Examination of the Arbitrage Pricing Theory: Using Japanese Data," unpublished manuscript, Yale University (1989).

Ingersoll, Jonathan, *Theory of Financial Decision Making*. Totowa, NJ: Rowman and Littlefield, 1987.

King, Benjamin, "Market and Stock Price Factors in Stock Price Behavior," *Journal of Business* 39, 139–140 (June 1966).

Markowitz, Harry, *Portfolio Selection: Efficient Diversification of Investments*. New York: John Wiley and Sons 1959.

Roll, Richard and Stephen Ross, "An Empirical Investigation of the Arbitrage Pricing Theory," *Journal of Finance* 35 (5), 1073–1103 (December 1980).

Ross, Stephen, "Mutual Fund Separation in Financial Theory—The Separating Distribution," *Journal of Economic Theory* 17, (April 1978).

Rothschild, Michael and Joseph Stiglitz, "Increasing Risk: A Definition," *Journal of Economic Theory* 2, 225–243 (September 1982).

Treynor, Jack and Fischer Black, "How to Use Security Analysis to Improve Portfolio Selection," *Journal of Business* 46, 66–86, (January 1973).

Multi-period Analysis

15 Dynamic Programming Applications in Finance

Edwin J. Elton and Martin J. Gruber

Most of the analytical work in the field of corporation finance has been based upon static analysis. The impact of current decisions on future decisions or the interrelationship of current decisions with future decisions is rarely considered. The purpose of this paper is to explore a relatively new tool—dynamic programming (or recursive optimization) which can be used to formulate and solve problems where inter-temporal relationships are important.

This paper is divided into three sections. The first two sections will present applications of dynamic programming to the bond refinancing decision. This particular problem was selected, not only because it is of interest to almost all corporations, but because its solution leads to an exploration of many of the attributes of dynamic programming.[1] The problem is rich enough so that under alternative realistic assumptions about the type of information which management employs and the time span over which management plans, solutions can be reached which both demonstrate different types of dynamic programming models and illustrate the sensitivity of optimal solutions to management behavior.

The third section of this paper will discuss present and potential applications of dynamic programming to other problems in business finance. First, the aspects of a problem which make it suitable for solution via dynamic programming will be presented. Next several recent applications of dynamic programming to financial management will be reviewed. Finally, areas of potential application will be delineated.

I The Bond Refunding Decision—A Simplified Example

Most corporate bonds contain a provision which allows the issuer to call the bonds before maturity upon repayment of principal plus a premium.

This provision raises a series of problems for the financial manager. First given that the firm has outstanding callable bonds should it call them today and if so with bonds of what maturity should it replace them? Second, what is the cost of following an optimum refunding policy over time? While there are a multitude of factors affecting the optimum timing and value of a call, the factor which has been singled out for special attention is the interest savings that can accrue to the firm through the execution of a call.[2] It is to this problem that we shall address our attention.

When a firm refunds a bond, it incurs a fixed charge equal to the call premium on the old bond plus the cost of floating a new bond. The refunding itself results in a change in future interest payments equal to the difference in interest payments between the old and the new bonds. With two exceptions, previous attempts to determine the optimum timing and/or value of a call have attempted to solve the bond refunding problem as a standard capital budgeting decision [8, 11, 41, 42].[3] One form of this solution is to refund in any period if the present value of the interest savings, over the life of the outstanding bond exceeds the cost of calling the old bond and floating the new bond.[4] A second form involves refunding in that period where the difference between the present value of the interest savings over the life of the original bond and the cost of calling the old bond and floating the new bond is a maximum. For the reasons discussed below either solution is likely to lead to wrong decisions.

If the firm views debt as a permanent component of its capital structure (or at least as a component with a life beyond that of its presently outstanding bonds) the firm might well wish to refund bonds when the present value calculation outlined above is negative. This might happen if interest rates in future periods were expected to be even higher than they are at the time a decision is being made. The present value calculation can also lead to incorrect solutions because it ignores the option of repetitive refunding. The opportunity to refund repetitively over time is what causes the bond refunding decision to be a perfect example of a recursive relationship which is amenable to solution via dynamic programming.[5]

In order to better understand the multiperiod character of the refunding decision and to gain insight into the dynamic programming formulation let us construct a simplistic bond refunding problem. More realistic (and more complex) problems will be discussed in the next section.

(1) Management will maintain a constant level of debt in its capital structure for 5 years after which it will have no debt. This will be referred to as a 5 year time horizon.

Table 15.1

Time	Interest rate
−2	5
−1	5
0	4
1	5
2	5
3	7
4	7

(2) Management will only issue callable bonds in $100 denominations and with a maturity of 3 years.

(3) Management is indifferent on the timing of flows.

(4) Floatation expenses on new debt involve a fixed charge of $2.00.

(5) The cost of calling the old debt is $2 if it is one year old and $1 if it is two years old. This applies at each decision point as well as at the horizon.

(6) The firm currently has a 3 year bond outstanding with a coupon rate of 5% and one year remaining to maturity.

(7) Management is willing to base its decision on the point estimates of future interest rates shown in Table 15.1

With these assumptions, the problem facing management can be represented by the decision tree shown in Figure 15.1. At each of 5 points management has to make a decision as to whether to keep or refund its outstanding bonds.

If we were to follow the tree diagram we could calculate the cost of any decision. For example, an initial decision to keep the outstanding bond involves a one period cost of $5, the interest payment on that bond. If instead the firm decided to refund, the cost would be $1 for calling a 2 year old bond, plus $2 for floating the new bond, plus the $4 interest payment on the new bond. One period later the firm again faces a decision. Assuming that it had initially refunded them the cost of the two alternatives would be:

(1) Keep; $4 interest payment

(2) Refund; $2 call penalty, $2 floatation expense and $5 interest payment.

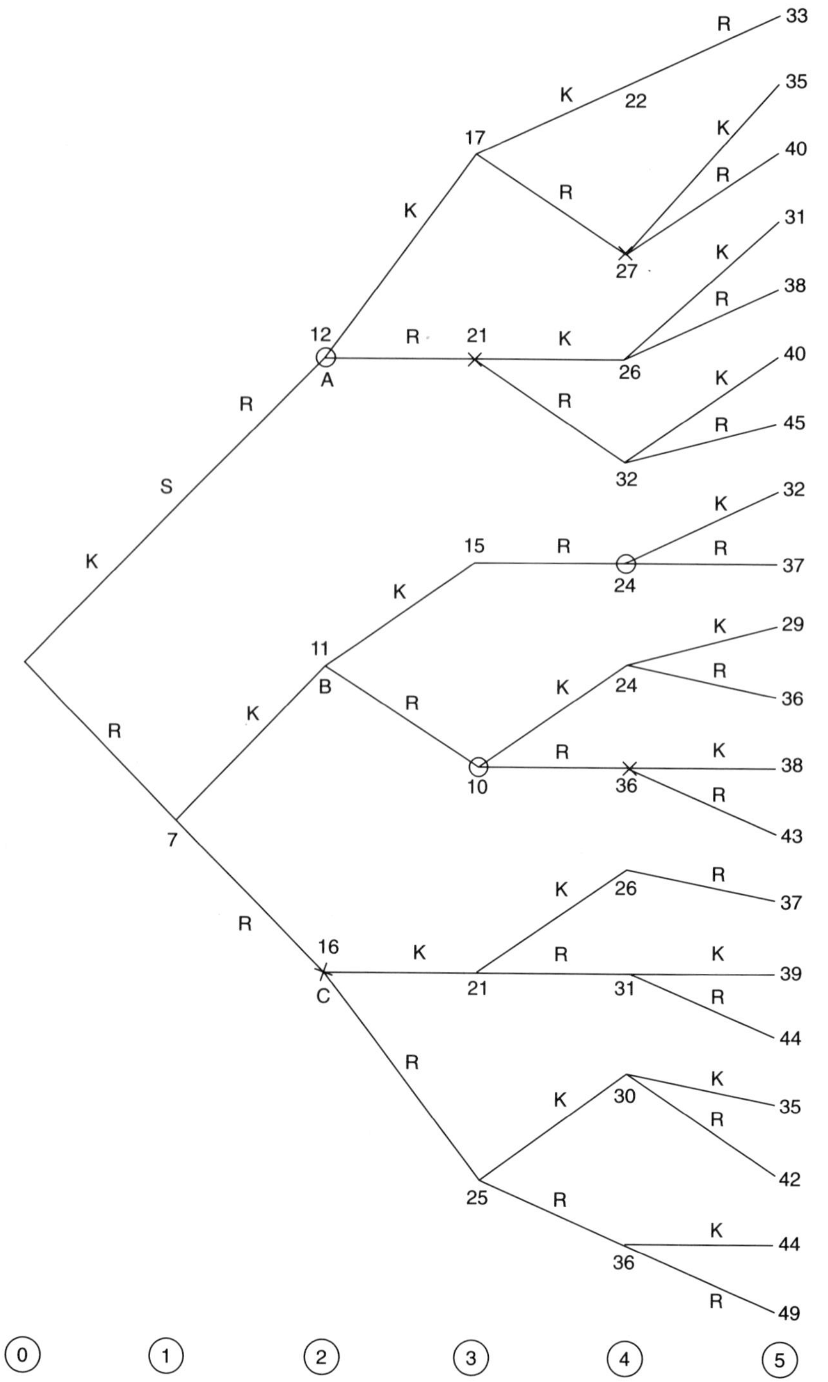
R
33
K
22
35
17
K
40
R
R
K
31
27
K
38
12
R
21
K
R
A
26
40
R
K
R
45
32
S
32
K
15
R
R
K
24
37
K
K
29
11
R
B
K
24
36
R
R
K
38
10
36
R
43
7
R
K
26
37
R
16
K
R
K
39
C
21
31
R
44
R
K
30
K
35
R
42
25
R
K
44
36
R
49
0
1
2
3
4
5

Figure 15.1

In this manner, we could trace out the costs of all feasible decision patterns for the 5 decision periods. We have done this in Figure 15.1. If we had the option of keeping or refunding at each decision point we would need $\Sigma_{i=1}^{5} 2^i + 2^5$ or 94 calculations to trace out all paths. However, since we cannot keep a bond once it has reached maturity, some of the branches of the decision tree can immediately be eliminated. Strategies including more than two successive keeps are infeasible because they call for a bond to remain outstanding past its maturity.[6] Eliminating all infeasible branches leaves us with 62 calculations.

An examination of the decision tree reveals that certain strategies dominate others. For example as shown in Figure 15.1 the firm has 3 nodes at decision point 2. Two of these nodes (*A* and *C*) involve the decision to keep or replace a one year old bond. Examining node *A* we see that if we replace this one year old bond we incur an added cost of \$9 (\$2 in call penalty, \$2 in floation expense and \$5 in interest expense) plus the old cost of \$12 incurred in reaching node 2 or a total of \$21. Examining node *C* reveals that replacing this one year old bond involves an added cost of \$9 plus the old cost of \$16 incurred in reaching node two.[7] Note that the new expense incurred in each case is the same. The additional cost incurred at any point depends only on the age of the bond and the decision made. The generality of this statement can be seen by tracing through the seven decision paths which emanate from node *A* and comparing them with the parallel decisions emanating from node *C*. Each of the seven pairs of costs differ by \$4, the difference in cost at time two.

The previous discussion can be summarized into a principle that will lead to considerable saving of computation time. The optimum pattern of decisions leading to a particular state is independent of the decisions to be made after that state is reached.[8] In the example cited above there were two ways to reach the position (state) of having a one year old bond outstanding at time two. The minimum cost of obtaining this state is \$12 (node *A*) and the higher cost path leading to node *C* can be ignored in all future decisions.

Let's apply this principle to the decision at time two. At this point we have two ways of ending up with a one year old bond, one with a cost of \$21 and one costing \$19. Since either path has the same future costs we eliminate the \$21 path. This elimination is noted by the *X* in Figure 15.1. Note that we could not eliminate the paths which lead to a two year old bond and to a three year old bond at the next decision since future costs would be different. In short, at any point we can eliminate all paths but one path resulting in a one year old bond at the next decision point, one path resulting in a two year old bond at the next decision point, and one path resulting in a three year old bond. Using the previously stated principle (which is the fundamental theorem of dynamic programming) we are able to reduce the calculations from 62 to 24.

As the reader might suspect the previous problem can be solved analytically rather than as a tree diagram. To do so, let's define some notation.

Let:

(1) $f_t(j)$ be the cost of having a bond of age j outstanding when t periods have elapsed if an optimum policy was followed.

(2) R_t be the interest rate at time t.

(3) $C(j)$ be the call penalty.

(4) F be the floatation expense.

The cost of following any policy before a decision is made at time zero can be denoted by f_0. This is equal to zero. If we start at time zero with a two year old bond containing a coupon rate of 5% we can make one of two decisions: keep the bond for another period or refund now. If we keep the bond we incur an interest cost of \$5. Therefore, $f_1(3)$, the cost of making a decision at time zero to have a three year bond outstanding at the end of the first year is R_{-2} or \$5.

If the bond is refunded the firm incurs a cost of buying back the old bond (\$1), the cost of floating a new bond (\$2), and the interest cost on the new bond (\$4).

$$f_1(1) = C(2) + F + R_0 = \$1 + \$2 + \$4 = \$7.$$

Next period we have three choices. First, we can keep the one year old bond which involves an interest cost of \$4 plus the cost of having a one year old bond at this point (\$7). Therefore

$$f_1(2) = R_0 + f(1) = \$4 + \$7 = \$11$$

Since we could refund the one year old bond or the three year old bond we have two possible values for $f_2(1)$.

$$f_2(1) = \text{minimum}\begin{bmatrix} C(1) + F + R_1 + f_1(1) = 2 + 2 + 5 + 7 = \$16 \\ C(3) + F + R_1 + f_1(3) = 0 + 2 + 5 + 5 = \$12. \end{bmatrix}$$

Notice that there are two ways we can get to the position of having a one year old bond outstanding at the end of the second decision period.

Since the optimum way to get to the position $f_2(1)$ is not affected by where we go from there we can eliminate the more expensive of these from further consideration.

We can proceed with this analysis using the general formulas.

$$f_0(j) = 0 \quad j = 1, 2, 3$$

$$f_t(3) = R_{t-3} + f_{t-1}(2)$$

$$f_t(2) = R_{t-2} + f_{t-1}(1)$$

$$f_t(1) = \text{Minimum}\ [C_j + F + R_{t-1} + f_{t-1}(j)]$$
$$j = 1, 2, 3$$

These formulas can be used to generate the numbers in Table 15.2. Note the 5 decisions made at period 5 are the same decisions indicated by arrows in Figure 15.1 and the optimum of \$29 is identical.

It might be appropriate at this time to show that the decision we have reached is different from that which would be reached via traditional analysis. The most commonly proposed criteria for making the refunding decision is to minimize costs over the life of the original bond.[9] Since the original bond only has one period until maturity, the decision would be to replace it or leave it outstanding according to which minimizes the cost to the firm in the first period. Not refunding gives a cost of \$5 while refunding involves a cost of \$7. The traditional analysis indicates that it is better not to refund. But as we have shown this decision results in higher costs over management's time horizon even though it had lower costs over one period.[10] It might appear that traditional analysis will always produce correct results if the life of the original bond coincides exactly with management's time horizon. However even in this case the possibility of multiple refundings means that the solutions produced by traditional analysis can be incorrect.

There is a second approach which can be used to solve the refunding decision via dynamic programming. Recursive optimization in a backward direction can be employed rather than recursive optimization in a forward direction. The theory of optimization proposed earlier can be restated: the optimum way of getting from a particular state to an end point is not a function of the path taken to that state. In fact the two theorems can be put together to yield a general theorem of recursive optimization: the optimum path between any two states is neither a function of how one gets to the first state nor where one goes from the second.

Table 15.2
Age of replaced bond

t	1	2	3	$f_t(1)$	$f_t(2)$	$f_t(3)$
	$F + C(1) + R_{t-1}$ $+f_{t-1}(1) =$	$F + C(2) + R_{t-1}$ $+f_{t-1}(2) =$	$F + C(3) + R_{t-1}$ $+f_{t-1}(3) =$	Minimum of replaced	$R_{t-2} + f_{t-1}(1) =$	$R_{t-3} + f_{t-1}(2) =$
1		$2 + 1 + 4 + 0 = 7$		7		$5 + 0 = 5$
2	$2 + 2 + 5 + 7 = 16$		$2 + 0 + 5 + 5 = 12$	12	$4 + 7 = 11$	
3	$2 + 2 + 5 + 12 = 21$	$2 + 1 + 5 + 11 = 19$		19	$5 + 12 = 17$	$4 + 11 = 15$
4	$2 + 2 + 7 + 19 = 30$	$2 + 1 + 7 + 17 = 27$	$2 + 0 + 7 + 15 = 24$	24	$5 + 19 = 24$	$5 + 17 = 22$
5	$2 + 2 + 7 + 24 = 35$	$2 + 1 + 7 + 24 = 34$	$2 + 0 + 7 + 22 = 31$	31	$7 + 24 = 31$	$5 + 24 = 29$
5+ (Call penalty)	$35 + 2 = 37$	$34 + 2 = 36$	$31 + 2 = 33$		$31 + 1 = 32$	$29 + 0 = 29$

To illustrate the process of backward optimization we would like to solve this simple example using a one equation system. The one equation system while conceptually more difficult is computationally much simpler and will be the way that will be used to solve the more realistic problems that follow. Instead of stating the problem as should the firm keep or refund a j year old bond in period t, we could reformulate it as given that the firm floats a bond in period t when should it refund again. If the firm knew this for every period but the current period it could then calculate the optimum time to refund a bond of any given age in the current period.

The optimum time to refund a brand new bond acquired in period four is of course at the horizon when it must be refunded. The cost involved is \$2 in floation to acquire the new bond, \$2 in call penalty at the horizon plus the \$7 interest charge or:

$$f_4 = \$2 + \$2 + \$7 = \$11$$

The optimum time to refund a brand new bond acquired in period three is either at period four or the horizon. If the firm calls at the horizon it incurs a cost of \$2 to float the new bond at period three, \$1 in call penalty and two interest payments of \$7 each. On the other hand, if it calls in period four it incurs \$2 to float the new bond, \$2 in call penalty, one interest payment of \$7, and the cost of the optimum policy from period four to the horizon. The firm should choose the least expensive so:

$$f_3 = \text{minimum}\begin{bmatrix} F + C(2) + 2R_3 = 2 + 1 + 14 = \$17 \\ F + C(1) + R_3 + f_4 = 2 + 2 + 7 + 11 = \$22 \end{bmatrix}$$

The other calculations are shown in Table 15.3. The general form is:[11]

for $t = T$

$$f_t = 0$$

for all $t < T$

$$f_t = \text{minimum } F + C(k) + kR_t + f_{t+k}.$$

$$k = 1, \ldots, (3, T - t)$$

Where:

(1) $(3, T - t)$ means the minimum of 3 years or the number of years to the horizon $(T - t)$;

(2) other symbols as before.

Table 15.3
Values for $F + C + \sum_{L=1}^{k} R_t^L + f_{t+k}$

t	f_t	$k = 1$	$k = 2$	$k = 3$
4	11	$2 + 2 + 7 + 0 = 11$		
3	17	$2 + 2 + 7 + 11 = 22$	$2 + 1 + 14 + 0 = 17$	
2	17	$2 + 2 + 5 + 17 = 26$	$2 + 1 + 10 + 11 = 24$	$2 + 0 + 15 + 0 = 17$
1	26	$2 + 2 + 5 + 17 = 26$	$2 + 1 + 10 + 17 = 30$	$2 + 0 + 15 + 11 = 28$
0	28	$2 + 2 + 4 + 26 = 34$	$2 + 1 + 8 + 17 = 28$	$2 + 0 + 12 + 17 = 31$

$$f_{\text{decision}} = \text{minimum}\begin{bmatrix} 1 + 28 \\ 5 + 26 \end{bmatrix} = 29$$

A second equation is necessary in order to incorporate starting conditions. The single equation presented above can be used to find the cost of floating a new bond at time zero, one, two, etc., however it does not incorporate the option of not refunding a bond which is outstanding at time period zero. To take this into consideration we must define a new term f_{decision} which represents the cost of maintaining debt until the horizon given the possibility of not refunding at time zero.

Since we assumed that the firm had a two year old bond outstanding at time 0 the firm had two options at time 0. It has the option of refunding the two year old bond immediately incurring costs of $C(1) + f_0$ or $\$1 + \$28 = \$29$. The second option was to let the outstanding bond mature incurring costs of $R_{-2} + f_1(1)$ or $\$5 + \$26 = \$31$. The first option is the more profitable one.

In general if j_0 is the age of the outstanding bond at time 0, f_{decision} can be expressed as:[12]

if $j_0 = 0$, then $f_{\text{decision}} = f_0$.

If $j_0 \neq 0$

$$f_{\text{decision}} = \text{minimum } f_k + C(j_0 + k) + \begin{bmatrix} 0 & \text{if } k = 0 \\ \sum_{i=1}^{k} R_{-j_0} & \text{if } k \neq 0 \end{bmatrix}$$

$$k = 0, \ldots, 3 - j_0$$

The number of calculations have been radically reduced from 62 using complete enumeration, to 24 working forwards, and comparing keep versus refund, and finally to 14 working backwards and asking when to refund (the one equation form of the dynamic programming problem).[13]

Having explored in detail a rather simplistic example in order to illustrate how dynamic programming works and why the bond refunding problem is a dynamic programming problem we will now turn to more realistic formulations of the bond refunding problem.

II The Generalized Bond Refunding Problem

In this section of the paper we will present several more realistic solutions to the bond refunding decision. These solutions differ from each other in terms of the type or amount of information which management is assumed to use and the time horizon over which management is assumed to plan. Before presenting analytical solutions it is desirable to present a more detailed discussion of the costs involved in the refunding decision.

A The Costs of Refunding

In order for the firm to refund its bonds it must incur a cost of calling the outstanding bonds (called a call premium). The call premium is usually stated as a function of the coupon rate on the debt and usually declines as maturity approaches. A. typical schedule of call premiums would be for the initial premium to be equal to one year's interest and to decline linearly to zero at maturity. At a point in time, the call premium on almost all callable bonds will be a function of the age of the bond, the interest rate at the time it was issued, and the original maturity of the bond.

When a firm sells a bond it incurs floatation charges. These floatation expenses usually vary with the size of the issue and often with the associated interest rate. Since we are holding the size of the issue constant we will assume in the rest of the paper that the only source of variation is the level of interest rates.

In deciding on whether to refund a bond or not the firm must decide on the proper discount rate to use in measuring the value of cash flows which accrue at different points in time. This is a rather complex issue. Several alternatives have been presented in the literature. These range from the firm's cost of capital to the riskless rate of interest.[14] The appropriate discount rate for management to use is the one that reflects the degree of risk inherent in the refunding decision. The decision is not a riskless decision because in the real world we would be uncertain about the level of future interest rates and therefore the actual costs of any refunding policy. At the other extreme it should not be the cost of capital for the risk of interest rate changes should be different from and smaller than the risks associated with the firm's assets.

The risks associated with the cash flows from refunding are the risk that the firm will default on its debt obligation (in which case it won't get the benefit of the refunding decision) and the risk of changes in interest rates. The premium that the market demands for bearing these risks is incorporated in the interest rate on corporate bonds. That is, the interest rate (yield) that must be offered on callable bonds of any particular maturity is the rate which the market demands for buying that bond given the possible loss from default and changes in interest rates (this includes the loss from a possible call). Thus we feel that the appropriate discount rate for the stream of cash flows that are generated from the decision to call any bond is the yield that must be offered to sell a bond of equal maturity. However, because the issue of the appropriate discount rate has been the subject of so much controversy we shall present all solutions in terms of a generalized discount rate for which the reader can substitute that rate which he feels is most appropriate.

In constructing all of the models in this section, we shall view the refunding decision as a discrete problem. While a firm could decide to call a bond at any moment in time the amount of data and level of analysis needed to make a decision makes it likely that management considers the decision at specified intervals of time. Since the call premium usually decreases after the coupon payment is due, (e.g., every year after the payment of even numbered coupon payments) one logical pattern of decision points is immediately after the payment of a coupon. We shall assume that management follows this time pattern in considering the refunding decision.

Having discussed some of the costs involved in the refunding decision, let's examine one set of such decisions. For the first group of problems we discuss, we will continue to assume that management acts on the basis of point estimates of future interest rates. In addition, at first we will continue our assumption that management has a fixed horizon during which they expect to maintain a given dollar value of debt in the firms capital structure and at the end of which they expect to retire all debt.[15] While most corporations do borrow on a permanent basis, a substantial minority retire debt.[16]

B Fixed Horizon with Point Estimates

Let us start by assuming that management intends to issue bonds of a particular maturity, M. However if the horizon is less than M years away, management will consider issuing either bonds of maturity M or debt instruments with a maturity equal to the number of years remaining until the horizon. Let:

m = a variable representing the actual maturity of the firm's bonds.

M = a constant representing the standard maturity.

R_t^m = the yield on a bond issued at time t with a maturity of m years.

$F(R_t^m)$ = the fixed cost of floating a bond carrying an interest rate of R_t^m.

$C(k, R_t^m, m)$ = the call premium on a bond k years of age, with an interest rate of R_t^m, and an original maturity of m years.

α_t = the discount factor used to equate the value of cash receipts and disbursements made at different points of time.[17]

T = the fixed horizon at which debt will be retired.

f_t = the minimum cost of having debt outstanding from time t until time T.

f_{decision} = the minimum cost of having debt outstanding from the current period until T given the characteristics of any bond that might be outstanding at time t.

The dynamic programming solution to this problem is:

$$f_T = 0 \tag{1}$$

for all t such that $T - M < t < T$

$$f_t = \text{minimum}\left[F(R_t^m) + \sum_{i=1}^{k} \alpha_{t+i}^i R_t^m + \alpha_{t+k}^k C(k, R_t^m, m) + \alpha_{t+k}^k f_{t+k}\right]$$

$$m = (T - t) \quad \text{or } M$$

$$k = 1, 2, \ldots, m \tag{2}$$

for all $t \leqslant T - M$ and $m = M$

$$f_t = \text{minimum}\left[F(R_t^m) + \sum_{i=1}^{k} \alpha_{t+i}^i R_t^m + \alpha_{t+k}^k C(k, R_t^m, m) + \alpha_{t+k}^k f_{t+k}\right]$$

$$k = 1, \ldots, m \tag{3}$$

If j_0 is defined as the age of the bond at t' and m_0 is defined as the maturity of the outstanding bond at t' then to reach a decision at t', we have:

If $j_0 = 0$ then $f_{\text{decision}} = f_{t'}$

If $j_0 \neq 0$

$$f_{\text{decision}} = \text{minimum } \alpha^k_{t'+k} f_{t'+k} + C(j_0 + k, R^{m_0}_{t'-j_0}, m_0)$$

$$+ \begin{bmatrix} 0 & \text{if } k = 0 \\ \sum_{i=1}^{k} \alpha^i_{t'+i} R^{m_0}_{t'-j_0} & \text{if } k \neq 0 \end{bmatrix}$$

$$k = 0, \ldots, m_0 - j_0 \qquad (4)$$

Equation (1) simply expresses the fact that from the horizon on (when all debt is eliminated) the firm incurs no debt charges. The second and third equations represent the minimum cost of maintaining debt from each year prior to the horizon until the horizon.

Both equations involve finding the minimum of the cost associated with issuing a new bond, and then calling this bond, plus the minimum cost of maintaining debt from the call date until the horizon. For example, in order to calculate the minimum cost at a point in time 40 years prior to the horizon, we would compare the cost of floating a bond and calling it in one year plus the cost of the optimum way to raise debt for 39 more years with the cost of floating a bond and calling it in two years plus the cost of the optimum way to raise debt for 38 more years. We would do this for all possible call dates up to and including the maturity of the bond. The four costs in both equations (2 and 3) represent the cost of floating the bond, the present value of the interest payment made on the bond until it is called, the present value of the call premium, and the present value of the minimum cost of maintaining debt from the call date to the horizon.

Equations (2) and (3) differ in one respect. Equation (3) only considers bonds of one maturity while equation (2) allows the firm to float bonds with a maturity equal to either the standard maturity or the time remaining to the end of the horizon.[18] Therefore in equation (2) the pattern of refunding is optimized with respect to the maturity of the bonds as well as the timing of calls.

Equation (4) incorporates starting conditions into the decision. Although $f_{t'}$ yields the optimum pattern of bond refunding providing no bond is

Table 15.4
Assume interest rates

	Maturity = 1			Maturity = 2			Maturity = 3			Maturity = 4		
Time period	r_1	r_2	Expected value	r_1	r_2	Expected value	r_1	r_2	Expected value	r_1	r_2	Expected value
0							4	6	5	4	6	5
1							4	6	5	5	7	6
2							5	7	6	5	8	6
3							5	7	6	5	8	6
4							5	7	6	4	7	5
5							4	6	5	4	7	5
6							4	6	5	3	5	4
7							3	5	4	3	5	4
8							4	6	5	5	7	6
9							4	6	5	4	6	5
10				7	9	8	6	8	7	5	7	6
11	7	9	8				6	8	7	6	8	7

outstanding at time t', it does not necessarily produce the best decisions if an outstanding bond exists. The outstanding bond changes the initial options and costs. For example if at t' a bond was outstanding with 2 years left to maturity the firm could call immediately and incur the cost of calling plus $f_{t'}$. On the other hand, it could wait one year to refund, incurring the interest cost on the old bond for one year, the cost of calling a year later and $f_{t'+1}$. Similarly the firm could wait 2 years to call and again change its costs. Equation (4) allows the firm to select the optimum strategy to follow given an outstanding bond with any number of years remaining to maturity.

The previous discussion can be further clarified with an example. Assume the firm has a 12 year horizon and is willing to base its financing decision on the interest rates shown in Table 15.4 under the column labeled Expected Value. Further assume that the standard bond maturity is 3 years, the call premiums are as shown in Table 15.5, the floatation expenses is \$2, and the discount factor is one.

Applying equations (1) through (4) yields Table 15.6. If the firm is to replace a bond at the beginning of the last period then it has the choice of issuing a bond with a one year maturity or one with a 3 year maturity. If it issues a 3 year bond it incurs \$2 in floatation expenses plus \$7 in

Table 15.5
Call premium

Remaining years to maturity	Call penalty
3	3
2	2
1	1
0	0

interest expense plus $2 for calling at the horizon or $11. If it issues a one year bond it incurs $2 in floatation expense plus $8 in interest expense or $10. The least expensive alternative is issuing a one year bond and calling at the horizon so that $f_1 = \$10$. If the firm wants to replace a bond two periods from the horizon, then it has the choice of issuing a three year bond and calling the next period, issuing a three year bond and calling at the horizon, or issuing a bond with a maturity of two years. If it issues a three year bond and calls the next period, the firm incurs $2 floatation expense, $7 interest expense, $2 call penalty (at the end of the period), and $10 representing the cost of the least expensive way of financing the last period or a total cost of $21. The cost of this alternative as well as the other alternatives is shown in Table 15.6. For period 10 the least expensive alternative is to issue a three year bond and call in two periods incurring a cost of $17. This becomes f_{10}.

How realistic is an example where the minimum cost involves calling at the horizon rather than issuing a bond that matures at the horizon? If the potential bondholders anticipate the call at the horizon than the yield on a three year callable bond must be the same as the yield on a two year bond and issuing a bond that matured at the horizon would have to be less expensive since it would save the expense of the call at the horizon.[19] If on the other hand, the bondholders did not perfectly anticipate the call and the yield curve were downward sloping, then issuing a bond which matures after the horizon and calling it could be the least expensive alternative. It would be the least expensive alternative if the interest saving on issuing a bond with a longer maturity (in the example 3 years) is greater than the call penalty. Since it seems unrealistic to assume that potential bondholders can perfectly anticipate the length of management's horizon and thus the timing of the final call issuing a bond which matures beyond the horizon may well be optimum.

Having determined the cost of the least expensive method of going from any period where the firm replaces a bond to the horizon, the firm is

Table 15.6
Values for $F + \sum_{l=1}^{k} \alpha^l R_t^m + \alpha^k C + \alpha^k f_{t+k}$

					$m = T - t$	
t	f_t	$k = 1$	$k = 2$	$k = 3$	$k = 1$	$k = 2$
11	10	$2 + 7 + 2 + 0 = 11$			$[2 + 8 + 0 + 0 = 10]$	
10	17	$2 + 7 + 2 + 10 = 21$	$[2 + 14 + 1 + 0 = 17]$			$2 + 16 + 0 + 0 = 18$
9	17	$[2 + 5 + 2 + 17 = 26]$	$2 + 10 + 1 + 10 = 23$	$(2 + 5 + 0 + 0 = 17)$		
8	26	$2 + 5 + 2 + 17 = 26$	$2 + 10 + 1 + 17 = 30$	$2 + 15 + 0 + 10 = 27$		
7	28	$2 + 4 + 2 + 26 = 34$	$(2 + 8 + 1 + 17 = 28)$	$2 + 12 + 0 + 17 = 31$		
6	34	$2 + 5 + 2 + 28 = 37$	$2 + 10 + 1 + 26 = 39$	$[2 + 15 + 0 + 17 = 34]$		
5	41	$2 + 5 + 2 + 34 = 43$	$(2 + 10 + 1 + 28 = 41)$	$2 + 15 + 0 + 26 = 43$		
4	48	$2 + 6 + 2 + 41 = 51$	$2 + 12 + 1 + 34 = 49$	$[2 + 18 + 0 + 28 = 48]$		
3	54	$2 + 6 + 2 + 48 = 58$	$2 + 12 + 1 + 41 = 56$	$2 + 18 + 0 + 34 = 54$		
2	61	$2 + 6 + 2 + 54 = 64$	$2 + 12 + 1 + 48 = 63$	$(2 + 18 + 0 + 41 = 61)$		
1	65	$2 + 5 + 2 + 61 = 70$	$2 + 10 + 1 + 54 = 67$	$[2 + 15 + 0 + 48 = 65]$		
0	71	$2 + 5 + 2 + 65 = 74$	$2 + 10 + 1 + 61 = 74$	$[2 + 15 + 0 + 54 = 71]$		

[ ] designates decision that minimizes cost.
( ) designates decision that minimizes cost and is expected to occur.

ready to make a decision. Assume it currently (time period 0) has a one year old bond outstanding with a coupon rate of 4% and two years remaining until it matures. Then, utilizing equation (4), the firm has three possible decisions: replace now, replace in one period or replace in two periods. If it replaces now, the firm incurs a call penalty of \$2 plus the cost of the optimum decision from the current period to the horizon given that a bond is replaced in the current period ($f_0 = \$71$) or a total cost of \$73. If it replaces next period, the firm incurs a call penalty of \$1, an interest expense of \$4 plus the cost of the optimum decision from the next period to the horizon given that a bond is replaced then (which is $f_1 = \$65$) producing a total cost of \$70. Finally if the firm replaces in two periods it incurs an interest cost of \$8 and a future cost of \$61 for a total of \$69. Therefore the firm should replace in period 2.

The firm should expect the bond it floats in period two to remain outstanding for three more years since the minimum value of f_2 (\$61) is associated with this decision. As can be seen from Table 15.6, the firm should expect to replace bonds in periods, 2, 5, 7 and 9 as well as at the horizon (T).

It is quite easy to generalize this solution to the case where management will consider floating bonds of more than one maturity.[20] The notation will remain the same as in the previous case except that M will now stand for the set of all maturities that the firm considers issuing and M' will stand for the longest maturity in the set.

Equations (1) and (4) remain the same. Equations (2) and (3) generalized for all allowable maturities become for all $t < T$

$$f_t = \text{minimum}\left[F(R_t^m) + \sum_{i=1}^{k} \alpha_{t+i}^{i} R_t^m + \alpha_{t+k}^{k} C(k, R_t^m, m) + \alpha_{t+k}^{k} f_{t+k}\right]$$

$$m \varepsilon M$$

and also

$$m = T - t$$

$$\text{for } T - t < M'$$

$$k = 1, \ldots, m \tag{5}$$

In this equation we are optimizing across all possible maturities as well as all possible call times.

These three equations (1), (4) and (5) allow the firm to decide on the optimum pattern of bond refunding over a finite horizon as well as the maturity of the bond it should issue at any refunding and the cost of pursuing this policy.[21] If we continue with the previous example except that we allow the firm to float a bond with either a three or four year maturity at any moment in time we can see that increasing management options can decrease the cost of maintaining debt.[22] The optimum policy for management to follow is to allow the initial bond to mature, in period 2, issue a four year bond and allow it to mature in period 6, issue a 4 year bond and call it in period 9, and issue a three year bond which matures at the horizon. Costs are reduced from \$71 in the fixed maturity case to \$68 in the variable maturity case.

C *Infinite Horizon with Point Estimates*

Up to now we have assumed that management was interested in making decisions over a finite horizon. It is more common for management to plan to have debt remain as a permanent component of the firm's capital structure. In this case management should optimize over an infinite horizon. The solution to the infinite horizon problem is made tenable by the fact that almost without exception the market's expectation of future interest rates is stable after some point in time (T). Evidence of this expectation is provided by the fact that almost all yield curves reach a constant level for long maturities.

Employing the same notation as in the previous case with the exception that T now stands for the point in time at which interest rates are expected to stabilize we can rewrite equation (5) as:

For $t \geqslant T$

$$f_t = \underset{\substack{m \varepsilon M \\ k=1,\ldots,m}}{\text{minimum}} \left[F(R_t^m) + \sum_{i=1}^{k} \alpha_{t+i}^i R_t^m + \alpha_{t+k}^k C(k, R_t^m, m) + \alpha_{t+k}^k f_{t+k} \right] \tag{6}$$

Since interest rates are assumed to be stable after T, it is reasonable to assume R is invariant with changes in maturity.[23] If R_t^m is constant then $F(R_t)$ and α_t are also constants. We shall use the subscript T to denote all three variables after the horizon. In addition the subscript of f_t is unnecessary since all the variables on the right side of equation (6) are in fact constants with respect to t. Thus equation (6) can be rewritten as:

$$f = \text{minimum}\left[F_T + \sum_{i=1}^{k} \alpha_T^i R_T + \alpha_T^k C(k, R_T^m, m) + \alpha_T^k f\right]$$

$$m \varepsilon M$$

$$k = 1, \ldots, m \tag{7}$$

Solving (7) for f yields:[24]

$$f = \text{minimum}\left[\frac{F_T + \alpha_T^k C(k, R_T^m, m)}{1 - \alpha_T^k} + \frac{\alpha_T}{1 - \alpha_T} R_T\right]$$

$$m \varepsilon M$$

$$k = 1, \ldots, m \tag{8}$$

An examination of equation (8) reveals that equation (8) is minimized if k and m are made as large as possible since call costs are zero and the present value of floatation expense is minimized.

Defining M' as the longest maturity the firm will issue and recognizing that call costs are equal to zero we have:[25]

For $t > T$

$$f_t = \frac{F_T}{1 - \alpha_T^{M'}} + \frac{\alpha_T}{1 - \alpha_T} R_T \tag{9}$$

This represents the cost of following the optimum policy of issuing bonds of maximum maturity and never refunding computed as of the time of the first refunding after T. To compute the cost of refunding before year T one simply employs equations (4) and (5). All we have really had to do to solve the infinite horizon model is to specify a set of ending conditions for equation (5). The optimum decisions for a firm to make will now consist of a specified set of refunding dates and associated specified maturities to some date past T plus a policy of always floating the maximum maturity bond and never calling after that date.[26]

To illustrate the application of the equations assume $\alpha = .8$, $R_T = 5\%$ the floatation expense is \$2, and the only possible maturities are 3 and 4 years. Then for $t > T$ we have:

$$f_t = \frac{2}{1 - (.8)^4} + \frac{.8}{1 - .8}(5) = 24.882$$

Assume the firm is willing to make explicit forecasts of future interest rates for 4 periods and that these rates are shown in Table 15.5 (under the headings, 0, 1, 2, 3). Further assume the call premium is given in Table 15.6 and floation expenses are \$2, and that a value for α of .8 is assumed to be appropriate for all periods.

Applying equations (4), (5) and (9) shows that if the firm had two years remaining on a bond with a coupon rate of 4%, it would allow the outstanding bond to mature and replace it with a 4 year bond, after which it would always float 4 year bonds and allow them to remain outstanding until maturity. The total expected cost of this policy would be \$22.63.

D Finite Horizon under Risk

Up to this point we have assumed that management while recognizing that risk was present in the refunding decision would make that decision on the basis of point estimates (expected values) of future interest rates. Now let us assume that management is willing to employ information about the distribution of future interest rates in making its refunding decision.

More specifically let us assume that management is willing to estimate the probability associated with the occurrence of each possible yield curve for each period in which it will face a refunding decision.

We will again start with the case of decisions over a finite horizon. Let:

M = the set of maturities which management considers offering.

M' = the maximum maturity management considers offering (the largest element in the set M).

m = a particular maturity (an element of the set M).

R_i^* = a random variable representing the level of the yield curve at a particular point in time.[27] R_i^* is always expressed in terms of one year rates.

R^* = a particular level for the yield curve. (i.e., one particular R_i^*). R^* is always expressed in terms of a one year rate.

$f_t(R^*)$ = the minimum cost of having bonds outstanding from period t until the horizon given the occurrence of yield curve R^* at time t.

$d_q^t(R_t^m, m)$ = the minimum cost of having bonds outstanding from year $t+q$ to the horizon given that a bond of maturity m bearing an interest rate R_t^m is floated in year t and is left outstanding q years or longer.

$P_q(R_i^*)$ = the probability of yield curve R_i^* occurring at time $t+q$

$P_q(R_i^*/R^*)$ = the probability of yield curve R_i^* occurring at time $t+q$ given that the yield at time t is R^*.

T = the horizon year after which the firm is assumed to have no debt in its capital structure.

$[(m-1),(T-t)]$ = is defined as the minimum of $(m-1)$ and $(T-t)$.

All other terms as before.

We can now write the recursive relationship for the cost of debt to the horizon. Before doing so, let us make one more assumption in the interest of realism. Assume that management is willing to sell non-standard maturities (Maturities not contained in the set M) as the horizon approaches in order to allow the bonds to mature at the horizon.[28] For all $t \geqslant T$

$$f_t = 0$$

for all $t < T$ and all R^*

$$f_t(R^*) = \text{minimum } [F(R_t^m) + \alpha_{t+1}R_t^m + \alpha_{t+1}^k d_1^t(R_t^m, m)]$$

$$_{m\varepsilon}M \text{ or } T-t \quad \text{if } M' > T-t$$

$$_{m\varepsilon}M \text{ if } M' \leqslant T-t. \tag{12}$$

For $q = m$

$$d_m^t(R_t^m, m) = \sum_{R_i^*} [f_{t+m}(R_i^*)][P_{t+m}(R_i^*)]$$

$$\text{for} \quad q = m-1, \ldots, 1 \tag{10}$$

$$d_q^t(R_t^m, m) = \Sigma P_{t+q}(R_i^*)[f_{t+q}(R_i^*) + C(q, R_t^m, m)]$$

$$+ [1 - \Sigma P_{t+q}(R_i^*)[\alpha_{t+q+1}R_t^m + \alpha_{t+q+1}d_{q+1}(R_t^m, m)] \tag{11}$$

The summation is done for all cases where:

$$f_{t+q}(R_i^*) + C(q, R_t^m, m) < \alpha_{q+1}R_t^m + \alpha_{q+1}d_{q+1}(R_t^m, m)$$

if $j_0 = 0$, $f_{\text{decision}} = f_{t'}$

if $j_0 \neq 0$

$$f_{\text{decision}} = \text{minimum } \alpha^{k}_{t'+k} \sum_{R^*_i} [f_{t'+k}(R^*_i)][P(R^*_i)]$$

$$+ \alpha^{k}_{t'+k} C(j_0 + k, R^{m_0}_{t'-j_0}, m_0) + B]$$

$$k = 0 \ldots M_0 - j_0 \tag{13}$$

Where

$B = 0$ if $k = 0$

$B = \sum_{i=1}^{k} \alpha^{i}_{t'+1} R^{m_0}_{t'-j_0}$ if $k \neq 0$

Equations (10) and (11) express the minimum expected cost of having debt in the firm's capital structure from time $t+q$ to T given each possible level of interest rates at time t, maturity of bond issued at time t, and minimum time that the bond will be left outstanding (q). Equation (10) simply computes the expected costs of following an optimum refunding policy from the end of the maximum life of a bond issued at time t until the horizon. Equation (11) computes the same expected cost for all years of the bond's potential life. This latter equation has two terms. The first term represents the expected cost associated with calling the bond in year $t+q$ under those conditions where such a call is profitable. The limits over which the first term is summed insure that the cost of calling the bond is computed only under conditions where it is profitable to call. The second term of equation (11) represents the expected cost of maintaining debt from year $t+q$ to T under conditions where it is not profitable to call the bond in year q. For any time period t a value of equation (10) is computed for all possible levels of interest rates, and all possible maturities of bonds issued at t. Equation (12) is then used to minimize the expected cost of any refunding policy between year t and year T, with respect to both maturity issued and time until call, for each possible level of interest rates at time t. The quantity minimized is simply the sum of the cost of floating a bond at time t, plus the cost of paying interest on the bond until it is called, plus the expected cost of the optimal way of financing debt from the time the bond issued at time t is called until the horizon.

Equation (13) incorporates starting conditions into the decision. Once again the value of $f_{t'}(R^*)$ might not produce a minimum cost solution if the firm has a bond outstanding at t'. Instead, the option of keeping the outstanding bond for all periods up to its maturity must be considered rather then assuming (as we did in calculating $f_{t'}(R^*)$) that the bond will be refunded at the beginning of t'.

These 4 equations (10), (11), (12), (13) allow the firm to decide on an optimum pattern of bond refunding over a finite horizon, the maturity of the bond it should issue any time it refunds, and the cost of making optimum decisions. In a moment we will turn to an example of the decision to which this model will lead but before doing so we might note certain of its properties.

In the previous examples discussed, the decisions produced by the model were deterministic in nature and were of the form refund in year Y or don't refund in year Y. Now since the level of interest rates is assumed to be a stochastic variable, our decision rules are more complex. The decision will be of the following form: if a bond carries an interest rate of X_1, is of age X_2, and the level of interest rates is X_3 in year Y refund.

The logical question to raise is whether costs are lower or higher when the probability distribution of future interest rates is considered. The answer is that costs are lower. Throughout this paper, the firm is considered to be operating under the same degree of risk. Earlier the firm was assumed to be making decisions on the basis of expected values. Now the firm is assumed to use information about the entire probability distribution of future interest rates. Incorporation of extra information into the decision process should not lead to worse decisions.[29] In fact it usually leads to better decisions as shown below.

Let us continue with our previous example. Table 15.4 shows the possible levels of future interest rates. Taking expected values of the entries in Table 15.4 yields the interest rates used in previous examples. Once again the call premium is given by Table 15.5, the floatation expense is \$2, and the discount factor is assumed to be 1. Part of the results are shown in Table 15.7. In order to understand the use of the previous equations lets examine the entries for the high interest rate in period 6. Assume the firm will issue a three year bond. Then the value of equation (10) is \$17. This value represents the expected cost to the firm of holding the bond to maturity and following an optimum policy to the horizon. Holding the three year bond to maturity means that the firm must issue a new bond in period 9 at whatever interest rate prevails at that time. If the interest rate is low the expected cost is \$14. If it is high the expected cost is \$20. \$17 represents the average of these two figures. When the three year bond is two years old the firm has two choices. Keep the bond for

Table 15.7
Values for $F(R_t^m) + \alpha_{t+1}R_t^m + \alpha_{t+1}d_1^t(R_t^m, m)$

t	r^*	M	$f(r^*)$	d_4	d_3	d_2	d_1	*
9	Low	3	14					
		4						
9	High	3	20					
		4						
8	Low	3	22	0	10	14	17	23
		4		0	5	10	15	22
8	High	3	$26\frac{3}{4}$	0	10	15.5	18.75	26.75
		4		0	7	14	19	28
7	Low	3	24	0	16	17	20	25
		4		10	13	16	19	24
7	High	3	30	0	16	18	23	30
		4		10	15	18	23	30
6	Low	3	28	0	17	21	25	$2+4+25=31$
		4		16	17	20	23	$2+3+23=28$
6	High	3	34.5	0	17	23	27.5	$2+6+27.5=35.5$
		4		16	18	23	27.5	$2+5+27.5=34.5$

* Candidates for $F(R^*)$.

another year incurring a cost of \$6 in interest plus \$17 expected cost from when it matures to the horizon or the firm can refund at the rates that prevail in period 8. If the lower rate prevails then examining Table 15.7 shows that the firm incurs an expected cost of \$22 plus \$1 in call penalty while if the high rate prevails the expected cost is $\$26\frac{3}{4}$. If the low interest rate occurs in 8 the firm incurs a cost of \$23 whether it refunds or not. If the higher interest rate occurs the firm should not refund but wait for the next period. Since high interest rates are assumed as likely as low interest rates, the expected cost is an average of the two costs. We have just applied equation (11) to calculate d_2. To calculate d_1 we observe that, if the firm keeps the bond the second year, it incurs a cost of \$6 plus the expected cost from the second year to the horizon d_2 or $23 + 6 = \$29$. Refunding a one year old bond involves a call penalty of \$2 so that cost of refunding if low interest rates prevail in period 7 is $\$2 + \$24$ while with high interest rates it is $\$2 + \$30$. If low interest rates prevail, the firm should refund since expected costs are less, otherwise it should keep the bond. The expected cost from period 7 to the horizon when a bond is issued in 6 is an average of the two costs or $27\frac{1}{2}$ and is symbolized by d_1.

Having applied equation (11) to obtain the d's we are now ready to calculate one candidate for minimum f. Applying equation (12) shows this is the floatation expenses \$2 plus interest costs \$6 plus the optimum from period 8 to the horizon given that the firm refunds in 6 or d_1 or $\$27\frac{1}{2}$. Comparing this with the minimum obtainable from a 4 year shows that the four year bond is preferable.

Earlier we argued that utilizing information about the distribution of future interest rates rather than basing the decision on expected values should lead to lower cost decisions. To illustrate this in the context of the current example assume the firm has a three year bond outstanding with two years remaining to maturity. The optimum decision is to refund in two periods with a cost of $\$65\frac{465}{512}$. This compares to a cost, of \$68 when the firm is assumed to base its decision on expected values.

As argued earlier decision rules are more complex when the firm utilizes information about the distribution of future interest rates. However it is not as complex as might first be expected since:

(1) If the optimum decision is for the firm to refund at an interest rate R^* it is also optimum for the firm to refund at an interest rate R where $R < R^*$.

(2) If the firm should keep the old bond at an interest rate R, it should also keep at a rate R^* where $R^* > R$.

(3) If the % change in the call penalty is invariant with respect to the maturity then the firm should issue the bond with the longest maturity providing the yield curve is flat or downward sloping.

E Infinite Horizon

Let us now extend the analysis of the refunding decision which employs information about the probability distribution of future returns to the case in which management expects to maintain debt in the firm's capital structure into the indefinite future.

Again we will assume that management has specific expectations about interest rates in each period up to some horizon year T. Now these expectations will be in the form of a group of possible yield curves in each year and a probability associated with each yield curve in the group (as in the case just discussed).[30] The question remains as to management's expectations about interest rates in the years beyond the horizon. In the earlier cases we assumed that management had an expected interest rate which would prevail from year T onward. In this case we are going to make a more complex assumption: that management expects interest rates to follow a Markov Process from the horizon on and will estimate the transition probabilities of this process. The Markov assumption implies that the probability of a particular interest rate existing in period t is a function of the interest rate which existed in period $t-1$. The Markov assumption is appealing for many reasons. As Pye [30] has shown, it is consistent with data on observed yield curves and with the empirical work on term structure performed by Meiselman. Secondly, it is a very rich assumption in the sense that the general model presented in terms of the Markov process can be used to solve problems where the assumption about future interest rates are much simpler. For example, a natural analogy to the expected value case would be to assume that interest rates after year T can take on one of a group of values in each period. This can be handled within the Markov model simply by making all column transition probabilities the same.

Employing the same notation as the previous case. For $t \geqslant T$

$$f(R^*) = \text{minimum}\left[F(R^m) + \sum_{l=1}^{k} \alpha^l R^m + \alpha^k d_k(R^m, m)\right]$$

$$_{m\varepsilon}M$$

$$k = m-1, \ldots, 1 \tag{16}$$

$$d_m(R^m, m) = \sum_{R_i^*}[f(R_i^*)][P_m(R_i^*/R^*)] \tag{14}$$

For $q = m-1, \ldots, 1$

$$d_q(R^m, m) = \Sigma P_q(R_i^*/R^*)[f(R_i^*) + C(q, R^m, m)] + [1 - \Sigma P_q(R_i^*/R^*)][\alpha R^m + \alpha d_{q+1}(R^m, m)] \tag{15}$$

The summation is done for all cases where:

$$f(R_i^*) + C(q, R^m, m) < \alpha R^m + \alpha d_{q+1}(R^m, m)$$

These equations represent a generalization of the finite case equations to the infinite case. The subscript t is missing from all variables because given R^* their value should not be a function of the year in which the bond was floated (since we have assumed that interest rates follow a Markov process). That is, given a particular interest rate in any period (t) after T, the occurrance of any interest rate a fixed number of periods later is invariant with respect to t. For the same reasons, α should not be affected by t. We can remove the subscript t from $f_t(R^*)$ because we can show that a Markov process will yield a stationary optimum policy over time.

This set of equations can be used to arrive at a set of $f(R^*)$ for any value of R^*. The Markov property of interest rates has been used to determine equations (14), (15), (16). The solution to this set of equations is not as obvious as it has been in the previous cases. Appendix I uses the Markov property of interest rates to both simplify the structure of these equations and to show how linear programming can be used to arrive at optimum values for $f(R^*)$. These values can then be set equal to all $f_t(R^*)$ for $T \leqslant t \leqslant T + m - 1$ and a solution arrived at for the refunding decision by the recursive use of equations (10, 11, 12, and 13).

III Other Applications of Dynamic Programming

In the first two sections of this paper, we formulated and solved a group of dynamic programming problems involving both deterministic and stochastic data over finite as well as infinite horizons. In this section, we will discuss several recent applications of dynamic programming to financial problems and delineate some areas where it should have future application. But, before doing so, let us briefly review those qualities of a problem which make it suitable for solution via dynamic programming.

Dynamic programming is often called recursive optimization. This more descriptive term serves to delineate problems which are amenable to solution via dynamic programming: namely those which can be expressed by means of a recursive formulation. The total problem must be amenable to disaggregation into a series of subproblems or stages (or decision nodes). Furthermore, the subproblems must be interrelated, or there is no need to employ recursive optimization.[31]

The bond refunding problem we solved in the first section of this paper serves as an excellent example of this recursive optimization. The overall problem was to identify the best time (either over a finite or an infinite horizon) to call and float bonds. The problem could be disaggregated into a series of subproblems: given that a bond is floated in year t, what should be its maturity and how long should it be left outstanding?

The stage of the system was identified as the time remaining until the end of the decision process. An optimum decision could be made with respect to refunding at any stage by minimizing the cost of leaving a bond floated at that stage outstanding for various amounts of time plus the minimum cost of debt financing from the call date until the horizon.

This process is repeated, recursively optimizing backwards in time until a decision as to refunding at the present point in time is reached. The optimum refunding decision at t is not independent of the decisions reached at other times since the choice between allowing a bond floated in year t to remain outstanding for k or $k+1$ years is affected by the relative cost of maintaining debt from year $t+k$ and year $t+k+1$ on. While decisions are not independent over time, they can be reached by considering each stage recursively.

The recursive nature of the bond refunding problem is not difficult to see, for the disaggregation of a problem into a series of subproblems which occur sequentially in time seems to be a natural process. But there are many problems which can be converted into a recursive decision process, where the sequencing pattern is not so obvious. Perhaps the most commonly encountered of these is the class of problem involving the allocation of a scarce resource among competitive uses. As an example, let us assume that we were faced with allocating Y dollars among T subsidiaries, where the return from allocating y_t dollars to subsidiary (t) is given by $R_t(y_t)$. Then, starting with any subsidiary, we could determine the return from giving it any amount of funds from $y = 0, \ldots, Y$. A second subsidiary can then be added and the return from assigning various amounts of money to it (from 0 to Y) and the remainder to the first subsidiary can be calculated (remember, we have already calculated the return of assigning all sums of money to the first subsidiary). When we add the third subsidiary, we follow the same procedure, making use of the optimum way to allocate any remaining sums of money among the first two subsidiaries. Our recursive relationship would be:

$$f_t(y) = \underset{y_t}{\text{maximum}}\ [R_t(y_t + f_{t-1}(Y - y_t)] \quad \text{for } t = 1, 2, 3, \ldots, T$$

where $y_t = 1, 2, \ldots, Y$.

This formulation will distribute the scarce resource (money) among all possible uses (subsidiaries). The order in which the uses are considered does not affect the solution. The problem has been broken into stages by adding competitive uses one at a time.[32]

Having presented the general approach of dynamic programming, let us turn to a discussion of some of the promising applications of dynamic programming to financial problems. In this section we shall review, in some detail four applications of dynamic programming to areas of financial management.

A Accounts Receivable Management

As pointed out several times in this paper, dynamic programming can often be applied to solve problems involving interdependent decisions in more than one period. The decision to grant credit to individual customers is such a decision. However, it is normally solved by considering only the profit in the first period. This calculation is usually made by comparing the product of the expected revenue from an order times the probability of payment with the product of the incremental cost times the probability of non-collection.[33] If each future decision involved an exact replica of the first then the decision maker could safely ignore future decisions.

Bierman and Hausman [7] suggest that future decisions are not exact replicas of the first since when future decisions are made, a history of past payments will be available allowing the decision maker to better estimate the probability of collection. In fact, even if the expected return from the first decision is negative, the value of the information acquired about customers' credit worthiness may be so large as to make the extension of credit desirable.

Let us set up a hypothetical two period example to show how considering the dynamic element of the collection process, even for as short a time as two periods, can change the optimum decision. Assume the following:

(1) The customer will purchase \$100 of goods in each of two periods if credit is granted.

(2) The marginal cost of making and selling the goods is \$54.

(3) The initial estimate of the probability of payment is 50%.

(4) If a customer repays credit the first time the probability of his repaying again is estimated at 75%.[34]

(5) If a customer fails to repay credit the probability of his repaying a subsequent credit sale is estimated at 25%.[34]

The traditional way to solve this problem has been to compare the expected return of the two alternative firm decisions at time one neglecting the effect of these decisions in period two. The expected revenue from the alternative of not granting credit is the expected profit from collection minus the expected loss on uncollected accounts or $.50(100 - 54) + .50(-54) = -4$. Note granting credit would seem to be the preferred course of action.

If we now consider that the collection pattern in the first period allows improved (and more profitable) decisions in the second period we reach a different conclusion. For those customers who did not repay in the first period the expected revenue from a subsequent extension of credit is $.25(100 - 54) + .75(-54) = -29$. The expected revenue from not extending credit is zero. The expected revenue from the extension of credit to those who repaid in the first period is $.75(100 - 54) - .25(54) = 21$. Thus we would extend credit to these customers. The correct solution to the two period example involves summing the expected revenue from extending credit in the first period and the expected revenue from following an optimum policy in the second period.[35] The expected revenue from the optimal policy in the second period is $.50(21) = 10.50$ from extending credit to that 50% of the customers who repaid in the first period plus 0 from not extending credit to those customers who did not repay in the first period. Thus the expected revenue from extending credit in the first period and following an optimum policy in the second is $-4 + 10.50$ or 6.50 and credit should be extended to customers in the first period.

It is obvious that management must extend this analysis to more than two periods. This can be done quite simply within a dynamic programming framework through backward recursive optimization. For any point in time (t) we can solve for the optimal credit decision (and its associated revenue) for any probability of repayment simply by maximizing the sum of the revenue from following a particular policy at t plus the expected revenue from following an optimum policy from time $t + 1$ on.

Bierman and Hausman [7] present such a formulation of the credit granting problem. Their solution is of particular interest because it includes an analytical scheme for the revision of collection probabilities as more experience is gained on individual accounts. In addition, they extend their analysis to include the decision as to the optimal amount of credit to extend to any customer.

B Cash Management

The cash management problem is very similar to the problem of inventory management, one of the areas where dynamic programming was first applied. Both involve the balancing of understock costs, transaction costs, and holding costs. Both involve, in the presence of risk, a probability distribution of demand (or deletions from stock). Perhaps the major difference between the two problems is that the random changes in the level of cash can be positive as well as negative. In order to set up the recursive relationship let us define each of the costs involved in cash management.

Transfer costs include the costs of both increasing and decreasing the level of cash on hand. If the firm moves from some cash level i to another cash level j the transfer costs are given by

$$\text{Transfer cost } T(i,j) = \begin{cases} (T_u + t_u)(j-i) & \text{if } j > i \\ (0) & \text{if } j = i \\ (T_d + t_d)(i-j) & \text{if } j < i \end{cases}$$

In these expressions T_u and T_d represent the fixed cost of increasing or decreasing the level of the cash balance and t_u and t_d represent the marginal costs per dollar of change.

Holding and understock costs are usually assumed to be a function of the level of cash on hand at the end of a decision period.[36] If we assume that the firm moves to a cash position j at the beginning of the decision period and that demand for cash is described by the density function $\pi(E)$ then the holding and understock costs are given by

$$\text{Holding cost } H(j) = \int_{-\infty}^{j-m} h([j-m]-E)\pi(E)\,dE$$

$$\text{Understock cost } U(j) = \int_{j-m}^{\infty} u(E-(j-m))\pi(E)\,dE$$

In these expressions h and u represent, respectively, the marginal cost of having a cash position above or below a specified cash level, e.g., above or below a cash balance (m) which the firm has agreed to maintain with its banks.

The cash problem is a recursive relationship because changes in the level of cash in one period affect costs in subsequent periods. The recursive relationships for the finite case can be written as:

$$f_t(i) = \underset{j}{\text{minimum}}\left[T(i,j) + H(j) + U(j) + \alpha \int_{-\infty}^{\infty} f_{t+1}(j-E)\pi(E)\,dE\right]. \qquad (17)$$

Where α is the appropriate discount rate.

All of the authors cited above examined some form of this equation for the finite and infinite case.[37]

Each author has tried one or more assumptions about the cost structures involved in the cash management decisions. For example cases were examined where T_u, T_d, and m are separately and simultaneously set equal to zero. Each has derived a specific form of equation (17) for the set of cost assumptions being made. Each has then taken this specific form and from it derived the relevant characteristics of the optimal cash management policy. Collectively the authors have provided both a series of models and a series of policies which can be used to solve the cash management problem under almost every conceivable set of cost structures. It is interesting to note that the form of the optimum policy as well as the optimum amount of cash to have on hand changes with the type of costs assumed.

Before leaving the discussion of the application of dynamic programming models to the cash management decision mention should be made of one final model.

Dallenback and Archer [13] have taken a broader approach to the problem of cash management.[38] They recognize that the cash balance can be modified from more than one source and that these sources have different transaction and opportunity (holding) costs. Thus they minimize a recursive cost relationship with respect to the change in cash balances from each possible source rather than just in terms of the total cash balance.

C *Asset Selection: The Replacement Problem*

The literature discussing optimal replacement policy is too extensive to review in detail here. Rather we shall present the essential nature of the problem and show why it is amenable to solution via dynamic programming.

The asset selection problem is often viewed as the decision on whether or not to purchase a particular asset. An alternative (and better) way to view the problem is as the decision on whether or not to purchase a service (the service the asset performs) for a particular amount of time. If the service of the asset is desired for a period of time which differs from the optimum life of the asset then the problem involves a series of interdependent decisions which are easily solved via dynamic programming.[39] The problem can be restated as: given management's time horizon (the length of time over which they desire services from the machine) when should they replace the machine; and if they replace it at the optimum time, how profitable is it to purchase the type of service offered by the machine. This is directly analogous to the refunding decision discussed earlier. Instead of asking when to buy back a bond and sell a new one we are asking when to sell a machine and buy a new one. Exactly the same types of interdependencies are involved. The recursive relationship can be written as follows:

$$f_t = \text{minimum}\left[\sum_{i=1}^{k} \alpha^{i-1} \rho_{t,t+i} + \alpha^k f_{t+k}\right]$$

$$k = 1, 2, \ldots, N \tag{18}$$

Where

f_t = the present value of an optimum policy from year t to the horizon.

$\rho_{t,t+i}$ = the cash flow (including salvage value and purchase cost) associated with operating a machine in period $t+i$ which was purchased at time t.

N = the maximum life of a machine.

Equation (18) has been utilized by [5] and [33] among others to solve the replacement problem.

D Portfolio Analysis

The application of dynamic programming to the inter-temporal consumption investment decision has received a large amount of attention in the last few years.[40] The problem is usually stated as given a series of random one period returns, an inter-temporal utility function, and an initial wealth, what pattern of consumption withdrawals maximizes overall utility. After setting up a dynamic programming representation of this problem, the authors then derive propositions about the form of optimal behavior with particular emphasis on the applicability (for the multi-period context) of propositions derived from one period portfolio models. Hakansson's work [18] is typical of this approach. Hakansson assumes that the overall utility function is of the additive form.

$$U(C_{1,\ldots,}C_{t,\ldots}) = \sum_{t=1}^{\infty} \alpha^{t-1} U(C_t)$$

Therefore, utility received from consumption in any one period is independent of the utility received in any other period. This leads to the following recursive relationship:

$$f_j(X_j) = \underset{C_j}{\text{maximum}}\ [U(C_j) + \alpha E[f_{j+1}(X_{j+1})]] \tag{19}$$

Where

(1) X_j = wealth in period j.

(2) C_j = consumption in period j.

(3) $U(C_j)$ = utility of consumption in period j.

(4) $f_j(X_j)$ = minimum expected utility from period j to the horizon.

(5) α = the appropriate discount rate.

The reader should note X_{j+1} is a random variable constrained by the expected return in the period and the consumption decision. Consequently equation (19) states: for each possible initial starting wealth X_j determine the maximum utility obtainable from a combination of withdrawals in the jth period C_j and withdrawals in all subsequent periods $E\,(f_{j+1}(X_{j+1}))$. The last term is a random variable that depends on the actual return from the investments, the wealth at the start of the jth period (X_j) and the consumption in the jth period. Chen, Jen, and Zionts [9] have extended the dynamic approach to portfolio analysis to include transaction costs. Their model, while similar to that described above, can produce results which are quite different because it includes as part of the investor return the cost of revising a portfolio in all subsequent periods. It is doubtful that any of the authors intend these models to be used directly by investors for their portfolio decision. Rather, their usefulness comes about from the power of the propositions that can be derived about investor behavior and the guidance this provides to investors in making one period decisions. As is the case for most dynamic programming problems, the decisions reached assuming a one period horizon may well be different from the one period decision which is optimum with a longer horizon.

E *Potential Applications of Dynamic Programming*

Having discussed the principles of dynamic programming in some detail and presented four successful applications of dynamic programming to financial problems, it seems appropriate, in closing, to delineate some further areas of potential application.[41] This task, while it might seem easy, is in fact difficult. It seems easy, for the principle of recursive optimization means that dynamic programming might profitably be applied anytime a problem can be disaggregated into a series of interrelated problems. But the multitude of financial problems that fit this description prevents the problems (much less the solutions) from being described in any finite amount of space. All we can do is reiterate some of the types of problems to which dynamic programming has been applied and mention a few areas in finance that clearly are of each type.

As we have seen, decisions which are made repetitively over time often lend themselves to formulation via dynamic programming. This suggests that all decisions involving the timing of financing might be viewed in terms of recursive optimization. We have already done so with the bond refunding decision. It might also be done with respect to the timing of other sources and uses of capital, e.g., equity sales or share repurchase. In fact, the problem of the optimum mix of funds over time might well lend itself to dynamic formulation. Furthermore, dynamic programming might lend insight into other areas where repetitive decisions are made, such as inventory management, accounts receivable management, accounts payable management, and cash management. Aspects of all of these areas have already been studied through dynamic programming, but further applications should prove profitable. For example, Bierman and Hausman [7] studied one aspect of accounts receivable management as a recursive process. However, their findings also strongly suggest that credit evaluation techniques (e.g., descriminate analysis) and collection techniques have been incorrectly evaluated; the effect on future returns has been ignored. The ability of dynamic programming to decompose a complex process which takes place over time into a series of simpler or shorter processes suggests that it should prove a useful tool in both forecasting and control, two areas with which the financial executive is deeply concerned. While some work has been done in the forecasting area, this field is still largely unexplored.[42]

Dynamic programming also provides insight into problems, which while not repetitive over time, can be disaggregated into a series of smaller problems. We have already seen this for the case of allocating scarce resources among competitive uses. The applications of this type of model are also multiple. One of the prime functions of the financial manager is to allocate a scarce resource (cash) among competitive uses. We have already examined the use of recursive optimization in allocating budgeted funds among alternative capital projects (or subsidiaries). Similar analysis would apply to the problem of (a) allocating cash (demand deposits) among banks to maximize bank services, (b) the geographic location of lock boxes and (c) the optimum allocation of overdue credit accounts among collection personnel.[43]

In the recent past, economists have turned more and more from one period static equilibrium models to dynamic processes. It is only recently that financial researchers have realized that financial decisions must be viewed in a dynamic context. As this realization grows, the application of recursive optimization to financial problems should increase markedly.

Appendix I

The Solution of an Infinite Dynamic Programming Problem with Markov Probabilities

If transition probabilities are stationary over time (interest rates follow a Markov process) then it has been shown that there is a unique series of policies which will produce minimum costs. While the optimum policy can be found through an iterative solution in policy space, a solution can be found more directly through use of a linear programming algorithm. Any stochastic dynamic programming problem with Markov probabilities has a corresponding linear programming formulation.[44] Equations (15, 16 and 17) in the text can be transposed to the following linear programming problem.

Maximize

$$\sum_{i=1}^{N} C_i f(R_i^*)$$

Subject to

$$f(R^*) \leqslant F(R^m) + \sum_{l=1}^{k} \alpha^l R^m + \alpha^k d_k(R_m, m)$$

$$k = m - 1, \ldots, 1 \text{ and for all } m \varepsilon M$$

$$d_m(R^m, m) = \sum_{i=1}^{N} [f(R_i^*)][P_m(R_i^*/R^*)]$$

$$\text{for } q = m - 1, \ldots, 1$$

$$d_q(R^m, m) \leqslant \sum_{i=1}^{j} P_q(R_i^*/R^*)[f(R_i^*) + C(q, R^m, m)]$$

$$+ [1 - \Sigma P_q(R_i^*/R^*)][\alpha R^m + \alpha d_{q+1}(R^m, m)]$$

$$\text{for } j = 0, \ldots, N$$

Where

$$\sum_{i=1}^{j} P_q(R_i^*/R^*) = 0 \quad \text{for } j = 0.$$

Notes

1. The problem is also of interest for although it has been widely treated in the literature [8, 11, 21, 29, 31, 42] it has almost always been solved as a static non-repetitive decision—a formulation that leads to non-optimal decisions. The two exceptions to this are the work of Weingartner [38] and Kalymon [24]. These two authors present models which are similar to the models presented here. The differences will be discussed in what follows.

2. These reasons include the desire to change a firm's capital structure and to maintain flexibility. For a more detailed discussion of additional reasons for employing a call provision, see [31] and [42].

3. The two exceptions to this are Weingartner [38] and Kalyman [24].

4. This solution has been advocated by [41]. Another proposal [8] resembles this except that it uses the present value of interest savings over the life of the new bond. This too can lead to incorrect decisions.

5. The recursive nature of the bond refunding problem was first recognized by Weingartner [38].

6. When a bond is refunded it is one year old at the end of the refund period. It becomes two years old at the end of the first keep period and three years old at the end of the second. Therefore a three year old bond would be designated by refund, keep and keep.

7. A similar conclusion is reached if we examine the keep option.

8. A state is defined by specifying the value of the variables which affect costs in subsequent periods. In this example the only variable that affects future costs is the age of the bond.

9. The criterion is to minimize the discounted value of costs. We have assumed a discount rate of zero here, which although a naive assumption will not affect the conclusions we are about to reach.

10. This analysis can also be looked upon as a specific demonstration of the general principal that the policy which minimizes costs over a time horizon varies with the length of the horizon itself.

11. A two equation form of the bond refunding problem is discussed in Weingartner [38].

12. Of course j_0 could also equal 3.

13. The two equation system working backward would require 20 calculations so that the majority of the saving can be attributed to using one equation.

14. See [8, 11, 12, 21, 29, 30, 34, 38, 42] for expositions of different points of view.

15. We will use the one equation form of the dynamic programming solution throughout the rest of this paper. We demonstrated in the last section of the paper that for a very simple example this involves less computation than the two equation form. It also involves less computation for all the cases presented throughout the rest of this paper.

16. Hickman found that 41% of the bonds retired in the period 1900–1943 were not refunded. See [20], p. 13.

17. See the earlier discussion of possible values for α_t.

18. A two equation solution to the form of the bond refunding problem just discussed has been presented by Weingartner [38]. However he did not allow the option of floating bonds of standard maturity just prior to the horizon. As we show below preclusion of this option can lead to non optimum decisions. Furthermore the use of the two equation rather than a one equation solution to this problem leads to increased calculations.

19. Yield is being used rather than coupon rate since the callable bond would be retired at a price greater than par.

20. Once again Weingartner [38] solved a similar problem. The differences between our solution and Weingartner's are enumerated in footnote 18.

21. Actually this decision is only optimum given the type of information management is assumed to use. As we shall see later if management makes use of the entire distribution of possible interest rates better decisions might well be made.

22. The relevant costs are presented in Tables 15.4 and 15.5.

23. Modifications where this does not hold are straightforward.

24. This same expression could be derived by repetitive substitution of this expression for f_{t+k}, f_{t+2k}, etc. and solved as the sum of a geometric series. For proof that the optimum policy is stationary as this expression suggests see [4 and 35].

25. The subscript t has been added as a convenience for substitution in the recursive relationship presented below.

26. Once again Weingartner [38] solved a similar problems the differences between our solution and Weingartner's are enumerated in footnote 18.

27. We are assuming that once the level of the yield curve is specified the full yield curve is known. Variation where this is not true are easy to incorporate into the decisions but require enormous amounts of input data.

28. The models presented in the next two sections are similar to those presented by Kalyman [24]. Differences arise in that our model is computationally more efficient, is more general in our assumptions about the movement of interest rates over time, and incorporates more realistic and ending conditions.

29. Inclusion of the probability distribution of future interest rates can lead to worse decisions if the distribution have been completely misestimated.

30. This assumption can be relaxed see note (27).

31. If the subproblems are not interdependent, we could reach a solution to each problem separately, and there would be no need to make use of a recursive relationship.

32. An example of this type of formulation is Weingartner [37] and Nemhauser and Ullmann's [28] solution to the problem of asset selection under capital rationing.

33. For example see the discussion contained in (6).

34. Note that in the second period the probability of payment is still 50% for the population of all customers. Future decisions are improved not because the probability of collection

changes for the population as a whole but because the decision maker is better able to discriminate between the good and bad customers.

35. Discounting is a trivial but necessary addition.

36. Eppen and Fama [14] and [15] assume these costs depend on beginning rather than ending cash balances. The more common assumption has been made by [17] and [27].

37. As in the example presented earlier in this paper the infinite case was solved as a linear programming problem.

38. They constructed their model to solve the cash management problem for a bank. However, the model is applicable to a corporation with very little modification.

39. If we were not going to replace the asset with a new one it would have an optimum life determined by that point in time (t) when the revenue from operating the machine one more period was exceeded by the decrease in salvage value which resulted from operating it one more year plus the one period return that could have been earned on the salvage value of the machine at time t.

40. See Mossin [26], Hakansson [28], Fama [16], and Chen, Jen, and Zionts [9].

41. It should be kept in mind that, though great insight into a problem may be gained by formulating it as a dynamic programming problem, the most efficient solution technique might be any one of a number of mathematical techniques.

42. See Beckmann [1].

43. The problem of optimal location of lock boxes is analogous to the warehouse location problem which has been solved as a dynamic programming problem. See [3].

44. See [22] and [35] for a discussion of the transformation of a dynamic programming problem to a linear programming form.

References

1. Beckmann. *Dynamic Programming of Economic Decisions* (New York: Springer-Verlag) 1968.

2. Richard Bellman. "Equipment Replacement Policy," *Journal of The Society for Industrial and Applied Mathematics*, Vol. 3, No. 3, (September, 1955), pp. 133–136.

3. Richard Bellman. "On the Theory of Dynamic Programming—A Warehouse Problem," *Management Science*, Vol. 2, No. 3 (April, 1956), pp. 272.

4. Richard Bellman. *Dynamic Programming* (Princeton University Press; Princeton, N.J.), 1957.

5. Richard Bellman and Dreyfus. *Applied Dynamic Programming* (Princeton University Press; Princeton, N.J.), 1962.

6. William Beranek. *Analysis for Financial Decisions* (R. D. Irwin; Homewood, Ill.), 1963.

7. Harold Bierman and Warren Hausman. "The Credit Granting Decision," *Management Science*, Vol. 16, No. 8 (April, 1970), pp. B519–B532.

8. Oswald Bowlin. "The Refunding Decision," *Journal of Finance*, Vol. XXI (March, 1966), pp. 55–68.

9. Andrew Chen, Frank Jen and Stanley Zionts. "The Optional Portfolio Revision Policy," Forthcoming *Journal of Business.*

10. Andrew Chen, Frank Jen and Stanley Zionts. "Transition Models for Portfolio Planning with Stochastic Cash Demand," Unpublished Manuscript.

11. Jerome Cohen and Sidney Robbins. *The Financial Manager: Basic Aspects of Financial Administration* (Harper and Row; New York, N.Y.), 1966.

12. Jean Crockett. "A Technical Note on the Value of a Call Privilege," in [21].

13. Hans Daellenbach and Stephen Archer. "The Optional Bank Liquidity: A Multi-Period Stochastic Model," *Journal of Financial and Quantitative Analysis,* Vol. IV, No. 3 (September, 1969), pp. 329–343.

14. Gary Eppen and Eugene Fama. "Cash Balance and Simple Dynamic Portfolio Problems with Proportional Costs," *International Economic Review,* Vol. 10, No. 2 (June, 1969), pp. 119–133.

15. Gary Eppen and Eugene Fama. "Solutions for Cash Balance and Simple Dynamic Portfolio Problems," *Journal of Business,* Vol. XLI (January, 1969), pp. 94–112.

16. Eugene Fama. "Multiperiod Consumption-Investment Decisions," *American Economic Review,* Vol. LX, No. 1 (March, 1970), pp. 163–174.

17. Nadia Girgis. "Optional Cash Balance Levels," *Management Science,* Vol. 15, No. 3 (November, 1968), pp. 130–140.

18. Niles Hakansson. "Optional Investment and Consumption Strategies Under Risk for a Class of Utility Functions," Forthcoming *Econometria.*

19. Niles Hakansson. "Optional Investment and Consumptions Strategies Under Risk, an Uncertain Lifetime, and Insurance," *International Economic Review,* Vol. X, No. 3 (October, 1969), pp. 443–466.

20. W. B. Hickman. *Corporate Bonds: Quality and Investment Performance,* Occasional Paper 59 (National Bureau of Economic Research; New York, N.Y.), 1959.

21. Arleigh Hess and Willis Winn. *The Value of the Call Privilege* (University of Pennsylvania Press; Philadelphia, Penn.), 1962.

22. Ronald Howard. *Dynamic Programming and Markov Prfocesses* (M.I.T. Press; Cambridge, Mass.).

23. Frank Jen and James Wert. "The Effects of Call Risk on Corporate Bond Yields," *Journal of Finance,* Vol. XXII (December, 1967), pp. 637–652.

24. Basil A. Kalyman. "The Bond Refunding Problem with Stochastic Interest Rates," A talk delivered at the 1970 International Meetings of T.I.M.S. in London.

25. Fred Levy. "An Application of Hueristic Problem Solving to Accounts Receivable Management," *Management Science,* Vol. XII (February, 1966), pp. 236–244.

26. Jon Mossin. "Optional Multi-Period Portfolio Policies," *Journal of Business,* Vol. 41 (April, 1968), pp. 215–299.

27. Edwin Neave. "The Stochastic Cash Balance Problem with Fixed Costs for Increases and Decreases," *Management Science,* Vol. 16, No. 7 (March, 1970), pp. 472–490.

28. G. L. Nemhauser and Z. Ullmann. "Discrete Dynamic Programming and Capital Allocation," *Management Science*, Vol. 15, No. 9 (May, 1969), pp. 494–505.

29. Gordon Pye. "The Values of the Call Options on a Bond," *Journal of Political Economy*, Vol. LXXIV (April, 1966), pp. 200–205.

30. Gordon Pye. "Markov Model of the Term Structure," *Quarterly Journal of Economics*, Vol. LXXX, No. 1 (February, 1966), pp. 60–72.

31. Gordon Pye. "The Value of Call Deferement on a Bond: Some Empirical Results," *Journal of Finance*, Vol. XXII (December, 1967), pp. 623–636.

32. Paul Samuelson. "Lifetime Portfolio Selection by Dynamic Stochastic Programming," *The Review of Economics and Statistics*, Vol. LI, No. 3 (August 1969), pp. 239–246.

33. Richard Stapleton. "The Application of Dynamic Programming to The Replacement Problem," Unpublished Manuscript, Sheffield University; Sheffield, England.

34. James C. Van Horne. *Financial Management and Policy* (Prentice-Hall; Englewood Cliffs, N.J.), 1968.

35. Harvey Wagner. *Principals of Operations Research* (Prentice-Hall; Englewood Cliffs, N.J.), 1969.

36. H. Martin Weingartner "Equipment Replacement Analysis: A Note on the Optimum Investment Period," *Industrial Management Review*, Vol. 7, No. 1 (Fall, 1965), pp. 47–50.

37. H. Martin Weingartner. "Capital Budgeting of Interrelated Projects: Survey and Synthesis," *Management Science*, Vol. 12, No. 7 (March, 1966), pp. 485–516.

38. H. Martin Weingartner. "Optimal Timing of Bond Refunding," *Management Science*, Vol. 13, No. 7 (March, 1967), pp. 511–524.

39. H. Martin Weingartner and David Ness. "Methods for the Solution of the Multi-Dimensional 0/1 Knapsack Problem," *Operations Research*, Vol. 15, No. 1 (January–February, 1967), pp. 83–103.

40. H. Martin Weingartner. *Mathematical Porgramming and the Analysis of Capital Budgeting Problems* (Markham Publishing Company; Chicago, Ill., 1967).

41. Fred Weston and Eugene Brigham. *Managerial Finance* (Holt, Rinehart, and Winston; N.Y., 1969).

42. Willis Winn and Arleigh Hess. "The Value of the Call Privilege," *Journal of Finance*, Vol. XIV (May 1959), pp. 182–195.

16

On the Optimality of Some Multi-Period Portfolio Selection Criteria

Edwin J. Elton and Martin J. Gruber

Criteria for portfolio selection have received a great deal of attention in the recent economic literature. Modern portfolio analysis has its origin in the work of Markowitz, who specified the portfolio problem in terms of the one-period means and variances of returns.[1] However, most portfolio problems are multiperiod. The appropriateness of one-period analysis for this class of problems has been seriously questioned in recent years.[2] As a result, several alternative decision rules and modification of the one-period analysis have been proposed.

The purpose of this paper is to evaluate two proposals that have received wide attention in the economic literature. The first involves selecting portfolios on the basis of the geometric mean of future multiperiod returns. The second involves selecting portfolios on the basis of the expected utility of multiperiod returns.[3] We shall show that, when the ability of the investor to revise his portfolio is considered, each of these rules is only appropriate under a very restrictive set of conditions.

In order to evaluate any portfolio selection rule, it is necessary to establish a goal for portfolio management. In this paper, we will assume that the goal of portfolio managers is to maximize the expected utility of the investor's wealth at some terminal date. We have selected this goal because (1) the decision rules we will investigate were devised to achieve this goal, (2) the goal is appropriate for many real portfolio problems (such as retirement portfolios), and (3) this goal has been assumed by many other authors.[4]

Once this goal has been established, we can define the portfolio problem as the development of decision rules for selecting a sequence of portfolios over time to maximize the expected utility of terminal wealth. The optimum sequence of portfolios can depend on the expected results of portfolios held prior to the horizon as well as the distribution of returns over the entire horizon.[5]

The rest of this paper will examine the two decision rules mentioned above and will delineate conditions under which they will lead to the maximization of the expected utility of terminal wealth. In Section I we examine the geometric mean return criteria both when return distributions are unchanging over time and when they change in a regular pattern. In Section II we perform the same analysis, for the criteria maximize the utility of T-period returns. The analysis in this paper differs from much of the previous work that has been done on portfolio management in that we explicitly allow for portfolio revision over time.

I Conditions for Optimality of the Geometric Mean Return

A criterion for ranking portfolios that has received a great deal of attention in the economic literature and has attracted an increasing number of supporters is the geometric mean return.[6] The purpose of this section is to delineate those types of investor utility functions for which the geometric mean return is an appropriate portfolio selection criterion. Throughout this paper the appropriateness of a criterion will be judged by its ability to select that sequence of portfolios that maximizes the expected utility of terminal wealth. This section will be divided into two parts. In the first part, we will examine the suitability of the geometric mean under the assumption that the distribution of returns in all future periods (until the horizon) is expected to be the same and the return in one period is independent of the return in all others. These are the assumptions that proponents of the geometric mean have usually made in defending its use. Furthermore, these assumptions have received theoretical and empirical support from proponents of the strict form of the random walk theory.[7] In the second part of this section, we will relax the assumption of equal return distributions and reexamine the suitability of the geometric mean.

To define the geometric mean, let R_{it} be a random variable equal to 1 plus the return, where t is a period index and i denotes a particular return; P_{it} be the probability of R_{it} occurring; and T be the number of periods in the investor's time horizon. Then for the one-period horizon, the geometric mean return is given by

$$\prod_{i1} R_{i1}^{P_{i1}}. \tag{1}$$

The geometric mean return over a two-period horizon is given by

$$\left(\prod_{i1}\prod_{i2} R_{i1}^{P_{i1}} R_{i2}^{P_{i2}}\right)^{1/2}$$

For a T-period horizon this generalizes as

$$\left(\prod_{i1}\prod_{i2}\prod_{i3}\cdots\prod_{iT} R_{i1}^{P_{i1}} R_{i2}^{P_{i2}} R_{i3}^{P_{i3}} \ldots R_{iT}^{P_{iT}}\right)^{1/T}. \tag{2}$$

A Return Distributions Stable over Time

If the expected distribution of returns is the same in each period, equation (2) becomes

$$\left(\prod_{i1}\prod_{i1}\cdots\prod_{i1} R_{i1}^{P_{i1}} R_{i1}^{P_{i1}} \ldots R_{i1}^{P_{i1}}\right)^{1/T} = \prod_{i1} R_{i1}^{P_{i1}}. \tag{3}$$

Note that equation (3) is identical to equation (1). Furthermore, equation (3) represents the ranking of all portfolios, regardless of the number of years left to the horizon. Thus, the ranking associated with any portfolio will be the same in each future period. The investor who uses the geometric mean would choose that portfolio which maximizes (3) and revise his portfolio at the beginning of each period (2 through T) in order to restore the percentage of each asset in his portfolio to the initial level. From this point on, a policy which calls for portfolios to be revised so as to hold the percentage invested in each asset constant over time will be called a constant percentage portfolio policy. Thus, given constant return distributions over time, a necessary but not sufficient condition for the geometric mean to be an optimum decision criterion is the presence of a utility function that calls for a constant percentage portfolio policy to be optimum. Mossin has shown that there are only two classes of utility functions (log and power) that have this property.[8] Furthermore, he has shown that these functions produce the same ranking of portfolios whether utility is expressed in terms of return or wealth. We have chosen to perform our analysis in terms of return distributions because this is consistent with the bulk of the literature on portfolio analysis.

Most economists would further restrict utility functions in order to ensure increasing utility of wealth and risk avoidance [i.e., $u'(w) > 0$ and $u''(w) < 0$]. If we assume these properties, then the functions of interest can be written as[9]

$$U(w) = R, \qquad \gamma = 1 \qquad \text{log function,}$$

$$\left.\begin{aligned} U(w) &= -R^{1-\gamma}, \qquad \gamma > 1 \\ U(w) &= R^{1-\gamma}, \qquad 0 < \gamma < 1 \end{aligned}\right\} \text{ power function.}$$

While the existence of any of these utility functions is a necessary condition for the geometric mean to be an optimum criterion, the sufficient condition for optimality is that the maximization of the geometric mean lead to the maximization of the utility of terminal wealth. In investigating the sufficient condition, we shall make use of another special property of the log and power utility functions. As Mossin has shown for either of these functions, the portfolio which maximizes the expected utility of first-period returns is identical to the optimal portfolio resulting from a T-period dynamic programming solution which maximizes the expected utility of terminal wealth.[10] This is true, though the dynamic programming solution considers all possible portfolios over all possible holding periods. Therefore, if the geometric mean leads to the same ranking of portfolios as the expected utility of first-period returns using the log or power utility function, then the geometric mean also leads to the same ranking as that produced by a T-period dynamic programming solution that allows the percentage of the portfolio invested in each asset to be changed over time.

1. *Log utility function.*—The expected utility of first-period returns for log utility functions is

$$\sum_{i1} P_{i1} \ln R_{i1}. \tag{4}$$

The geometric mean will produce identical rankings of portfolios, providing there is some monotonic transformation of equation (3) that yields equation (4). If the expected utility produced by equation (4) is a monotonic transformation of a decision criterion (such as the geometric mean), then the ranking of portfolios by the utility function will be identical to the ranking by the decision criterion and the same optimum will exist for both functions. One such monotonic transformation is the log function.[11] Since the log of a larger number will always be larger than the log of a smaller number, if the expected utility produced by a utility function is the log of the rating produced by a decision criterion, order will be preserved and the same portfolio will be selected as optimum by both criteria. If we take logs of the geometric mean (eq. [3]), we get

$$\ln \prod_{i1} R_{i1}^{P_{i1}} = \sum_{i1} P_{i1} \ln R_{i1}. \tag{5}$$

Since equation (5) equals equation (4) and since the log function is monotonic, the ranking given by the geometric mean must always be

Table 16.1

	Return	Probability
Portfolio A	1.0	.25
	1.5	.50
	2.0	.25
Portfolio B	1.2	.25
	1.4	.50
	1.6	.25

identical to the ranking given by the log utility function. Thus, when portfolio revision is considered, the geometric mean is an appropriate decision criteria when the investor's utility function is of the log form and the distribution of returns in all future periods are the same.

2. *Power function.*—In the following discussion we will show that, when portfolio revision is allowed, the geometric mean can lead to a ranking of portfolios different from that of a utility function which has the form of a power function. It is more difficult to prove that a decision criterion and a utility function lead to different rankings than it is to prove that they lead to the same ranking. Since it would be tedious (and an almost infinite task) to prove inequality under every possible monotonic transform, we will present an example of two portfolios and show that the geometric mean and the power function can lead to different rankings and are therefore not equivalent.

Consider the two portfolios described in table 16.1. Furthermore, assume that the appropriate utility function is $-R^{-2}$, that is, $\gamma = 3$. The geometric mean return for portfolio A is 1.459, while for portfolio B it is 1.400. The value of the power utility function for portfolio A is -0.535, while for B it is -0.526. Thus, the geometric mean selected A as a superior portfolio while the power utility function selected B. In this example, if the investor's utility function were of the form $R^{1-\gamma}$ with γ equal to 3, the geometric mean would lead to an incorrect ranking.

B Unequal Return Distributions over Time

Up to this point, we have shown that if returns in all future periods are identically distributed, maximizing the geometric mean leads to the selection of the same portfolio as a T-period dynamic programming problem with an objective of maximizing terminal wealth if, and only if, the utility function is of the log form. Now we will extend the analysis to show under what alternative return patterns the geometric mean is appropriate when the investor's utility is of the log form.[12]

Mossin has shown that when utility functions are of the log form, myopic portfolio decisions can be made. If utility is of the log form, then the ranking of portfolios for the tth period is given by

$$\sum P_{it} \ln R_{it}. \tag{6}$$

If we use the geometric mean criteria, then the ranking for the tth period is

$$\prod_{it}\prod_{it+2}\prod_{it+1}\cdots\prod_{iT}(R_{it}^{P_{it}} R_{it+1}^{P_{it+1}} R_{it+2}^{P_{it+2}} \cdots R_{it}^{P_{iT}})^{1/(T-t+1)}. \tag{7}$$

If all $R_{it} = C_t R_{i1}^{C'_t}$ and $P_{it} = P_{i1}$, when C_t and C'_t are constants, then log utility functions and the geometric mean will lead to the same ranking of portfolios.

To show this, note that if the two functions are to lead to the same ranking of portfolios, they must do so in every period. We can take logs of equation (7) without changing its ranking, since the log is a monotonic function. So (7) becomes

$$1/(T-t+1)\left(\sum_{it} P_{it} \ln R_{it} + \sum_{it+1} P_{it+1} \ln R_{it+1} \right.$$
$$\left. + \sum_{it+2} P_{it+2} \ln R_{it+2} + \cdots + \sum_{iT} P_{iT} \ln R_{iT}\right).$$

If all $R_{it} = C_t R_{i1}^{C'_t}$, then this equation can be written as

$$1/(T-t+1)\left(\sum_{i1} P_{i1} \ln C_t R_{i1}^{C'_t} \right.$$
$$\left. + \sum_{i1} P_{i1} \ln C_{t+1} R_{i1}^{C'_{t+1}} + \cdots \sum P_{i1} \ln C_T R_{i1}^{C'_T}\right).$$

Simplifying yields

$$1/(T-t+1)(\ln C_t + \ln C_{t+1} + \cdots + \ln C_T)$$
$$+ 1/(T-t+1)(C'_t + C'_{t+1} + \cdots + C'_T) \sum_{i1} P_{i1} \ln R_{i1}. \tag{8}$$

Substituting $R_{it} = C_t R_{i1}^{C'_t}$ into equation (6) yields

$$\ln C_t + C'_t \sum_{i1} P_{i1} \ln R_{i1}. \tag{9}$$

Since (8) is just a linear transform of (9), the geometric mean is a valid criterion for portfolio choice when the investor's utility function is logarithmic and the distribution of returns in each future period are first-period returns raised to a power, or multiplied by a constant, or both.

In this section we have shown that, if return distributions are constant over time, the geometric mean will only lead to maximization of investor wealth provided that the investor's utility function is logarithmic.[13] Furthermore, if the investor's utility function is logarithmic, the geometric mean will be an appropriate decision criterion provided that the distribution of returns in any period is expected to be the first-period returns multiplied by a constant, or raised to a power, or both multiplied by a constant and raised to a power. All of these proofs have assumed that the investor has the ability to revise this portfolio at the end of each period.

II Conditions for the Optimality of T-Period Returns

A second criterion which has been suggested to maximize the expected utility of terminal wealth is to base the investment decision on the maximization of the expected utility of T-period returns. In this section we will show that, when portfolio revision is allowed, only under very special conditions will the use of T-period returns lead to optimal investment decisions. To do so, we will examine three forms of utility functions: logarithmic, power, and quadratic.[14] We will initially examine the case where the probability distributions of returns are equal in each period and where returns are independent from period to period.[15] This will be followed by a section discussing more general results. Note that the assumption of equal return distributions encompasses many situations discussed in standard portfolio theory. For example, assume that an individual wishes to maximize wealth over 2 years, short-run prospects equal long-run prospects (same distribution of returns in each period), and no new information is forthcoming over the 2 years. There is general agreement that in this situation the same portfolio should be held over the full period and, if utility is quadratic, the optimum portfolio can be determined using standard mean-variance analysis of 2-year returns. It is shown in this section that this result is incorrect and that generating a mean-variance efficient frontier using 2-year returns, while appropriate if utility is logarithmic or power and returns normally distributed, is inappropriate if utility is quadratic.

The expected utility of T-period returns can be expressed as

$$E[U(z)] = \sum_{i1}\sum_{i2}\cdots\sum_{iT} P_{i1}P_{i2}\ldots P_{iT}U(R_{i1}R_{i2}\ldots R_{iT}), \tag{10}$$

where z is T-period returns and all other terms are as previously defined.

Mossin has shown that for logarithmic and power utility functions, maximization of the expected utility of the first-period returns leads to the same portfolio decisions as maximization of the expected utility of terminal wealth at the end of T-periods.[16] If for these functions we can extend Mossin's analysis to show that the expected utility of T-period returns can be expressed as a monotonic transform of the expected utility of one-period returns, then maximization of the expected utility of T-period returns also leads to the same portfolio decisions as the maximization of the expected utility of terminal wealth.

If utilities are logarithmic, equation (10) becomes

$$E[U(z)] = \sum_{i1}\sum_{i2}\cdots\sum_{iT} P_{i1}P_{i2}\ldots P_{iT}\ln(R_{i1}R_{i2}\ldots R_{iT}).$$

Using the assumption of independent and identical return distributions over time, this equation becomes[17]

$$E[U(z)] = T\sum_{i1} P_{i1}\ln R_{i1}. \tag{11}$$

The right-hand side of equation (11) is simply T times the expected utility of first-period returns.

If utilities are power functions, equation (10) becomes

$$E[U(z)] = \sum_{i1}\sum_{i2}\cdots\sum_{iT} P_{i1}P_{i2}\ldots P_{iT}(R_{i1}R_{i2}\ldots R_{iT})^{1-\gamma}.$$

Using the assumption of independent and identical return distributions over time, this equation becomes[18]

$$E[U(z) = \left(\sum_{i1} P_{i1}R_{i1}^{1-\gamma}\right)^{T}. \tag{12}$$

The right-hand side of equation (12) is simply the expected utility of first-period returns raised to the Tth power.

Since multiplying any series of positive numbers by a constant or raising the series to a power greater than 1 preserves order, the ranking of expected utility by T-period returns is identical to the ranking by one-period returns when utility functions are either of the log or the power form. Since ranking on the basis of the expected utility of one-period returns is consistent with maximizing the expected utility of terminal wealth, ranking on the basis of the expected utility of T-period returns is also consistent with maximizing the expected utility of terminal wealth.

A *Quadratic Utility Functions with Constant Returns*

To show that maximizing the utility of T-period returns with a quadratic utility function leads, in general, to different portfolio decisions from that set of portfolios which maximizes the expected utility of terminal wealth, we will consider a two-period two-asset case. This requires a change in notation, since we will be working directly with the return on individual assets. Let R_{it} = the return in period t on asset i, where $i = 1, 2$, and $t = 1, 2$; W_0 = the initial wealth of the investor; W_2 = the final wealth of the investor; R = the return earned by investing over the two periods; E_i = the expected one-period return of asset i (no period subscript is necessary since the distribution of returns are assumed equal in each period); and V_i = the variance of the one-period return of asset i (no period subscript is necessary since the distributions of returns are assumed equal in each period).

We can represent the investor's quadratic utility function as

$$U(W_2) = W_2 - \alpha W_2^2.$$

By defining B as αW_0, we can state this in the equivalent form

$$U(R) = R - BR^2. \tag{13}$$

Mossin has shown that the dynamic programming solution that maximizes this utility function calls for the fraction (k) of the initial assets invested in security 1 to be given by[19]

$$k = \frac{(E_1 - E_2)[V_1(1+E_2) + V_2(1+E_1)]}{2\beta[V_1(1+E_2)^2 + V_2(1+E_1)^2 + V_1V_2][V_1 + V_2 + (E_1 - E_2)^2]} - \frac{(1+E_2)(E_1 - E_2) - V_2}{V_1 + V_2 + (E_1 - E_2)^2}. \tag{14}$$

If maximizing the expected utility of two-period returns leads to the same initial portfolio, it is a satisfactory decision rule. If it leads to any other initial portfolio, it will produce lower expected utility of terminal wealth and must be rejected as a decision rule.

We can define the two-period return for any constant percentage portfolio policy as

$$R = [(1 + X_{21}) + k(X_{11} - X_{21})][(1 + X_{22}) + k(X_{12} - X_{22})]. \tag{15}$$

Substituting (15) into (13), taking expected values and differentiating with respect to k, yields

$$\begin{aligned}
&- k^3[V_1 + V_2 + (E_1 - E_2)^2]^2 2\beta \\
&- k^2[V_1 + V_2 + (E_1 - E_2)^2][-V_2 + (1 + E_2)(E_1 - E_2)]6\beta, \\
&- k\{[V_1 + V_2 + (E_1 - E_2)^2][V_2 + (1 + E_2)^2]2\beta \\
&\qquad + [-V_2 + (1 + E_2)(E_1 - E_2)]^2 4\beta - (E_1 - E_2)^2\}, \\
&- [-V_2 + (1 + E_2)(E_1 - E_2)][V_2 + (1 + E_2)^2](-2\beta) \\
&\qquad + (1 + E_2)(E_1 - E_2).
\end{aligned} \tag{16}$$

Substituting equation (14) into equation (16) reveals that the optimum k as defined by (14) is not a root of equation (16). Thus, maximizing the utility of T-period returns will lead to nonoptimum portfolios if the investor's utility function is quadratic.

The above analysis has important implications for portfolio selection. The selection of portfolios that maximize the expected value of a utility function in terms of return and risk (standard deviation or variance) has been deemed appropriate whenever either utility functions are quadratic or returns are normally distributed.[20] The appropriate distribution of returns to examine has often been defined in terms of the horizon with which the investor is concerned.[21]

As shown in Part A of this section, if an investor can revise his portfolio before the horizon and has a quadratic utility function, then maximizing the expected utility of T-period returns is inconsistent with maximizing terminal wealth at the end of T-periods. In fact, if return distributions are uniform through time, it is only appropriate to maximize utility in terms of horizon returns if the utility function is either of the log or the power form. Furthermore, restricting the analysis to means and variances for log and power functions is only consistent with maximizing utility if returns are normally distributed. Thus, for the standard Markowitz efficient frontier to be meaningful in terms of an investor maximizing the utility of terminal wealth over any time span within which he can trade, (1) his utility function must be of the power or log form (it cannot be quadratic) and (2) returns must be normally distributed.

B The Optimality of Maximizing N-Period Returns When the Distribution of Returns Varies from Period to Period

In this section we will relax the assumption that return distributions are constant and show that there are still situations where the maximization of T-period returns leads to optimum decisions.[22] This result conflicts with Mossin's assertion that return distribution must be the same in each period for a stationary policy.[23]

Earlier we showed that if utility is logarithmic the utility of T-period returns is[24]

$$E[U(z)] = \sum_{i1} P_{i1} \ln R_{i1} + \sum_{i2} P_{i2} \ln R_{i2} + \cdots + \sum_{iT} P_{iT} \ln R_{iT}. \tag{17}$$

If $R_{it} = C_t R_{i1}^{C'_t}$ and $P_{it} = P_{i1}$, then maximizing the expected utility of T-period returns leads to the same portfolio decisions as maximizing terminal wealth. To show this, substitute $R_{it} = C_t R_{i1}^{C'_t}$ into equation (17):

$$\begin{aligned} E[U(z)] &= \sum_{i1} P_{i1} \ln R_{i1} + \sum_{i1} P_{i1} \ln C_2 R_{i1}^{C_2} + \cdots + \sum_{i1} P_{il} \ln C_T R_{i1}^{C'_T} \\ &= C' \sum_{i1} \ln R_{i1} + C, \end{aligned}$$

where

$$C = 1 + \sum_{i1} P_{i1} \ln C_2 + \sum_{i1} P_{i1} \ln C_3 + \cdots + \sum_{i1} P_{i1} \ln C_T = \ln(C_2 C_3 \ldots C_T),$$

$$C' = 1 + C'_2 + C'_3 + \cdots + C'_T.$$

Since $E[U(z)]$ is a linear function of the expected utility of one-period returns, portfolio decisions based on T-period returns are identical to portfolio decisions based on one-period returns. As discussed earlier, for logarithmic utility functions this implies that decisions based on T-period returns are identical to those based on terminal wealth.

Note also that the optimal portfolio decision is not a function of T. Therefore, subsequent decisions would be identical to the initial decision if expectations regarding return distributions were maintained. A similar result holds if utility functions are a power series. The utility of T-period returns is[25]

$$E[u(z)] = \left(\sum_{i1} P_{i1} R_{i1}^{1-\gamma}\right)\left(\sum_{i2} P_{i2} R_{i2}^{1-\gamma}\right)\cdots\left(\sum_{iT} P_{iT} R_{iT}^{1-\gamma}\right). \tag{18}$$

Assume that $R_{it} = C_t'' R_{i1}$ and $P_{it} = P_{i1}$. Substituting into equation (18) yields

$$\begin{aligned} E[u(z)] &= \left(\sum_{i1} P_{i1} R_{i1}^{1-\gamma}\right)\left(\sum_{i1} P_{i1} C_2'' R_{i1}^{1-\gamma}\right)\cdots\left(\sum_{i1} P_{i1} C_T'' R_{i1}^{1-\gamma}\right), \\ E[U(z) &= C''\left(\sum_{i1} P_{i1} R_{i1}^{1-\gamma}\right)^T = C''\{E[u(R_i)]\}^T, \end{aligned} \tag{19}$$

where $C'' = (C_2'' C_3'' \ldots C_T'')$.

By now-familiar reasoning, equation (19) shows that the ranking of portfolios by T-period returns is identical to the ranking by one-period returns and hence identical to the ranking by terminal wealth.[26]

Once again the optimal portfolio is not a function of T, and if expectations concerning return distributions are maintained, the policy is stationary over time.[27]

III Conclusion

The analysis performed in this paper demonstrates that, when portfolio revision is considered, portfolio decisions based on either the expected utility of multiperiod returns or the geometric mean of multiperiod returns are often different from and inferior to decisions based on consideration of returns sequentially over time. This is true even when the distribution of returns is expected to be identical in each future period. The conditions under which the geometric mean and the utility of multiperiod returns are appropriate portfolio selection criteria are delineated in the paper.

Closely associated with the analysis in this paper is the problem of deciding the optimum frequency for portfolio revision. Many authors have contended that the frequency of portfolio revision should be exclusively a function of the frequency with which new information arises or expectations concerning return distributions change.[28] However, as shown in this paper, even if no new information is expected to arise over time, and even if the distribution of returns is expected to be identical in each future period, changing the portfolio will increase the expected utility of terminal wealth if the investor's utility is neither of the log nor of the power function form.[29] This results from changes in investor wealth over time which cause the investor to change his risk preferences and so the composition of his portfolio. In fact, in the absence of revision costs, the maximization of the expected utility of terminal wealth calls for a continuous revision of the investor's portfolio.

Notes

The initial research for this paper was funded by the Institute for Quantitative Research in Finance.

1. Harry Markowitz, *Portfolio Selection* (New York: John Wiley & Sons, 1959).

2. See Nils H. Hakansson, "Capital Growth and the Mean-Variance Approach to Portfolio Selection," *Journal of Financial and Quantitative Analysis* 6 (January 1971): 517–55; "Optimal Investment and Consumption Strategies under Risk for a Class of Utility Functions," *Econometrica* 38 (September 1970): 587– 607; and Jan Mossin, "Optimal Multi-Period Portfolio Policies," *Journal of Business* 41 (April 1968): 215–29. In addition, Markowitz laid the groundwork for some of this latter attack on his one-period model by exploring the dynamic nature of portfolio management policy.

3. This can be thought of as consistent with a Markowitz analysis where the risk and return for a portfolio is defined as the multiperiod risk and return.

4. Hakansson, "Optimal Investment," and Mossin.

5. A decision rule that naturally suggests itself is to solve a sequence of one-period portfolio problems. The fact that this decision rule generally leads to incorrect decisions, as well as the specific conditions under which it will lead to optimum decisions, has already been documented (see Hakansson, "Capital Growth" and "Optimal Investment," and Mossin).

6. Among its supporters are Henry Latane, "Criteria for Choice among Risky Ventures," *Journal of Political Economy* 67 (April 1959): 144–55; Henry Latane and Donald Tuttle, *Security Analysis and Portfolio Analysis* (New York: Ronald Press, 1970); Hakansson, "Optimal Investment"; and J. B. Williams, "Speculation and the Carry-over," *Quarterly Journal of Economics* 50 (May 1936): 436–55.

7. See Eugene F. Fama, "Efficient Capital Markets: A Review of Theory and Empirical Work," *Journal of Finance* 20 (January 1965): 383–417.

8. Mossin.

9. These functions involve constant relative risk aversion in the Pratt-Arrow sense. That is, $[U''(R)R]/[U'(R)] = -\gamma$, where γ is the coefficient of relative risk aversion and is a constant.

10. See Mossin.

11. If R could take on negative values, the log function would not be monotonic. However, since R is 1 plus the rate of return and since the rate of return can never be smaller than

-100 percent, the smallest value R can take on is zero. Since R can never take on negative values, the log function is monotonic.

12. For almost any utility function, there is a specific pattern of returns which will cause the geometric mean to give the same ranking of portfolios as does the utility function. However, in the case of the log function, there is a class of return patterns that leads to the same ranking.

13. We are assuming the security outcomes are independent of the investor's personal wealth (i.e., the investor is not large enough to affect the market). If this is not true, serious complications occur.

14. The log and power functions were chosen because they produce optimum decisions that are independent of wealth. The quadratic was chosen because it is the most commonly used utility function in portfolio theory and because it is representative of that class of utility functions under which relative risk aversion is not constant.

15. The assumption of independence is consistent with the random walk theory.

16. See Mossin. The possible combinations of terminal wealth that are considered are those that are produced by all combinations of securities for all possible holding periods.

17. With the log utility function, the expected utility of T-period returns is

$$E[U(z)] = \sum_{i1}\sum_{i2}\cdots\sum_{iT} P_{i1}P_{i2}\ldots P_{iT}\ln(R_{i1}R_{i2}\ldots R_{iT})$$

or

$$E[U(z)] = \sum_{i1}\sum_{i2}\cdots\sum_{iT} P_{i1}P_{i2}\ldots P_{iT}(\ln R_{i1} + \ln R_{i2} + \cdots + \ln R_{iT}).$$

Consider the first term:

$$\sum_{i1}\sum_{i2}\cdots\sum_{iT} P_{i1}P_{i2}\ldots P_{iT}\ln R_{i1}.$$

Since $\sum_{it} P_{it} = 1$ and since we are assuming independence, this expression simplifies to

$$\sum_{i1} P_{i1}\ln(R_{i1}).$$

Applying the same simplification to each term in the initial equation yields

$$E[U(z)] = \sum_{i1} P_{i1}\ln R_{i1} + \sum_{i2} P_{i2}\ln R_{i2} + \cdots + \sum_{iT} P_{iT}\ln R_{iT}.$$

If $R_{ij} = R_{i1}$ and $P_{ij} = P_{i1}$ for all i (constant probability distribution of returns over time), this equation reduces to

$$E[U(z)] = T\sum_{i1} P_{i1}\ln R_{i1}.$$

18. With the power utility function, the expected utility of T-period returns is

$$E[U(z)] = \sum_{i1}\sum_{i2}\cdots\sum_{iT} P_{i1}P_{i2}\ldots P_{iT}(R_{i1}R_{i2}\ldots R_{iT})^{1-\gamma}.$$

This simplifies to

$$E[U(z)] = \left(\sum_{i1} P_{i1}R_{i1}^{1-\gamma}\right)\left(\sum_{i2} P_{i2}R_{i2}^{1-\gamma}\right)\cdots\left(\sum_{iT} P_{iT}R_{iT}^{1-\gamma}\right).$$

Setting $R_{ij} = R_{i1}$ and $P_{ij} = P_{i1}$ for all j, we have

$$E[U(z)] = \left(\sum_{i1} P_{i1} R_{i1}^{1-\gamma}\right)\left(\sum_{i1} P_{i1} R_{i1}^{1-\gamma}\right)\cdots\left(\sum_{i1} P_{i1} R_{i1}^{1-\gamma}\right),$$

$$E[U(z)] = \left(\sum_{i1} P_{i1} R_{i1}^{1-\gamma}\right)^{T}.$$

19. While Mossin does not explicitly present this expression, he describes the methodology needed to derive it and presents a numerical example utilizing this expression.

20. Originally it was believed that any two-parameter distribution was appropriate. However, it has been pointed out that the normal distribution is the only distribution that has the property that the form of the distribution is maintained under linear transform (see K. Borch, "A Note on Uncertainty and Indifference Curves," *Review of Economic Studies* 36 [1969]: 473–507; M. S. Feldstein, "Mean-Variance Analysis in the Theory of Liquidity Preference and Portfolio Analysis," *Review of Economic Studies* 36 [January 1969]: 5–12; and James Tobin, "Comment on Borch and Feldstein," *Review of Economic Studies* 36 [January 1969]: 13–15).

21. The alternative formation is in terms of one-period returns. This also leads to incorrect decisions (see Hakansson, "Capital Growth," and Mossin).

22. We will continue to assume that returns are independent over time.

23. See Mossin, p. 228.

24. See n. 17 above.

25. See n. 18 above.

26. There are, of course, a number of patterns that can cause eq. (22) to be a monotonic transform of first-period returns. If T were an odd number and if $R_{ij} = 1/R_{i(j+1)}$, then eq. (22) would be identical to first-period returns. Other such patterns are possible.

27. Again, this conflicts with Mossin's result (see Mossin, p. 228).

28. See Keith Smith, *Portfolio Management* (New York: Holt, Rinehart & Winston, 1971).

29. Even if it is of the log or power function form, expected changes in the distribution of returns lead to revision in the absence of new information.

17 The Multi-Period Consumption Investment Problem and Single Period Analysis

Edwin J. Elton and Martin J. Gruber

In recent years multi-period consumption investment models have received increasing attention in the economic literature. This represents a departure from economists' early preoccupation with single-period models. Given the vast number of normative and descriptive models which have been derived based on the assumption that single-period decisions were appropriate, it would be fortuitous if the multi-period formulation of the problem led to results which were consistent with those produced by single-period models. The purpose of this paper is to synthesize the work that has been done on the multi-period consumption–investment decision in order to examine the implications for the validity of single-period models in the multi-period setting. Throughout this paper we will assume that the investor's objective is maximization of multi-period consumption. This objective function is sufficiently general to encompass all multi-period objective functions.[1]

I Single-period Analysis

Analysis of the single-period consumption investment decision has led to the development of:

1. Normative portfolio theory.
2. A general equilibrium theory of the pricing of risky assets.
3. Techniques for evaluating portfolio performance.
4. Descriptive and normative models of the behaviour of financial institutions.

The body of theory and formal models in each of these areas is based on assumptions about the single-period utility function. Some of the analysis assumes that single-period utility functions are concave, some assumes that we know the form of the function (though the form is not restricted), and some assumes that utility functions are of a particular form. In this section of the paper we shall examine the assumptions which must be made about single-period utilities to lead to the results listed above. In the next sections of this paper we will show that solution of the multi-period investment consumption problem often leads to a derived one-period utility function and we shall discuss those conditions under which this derived function is consistent with the theory discussed in this section.

Markowitz [25] and Tobin [38] proved that if returns were normally distributed and the investor's utility function were concave, then an investor would maximize his expected single-period utility if he minimized standard deviation of returns for any level of expected return and maximized expected return for any level of standard deviation of return (the efficient set theorem). He further showed that independent of the distribution of returns, the same decision rule maximizes the expected value of single-period utility if the investor's utility function is quadratic.

Other researchers have attempted to arrive at an efficient set theory which is appropriate under alternative assumptions about return distributions and/or single-period utility functions.[2] Two alternative assumptions about the distribution of returns have been studied extensively; returns are nonnormal stable Paretian or log normal. Fama [10] has shown that if returns are symmetric stable Paretian and if utility functions are concave, an efficient set theorem can be derived analogous to the one described earlier. Elton and Gruber [5] have shown that if returns on portfolios are log normally distributed, portfolios which maximize expected utility must lie on an exterior boundary in mean variance space for any concave utility function. Furthermore, once the functional form of the single period utility function is known, that section of the boundary curve in mean variance space which is efficient can be delineated and the properties of optimum portfolios inferred.

One additional assumption has been made concerning utility functions. It has been shown by Elton and Gruber [8] that if utility is logarithmic, maximization of the geometric mean is equivalent to maximizing expected utility. Furthermore, they [6] have shown that if returns are log normally distributed, the optimum portfolio is part of the efficient set.

General equilibrium theory for the pricing of risky assets is an extremely powerful tool that has been used to prove propositions about efficient capital markets and theorems concerning normative behaviour of firms (e.g. investment decisions and optimum capital structure). The original theory [24 and 35] was derived using the assumptions under which Tobin derived the efficient set theorem, concave utility functions with normally distributed returns or quadratic utility functions. Fama [10] has derived a general equilibrium theory assuming that utility functions are concave and returns follow a symmetric non-normal stable Paretian distribution. Finally, Merton [26] has derived a general equilibrium theory when returns are log normally distributed. He requires that the utility functions have hyperbolic absolute risk aversion. Of special interest for the later discussion is that the log and power functions are members of this class.

General equilibrium theory is the basis of the literature on portfolio evaluation. Therefore, the same conclusions concerning utility functions are applicable for this literature. Normative and descriptive models of institutional behaviour [17, 18, and 19] are based on the original Markowitz–Tobin analysis. The recent developments concerning alternative distributional assumptions have not been incorporated. Hence, the original assumptions underlying the efficient set theorem are necessary to this body of literature.

As just discussed, the single period consumption–investment literature makes one of three alternative assumptions about the investor's utility function:

1. It is concave.
2. It has a known functional form, but it need not be of any special type.
3. It has a particular functional form (i.e. log or power).

Which of these assumptions are made in each model is reviewed in Table 17.1. In the next section we will show which multi-period consumption–investment models are consistent with each of these assumptions about single period models.

II Multi-period Portfolio Analysis with A General Utility Function

In constructing a general function to represent the utility of life-time consumption, one should consider possible interdependencies between the utility of a dollar amount of consumption in one period and the level of consumption in any other period, as well as the effect of external conditions on the value of consumption. For example, the utility of a particular level of consumption in any year may well be a function of an individual's past level of consumption as well as his anticipated future levels of consumption. In addition, the utility of a particular level of consumption may

Table 17.1

Problem	Distributional assumption	Utility function assumption
1. Normative portfolio theory		
A. Markowitz [25]–Tobin [38]	Normal	Concave
B. Markowitz [25]–Tobin [38]	None	Quadratic
C. Fama [10]	Symmetric stable	Concave
D. Elton–Gruber [5]	Log normal	Known
E. Elton–Gruber [8]	None	Log
2. General equilibrium theory		
A. Sharpe [35]–Lintner [24]	Normal	Concave
B. Sharpe [35]–Lintner [24]	None	Quadratic
C. Fama [10]	Symmetric stable Paretian	Concave
D. Merton [26]	Log normal	Hyperbolic absolute risk aversion
3. Portfolio evaluation		
A. Sharpe [36]–Treynor [37]–Jensen [21]	Normal	Concave
B. Sharpe [36]–Treynor [37]–Jensen [21]	None	Quadratic
C. Jensen [21]	Stable Paretian	Concave
4. Descriptive and normative models		
1. Various authors*	Normal	Concave
2. Various authors*	None	Quadratic

* The studies here are too numerous to list. Typical examples can be found in the three volumes edited by Hester and Tobin [17], [18], and [19]. See especially [18].

be state dependent in the sense that the utility of particular dollar level of consumption varies with conditions in the investor's environment. A general utility function which incorporates both temporal independencies between consumption levels and independencies with external factors can be written as:[3]

$$U(c_1, c_2, \ldots, c_k, \ldots, c_{T-1}, c_T \mid \phi_T)$$

1. c_t is consumption in period t, where t goes from 1 (birth) the time at which the initial consumption decision is made to the time at which a bequest is left upon death T. Time period $T-1$ is the time in which the last portfolio decision is made. Time period k is the time period in which the investor currently faces a decision.

2. ϕ_t is a vector giving the information available at the time that the consumption decision c_t is made.

The problem situation facing the investor is defined as follows. In each period the investor must decide on how much to consume and how to allocate the remaining funds among alternative investment opportunities. These investment opportunities consist of securities whose return is a random variable and a safe investment earning a known rate of interest. Furthermore, the investor has a known income stream that will be available over time.[4] This income stream can be thought of as return from employment. The investment and consumption decisions are made in each period until a known horizon, at which time all remaining wealth in the form of a bequest is consumed.[5] Taxes and transaction costs are assumed to be zero.[6]

The wealth at time $t+1$ is the value at $t+1$ of the investment portfolio selected at t or

$$W_{t+1} = \sum_{i=2}^{m} \beta_{it}(\phi_{t+1})z_{it} + r_t z_{1t} + y_t$$

where

1. $\beta_{it}(\phi_{t+1})$ is one plus the return on a dollar invested in asset i for period t. It is a function of all information which will exist at time $t+1$. Since at time t, this information set is a random variable, β_{it} itself is a random variable.
2. z_{it} is the dollar amount invested in asset i in period t.
3. r_t is one plus the return on a riskless investment.[7]
4. y_t is the non-investment income received between time t and $t+1$.

This equation simply states that the cash available at time $t+1$ is equal to the value of the $m-1$ risky assets the investor purchases at t, plus the value of the investment in the riskless asset plus the non-investment income received between time t and $t+1$.

The dollar amount invested at any time (t) is limited to wealth less consumption at time t or $\sum_{i=1}^{m} z_{it} = W_t - c_t$. Substituting this into the previous equation, we can derive an expression for wealth in $t+1$ as a function of wealth and consumption in t.

$$W_{t+1} = \sum_{i=2}^{m} [\beta_{it}(\phi_{t+1}) - r_t]z_{it} + (W_t - c_t)r_t + y_t. \tag{1}$$

We are now ready to derive the recursive relationship. The utility function given earlier is the end condition, that is

$$f_T(c_1, c_2, \ldots, c_{T-1}, W_T \mid \phi_T) = U(c_1, c_2 \ldots, c_{T-1}, c_T \mid \phi_T).$$

This holds for all c_i, W_T, and elements of the vector ϕ_T. This expression gives the utility of lifetime consumption for all possible consumption patterns and states of the world. The recursive relationship for period $T-1$ is

$$f_{T-1}(c_1, c_2, \ldots, c_{T-2}, W_{T-1} \mid \phi_{T-1}) = \max_{z_{iT-1} c_{T-1}} E[f_T(c_1, c_2, \ldots, c_{T-1}, W_T \mid \phi_T)] \tag{2}$$

where the expected value is taken over all levels of ϕ_T and where the recursive relationship is calculated for all values of c_i where $i = 1, \ldots T-2$; all W_{T-1}; and all elements of the vector ϕ_{T-1}.

Note that the maximization is performed with respect to the optimum level of consumption in period $T-1$ and the optimum level of investment in each possible asset at time $T-1$.[8] These are the only decision variables in equations (1) and (2).

For an arbitrary time t, the recursive relationship becomes

$$f_t(c_1, c_2, \ldots, c_{t-1}, W_t \mid \phi_t) = \max_{z_{it} c_t} E[f_{t+1}(c_1, c_2, \ldots, c_t, W_{t+1} \mid \phi_{t+1})]. \tag{3}$$

Subject to equation (1) for all c_i, all W_t, and all ϕ_t.

To understand this equation, examine the meaning of

$$f_{t+1}(c_1, c_2, \ldots, c_t, W_{t+1} \mid \phi_{t+1}).$$

This function gives the maximum expected utility from period $t+1$ to the horizon given

1. Any particular consumption patten in periods 1 to t.
2. Any particular level of investor's wealth in $t+1$.
3. An optimum consumption plan and portfolio strategy from $t+2$ to the horizon.

Equation (3) allows us to move back in time by repetitively selecting the optimum consumption and investment mix at t, so that for any consumption level from 1 to $t-1$ and for any wealth level at t, the expected utility of lifetime consumption is maximized.

Equation (3) together with equation (1) represents the generalized dynamic programming formulation of the multi-period portfolio problem when the objective function is to maximize the expected utility of multi-period consumption. We can reformulate equation (3) in terms of an investor facing a decision at a point in time k. All consumption in previous periods is known at time k so that a utility function can be stated entirely in terms of future consumption. Equation (3) becomes

$$f_k^*(W_k \mid \phi_k) = \max_{z_{ik}c_k} E[f_{k+1}^*(c_k, W_{k+1} \mid \phi_{k+1})] \tag{4}$$

where the asterisk on f^* indicates that all consumption which has already taken place $(c_1, \ldots, c_{k-1})$ is incorporated in the function.

Examination of equation (4) reveals that even in the most general formulation of the multi-period consumption investment decision, the problem can be reduced to a single-period problem. That is equation (4) just involves the maximization of a function in terms of one-period decision parameters. However, two facets of the analysis are of interest. To derive f_{k+1}^* one had to specify all future investment opportunities (not just one-period opportunities), and all information sets. Thus f_{k+1}^* is a derived function which in turn is a function of the above-mentioned variables. The question remains that if having derived f_{k+1}^*, this one-period utility function has the properties necessary for the type of analysis outlined in the first section. The answer to this is *no*. The form of the one-period utility function that is relevant depends upon the value of ϕ_{k+1}. The same level of wealth can have different utility depending on the state of the world. This rules out any evaluation or asset selection scheme that does not consider state dependencies. If utilities are formulated this way one must reject all of the decision models discussed in the first part of this paper and use state preference theory.

If the state dependency of utilities is eliminated, then this problem would resemble a one-period problem. Fama [9] argues that the utility function would not be state dependent if the following conditions hold:

1. The consumer's tastes for particular consumption goods and services are independent of the state of the world.
2. The consumer acts as if consumption opportunities in terms of goods and their prices are known at the beginning of any previous period.
3. The consumer acts as if the distribution of one-period returns on all assets is known at the beginning of any previous period.

If these conditions hold, then equation (4) can be written as

$$f_k^*(W_k) = \max_{z_{ik}c_k} E[f_{k+1}^*(c_k, W_{k+1})]. \tag{5}$$

This equation is formally equivalent to the one-period problem. If we call the functional relationship $f^*_{k+1}(\ )$ a utility function, then in both the one-period problem and the equation above, the decision-maker maximizes the expected value of the utility of current consumption and terminal wealth. Thus, although the decision-maker has derived the utility function via dynamic programming (employing information concerning future investment opportunities and a multi-period utility function), each period's decision is identical in form to that engaged in by a one-period expected utility maximizer.

This in itself says very little, since without further assumptions the previous equation provides no insight into the functional form of the one-period utility function. In particular, without further assumptions the utility function derived by dynamic programming need not bear any resemblance to a utility function that is considered reasonable in a one-period case. Its derivatives could have any sign, its functional form cannot be specified. In particular none of the conditions discussed in the first section need be fulfilled.

However, if we assume that the utility function for multi-period consumption is monotonically increasing and strictly concave with respect to each period's consumption, then as Fama has shown, the derived one-period utility function has these same properties. The essential reason is that the expected value function involves taking a weighted average of concave functions and the sum of concave functions is concave. Monotonicity is easy to understand since if an extra dollar is available for current wealth, it can be consumed leaving the same decisions in future periods feasible. Since we have assumed that the multi-period functions are monotonically increasing, this must yield higher utility.

The knowledge that the multi-period decision-maker faces a monotonically increasing concave derived utility function in each period is sufficient to validate the optimality of several two-period models under alternative distributional assumptions. For example, if returns follow a normal distribution and derived utility functions are concave, then the normative portfolio theories proported by Markowitz [25]–Tobin [38], the Sharpe [35]–Lintner [24] general equilibrium theories, the Sharpe [36]–Jensen [21]–Treynor [37] portfolio evaluation literature, and most of the literature on descriptive and normative behaviour of institutions is valid in a multi-period setting. Similarly, if returns follow a symmetric non-normal stable Paretian distribution, the normative portfolio theory and general equilibrium theory of Fama [10] and the portfolio evaluation models of Jensen [21] are suitable for multi-period decision-makers.

Although for many purposes the knowledge that the decision-maker should maximize the expected utility of a concave monotonically increasing function is sufficient, for other decisions some knowledge concerning the possible functional form of the utility function is necessary. Without further assumptions no statements are possible. In particular, there is no reason to believe that the derived utility function of equation (5) bears any resemblance to functions that can be justified in one-period decisions. However, the introduction of separable utility functions allows stronger conclusions to be drawn.

III The Analysis with Separable Utility Functions

The multi-period portfolio problem with intermediate consumption becomes much more tractable if we continue to assume that utility is independent of the information set (state of the world) and, in addition, we accept the assumption that utility functions are separable.[9] Under the assumption of separable utilities, the utility of a level of consumption in any period is unrelated to the past or future level of consumption. Thus, the utility of consumption from period t onward (until death in year T) can be defined as

$$\begin{aligned} U(c_t, c_{t+1}, \ldots, c_{T-1}, W_T) = u(c_t) &+ \alpha_t u(c_{t+1}) + \alpha_t \alpha_{t+1} u(c_{t+2}) \\ &+ \cdots + \alpha_t \alpha_{t+1} \cdots \alpha_{T-2} u(c_{T-1}) \\ &+ \alpha_t \alpha_{t+1} \cdots \alpha_{T-1} u(W_T) \end{aligned} \tag{6}$$

where

α_t is the appropriate discount factor for period t.

W_T is terminal wealth in the form of a bequest.

We will continue to assume the problem situation described in Section II. In addition, equation (1) continues to hold except that $\beta_{it}(\phi_t)$ is replaced by β_{it} since we are assuming no state dependency.

We are now ready to derive the recursive relationship. Let $f_t(W_t)$ be the expected utility of consumption from period t to the horizon if W_t dollars in wealth are available at t. Then from equation (6) $f_t(W_t)$ is equal to

$$\begin{aligned} f_t(W_t) = \max E[u(c_t) &+ \alpha_t u(c_{t+1}) + \alpha_t \alpha_{t+1} u(c_{t+2}) \\ &+ \cdots + \alpha_t \alpha_{t+1} \cdots \alpha_{T-1} u(W_T)]. \end{aligned} \tag{7}$$

If we assume the β_{it} are independent over time (the random walk assumption) then using the principal of optimality equation (7) can be written as

$$f_t(W_t) = \max_{c_t z_{it}} [[u(c_t) + \alpha_t E f_{t+1}(W_{t+1})]] \tag{8}$$

subject to $\quad W_{t+1} = \sum_{i=2}^{m} (\beta_{it} - r_t) z_{it} + r_t(W_t - c_t) + y_t.$

An examination of equation (8) shows that the only decision variables are consumption c_t and the dollar amount placed in the assets z_{it} since r_t, W_t, y_t, and β_{it} are either known quantities or have known probability distributions. Therefore, the maximum is over the variables that are indicated in the recursive relationship. The right side of equation (8) is composed of two terms. The first term is the utility of consuming c_t dollars in period t and the second term is the expected utility of consumption from $t+1$ to the horizon if W_{t+1} dollars are available in $t+1$.

To solve equation (8), the decision-maker must solve a problem with the same decision variables and format as the one-period problem. In both cases, the decision-maker is selecting a portfolio to maximize the utility of current consumption plus future wealth. This should not be surprising, since this decision problem is simply a special case of the decision problem presented earlier. However, this simplified decision model yields more results. The right side of equation (8) involves linear operations. The expected value operator is a linear average of the $f_{t+1}(W_{t+1})$ and this is added to the utility of current consumption. Since $f_T(W_T)$ is a linear average of the terminal utility, all earlier $f_t(W_t)$ are also linear averages of utility functions. The following conclusion can now be stated.

The investor described above will face a series of single-period portfolio problems which has an objective function of the same functional form as the utility function for consumption in each future period, if a linear combination of these individual utility functions preserves the form. As discussed in Section I, knowledge concerning functional form is important in many applications of consumption-investment models. For example, if returns are log normally distributed then the single-period portfolio theory of Elton and Gruber [5] will apply. Furthermore, if the form of the distribution once known fits the appropriate category then the general equilibrium theory of Merton [26] may apply.

Further simplication of the multi-period investment consumption problem is possible if utility functions are assumed to be of the log or power form. These functions have received a lot of attention in the economic literature for they are the only utility functions consistent with constant relative risk aversion. In addition, these functions allow the (percentage) composition of optimal portfolios to be completely independent of wealth and consumption and lead to greatly simplified decision rules.

IV Solution to the Recursive Relationship with Log and Power Utility Functions

It is well known that utility functions of the following form exhibit constant relative risk aversion increasing utility of wealth and marginal decreasing utility of wealth[10]

$$u(W) = \ln W \qquad \text{for } \gamma = 1$$

$$u(W) = -W^{1-\gamma} \qquad \text{for } \gamma > 1$$

$$u(W) = W^{1-\gamma} \qquad \text{for } 0 < \gamma < 1.$$

Employing any of these utility functions in conjunction with equations (1) and (8) vastly simplifies both the computation and interpretation of the multi-period portfolio problem. It is well known (for example, Mossin [28], or Hakansson [15]) that under either of these utility functions, portfolio composition (in percentage terms) is completely independent of the level of wealth. Furthermore, Hakansson [15] has shown that when the multi-period utility function is assumed additively separable and single-period utility functions are of the log or power form, then the derived utility function for each period will be a linear transformation of the single-period utility function. Thus that portfolio which maximizes the single-period utility function will also maximize the multi-period utility function.[11] In short, any optimal single-period portfolio decision will be optimum in the multi-period setting. We have now come full circle. If utility functions are additive separable and are of the log or power form, then any model of portfolio analysis, general equilibrium, portfolio evaluation or institutional behaviour which is appropriate for a single-period decision (given the distribution of returns) will be appropriate for a multi-period decision.

V Conclusion

In this paper we have constructed a general dynamic programming model of the multi-period portfolio problem when the investor is assumed to act so as to maximize the expected utility of lifetime consumption. The implications of this model for the vast literature on the single-period consumption–investment decision are explored. Even under the most general assumptions about utility functions, a one-period utility function can be *derived* under which the investor will act in a manner indistinguishable from a one-period decision-maker. However, as long as the multi-period utility function is assumed to be state dependent, single-period models which do not incorporate this property are inappropriate. Even if the assumption that the multi-period utility function is state dependent is dropped, the form of the derived one-period utility function might differ from both the form of the utility function for multi-period consumption and any utility function that is considered appropriate for single-period decision makers. However, if the multi-period consumption function is concave and monotonically increasing with wealth, the derived single-period function will have these same properties. Once these properties are established, many of the models which were developed for single-period analysis become appropriate.

In order to derive additional conclusions from the model, it was necessary to assume that the multi-period consumption function was separable. Under this assumption, the derived utility function for any single period will have the same form as the utility function for consumption in any period, if taking linear combinations of these utility functions preserves the form. This allows still more single-period models to be applicable for the multi-period case. Finally, if the investor's utility function for consumption in each period is of the log or power form, then the composition of each period's portfolio can be selected on the basis of single-period information about securities. In this case, any single-period model which is consistent with a single-period utility function of the type under study is appropriate for the multi-period portfolio problem.

Notes

1. Variations of this objective function have been studied by [2], [3], [4], [9], [11], [12], [13], [14], [15], [16], [22], [23], [26], [27], [28], [29], [31], [32], [33], [34]. This function is general enough to include the more specific objective function, maximize the utility of terminal wealth.

2. This work has been motivated by the fact that empirical evidence is not consistent with normally distributed returns and the quadratic utility function assumes increasing absolute risk aversion.

3. Fama [9] has analysed this problem extensively. The analysis in this section draws on his work.

4. If the reader wishes to delete non-investment income from the analysis in this section, he merely has to set all y_t equal to zero. This analysis could also be performed with a stochastic exogeneous income stream rather than a deterministic one. However, the computational implications of such a model are quite complex.

5. Generalizations to incorporate uncertainty concerning death are trivial involving only notational changes. See Fama [9].

6. Some authors (e.g., Hakansson [15], p. 445) argue that taxes and transaction costs can be proportional to the dollar amount invested and still be included in β_{it}. For this to be true, the taxes and transaction costs would have to be incurred irrespective of previous or future investments. In other words, the same taxes and transaction costs would have to be incurred irrespective of whether the security was held in the previous period or world be held in future periods. Such an assumption adds no realism.

7. The assumption of the existence of a riskless rate of interest is made throughout this paper and does not affect any of the analysis. It is a conventional assumption and we have made it here. The reader who wishes can set this term equal to zero.

8. To see that z_{iT-1} and c_{T-1} are the variables over which the maximum is taken, examine equation (1) where $t+1$ is set equal T. $\beta_{iT-1}(\phi_T)$ has a known probability distribution, while r_{T-1} is a known (deterministic) variable. C_1 to C_{T-2} and W_{T-1} are also known since they are state variables. Therefore, the decision variables are z_{iT-1} and c_{T-1}.

9. This is the assumption that is implicitly or explicitly made in the work of Samuelson [31], Merton [26] and [27], Hakansson [12], [14], [15], and [16], and Phelps [29]. The limitations of the assumption of separable utility functions are well known and need no further elaboration here.

10. These three functions are the only functions which exhibit:

a. Constant relative risk aversion $Wu''(W)/u'(W) = \gamma$.

b. Increasing utility of wealth $u'(W) > 0$.

c. Decreasing marginal utility of wealth $u''(W) < 0$.

11. The reader should note that while the utility functions under study allow the composition of the optimal portfolio to be determined solely on the basis of the single-period utility function and information about single-period returns, the optimum dollar amount to consume in any period is a function of information for all future periods. For a discussion of the optimum allocation of wealth between consumption and investment, see Hakansson [15].

References

1. Arrow, Kenneth, 'Aspects of the theory of risk bearing', Yrjö Jahnsson lectures. Helsinki: The Yrjö Jahnsson Foundation, 1965.

2. Chen, Andrew, Jen, Frank, and Zionts, Stanley, 'The optimal portfolio revision policy', *Journal of Business*, vol. 64, no. 1 (Jan. 1971), pp. 51–61.

3. Dreze, J. H., and Modigliani, F., 'Consumption decisions under uncertainty', CORE discussion paper no. 6906, Université Catholique de Louvain, 1969.

4. Elton, Edwin, J., and Gruber, Martin J., 'Dynamic programming models in finance', *Journal of Finance*, vol. 26, no. 2 (May 1971), pp. 473, 505.

5. ——— ——— 'Portfolio theory when investment relatives are lognormally distributed', Forthcoming *Journal of Finance.*

6. ——— ——— 'On the maximization of the geometric mean with lognormal return distributions', forthcoming in *Management Science.*

7. ——— ——— *Security Evaluation and Portfolio Analysis* (Prentice-Hall; Englewood Cliffs, New Jersey), Jan. 1972.

8. ——— ——— 'On the optimality of some multi-period portfolio selection criteria', forthcoming in *Journal of Business.*

9. Fama, Eugene, 'Multi-period consumption-investment decisions', *American Economic Review*, vol. 60 (Mar. 1970), pp. 163–74.

10. ——— 'Risk, return and equilibrium', *Journal of Political Economy*, vol. 79, no. 1 (Jan./Feb. 1971), pp. 30–55.

11. Hagen, Kåre, 'On the problem of optimal consumption and investment policies over time', *The Swedish Journal of Economics*, vol. 74, no. 2 (June 1972). pp. 201–20.

12. Hakansson, Nils, 'Optimal investment and consumption strategies under risk for a class of utility functions', *Econometrica*, vol. 38 (Sept. 1970), pp. 587–607.

13. ——— 'On optimal myopic portfolio policies with and without serial correlation of yields', *Journal of Business*, vol. 44, no. 3 (July 1971), pp. 324–35.

14. ——— 'Risk disposition and the separation property in portfolio selection', *Journal of Financial and Quantitative Analysis*, vol. 4, no. 4 (Dec. 1969), pp. 401–16.

15. ——— 'Optimal investment and consumption under risk: an uncertain lifetime and insurance', *International Economic Review*, vol. 10, no. 3 (Oct. 1969), pp. 443–66.

16. ——— 'An induced theory of the firm under risk: the pure mutual fund', *Journal of Financial and Quantitative Analysis*, vol. 3, no. 2 (June 1970), pp. 155–78.

17. Hester, Donald, and Tobin, James, Editors, *Risk Aversion and Portfolio Choice.* John Wiley and Sons; New York, New York, 1967.

18. ——— ——— Editors, *Studies of Portfolio Behavior.* John Wiley and Sons; New York, New York, 1967.

19. ——— ——— Editors, *Financial Markets and Economic Activity.* John Wiley and Sons; New York, New York, 1967.

20. Hirshleifer, Jack, *Investment Interest Capital.* Prentice-Hall: Englewood Cliffs, New Jersey, 1970.

21. Jensen, Mike, 'Risk, the pricing of capital assets and the evaluation of investment portfolios', *Journal of Business*, vol. 42, no. 2 (Apr. 1969), pp. 167–277.

22. Latane, Henry, 'Criteria for choice among risky ventures', *Journal of Political Economy*, vol. 67 (Apr. 1959), pp. 144–55.

23. Leland, H., 'Saving and uncertainty: the precautionary demand for saving', *Quarterly Journal of Economics*, vol. 82, no. 3 (Aug. 1968), pp. 465–72.

24. Lintner, John, 'Security prices, risk and maximal gains from diversification', *Journal of Finance*, vol. 20, no. 5 (Dec. 1965), pp. 587–616.

25. Markowitz, H. M., 'Portfolio Selection', *Journal of Finance*, vol. 7, no. 1, (Mar. 1952), pp. 77–91.

26. Merton, Robert, 'Optimal consumption and portfolio rules in a continuous time model', *Journal of Economic Theory*, vol. 3, no. 4 (Dec. 1971), pp. 373–413.

27. ——— 'Lifetime portfolio selection under uncertainty: the continuous time case', *Review of Economics and Statistics*, vol. 50 (Aug. 1969), pp. 247–57.

28. Mossin, Jan, 'Optimal multi-period portfolio policies', *Journal of Business*, vol. 41 (Apr. 1968), pp. 215–29.

29. Phelps, Edmund, 'The accumulation of risky capital: a sequential utility analysis', *Econometrica*, vol. 30 (Oct. 1962), pp. 729–43.

30. Pratt, John, 'Risk aversion in the small and in the large', *Econometrica*, vol. 32, nos. 1–2 (Jan.–Apr. 1964), pp. 122–36.

31. Samuelson, Paul, 'Lifetime portfolio selection by dynamic stochastic programming', *Review of Economics and Statistics*, vol. 50 (Aug. 1969), pp. 239–46.

32. Sandmo, A., 'Portfolio choice in a theory of savings', *Swedish Journal of Economics*, vol. 70, no. 2 (June 1968), pp. 106–22.

33. ——— 'Capital risk, consumption and portfolio choice', *Econometrica*, forthcoming.

34. ——— 'The effect of uncertainty on savings decisions', *The Review of Economic Studies*, forthcoming.

35. Sharpe, William, 'Capital asset prices: a theory of market equilibrium under conditions of risk', *Journal of Finance*, vol. 19, no. 4 (Sept. 1964), pp. 425–42.

36. ——— 'Mutual fund performance', *Journal of Business*, vol. 39, no. 1, part 2 (Jan. 1966), pp. 119–38.

37. Treynor, Jack, 'How to rate management of investment funds', *Harvard Business Review*, vol. 43, no. 1 (Jan./Feb. 1968), pp. 63–75.

38. Tobin, James, 'Liquidity preference as a behaviour towards risk', *Review of Economic Studies*, vol. 25, no. 67 (February 1958), pp. 65–87.

IV Equilibrium

In this section we explore some of our research on equilibrium models. The essay on portfolio analysis with a nonnormal, multi-index, return-generating process discussed in the prior section could well be placed in this section. The first chapter on nonstandard CAPMs and the market portfolio is in some sense a survey of the literature on non-Sharpe Lintner CAPMs. In another sense, it shows that all nonstandard CAPMs can be easily derived from an assumption of a different market portfolio being efficient. The choice between them rests on what is included in the market portfolio. For example, if the efficient market portfolio includes nontraded assets, then we can derive the version of the CAPM for nontraded assets. If the market portfolio includes international assets, then we can derive one of the international CAPMs. The article can be seen as a generalization of the Roll proof that if the market portfolio is efficient, then the standard CAPM follows to similar proofs for more complete definitions of the market. It can also be viewed as a handy way to learn all of the non-standard CAPMs, since having mastered one proof, all follow in a parallel fashion.

The second chapter examines an equilibrium model when an asset's ability to hedge against inflation risk affects its equilibrium pricing. Prior models involving inflation had all been derived in the mean-variance framework. Investors were assumed to care about the mean and variance of real returns. Inflation entered the return-generating process because it affected the mean and variance of real returns, however, it was not priced because of hedge characteristics. A stock that was a perfect hedge against inflation would have the same expected return as one that was not, providing it had the same covariance with the market. In this article we argue that the hedge characteristics of a stock should affect its expected return and derive an equilibrium model when it does.

The last chapter in the section is somewhat different from the prior two. First, it is empirical. Second, it deals with a specific problem: the testing of asset-pricing models. The specific issue is how to determine the number of factors in the return-generating process. We generate return series that have the same characteristics as actual return series but for which we know the underlying return-generating process. We then use standard tests of the number of factors and the number of priced factors. We find that standard procedures for testing for the number of factors and the number of priced factors result in too many factors being accepted relative to the true model.

18

Non-Standard C.A.P.M.s and the Market Portfolio

Edwin J. Elton and Martin J. Gruber

Richard Roll (8) changed our way of thinking about the CAPM model, both in terms of theoretical content and empirical testing. One of Roll's key contributions was to show that if the market portfolio were efficient, the Sharpe-Lintner-Mossin or zero beta form of the CAPM *must* follow.

The purpose of this article is to extend Roll's work to non-standard forms of the CAPM. In recent years, the literature has contained over a dozen extensions of the simple CAPM. Of particular interest have been models which incorporate uncertain inflation, differential taxes on income and capital gains, heterogenous expectations, non-marketable assets, missing assets and international securities. In this article we will show that models that have been proposed in each of these areas follow directly from the assumption that investors act as if some particular market portfolio is efficient. We believe that doing so is important for several reasons. First, it is a generalization of Roll's work which shows that his analysis and many of his conclusions can be extended well beyond his initial contribution. Second, it allows us to derive alternative equilibrium models using only algebra in a very simple and straightforward way. Furthermore, since the derivations are almost exactly parallel, having mastered one, the reader can move easily through the others. Third, we show that the differences between most non-standard forms of the CAPM come about from a difference in which market portfolio is assumed efficient and an assumption about how to change from the definition of returns used to define the market portfolio to the usual meaning of returns (dividends plus capital gains). This analysis highlights exactly what are the differences between models and shows that many of the asserted differences are nonexistent.

The final reason this paper is important is that it stresses that each model arises directly from the efficiency of a *particular* version of the market portfolio. Therefore, on a theoretical level, one can think about which version of a portfolio is likely to be efficient and on an empirical level the correctness of any model is likely to be decided by which "market portfolio" is efficient.

The following sections of the paper are divided by type of non-standard CAPM. The types discussed incorporate non-marketable assets, international assets, inflation, taxes, and heterogenous expectations.

I The Effect of Missing and Non-Marketable Assets

Mayers (7) derived the impact of both missing and nonmarketable assets on general equilibrium returns. Actually Mayers' treatment of the missing asset case was the first demonstration of the type of derivation we shall use throughout the remainder of this paper.

In the case of missing assets the goal is to express equilibrium in terms of the characteristics of the set of assets which has improperly been excluded from the market portfolio as well as the characteristics of the set of assets which has been included:

Let

r'_M be the return on all assets—the true market return

r_M be the return on those assets which have been included in the incomplete definition of the market portfolio

r_H be the return on those assets which have been inappropriately excluded from the definition of the market portfolio

P_M be the market value (at the beginning of the period) of all assets included in the incomplete definition of the market portfolio

P_H be the market value (at the beginning of the period) of all assets inappropriately excluded from the market portfolio

r_i be the return in asset i

r_F be the riskless lending and borrowing rate

β'_i be the Beta coefficient between the return on asset i and the true market portfolio

Following Roll or Mayer the true market portfolio should be efficient and in the presence of unlimited riskless lending and borrowing a version of the standard CAPM holds

$$\bar{r}_i = r_F + \frac{\text{cov}(r_i r'_M)}{\text{var}(r'_M)}(\bar{r}'_M - r_F) \tag{1}$$

The return on the true market portfolio is simply a weighted average of the return on the misestimated market portfolio and the missing assets as follows:

$$r'_M = \frac{P_M}{P_H + P_M} r_M + \frac{P_H}{P_H + P_M} r_H \tag{2}$$

substituting equation (2) into equation (1) and simplifying

$$\bar{r}_i = r_F + \left[(\bar{r}_M - r_F) + \left(\frac{P_H}{P_M}\right)(\bar{r}_H - r_F) \right] \times \frac{\operatorname{cov}(r_i r_M) + \left(\frac{P_H}{P_M}\right)\operatorname{cov}(r_i r_H)}{\operatorname{var}(r_M) + 2\left(\frac{P_H}{P_M}\right)\operatorname{cov}(r_H r_M) + \left(\frac{P_H}{P_M}\right)^2 \operatorname{var}(r_H)} \tag{3}$$

This equation must hold for all risky assets, including the market portfolio of risky assets. Setting $\bar{r}_i = \bar{r}_M$ and rearranging

$$\frac{\frac{P_H}{P_M}(\bar{r}_H - r_F)}{\operatorname{var}(r_M) + 2\frac{P_H}{P_M}\operatorname{cov}(r_H r_M) + \left(\frac{P_H}{P_M}\right)^2 \operatorname{var}(r_H)} = \frac{\bar{r}_M - r_F}{\operatorname{var}(r_M) + \frac{P_H}{P_M}\operatorname{cov}(r_M r_H)} \tag{4}$$

Substituting equation (4) into equation (3) yields

$$\bar{r}_i = r_F + \frac{\bar{r}_M - r_F}{\operatorname{var}(r_M) + \frac{P_H}{P_M}\operatorname{cov}(r_H r_M)} \left[\operatorname{cov}(r_i r_M) + \frac{P_H}{P_M}\operatorname{cov}(r_i r_H) \right] \tag{5}$$

This is simply the return form of Mayers [7] equation (27) which is expressed in terms of prices. This analysis is very similar to the analysis presented in Mayers [7]. The major reason for including it is that it exactly parallels several of the proofs that follow in latter sections of this article but is less complex.

Now let us derive the relationship for non-marketable assets. Let r'_M now stand for the return on the aggregate of all risky assets including non-marketable assets, the subscript $_H$ stand for non-marketable risky assets and r_M stand for the portfolio of risky marketable assets.[1] Let r_{pi} be the return on investor i's optimum portfolio which includes marketable and non-marketable assets. Then following Roll for any marketable asset we can write[2]

$\bar{r}_k = r_F + \lambda_i \operatorname{cov}(r_{pi} r_k)$

λ_i is a coefficient representing the ratio of excess return to variance on the optimum portfolio held by investor i (6)

Define w_i as the dollars of wealth which investor i will place in risky assets (including non-marketable risky assets). Dividing both sides of equation (6) by λ_i and multiplying both sides by w_i

$$\frac{w_i}{\lambda_i}(\bar{r}_k - r_F) = \operatorname{cov}(r_k, w_i r_{pi})$$

Dividing both sides of this equation by $\sum_i w_i$ summing over all i and recognizing that $(\sum_i w_i r_{pi})/(\sum_i w_i) = r'_M$ (since the sum of all risky assets is the market portfolio of risky assets) we obtain after rearranging

$$\bar{r}_k = r_F + \frac{\sum_i w_i}{\sum_i \frac{w_i}{\lambda_i}} \operatorname{cov}(r_k r'_M) \tag{7}$$

This equation must hold for all marketable risky assets or portfolios of marketable risky assets. It does not have to hold for non-marketable risky assets because equation (6) did not have to hold for non-marketable assets. One portfolio it must hold for is the market portfolio of all marketable risky assets. Using equation (7) to define $\bar{r}_M$, solving for $(\sum_i w_i)/(\sum_i (w_i/\lambda_i))$ and substituting into (7) we obtain

$$\bar{r}_k = r_F + \frac{\operatorname{cov}(r_k r'_M)}{\operatorname{cov}(r_M r'_M)}(\bar{r}_M - r_F)$$

Recall that

$$\operatorname{cov}(r_k r'_M) = \frac{P_M}{P_M + P_H}\operatorname{cov}(r_k r_M) + \frac{P_H}{P_M + P_H}\operatorname{cov}(r_k r_H)$$

and

$$\operatorname{cov}(r_M r'_M) = \frac{P_M}{P_M + P_H}\operatorname{var}(r_M) + \frac{P_H}{P_M + P_H}\operatorname{cov}(r_M r_H).$$

Substituting these two expressions into the previous equation and simplifying

$$\bar{r}_k = r_F + \frac{\bar{r}_M - r_F}{\operatorname{var}(r_M) + \frac{P_H}{P_M}\operatorname{cov}(r_M r_H)}\left[\operatorname{cov}(r_k r_M) + \frac{P_H}{P_M}\operatorname{cov}(r_k r_H)\right]$$

which is essentially equation (5) with the definition of the terms modified as explained above. This is the general equilibrium equation presented in Mayers [7] equation (20) page 230. The other versions of the general equilibrium relationships presented in Mayers are just algebraic manipulations of this equation.

II International C.A.P.M.

Three of the best known and most often quoted C.A.P.M.s are the models presented by Grauer, Litzenberger and Stehle [4]. Solnick [14], and Senbet (11). These models are concerned with exchange risk and the effect of exchange risk on both the price of goods and the return on assets.

Solnick assumes that investors consume a domestic good but can invest in their own assets and assets of other countries. Exchange rate risk adds to the uncertainty of the return of foreign assets. However, Solnick argues that this risk can be eliminated through the use of lending in some countries and borrowing in others. This differentiates Solnick's model from other models discussed in this section.

Grauer, Litzenberger, and Stehle [4] assume that all assets and all commodities are freely traded. Exchange rate fluctuations are simply changes in the relative prices of the goods offered by the various countries. This results in the value of a security not being affected by the country of domicile of the investor.

Senbet does not make an explicit assumption about the prices of consumption goods and exchange rate movements. Rather, he assumes the existence of a supercurrency which can be used to price all goods and local currencies.

A Solnick Model

Solnick's C.A.P.M. follows from two assumptions. The first is that investors can eliminate exchange risk through hedging. The second is that investors consume only in their own country. Since investors only consume in their home currency, the appropriate way in which to examine portfolio returns is in units of the investor's home currency. Thus the relevant efficient frontier for any investor will be in units of his or her home currency. Domestic assets are already in the appropriate units. Foreign assets are converted to the appropriate units by hedging activity that eliminates exchange risk.

All investors are assumed to have homogeneous expectations regarding both an asset's return in its home currency and exchange rate fluctuations. These two assumptions together imply that investors in any one country have homogeneous expectations about returns on foreign securities as well as domestic securities, both before and after hedging to eliminate exchange risk. Thus all investors in any one country face the same frontier of risky securities. Furthermore, a riskless lending and borrowing rate is assumed to exist in each country although the rate may differ between countries. Homogeneous expectations and riskless lending and borrowing insure that a single portfolio is optimal for all investors in any one country (though it may differ between countries).

Under the conditions just discussed, from Roll's analysis the Sharpe-Lintner model must hold with respect to the optimal portfolio held by the investors in any country (e.g. country k). If we let r_k^* be the return on the optimal portfolio for an investor living in country k given that the appropriate hedged situation is taken, then

$$\bar{r}_{ik}^* - r_{Fk} = \frac{\text{cov}(r_{ik}^* r_k^*)}{\text{var}(r_k^*)} - (\bar{r}_k^* - r_{Fk})$$

where

1. $\bar{r}_{ik}^*$ is the return on asset i to an investor in country k given that he has hedged away exchange risk.
2. r_{FK} is the riskless lending and borrowing rate in country k

If r_i is the return on an asset of country k in units of its own currency, then $r_i = r_{ik}^*$ and for assets of country k and we have

$$\bar{r}_i - r_{Fk} = \frac{\text{cov}(r_i r_k^*)}{\text{var}(r_k^*)} - (\bar{r}_k^* - r_{Fk}) \tag{8}$$

To get from this equation to Solnick's final equation it is necessary to define the hedging strategy. Solnick's hedge consists of borrowing a sum of money in the foreign market equal to the amount of assets purchased in that country and investing the proceeds from the loan in the domestic riskless asset. Thus any loss on the foreign investment due to exchange rates should be approximately offset by gains on the foreign debt while gains on investment from changes in exchange rates are offset by losses on the foreign debt.

Let r_k be the return on the optimal portfolio for an investor in country k when the return on each security is defined in its own (home) currency. Then, the after hedged return on the portfolio selected by investors in k is related to the before hedged return as shown below.

$$\bar{r}_k^* = \bar{r}_k - \sum_{\substack{j=1 \\ j \neq k}}^{N} W_j^k r_{Fj} + \sum_{\substack{j=1 \\ j \neq k}}^{N} W_j^k r_{Fk} = \bar{r}_k - \sum\nolimits_{j=1}^{N} W_j^k r_{Fj} + r_{Fk} \tag{9}$$

(1) W_j is the proportion of total wealth (across all countries) invested in the assets of country j

(2) W_j^k is the proportion of their wealth which investors from country k invest in country j

(3) $N =$ the total number of countries

substituting equation (9) into equation (8) yields:

$$\bar{r}_i - r_{Fk} = \frac{\operatorname{cov}(r_i r_k)}{\operatorname{var}(r_k)} \left(\bar{r}_k - \sum\nolimits_{j=1}^{N} W_j^k r_{Fj} \right) \tag{10}$$

Note that we have dropped the asterisk in variance and covariance terms. This is permissible since the substitution into these expression for r_k^* involves r_k and constant (non-stochastic) terms and the constant terms drop out in taking expected values. Defining λ_k as

$$\frac{\left(\bar{r}_k - \sum_{j=1}^{N} W_j^k r_{Fj} \right)}{\operatorname{var}(r_k)}$$

Multiplying both sides by W_k/λ_k, summing, recalling $\sum_{k=1}^{N} W_k r_k = r_M$ and rearranging yields

$$\bar{r}_i - r_{Fk} = \frac{1}{\sum_k^N \frac{W_k}{\lambda_k}} \operatorname{cov}(r_i r_M)$$

Solving this for the market portfolio and using this to estimate the summation containing (W_k/λ_k)

$$\bar{r}_i - r_{Fk} = \frac{\operatorname{cov}(r_i r_M)}{\operatorname{var}(r_M)} (\bar{r}_M - r_{FM}) \tag{11}$$

This is Solnick's C.A.P.M. and his equation (16).

B Senbet Model

In Senbet's [11] model, each investor can consume a basket of goods including both domestic and foreign commodities. Similarly, each investor is free to invest in both domestic and international assets. The unique aspect of Senbet's model is that exchange rates are defined in terms of a "token supercurrency" or numeraire.[3] Wealth expressed in the numeraire represents real purchasing power and the investor should be concerned with the terminal value of his wealth in terms of real purchasing power. Investment risk arises from changes in the number of units of the numeraire currency that a unit of a particular local currency will command and from the risk associated with the returns from any asset denominated in its local currency.

Senbet assumes homogenous expectations concerning both asset values one period hence expressed in units of the asset's own currency and exchange rates between each currency and the numeraire currency. These assumptions imply homogeneous expectations with respect to asset returns expressed in units of the numeraire currency. Thus, all investors face the same efficient frontier.

Senbet assumes a lending and borrowing rate that is riskless in the currency in which it is denominated, but is, of course, risky in the numeraire currency. Thus each investor will hold a different portfolio on the efficient frontier constructed in the numeraire currency. However, since 1) each investor will select an efficient portfolio from the same efficient frontier, 2) the aggregate of all investors' portfolios must be the market portfolio, and 3) combinations of efficient portfolios are efficient, the market portfolio (expressed in the numeraire) must be efficient.[4]

As Roll [8] has shown, if the market portfolio is efficient and there is no riskless lending and borrowing, the zero Beta form of the C.A.P.M. holds, or

$$\bar{R}_i - \bar{R}_z = \frac{\operatorname{cov}(R_i R_M)}{\operatorname{var}(R_M)}(\bar{R}_M - \bar{R}_Z) \qquad (12)$$

where capital letters are used to denote that the relevant variables are defined in terms of the numeraire currency.[5]

Define R_{Fi} as the return in the numeraire currency of the riskless asset of the country to which asset i belongs. Then equation (12) becomes

$$\bar{R}_{Fi} - \bar{R}_Z = \beta_{Fi}(\bar{R}_M - \bar{R}_Z)$$

Solving for $\bar{R}_Z$

$$\bar{R}_Z = \frac{\bar{R}_{Fi} - \beta_{Fi}\bar{R}_M}{1 - \beta_{Fi}}$$

Eliminating $\bar{R}_Z$ by substituting the expression for $\bar{R}_Z$ into equation (12) and simplifying yields

$$\bar{R}_i = \bar{R}_{Fi} + \frac{\beta_i - \beta_{Fi}}{1 - \beta_{Fi}}(\bar{R}_M - \bar{R}_{Fi}) \tag{13}$$

There is a nominally riskless asset for each currency. Define R_{FM} as the return on a portfolio of nominally riskless assets where the weights represent the proportion that each country's risky assets represents of the world market portfolio. Since this has the same weights as the market portfolio, its change in purchasing power is the same as the change in the purchasing power of the market portfolio. This asset is, of course, risky in terms of the numeraire currency and equation (13) must hold with respect to this asset. Utilizing equation (13) to get a relationship between R_{FM} and R_{Fi}, solving for R_{Fi} and substituting for the R_{Fi} in the term involving $\bar{R}_M$ in equation (13) and simplifying this equation

$$\bar{R}_i = \bar{R}_{Fi} + \frac{\beta_i - \beta_{Fi}}{1 - \beta_{FM}}(\bar{R}_M - \bar{R}_{FM}) \tag{14}$$

To get from this equation to Senbet's final model, we must first express returns defined in the numeraire currency in terms of returns expressed in each asset's own local currency.

If we let π_i be the change in the purchasing power, in terms of the numeraire currency, of the currency for the country to which asset i belongs, then[6]

$$R_i = r_i - \pi_i \tag{15}$$

and

$$R_{Fi} = r_{Fi} - \pi_i \tag{16}$$

If π_M is the change in the purchasing power of the market portfolio in terms of the numeraire currency, then

$$R_M = r_M - \pi_M \tag{17}$$

and

$$R_{FM} = r_{FM} - \pi_M \tag{18}$$

Note that the π's have different subscripts since each of the assets or portfolios involve different amounts of exchange risk. Utilizing the above expressions we have

1. $\text{Cov}(R_i R_M) = \text{cov}(r_i r_M) - \text{cov}(r_i \pi_M) - \text{cov}(\pi_i r_M) + \text{cov}(\pi_i \pi_M)$ (19)
2. $\text{var}(R_M) = \text{var}(r_M) - 2\text{cov}(r_M \pi_M) + \text{var}(\pi_M)$ (20)

3. $\text{cov}(R_{FM}R_M) = -\text{cov}(\pi_M r_M) + \text{var}(\pi_M)$ (21)

4. $\text{cov}(R_{Fi}R_M) = -\text{cov}(\pi_i r_M) + \text{cov}(\pi_i \pi_M)$ (22)

Substituting equations (15), (16), (17), (18), (19), (20), (21), and (22) into equation (14) yields:

$$\bar{r}_i - \bar{\pi}_i = r_{Fi} - \bar{\pi}_i + \frac{\text{cov}(r_i r_M) - \text{cov}(r_i \pi_M)}{\text{var}(r_M) - \text{cov}(r_M \pi_M)}[(\bar{r}_M - \bar{\pi}_M) - (r_{FM} - \bar{\pi}_M)]$$

Simplifying yields:

$$\bar{r}_i - r_{Fi} = \frac{\text{cov}(r_i r_M) - \text{cov}(r_i \pi_M)}{\text{var}(r_M) - \text{cov}(r_M \pi_M)}(\bar{r}_M - r_{FM})$$

This is Senbet's (11) and Senbet and Chen's (12) C.A.P.M. and is Senbet's equation (4), page 459.

C *Grauer, Litzenberger, and Stehle Model*

Grauer, Litzenberger, and Stehle [4] have developed an international capital asset pricing model based on free international transferability of goods and assets. All investors have homogeneous expectations about return on the assets expressed in the asset's own currency. Furthermore, there is one international market basket that serves as a price index.

Grauer, Litzenberger, and Stehle assume that investors look at real returns; that is, returns after adjusting for the effect of inflation. Since the same price index is applicable to all investors and since they are assumed to have homogeneous expectations with respect to the index and asset returns, all investors have homogeneous expectations with respect to real returns. Additionally, Grauer, Litzenberger, and Stehle assume a common riskless lending and borrowing rate in real terms. With homogeneous expectations concerning real returns and a real riskless and borrowing rate, the market portfolio is the tangency portfolio and as Roll has shown, this implies the Sharpe-Lintner C.A.P.M. This is the equation that Grauer, Litzenberger, and Stehle derived on page 242. Note that the GLS equation is expressed in real returns rather than in nominal returns. Thus it is simpler than the previous international asset pricing models.

III Inflation and Equilibrium Returns

Two of the best known and most often quoted articles on uncertain inflation and equilibrium prices are Friend, Landskroner, and Losq [3] (hereafter FL&L) and Chen and Boness [2] (hereafter C&B). The results of both sets of authors follow directly from the assumption that a particular definition of the market portfolio is efficient. Differences in their results stem entirely from differences in the way they have incorporated inflation in their analysis and their treatment of the statistical process generating returns and inflation.

FL&L assume that nominal returns and inflation are both generated by a continuous Gaussian (Wiener) process, while C&B assume discrete returns. The equation used by FL&L to relate real returns to nominal returns is simply the continuous analog of the equation used by C&B. However, each set of authors approximates this equation differently, and uses different approximations for the cross-product terms involving inflation and security returns.

Both sets of authors assume investors use real returns to choose between portfolios. Investors are interested in maximizing their utility of end of period wealth. In a world of inflation, they should be interested in maximizing the utility of the purchasing power of end of period wealth or utility of wealth defined in real terms. Both sets of authors, by assuming homogeneous expectations with respect to both nominal returns and inflation rates, imply that investors have homogeneous expectations concerning real returns. Thus, all investors face the same efficient frontier. Without riskless lending and borrowing in real terms, investors will in general select different efficient portfolios. However, combinations of efficient portfolios are efficient. Since the market portfolio is a combination of all investors' efficient portfolios, the market portfolio is efficient.

If we denote the market portfolio by M', we can think of it as the portfolio of all assets which are risky in real terms. Note that this portfolio includes assets which are riskless in nominal terms. As Roll has shown, the Zero Beta C.A.P.M. must hold with respect to M'. Thus,

$$\bar{R}_i = \bar{R}_Z + \beta_i'(\bar{R}_M' - \bar{R}_Z) \tag{23}$$

$\bar{R}_i$ is the expected real return on stock i.

$\bar{R}_M'$ is the expected real return on the market portfolio of all securities which are risky in real terms.

$\bar{R}_Z$ is the expected return on a portfolio which has returns uncorrelated with M' in real terms.

β_i' is $\text{cov}(R_i R_M')$ divided by $\text{var}(R_M')$

Note that the nominally riskelss asset must be risky in real terms. Thus equation (23) must describe the real return on the riskless asset. Using this relationship to get an expression for $\bar{R}_Z$ and substituting into equation (23) yields

$$\bar{R}_i = R_F + \frac{\operatorname{cov}(R_i, R'_M) - \operatorname{cov}(R_F, R'_M)}{\operatorname{var}(R'_M) - \operatorname{cov}(R_F, R'_M)} (\bar{R}'_M - R_F). \tag{24}$$

C&B related real and nominal returns by

$$R_i = r_i - \pi. \tag{25}$$

Using this approximation and $R'_M = \alpha R_M + (1-\alpha)R_F$ we have

$$\operatorname{cov}(R_i, R'_M) = \alpha \operatorname{cov}(r_i, r_M) - \alpha \operatorname{cov}(r_M, \pi) - \operatorname{cov}(r_i, \pi) + \operatorname{var}(\pi) \tag{26}$$

$$\operatorname{cov}(R_F, R'_M) = -\alpha \operatorname{cov}(r_M, \pi) + \operatorname{var}(\pi), \tag{27}$$

and

$$\operatorname{var}(R'_M) = \alpha^2 \operatorname{var}(r_M) - 2\alpha \operatorname{cov}(r_M, \pi) + \operatorname{var}(\pi) \tag{28}$$

Substituting these expressions and (25) into (24) and rearranging yields

$$\bar{r}_i = r_F + \frac{\operatorname{cov}(r_i, r_M) - \dfrac{\operatorname{cov}(r_i, \pi)}{\alpha}}{\operatorname{var}(r_M) - \dfrac{\operatorname{cov}(r_M, \pi)}{\alpha}} (\bar{r}_M - r_F) \tag{29}$$

This is exactly the C.A.P.M. presented by C&B [2] in their equation (7a) which is equivalent to their equation (7).

The FL&L approximation is

1. $\bar{R}_i = \bar{r}_i - \bar{\pi} - \operatorname{cov}(r_i, \pi)$,
2. $R_i\,dt = \bar{r}_i\,dt + \sqrt{\operatorname{var}(r_i)}\,Y_i\sqrt{dt} - \bar{\pi}\,dt - \sqrt{\operatorname{var}(\pi)}\,Y_\pi\sqrt{dt} - \sqrt{\operatorname{var}(r_i)\operatorname{var}(\pi)}\cdot Y_i Y_\pi\,dt + \operatorname{var}(\pi)\,Y_\pi^2\,dt$,

and

3. all terms involving dt to a power greater than $\frac{3}{2}$ can be ignored.

The FL&L expressions are all in continuous time, $\operatorname{cov}(r_i, \pi)$ is the continuous covariance between r_i and π, $\operatorname{var}(\pi)$ and $\operatorname{var}(r_i)$ are variances, Y's are standard normal variates and dt is the derivative of time. With these definitions one obtains the same variance-covariance expressions which are given in (26), (27) and (28) with the qualification that they are in continuous time. Using $R'_M = R_M + (1-\alpha)R_F$ and condition 1 and substituting (26), (27) and (28) in equation (24) and simplifying yields

$$\bar{r}_i - \text{cov}(r_i, \pi) = r_F + \frac{\text{cov}(r_i, r_M) - \dfrac{\text{cov}(r_i, \pi)}{\alpha}}{\text{var}(r_M) - \dfrac{\text{cov}(r_M, \pi)}{\alpha}} (\bar{r}_M - r_F - \text{cov}(r_M, \pi)) \tag{30}$$

This is exactly the C.A.P.M. presented by FL&L in their equation (12). The proofs above make it clear that the difference between equations (29) and (30) derive primarily because of the difference in the relationship between expected real returns and nominal returns assumed by FL&L and C&B.

IV Differential Taxes

Brennan [1] derived the first general equilibrium model that incorporated differential taxes on income and capital gains. Brennan derived his results from the maximization of investor utilities and market clearing conditions. We should and do get Brennan's result utilizing Roll's [8] insight and a little algebra. Brennan assumes homogeneous expectations with respect to pre-tax returns and a common riskless lending and borrowing rate.

Furthermore he assumes investors make their portfolio choices in terms of after-tax returns. The rate of taxation is independent of return, and taxes on losses and borrowing are treated as a subsidy. Furthermore the rate of taxation may differ between investors. Investors in different tax brackets will face a different efficient frontier and a different riskless lending and borrowing rate in the relevant after tax terms. Consequently Roll's [9] insight must be utilized in a slightly different manner than in prior sections. With a constant lending and borrowing rate the tangency portfolio is optimal for each investor and Roll's insight is that the Sharpe Lintner equation holds between each asset's expected after tax return and each investor's tangency portfolio thus for investor i,

$$\bar{R}_{ik} = R_{iF} + \beta_{k,ip}(\bar{R}_{ip} - R_{iF}) \tag{31}$$

where capital letters denote after tax values, the i subscript indicates investor i; and the ip subscript indicates the optimum portfolio of investor i.

Let lower case r's be before-tax returns, d_k be a securities dividend yield, t_{oi} the ordinary income tax rate of investor i, and t_{ci} the capital gains rate then

$$R_{ik} = (r_k - d_k)(1 - t_{ci}) + d_k(1 - t_{oi}) = r_k(1 - t_{ci}) - d_k(t_{oi} - t_{ci})$$

$$R_{iF} = r_F(1 - t_{oi})$$

Note that since there are homogeneous assumptions about pre-tax returns there is no i subscript on the before-tax terms. Making Brennan's assumption that dividends are riskless, we can substitute the expression for after-tax returns into equation (31) to obtain

$$(\bar{r}_k - r_F)(1 - t_{ci}) - (d_k - r_F)(t_{oi} - t_{ci})$$
$$= [(\bar{r}_{ip} - r_F)(1 - t_{ci}) - (d_{ip} - r_F)(t_{oi} - t_{ci})] \frac{\text{cov}(r_k(1 - t_{ci}), r_{ip}(1 - t_{ci}))}{\text{var}(r_{ip}(1 - t_{ci}))}$$

Define t_i as $\dfrac{t_{oi} - t_{ci}}{1 - t_{ci}}$. Dividing both sides of the above equation by $(1 - t_{ci})$ and dividing both the covariance and variance term by $(1 - t_{ci})^2$ yields

$$\bar{r}_k = r_F + [(\bar{r}_{ip} - r_F) - (d_{ip} - r_F)t_i] \frac{\text{cov}(r_k, r_{ip})}{\text{var}(r_{ip})} + (d_k - r_F)t_i$$

defining λ_i as $\dfrac{(\bar{r}_{ip} - r_F) - (d_{ip} - r_F)t_i}{\text{var}(r_{ip})}$ and rearranging yields

$$\frac{1}{\lambda_i}(\bar{r}_k - r_F) - \frac{t_i}{\lambda_i}(d_k - r_F) = \text{cov}(r_k, r_{ip}) \tag{32}$$

Define w_i as the fraction of the total investment in risky assets which is made by investor i. Multiplying both sides of equation (32) by w_i suming across all investors and recognizing that $\sum_i w_i r_{ip} = r_M$ where r_M is the return on the market portfolio yields

$$\sum_i \frac{w_i}{\lambda_i}(\bar{r}_k - r_F) - \sum_i \frac{w_i t_i}{\lambda_i}(d_k - r_F) = \text{cov}(r_k r_M) \tag{33}$$

Define

$$1.\ \lambda = \sum_i \frac{\lambda_i}{w_i} \qquad \text{and} \qquad 2.\ T_M = \sum_i \frac{w_i t_i}{\lambda_i} \Big/ \sum_i \frac{w_i}{\lambda_i}$$

then equation (33) can be written as

$$(\bar{r}_k - r_F) - (d_k - r_F)T_M = \lambda\ \text{cov}(r_k r_M) \tag{34}$$

This equation holds for each security and thus must hold for the market, therefore,

$$\lambda = \frac{(\bar{r}_M - r_F) - (d_M - r_F)T_M}{\sigma_M^2} \tag{35}$$

Equation (34) and (35) are the versions of the general equilibrium equation presented by Brennan [1].

V Heterogeneous Expectations

The best known research specifying equilibrium relationships when investors hold heterogeneous expectations about expected payoffs, variances and covariances are Lintner [5] and Rabinovitch and Owen [9] and Sharpe [13]. In previous sections we derived equilibrium relationships by showing that a relevant measure of the market portfolio was efficient. In dealing with heterogeneous expectations, Roll's insight has to be employed differently for the meaning of the market portfolio is not clear. Although later we will see that under certain restrictive assumptions about utility it can be employed in a manner parallel to other sections of this paper.

To start this section we will assume that each investor i holds some portfolio which he or she believes will be ex-post efficient. If the investor believes this portfolio is efficient, then the expected return on any security must be related to the return on this portfolio by a linear equation like equation (6).

Expressing this equation in terms of prices using matrix notation we have

$$\frac{1}{R_F}{}_0P = {}_1\bar{P}_i - \frac{1}{t_i}\sum\nolimits_i X_i$$

${}_0P$ = the N component vector of present prices.

${}_1\bar{P}_i$ = the N component vector of the payoff expected by investor i from each stock.

X_i = the N component vector of shares held by investor i.

$\sum_i$ = the NXN variance covariance matrix of the payoffs from securities as perceived by the ith investor.

Rearranging,

$$\frac{1}{R_F}t_i\sum\nolimits_i^{-1}{}_0P = t_i\sum\nolimits_i^{-1}{}_1\bar{P}_i - X_i$$

Summing over all investors, recognizing that $\sum_i X_i = n$ where n is the N component vector of the number of shares outstanding for each stock, and solving for $\frac{1}{R_F}{}_0P$, we obtain

$$\frac{1}{R_F}\,{}_0P = \left[\sum_i t_i \Sigma_i^{-1}\right]^{-1}\left[\sum_i t_i \Sigma_i^{-1}\,{}_1\bar{P}_i - n\right]$$

This is exactly the result obtained by Rabinovitch and Owen, equation (6), page 578.

Litner has two principal results. The first can be shown to follow trivially from Rabinovitch and Owen.[7] Lintner has derived his results under a special form of the investor utility function, namely, $u^i(w_i) = -e^{-a_i w_i}$. Where a is the coefficient of absolute risk aversion which is constant. It is well known that with the negative exponential utility function $(1/t_i)$ in our equation will equal a_i. Making this substitution, we get Lintner's equation (10), page 362.

The use of the negative exponential function is more important in Lintner's derivation in that it leads to a second result not found in Rabinovitch and Owen. The negative exponential utility function allows individual utilities to be aggregated and thus allows the assertion of a market utility function. Furthermore, we know that this market utility function will be a negative exponential function. This means that we can "suppose that the market as a whole acts as a single composite 'price-taker'."[8] Thus, there is some market portfolio which must be efficient. Thus, from Roll's results we can write:

$$r_{mj} = r_F + \frac{\bar{r}_m - r_F}{\text{var}(r_m)}\text{cov}(r_{mj}, r_m) \tag{36}$$

where the subscript m standing alone indicates the market's expectations about the market portfolio while the double subscript mj indicates the market's belief about security j. Switching this to price form yields Lintner's equation (5m) (i), page 358.

Before closing this section we should say a few words about Sharpe's derivation of equilibrium with heterogeneous expectations. If one takes equation (36) and aggregates across all investors, one gets with the appropriate change in notation the equilibrium result presented by Sharpe in Appendix D, page 292.

Notes

1. We follow Mayers in treating r_H and P_H as observable variables for expository purposes. This proof differs from that presented in Mayers.

2. Note this expression does not hold for any non-marketable asset. An investor can not purchase and sell the non-marketable assets. Thus if derivatives were taken to arrive at an equation like this for non-marketable assets a Lagrangian multiplier associated with each asset would be included in the expression.

3. To understand the concept of a numeraire currency, think in terms of a market basket of goods and services. The numeraire currency is a unit of the market basket and the value of all currencies is expressed in terms of how many units of the market basket a unit of that currency will purchase.

4. See Roll [9] for a proof. None of the weights can be negative and the weights must sum to one. But this is, of course, true for the case in the text.

5. Senbet assumes that lending equals borrowing so that nominally riskless assets are not part of the market portfolio defined in the numeraire currency.

6. These expressions are approximations. The correct expression is $1 + R_i = (1 + r_i)/(1 + \pi_i)$. Expanding the expression in a Taylor series and ignoring all terms except the first two yields the expression given in the text.

7. Lintner's results were presented long before Rabinovitch and Owen's. We have presented Rabinovitch and Owen's results first because the Lintner results are a special case of these more general results.

8. Lintner, page 357.

References

1. Brennan, Michael, "Investor Taxes, Market Valuation and Corporate Financial Policy," *National Tax Journal* (December 1970).

2. Chen, Andres and Boness, James, "Effects of Uncertain Inflation on the Investment and Financing Decision of a Firm," *Journal of Finance*, Vol. 30, No. 2, (May, 1975), 469–485.

3. Friend, Irwin, Landskroner, Yoram, and Losq Etienne, "The Demand for Risky Assets Under Uncertain Inflation," *Journal of Finance*, Vol. 31, No. 5, (December 1976), pp. 1287–1299.

4. Grauer, Frederick, Litzenburger, Robert and Stehle, Richard, "Sharing Rules and Equilibrium in an International Capital Markets Under Uncertainty," *Journal of Financial Economics*, Vol. 3, (June 1976), pp. 233–256.

5. Lintner, John, "The Aggregation of Investors Diverse Judgements and Preferences in Purely Competitive Markets," *Journal of Financial and Quantitative Analysis*, Vol. 4, No. 4, (December 1969), pp. 347–400.

6. Lintner, John, "The Valuation of Risk Assets and the Selection of Risky Investments in Stock Portfolios and Capital Budgets," *Review of Economics and Statistics*, (February 1965).

7. Mayers, David, "Non-marketable Assets and Capital Market Equilibrium Under Uncertainty" in Jenson, Mike, *Studies in the Theory of Capital Markets* (Praeger: New York), 1972.

8. Roll, Richard, "A Critique of Asset Pricing Theory's Tests," *Journal of Financial Economics*, (March 1977), pp. 129–176.

9. Rabinovich, Ramon and Owen, Joel, "Non-homogeneous Expectations and Information in the Capital Asset Pricing Model," *Journal of Finance*, Vol. 33, No. 2, (May 1979), pp. 575–587.

10. Mossin, Jan, "Equilibrium in a Capital Asset Model," *Econometrica*, (October 1966).

11. Senbet, Lemma, "International Capital Market Equilibrium and the Multi-National Firm Financing and Investment Policies," *Journal of Financial and Quantitative Analysis,* Vol. 14, No. 3, (September 1979), pp. 455–477.

12. Senbet and Chen, Andrew, "International Purchasing Power Risk and Capital Market Equilibrium," Working Paper, Ohio State University, 1977.

13. Sharpe, William, *Portfolio Theory and Capital Markets* (McGraw-Hill: New York) 1970.

14. Solnick, Bruno, "An Equilibrium Model of the International Capital Market," *Journal of Economic Theory,* Vol. 8, (August 1974), pp. 500–524.

19

The Arbitrage Pricing Model and Returns on Assets Under Uncertain Inflation

Edwin Elton, Martin Gruber, and Joel Rentzler

The impact of inflation on equilibrium returns in capital markets has been the subject of several articles in recent years. Chen and Boness [1], Friend, Landskroner and Losq [4], Long [7] and Roll [13] have all constructed general equilibrium models which incorporate the impact of uncertain inflation on returns.[1] All of these authors have derived models in a mean-variance world utilizing methodologies similar to that first utilized by Mossin [9] or Merton [8].

The basic underlying tenet of mean-variance analysis is that for any given level of expected return investors wish to minimize the variance of return. In mean-variance equilibrium models the only risk that cannot be diversified away is the covariance of an asset's return with the market return. Assets which have the same covariance with the market have the same equilibrium required return. Thus in a mean-variance world if each member of the following pairs of assets had the same covariance with the market each member would have the same expected return:

(a) a stock which was a perfect hedge against inflation versus one which was not,

(b) a stock which was a perfect hedge against oil price changes versus one which was not,

(c) a security that hedged against interest rate changes versus one which did not.

In this article we break out of the limitations of the mean variance assumptions by utilizing the Arbitrage Pricing Theory (APT) of Ross [15], [16], [17]. This allows us to examine equilibrium returns when returns on alternative securities are impacted differentially by inflation and where investors care about (price) inflation sensitivity.

This paper will proceed as follows. In the first section we show that if the process generating real returns is affected by both the return on the market and the rate of inflation then a model for equilibrium real returns can be derived. Equilibrium real returns will be expressed in terms of the expected return on the market, the expected real return on a zero beta portfolio and the expected real return on an asset which is riskless in nominal terms. In the second section of this paper, we show that if either:

(1) the return generating process depends only on the market return or

(2) the return generating process depends on both the market return and inflation but the inflation factor is not priced,

then the arbitrage pricing model leads to results identical to the mean-variance inflation models which have been presented in the literature. Of special interest is the meaning and derivation of conditions under which a factor is not priced. In particular, we show that multiple factors can be priced using the Roll and Ross [14] testing procedure and the model still reduces to a mean-variance model. The third section expresses the equilibrium model in nominal terms. In the final section we compare our model with prior models and examine the implications for equilibrium prices and empirical testing.

The major purpose of this paper is the construction of richer descriptions of equilibrium under uncertain inflation. However, there is a second purpose which is at least as important. This concerns the role of the APT pricing model as a central model in the economics of uncertainty. The methodology of the APT involves an unspecified return generating process. Tests of the model [3], [10], [12] and [14] have attempted to identify the return generating process through empirical methods. As of this point in time, no economic rationale has been associated with the empirical processes which have been identified. While the empirical approach is one meaningful way to proceed with research on the APT model, we believe that the acceptance of this theory as the central equilibrium theory in finance must await the development of APT models defined in terms of factors which are not only statistically identifiable but which have economic meaning. This paper starts with an hypothesis which sets forth factors that might affect return in a world of uncertain inflation and shows how APT can be used to develop an equilibrium model in terms of observable variables. We do not claim to have developed the "best" description of the return generating process under inflation or to have captured all of the influences which might affect the return generating process. But we do illustrate how a model of the return generating process of the APT based on economic variables is converted to an equilibrium model. We believe this is a necessary complement to the empirical APT studies if the potential importance of APT as an equilibrium model is to be realized. In addition, we take comfort in our description of the return generating process from the fact that under simplifying assumptions about either the process itself or the pricing of the factors which generate the return, our equilibrium model reduces to the equilibrium models of Chen and Boness [1], Friend, Landskroner and Losq [4] and Roll [13] which were developed under uncertain inflation in a mean-variance framework.[2]

I Derivation of the Model

The simplest return generating process investigated in the literature (see Ross [15]) assumed a single factor return generated process where the single factor was the market. As noted in Roll and Ross [14], pages 1079–1080, although the market portfolio plays no special role whatsoever in the APT, "as a well diversified portfolio, indeed a convex combination of diversified portfolios, the market portfolio ... might serve as a substitute for one of the factors." Earlier Ross [15] suggested that it might be more appropriate to decompose the return process into real returns and a term or terms associated with inflation. In a world of uncertain inflation, investors should be concerned with real return and riskless arbitrage should be defined in terms of real returns.[3] Furthermore, under uncertain inflation we believe that returns on different assets would be affected differentially by inflation. Reasons advanced in support of this contention included the existence of differences in creditor-debtor positions, differences in contractual obligations at fixed prices, and differences in tax obligations.[4] The simplest model under which real returns are differentially related to the real returns on the market and uncertain inflation is a linear relationship of the form

$$R_i = \alpha_i + \beta_{1i} R'_M + \beta_{2i} \pi + \varepsilon_i$$

where subtracting $\bar{R}_i$ from this equation yields

$$R_i = \bar{R}_i + \beta_{1i}(R'_M - \bar{R}'_M) + \beta_{2i}(\pi - \bar{\pi}) + \varepsilon_i \tag{1}$$

Here:

1. R_i is the real return on a security,

2. R'_M is the real return on a "market" portfolio of all risky assets. This portfolio is composed of a fraction α of assets M which are risky in nominal returns and a fraction $(1 - \alpha)$ of an asset F riskless in nominal returns. Thus we are allowing for the possibility of a nominally riskless asset with a positive net supply,
3. π is the rate of inflation,
4. ε_i is a random error term,
5. β_{1i} is a measure of the sensitivity of the security's real return to a change in real return of the market index,
6. β_{2i} is a measure of the sensitivity of the security's real return to a change in the inflation rates,
7. Bars over random variables indicate expected values.

The only assumption made concerning the relationship between the market factor and the inflation factor is the absence of perfect correlation. Thus the market factor can be, and probably is, affected by inflation.

Equation (1) is a special case of the general equation used by Ross [15] to develop the arbitrage pricing model. To get our arbitrage pricing model we follow Ross in setting up an arbitrage portfolio. This portfolio involves zero net investment, zero systematic risk with both of the factors, and is sufficiently diversified that there is a negligible effect of ε_i on the portfolio risk. Such a riskless portfolio should have an expected return of zero. Since the vector of portfolio proportions is orthogonal to expected return and the betas, expected return can be expressed as a linear combination of the betas. If a's denote coefficients, this results in

$$\bar{R}_i = a_0 + \beta_{1i}a_1 + \beta_{2i}a_2. \tag{2}$$

There is nothing new in equation (2): it is identical to Ross' [15] equation (9.21) which was derived for the general case. The remainder of this section is a new extension of Ross' work in that the special form of equation (1) will be used to eliminate the a's and replace them with observable economic variables. If we define R_z as the return on a portfolio that is orthogonal to both R'_M and π then for this portfolio $\beta_{1Z} = \beta_{2Z} = 0$ and $\bar{R}_Z = a_0$.

In order to eliminate a_1 and a_2 we must first derive expressions for β_{1i} and β_{2i}. We have not made any assumption about the orthogonality of the two factors R'_M and π so that we should allow for the possibility of correlation between them. In order to determine β_{1i} and β_{2i}, first calculate $\operatorname{cov}(R_i, R'_M)$ and $\operatorname{cov}(R_i, \pi)$. Utilizing equation (1) for R_i we have[5]

$$\mathrm{cov}(R_i, R'_M) = E[((\bar{R}_i + \beta_{1i}(R'_M - \bar{R}'_M) + \beta_{2i}(\pi - \bar{\pi}) + \varepsilon_i) - \bar{R}_i)(R'_M - \bar{R}'_M)].$$

Without loss of generality we can assume that ε_i and R'_M are orthogonal. Thus

$$\mathrm{cov}(R_i, R'_M) = \beta_{1i}\mathrm{var}(R'_M) + \beta_{2i}\mathrm{cov}(R'_M, \pi).$$

Likewise

$$\mathrm{cov}(R_i, \pi) = \beta_{1i}\,\mathrm{cov}(R'_M, \pi) + \beta_{2i}\,\mathrm{var}(\pi).$$

Solving these equations for β_{1i} and β_{2i} results in

$$\beta_{1i} = \frac{\mathrm{cov}(R_i, R'_M)\,\mathrm{var}(\pi) - \mathrm{cov}(R'_M, \pi)\,\mathrm{cov}(R_i, \pi)}{\mathrm{var}(R'_M)\,\mathrm{var}(\pi) - (\mathrm{cov}(R'_M, \pi))^2} \tag{3}$$

and

$$\beta_{2i} = \frac{\mathrm{cov}(R_i, \pi)\,\mathrm{var}(R'_M) - \mathrm{cov}(R_i, R'_M)\,\mathrm{cov}(R'_M, \pi)}{\mathrm{var}(R'_M)\,\mathrm{var}(\pi) - (\mathrm{cov}(R'_m, \pi))^2}. \tag{4}$$

With these expressions we can determine the values of a_1 and a_2. Consider first the portfolio M'. Examining equation (3) shows that for this portfolio $\beta_{1i} = 1$ and examining equation (4) shows that $\beta_{2i} = 0$. Thus from equation (2) and the fact that $a_0 = \bar{R}_z$ we have

$$\bar{R}'_M = \bar{R}_z + a_1$$

or

$$a_1 = \bar{R}'_M - \bar{R}_z.$$

Likewise consider the nominally riskless asset. The only risk that affects the real return of this asset is due to inflation. In order to proceed further we need an expression relating real and nominal returns. We will utilize the Chen and Boness linkage. However, the same general equilibrium relationship would result from using the Friend, Landskroner and Losq linkage.[6] The Chen and Boness equation relating real and nominal returns is

$$R_i = r_i - \pi \tag{5}$$

where

r_i is the nominal return on asset i,

and

π is the inflation rate.

Utilizing this equation and recognizing that $\operatorname{cov}(r_F, \pi) = 0$ since r_F is nonstochastic

$$\operatorname{cov}(R_F, \pi) = E[((r_F - \bar{r}_F) - (\pi - \bar{\pi})), (\pi - \bar{\pi})]$$
$$= -\operatorname{var}(\pi).$$

Likewise

$$\operatorname{cov}(R_F, R'_M) = -\operatorname{cov}(R'_M, \pi).$$

With these substitutions an examination of equations (3) and (4) shows that for the nominally riskless asset $\beta_{1i} = 0$ and $\beta_{2i} = -1$. Thus we have

$$\bar{R}_F = \bar{R}_z - a_2$$

or

$$a_2 = (\bar{R}_z - \bar{R}_F).$$

This results in an arbitrage pricing model of

$$\bar{R}_i = \bar{R}_z + \beta_{1i}(\bar{R}'_M - \bar{R}_z) + \beta_{2i}(\bar{R}_z - \bar{R}_F) \tag{6}$$

which we will use in the rest of the paper.

II Relationship to Prior Models

Up to this point we have developed one model of equilibrium returns from the Ross arbitrage pricing model. However there are two conditions under which the equilibrium model derived from arbitrage pricing can be simplified. One is that the return generating process depends only on the market return. The other is that the return generating process depends on both the market return and inflation but that investors will not (*ceteris paribus*) pay a differential return for an asset that is a superior inflation hedge.

It is easy to deal with the first of these. If the return generating process is the single factor model

$$R_i = \bar{R}_i + \beta_{1i}(R'_M - \bar{R}'_M) + \varepsilon_i, \tag{7}$$

then as Ross has shown the equilibrium model is

$$\bar{R}_i = \bar{R}_z + \beta_{1i}(\bar{R}'_M - \bar{R}_z). \tag{8}$$

We would argue that this return generating process presented in equation (7) is less appropriate than that presented in equation (1) because both theory and empirical evidence support the fact that inflation has an independent effect on the returns on different assets beyond the market impact. As noted above, a number of theoretical hypotheses have been advanced in the literature as to why firms should have varying sensitivities to inflation.

The second condition under which the equilibrium model can be simplified is more subtle. The return generating process might be given by equation (1) but the market does not price (require a return for) any inflation risk above and beyond that captured by the market return. Shortly we will demonstrate that under either of these conditions the equilibrium model of equation (6) collapses to that of Chen and Boness (C&B), Friend, Landskroner and Losq (F, L&L), or Roll. Before we do so let us discuss why we believe inflation *should* be priced.

To see why inflation should be priced we must examine why the expected real return required by individuals should be a function of inflation. Let us look at a simple example of the conditions under which inflation risk would bear a market price. Consider the extreme case of an individual who consumed only goods that were extremely sensitive to changes in the price index while another individual consumed only goods which were relatively insensitive to changes in the price index. The investor whose consumption was sensitive to changes in the price index would prefer assets which gave exceptionally high returns in periods with a high rate of change in the price index while the other investor would not have such a preference. Because changes in the price index would not perfectly reflect changes in purchasing power for all individuals, inflation risk would be priced in the market.[7]

Another way to picture this difference is to note that if inflation risk were important to individuals then each investor's optimum portfolio should consist of a component that allows a modification of inflation risks according to the sensitivity of the pricing of his personal consumption basket to inflation. This is why, as we shall see, our general model of equation (6) leads to a three mutual fund theorem while the models which assume inflation risk is not priced—(C&B) and (F, L&L)—lead to a two mutual fund theorem. Let us now demonstrate that C&B, F, L&L and Roll can be derived from either of the two conditions.

A Demonstration that the Chen and Boness, Friend, Landskroner and Losq and Roll models can be derived from a single factor generating model

If returns are generated by the single factor model of equation (7) then as Ross has shown

$$\bar{R}_i = \bar{R}_z + \beta_i'(\bar{R}_M' - \bar{R}_z). \tag{8'}$$

where the β_i' is the response of asset i to the market when a second factor is excluded. This is Roll's equation at the bottom of page 922.[8] To get the C&B and F, L&L equation in real terms note that the nominally riskless asset is risky in real terms and thus equation (8′) must hold for R_F. Thus

$$\bar{R}_F = \bar{R}_z + \beta_F'(\bar{R}_M' - \bar{R}_z).$$

Solving for $\bar{R}_z$

$$\bar{R}_z = \frac{\bar{R}_F - \beta_F'\bar{R}_M'}{1 - \beta_F'}.$$

Substituting into equation (8′) yields

$$\bar{R}_i = \frac{\bar{R}_F - \beta_F'\bar{R}_M'}{1 - \beta_F'} + \beta_i'\bar{R}_M' - \beta_i'\left(\frac{\bar{R}_F - \beta_F'\bar{R}_M'}{1 - \beta_F'}\right).$$

Putting all terms on the right hand side of the equation over a common denominator, adding and subtracting $\beta_F'\bar{R}_F$ in the numerator and simplifying yields

$$\bar{R}_i = \bar{R}_F + \frac{\beta_i' - \beta_F'}{1 - \beta_F'}(\bar{R}_M' - \bar{R}_M).$$

Substituting $(\text{cov}(R_i, R_M'))/(\text{var}(R_M'))$ for β_i' and $(\text{cov}(R_F, R_M'))/(\text{var}(R_M'))$ for β_F' yields

$$\bar{R}_i = \bar{R}_F + \frac{\text{cov}(R_i, R_M') - \text{cov}(R_F, R_M')}{\text{var}(R_M') - \text{cov}(R_F, R_M')}(\bar{R}_M' - \bar{R}_F). \tag{9}$$

This is equivalent to C&B's and F, L&L's equations when they are expressed in real terms. Both of these sets of authors express their equilibrium relationship in nominal terms. Elsewhere [2], we show that when equation (9) is expressed in nominal terms it leads directly to the final equilibrium equations presented by C&B and F, L&L.

B Demonstration that the Chen and Boness, Friend, Landskroner and Losq and Roll models can be derived from the general model by assuming that inflation risk (beyond that captured by the market index) is not priced

Earlier we argued that mean-variance equilibrium models made the assumption that the only risk that mattered was the covariability with the market. Whether or not an asset provided a hedge against inflation was unimportant. In this section we will assume that an asset's return is generated by the two factor model given in equation (1). From this we already have derived the general equilibrium equation (6). We will now show that if inflation (beyond that captured in the market index) is not priced, then equation (6) reduces to the results presented by C&B, F, L&L and Roll. To do so we will impose on equation (6) the constraint that two assets which have the same covariance with the market have the same required return regardless of their covariance with inflation. As discussed at the end of this section, imposing this constraint is not equivalent to assuming that a_2 in equation (6) is equal to zero (i.e., that $\bar{R}_z = R_F$). The analysis of this section will clarify what is meant by a factor not being priced in the market. We are assuming returns are generated by two factors, the market return and inflation. However, we are assuming that investors do not care whether an asset is a good or poor hedge against inflation. *Ceteris paribus* they will not pay a differential premium for a stock with a negative β_{2i}. All they care about is the stock's covariability with the market.

To demonstrate these assertions define an asset L with the following characteristics:

1. $\operatorname{cov}(R_L, R'_M) = \operatorname{cov}(R_F, R'_M)$
2. $\operatorname{cov}(R_L, \pi) = 0$

Thus asset L has the same market related risk as the nominally riskless asset but its return is uncorrelated with inflation. Using these conditions to simplify the expressions for β_{1i} and β_{2i} presented in equations (3) and (4) the expected return for asset L derived from equation (6) becomes

$$\bar{R}_L = \bar{R}_z + \frac{\operatorname{cov}(R_F, R'_M)\operatorname{var}(\pi)}{\operatorname{var}(R'_M)\operatorname{var}(\pi) - (\operatorname{cov}(R'_M, \pi))^2}(\bar{R}'_M - \bar{R}_z)$$

$$- \frac{\operatorname{cov}(R_F, R'_M)\operatorname{cov}(\bar{R}'_M, \pi)}{\operatorname{var}(R'_M)\operatorname{var}(\pi) - (\operatorname{cov}(R'_M, \pi))^2}(\bar{R}_z - \bar{R}_F).$$

L and F have the same market risk. In the mean-variance world or when all that matters is market variability they should have the same expected return or $\bar{R}_F = \bar{R}_L$. Recalling that $\text{cov}(R_F, R'_M) = -\text{cov}(R'_M, \pi)$, substituting $\bar{R}_F$ for $\bar{R}_L$ and solving for $\bar{R}_z$ yields

$$\bar{R}_z = \bar{R}_F - \frac{\text{cov}(R_F, R'_M)\,\text{var}(\pi)}{(\text{var}(\pi))(\text{var}(R'_M) - \text{cov}(R_F, R'_M))}(\bar{R}_M - \bar{R}_F). \tag{10}$$

Examining equation (6) shows that the coefficients of β_{2i} is $(\bar{R}_Z - R_F)$. Since from equation (10) $\bar{R}_Z \neq R_F$, our assertion that the coefficient of $\beta_{21} \neq 0$ is validated. Substituting the expression for $\bar{R}_z$ into equation (6) and rearranging yields

$$\bar{R}_i = \bar{R}_F + \left(\beta_{1i} - \frac{\text{cov}(R_F, R'_M)\,\text{var}(\pi)}{\text{var}(\pi)(\text{var}(R'_M) - \text{cov}(R_F, R'_M))}(1 - \beta_{1i} + \beta_{2i})\right)(\bar{R}'_M - \bar{R}_F)$$

Simplifying we again get equation (9)

$$\bar{R}_i = \bar{R}_F + \frac{\text{cov}(R_i, R'_M) - \text{cov}(R_F, R'_M)}{\text{var}(R'_M) - \text{cov}(R_F, R'_M)}(\bar{R}'_M - \bar{R}_F) \tag{9}$$

which is the C&B, F, L&L and Roll equation in real terms.

A number of comments on the analysis in this section are in order. We simplified our asset pricing model to be consistent with mean-variance analysis by using the condition that two assets with the same covariance with the market would offer the same expected return regardless of their correlations with inflation. This is the economically meaningful definition of inflation not being priced. It is important to note that this is not equivalent to assuming that the second factor of equation (6) is not priced. If this second factor was not priced, a_2 would equal zero (i.e., $\bar{R}_Z = R_F$). However, as shown above, the conditions under which our model is equivalent to mean-variance analysis don't imply $\bar{R}_Z = R_F$ (see equation (10)). Thus, an arbitrage pricing model can be consistent with mean-variance analysis and still have more than one priced factor.[9] A number of recent papers have used the presence of multiple priced factors as evidence against the mean-variance CAPM. The discussion in this section should serve as a cautionary note for that conclusion.

III The Asset Pricing Model in Nominal Terms

In section I we derived the asset pricing model when real returns are affected by the market and inflation. The asset pricing model was presented in real terms. To facilitate comparison with other models and to examine implications of our model, it is necessary to express the model of equation (6) in nominal terms. This section utilizes the inflation conversion assumed by C&B and derives the nominal asset pricing model that results in some detail. The nominal model which results from utilizing F, L&L's inflation conversion is stated in the text. This choice should not be viewed by the reader as a preference on our part for the C&B approximation over the one used by F, L&L. The reason for deriving the C&B results in the body of this paper is that, although the derivations are analogous, using C&B's approximation makes the proofs less complex.

As already stated in equation (5), C&B relate nominal to real returns with the following expression

$$R_i = r_i - \pi.$$

This expression is an approximation to a more general expression relating real and nominal returns.[10] Employing this expression and recalling that $R'_M = \alpha R_M + (1-\alpha)R_F$ and that the return on asset F is non-stochastic in nominal terms we have

$$\operatorname{cov}(R_i, \pi) = \operatorname{cov}(r_i, \pi) - \operatorname{var}(\pi), \tag{11a}$$

$$\operatorname{cov}(R_i, R'_M) = \alpha \operatorname{cov}(r_i, r_M) - \operatorname{cov}(r_i, \pi) - \alpha \operatorname{cov}(r_M, \pi) + \operatorname{var}(\pi), \tag{11b}$$

$$\operatorname{cov}(R'_M, \pi) = \alpha \operatorname{cov}(r_M, \pi) - \operatorname{var}(\pi), \tag{11c}$$

and

$$\operatorname{var}(R'_M) = \alpha^2 \operatorname{var}(r_M) - 2\alpha \operatorname{cov}(r_M, \pi) + \operatorname{var}(\pi). \tag{11d}$$

Utilizing these four expressions and equations (3) and (4) for β_{1i} and β_{2i} yields

$$\beta_{1i} = \frac{[\operatorname{cov}(r_i, r_M)\operatorname{var}(\pi) - (\operatorname{cov}(r_i, \pi)\operatorname{cov}(r_M, \pi))]}{[\alpha \operatorname{var}(r_M)\operatorname{var}(\pi) - \alpha(\operatorname{cov}(r_M, \pi))^2]} \tag{12}$$

and

$$\begin{aligned}\beta_{2i} = {} & [\alpha \operatorname{cov}(r_i, \pi)\operatorname{var}(r_M) - \alpha \operatorname{var}(\pi)\operatorname{var}(r_M) - \alpha \operatorname{cov}(r_i, r_M)\operatorname{cov}(r_M, \pi) \\ & + \alpha(\operatorname{cov}(r_M, \pi))^2 - \operatorname{cov}(r_i, \pi)\operatorname{cov}(r_M, \pi) + \operatorname{cov}(r_i, r_M)\operatorname{var}(\pi)]/ \\ & [\alpha \operatorname{var}(r_M)\operatorname{var}(\pi) - \alpha(\operatorname{cov}(r_M, \pi))^2].\end{aligned} \tag{13}$$

Recall that the asset pricing model in real terms is

$$\bar{R}_i = \bar{R}_z + \beta_{1i}(\bar{R}'_M - \bar{R}_z) + \beta_{2i}(\bar{R}_z - \bar{R}_F). \tag{6}$$

Substituting in relationship (5) relating real to nominal returns and substituting $\alpha R_M + (1-\alpha)R_F$ for R'_M yields

$$\bar{r}_i = \bar{r}_z + \beta_{1i}(\alpha(\bar{r}_M - r_F) - (\bar{r}_z - r_F)) + \beta_{2i}(\bar{r}_z - r_F).$$

Adding and subtracting r_F and combining all terms involving $(\bar{r}_Z - r_F)$ gives

$$\bar{r}_i = r_F + \beta_{1i}\alpha(\bar{r}_M - r_F) + (1 - \beta_{1i} + \beta_{2i})(\bar{r}_z - r_F).$$

Substituting for β_{1i} and β_{2i} and simplifying yields

$$\begin{aligned}\bar{r}_i = r_F &+ \frac{\operatorname{cov}(r_i, r_M)\operatorname{var}(\pi) - \operatorname{cov}(r_i, \pi)\operatorname{cov}(r_M, \pi)}{\operatorname{var}(r_M)\operatorname{var}(\pi) - (\operatorname{cov}(r_M, \pi))^2}(\bar{r}_M - r_F) \\ &+ \frac{\operatorname{cov}(r_i, \pi)\operatorname{var}(r_M) - \operatorname{cov}(r_i, r_M)\operatorname{cov}(r_M, \pi)}{\operatorname{var}(r_M)\operatorname{var}(\pi) - (\operatorname{cov}(r_M, \pi))^2}(\bar{r}_z - r_F).\end{aligned} \tag{14}$$

This is the asset pricing model which results from an assumption that returns on securities are generated by a two-factor model (a market and an inflation factor) when the C&B approximation between real and nominal returns is used. If the F, L&L approximation is used the equilibrium equation becomes

$$\begin{aligned}\bar{r}_i = r_F &- \operatorname{cov}(r_i, \pi) \\ &+ \frac{\operatorname{cov}(r_i, r_M)\operatorname{var}(\pi) - \operatorname{cov}(r_i, \pi)(\operatorname{cov}(r_M, \pi)}{\operatorname{var}(r_M)\operatorname{var}(\pi) - (\operatorname{cov}(r_M, \pi))^2}(\bar{r}_M - r_F - \operatorname{cov}(r_M, \pi)) \\ &+ \frac{\operatorname{cov}(r_i, \pi)\operatorname{var}(r_M) - \operatorname{cov}(r_i, r_M)\operatorname{cov}(r_M, \pi)}{\operatorname{var}(r_M)\operatorname{var}(\pi) - (\operatorname{cov}(r_M, \pi))^2}(\bar{r}_z - r_F - \operatorname{cov}(r_z, \pi)).\end{aligned} \tag{15}$$

IV Implications

There are a number of differences between our model and earlier models which examined the impact of inflation on equilibrium returns. Our model, like those of C&B, F, L&L and Roll assume that investors use real returns to choose between assets. However ours, unlike prior models, assumes that investors are also concerned with an asset's response to inflation (its inflation hedge characteristics). Thus in the equilibrium equation expressed in real terms (equation (6)) the asset's hedge characteristics explicitly affect the securities equilibrium return. This is in contrast to earlier models (equation (9)). As previously discussed equation (9) results from either assuming asset's real returns are unaffected by inflation (except insofar as inflation affects the variability of the market) or that the only source of variability that affects a security's return is the covariability with a market index. While it is true that prior models expressed in nominal returns contained an inflation term this term was present only because it entered in the conversion from real to nominal terms and not because it affected an investor's choice between assets. In these earlier models the choice between assets can unambiguously be made in terms of means and variances of real returns. The covariance of the real return of any asset with inflation was a matter of no importance.

To examine the conditions under which our model leads to a different expression for expected real returns, equation (6) should be compared to equation (9). Letting the superscript "o" stand for our model and "p" for prior inflation models, an examination of when our model leads to higher expected returns involves examining the conditions when

$$\bar{R}_i^o - \bar{R}_i^p > 0.$$

Utilizing equations (3), (4), (6) and (8) yields the condition as

$$\beta_{2i}\left[-\frac{\mathrm{cov}(R'_M, \pi)}{\mathrm{var}(R'_M)}(\bar{R}'_M - \bar{R}_z) + (\bar{R}_z - \bar{R}_F)\right] > 0. \tag{16}$$

$\bar{R}'_M$ can be shown to be larger than $\bar{R}_z$ assuming risk aversion. Otherwise an arbitrage portfolio can be found with positive return. The sign of $(\bar{R}_z - \bar{R}_F)$ cannot be specified. It depends on investors' feelings toward inflation as manifested by the effect of inflation on their market baskets relative to the market basket used as the basis for calculating the rate of inflation in the return generating process. Thus the sign of (16) depends on the sign of β_{2i}, $\mathrm{cov}(R'_M, \pi)$ and $\bar{R}_z - \bar{R}_F$. Table 19.1 shows the possibilities for an asset whose real return is positively related to inflation (i.e., $\beta_{2i} > 0$). The entry "higher" means that our model leads to an asset

Table 19.1
The relationship of expected return on our model to prior models

	$\bar{R}_Z > \bar{R}_F$	$\bar{R}_Z = \bar{R}_F$	$\bar{R}_Z < \bar{R}_F$
$\mathrm{cov}(R'_M, \pi) > 0$	indeterminate	lower	lower
$\mathrm{cov}(R'_M, \pi) = 0$	higher	same	lower
$\mathrm{cov}(R'_M, \pi) < 0$	higher	higher	indeterminate

having a higher equilibrium expected return than that which would be predicted by the C&B or F, L&L models.

Empirical studies of the relationship between inflation and nominal returns have found that the nominal return on the market is negatively correlated (or occasionally uncorrelated) with inflation. This would imply $\mathrm{cov}(R'_M, \pi) < 0$. Examining the third row of Table 1 shows that in this case if $\bar{R}_z \geqslant \bar{R}_F$ then assets with positive correlation of their real return with inflation would require a higher real return in our equilibrium model than in prior models.

Another implication of having an asset's expected return affected by inflation is that the usual two fund theorem is replaced by a three fund theorem. Prior CAPM inflation models allowed an investor to achieve his desired portfolio by utilizing two mutual funds. Any two minimum variance portfolios would, of course, be equally good. However, a convenient choice would be the market and a portfolio uncorrelated with it in real terms. When assets' required returns are affected by inflation a three fund theorem replaces the two fund theorem. These funds are two minimum variance portfolios and a portfolio that is perfectly correlated with inflation. Once again there are a wide variety of choices. However, a convenient set of choices would be the market, a portfolio uncorrelated in real terms with both the real market return and inflation and the nominally riskless asset. Combinations of these three funds allow the investor to select the degree of market risk he desires while adjusting the degree of inflation exposure to a level that is optimum given his consumption preferences.

Notes

The authors would like to thank The Dexter Corporation, Windsor Locks, Connecticut for funding this research.
New York University.
Baruch College, CUNY.

1. Long's [7] paper is different from the other three. Long analyzes a multiperiod framework to derive a model that incorporates an intertemporally changing opportunity set and intertemporally changing interest rate. In his model equilibrium returns are affected by varying future interest rates and prices on each good. While it is an interesting model it differs from the model derived in this paper both by its complexity and its assumption of multivariate normality.

2. We are referring to that section of Roll's [13] paper in which he derives a CAPM. He clearly has other models that analyze the hedge characteristics of assets.

3. In particular, when we discuss arbitrage pricing and formulate zero risk strategies, these should be zero risk strategies in terms of real purchasing power.

4. See Lintner [6] and Reilly [11] for a fuller statement and some empirical evidence.

5. See any standard econometric text for an alternative derivation of equations (3) and (4).

6. The key relationship in demonstrating this is that under either approximation $\text{cov}(r_F, \pi) = \text{cov}(r_F, r_M) = 0$.

7. It might be worth pointing out that this discussion (namely the differential impact of measured inflation) is consistent with our earlier analysis. Despite the fact that alternative rates of inflation impact different investors-consumers differently, for any rate of inflation and market rate of return there is an equilibrium rate of return on each asset. At this equilibrium each investor and consumer is at a consumption-investment decision set which maximizes his utility. As Ross [17] has shown, the existence of equilibrium means the absence of arbitrage profits. Thus, an equation of the form of equation (2) must always follow from equation (1) as shown in Ross [17].

8. Actually, to get Roll's equation replace R'_M with R_M.

9. Another way to account for this seeming anomaly is to see that the β_{1i} that arises from the two factor returns generating process will in general be different from the $\beta_{1i}(\beta'_i)$ that will arise from the single factor returns generating process. If a_2 equals zero, inflation will still impact a_1 because of the way β_{1i} is measured.

10. See Chen and Boness [1] for a derivation. Also see Elton and Gruber [2] for a derivation and a comparison of the approximations used by Chen and Boness and those used by Friend, Landskroner and Losq. Chen and Boness relate nominal and real returns by the expression

$$(1 + R_i) = (1 + r_{2i})\frac{1}{1+\pi}.$$

They then approximate $\frac{1}{1+\pi}$ by expanding it in a Maclaurin series dropping all terms with powers greater than zero and assuming that πr_i is sufficiently small so it can be approximated as zero.

References

1. A. H. Chen and A. J. Boness. "Effects of Uncertain Inflation on the Investment and Financing Decisions of a Firm." *Journal of Finance* (May 1975), 469–83.

2. E. Elton and M. Gruber. "Non-standard C.A.P.M. and the Market Portfolio." Unpublished manuscript, NYU.

3. H. R. Fogler, J. Kise and J. Tipton. "Three Factors, Interest Rate Differentials and Stock Groups." *Journal of Finance* (May 1981), 323–35.

4. I. Friend, Y. Landskroner and E. Losq. "The Demand for Risky Assets under Uncertain Inflation." *Journal of Finance* (December 1976), 1278–97.

5. J. Lintner. "The Valuation of Risk Assets and the Selection of Risky Investments in Stock Portfolios and Capital Budgets." *Review of Economics and Statistics* (February 1965), 87–99.

6. ———. "Inflation and Security Returns." *Journal of Finance* (May 1975), 259–80.

7. J. B. Long, Jr. "Stock Prices, Inflation, and the Term Structure of Interest Rates." *Journal of Financial Economics* (July 1974), 131–70.

8. R. Merton. "An Intertemporal Capital Asset Pricing Model." *Econometrica* 41, No. 5 (September 1973), 867–88.

9. J. Mossin. "Equilibrium in a Capital Asset Market." *Econometrica* (October 1966), 768–83.

10. G. S. Oldfield, Jr. and R. Rogalski. "Treasury Bill Factors and Common Stock Returns." *Journal of Finance* (May 1981), 337–50.

11. F. Reilly. "Companies and Common Stocks as Inflation Hedges." *The Bulletin,* Graduate School of Business, NYU.

12. M. R. Reinganum. "The Arbitrage Pricing Theory: Some Empirical Results." *Journal of Finance* (May 1981), 313–21.

13. R. Roll. "Assets, Money and Commodity Price Inflation Under Uncertainty." *Journal of Money, Credit and Banking* (November 1973), 903–23.

14. ——— and S. Ross. "An Empirical Investigation of the Arbitrage Pricing Theory." *Journal of Finance* (December 1980), 1073–103.

15. S. Ross. "Return, Risk, and Arbitrage." In I. Friend and J. Bicksler (eds.), *Risk and Return in Finance*. Cambridge: Ballinger, 1977, 189–218.

16. ———. "The Arbitrage Theory of Capital Asset Pricing." *Journal of Economic Theory* 13 (December 1976), 341–60.

17. ———. "A Sample Approach to the Valuation of Risky Streams." *Journal of Business* (July 1978), 453–75.

20

On the Robustness of the Roll and Ross Arbitrage Pricing Theory

D. Chinhyung Cho,
Edwin J. Elton, and
Martin J. Gruber

Roll and Ross [6] have written what has quickly become the classic article on testing the Arbitrage Pricing Theory (APT) originally proposed by Ross [8]. They presented methods both for estimating the return generating process and for testing whether particular elements (factors) in the return generating process were priced in equilibrium. They found that more factors are priced than one would expect to be priced if the Capital Asset Pricing Model (CAPM) held.

Roll and Ross used maximum likelihood factor analysis to estimate both the number of factors generating returns and the factor loadings. Very little is known about the properties of the estimates obtained from maximum likelihood factor analysis or the sensitivity of the results to the characteristics of the underlying data. For example, Dhrymes, Friend, and Gultekin [2] have observed that the number of significant factors increases with the number of stocks employed in the factor analysis and that the tests of APT depend very much on how the stocks were grouped.

In this article, we examine the results produced by the Roll and Ross procedure when the return generating process is known. We simulate returns from a zero beta CAPM and allow the parameters of the return generating process to change quarterly in two distinct ways. First, we use Wilshire's fundamental betas, which are very similar to those used by Rosenberg and Marathe [7].[1] Then, we use betas that are estimated quarterly using historical daily return data. Extra factors may be identified for two reasons. First and foremost, if the betas themselves are related to a set of variables (factors) as they will be in our simulations, then the return generating process and the model explaining equilibrium returns may contain more than two factors. These extra factors will reflect the factors that influence betas.[2] Additional factors also may be identified simply due to random patterns in the data.

We find that, while the test procedure of Roll and Ross overstates the number of factors present in the return generating process for the simulated returns, the procedure has at most a slight tendency to overestimate the number of factors influencing equilibrium returns. Furthermore, for our simulated data, there were fewer factors identified as generating returns and fewer factors required to explain equilibrium returns than the numbers corresponding to actual data. Therefore, there do appear to be influences in the market that generate returns beyond those depicted in the zero beta CAPM.

I Test Procedures

In this section, first we will discuss our data file and sample period; second, our techniques for simulating returns consistent with the zero beta CAPM and also with actual historical returns; and third, the tests we did to compare our results with those of Roll and Ross.

A The Sample

Daily returns were taken from the Center for Research on Security Prices (CRSP) file for the period January 1, 1973 to September 30, 1980, a total of 1,770 days. This period is more current and slightly shorter than that used by Roll and Ross. Estimates of the daily riskless rate were based on daily quotations on new 90 day certificates of deposit.[3] The time period selected was the longest over which we could obtain daily quotations. Betas were generated from historical returns and from Wilshire. The Wilshire betas are fundamental betas estimated using techniques devised by Rosenberg and Marathe [7].

There were 2,016 securities listed on the New York or American Stock Exchanges on both January 1, 1973 and September 30, 1980. Since one source of betas was the set of fundamental betas generated by Wilshire, we eliminated stocks for which Wilshire did not estimate fundamental betas. There were 247 such stocks. We grouped the remaining stocks into 58 groups of 30 securities each. The grouping was done alphabetically on the basis of ticker symbols.[4] Data on the remaining 28 securities were discarded.

B Simulated Returns

Two different time series of daily returns were generated. For both series, it was assumed that the zero beta CAPM described expected returns. In one case, we used the quarterly betas along with the quarterly standard deviations of residuals for each individual stock that were supplied to us by Wilshire Associates. Wilshire generates a beta for each stock quarterly from fundamental factors. This beta changes quarterly with its level determined by such factors as historical beta, a set of fundamental factors, and industry membership. The Wilshire beta is a linear function of these variables. In addition to the Wilshire beta, we also used the historical betas and standard deviations of residuals that were estimated quarterly via the ordinary least square regression of $R_i - R_f$ on $R_m - R_f$, using the actual daily returns of the stock R_i and the actual daily returns of the value-weighted market index, R_m. This was done for each quarter in our sample period.[5]

We estimated the daily return for a zero beta portfolio, R_z, by adding an adjustment factor to the daily riskless rates. This was done for each set of simulated returns. To determine this adjustment factor, we first calculated α_i's for each stock i by subtracting $\beta_i(\overline{R_m - R_f})$ from $(\overline{R_i - R_f})$. Since, in either simulation, we had quarterly betas, this gave us quarterly alphas for each stock. The adjustment factor was determined by dividing the sum of alphas by the sum of one-minus betas. The summation was across all stocks and all quarters. This adjustment process ensures that the overall mean return for the actual and simulated returns during our sample period will be identical for the sample as a whole. Note that we do not get the same adjustment factor for both simulations.

To obtain an estimate of each stock's daily residual variance, we divided the quarterly residual variance by 60. This is an implicit assumption of 60 days for each quarter. For the simulation using Wilshire data, we adjusted the Wilshire estimates of quarterly residual variance so that they had the same mean and variance as those from actual returns.

In summary, for each stock we had a time series of quarterly betas, and standard deviations of residuals. Also, we had a time series of daily market returns (value-weighted) and daily riskless rates, and an adjustment factor that is a premium of $\overline{R_z}$ over $\overline{R_f}$. Even though some adjustments were made to force both actual and simulated returns to have similar levels of returns, these adjustments would not affect the characteristics of either set of return data because we still captured the variation in betas.

With the above estimates, we simulated daily return data for 1,770 days using

$$S_{it} = R_{zt} + \beta_{iq}(R_{mt} - R_{zt}) + \sigma_{it} e_{it}$$

$$R_{zt} = R_{ft} + \text{adjustment factor}$$

where S_{it} are simulated returns for stock i, R_{ft} are daily returns rates, R_{zt} are daily zero beta portfolio returns, β_{iq} are quarterly betas[6] for stock i, R_{mt} are actual daily value-weighted market returns, σ_{it} are daily standard deviations of residuals for stock i, and e_{it} are independent random numbers generated from the standardized normal distribution.[7]

C Determining the Number of Factors

Our factor analytic procedures and the test for number of factors were identical to those of Roll and Ross [6]. To obtain the factor loading estimates, we used the EFAP computer package on the adjusted variance-covariance matrices.[8] The adjustment consisted of dividing each element in the variance-covariance matrix by one-half of the largest variance among 30 stocks. The adjustment was made to reduce round-off errors. However, one should note that, because of these adjustments, the resulting betas were scaled down by a square root of one-half of the largest variance and the resulting unique variances were scaled down by one-half of the largest variance. This scaling has no effect on our conclusions except through the reduction in round-off errors.

One step in our procedure requires further clarification. In extracting factors from the data, we encountered a number of so-called Heywood cases. A Heywood case occurs when returns of a stock are perfectly correlated with a linear combination of the factor returns so that the unique variance of a stock is equal to zero. A unique variance is the variance of residuals after extracting the effects of factors from a stock's returns. These Heywood cases cause serious problems in estimating factor loadings unless some modifications are made [4], [5]. These problems arise because the maximum likelihood estimation requires an extraction of eigenvalues from a matrix $\psi^{-1/2}S\psi^{-1/2}$ where ψ is the diagonal matrix of unique variances and S is the sample variance-covariance matrix.

Since we felt it unlikely that a stock can be viewed as a perfect linear combination of underlying factors, we decided to remove the stocks that cause Heywood cases and reestimated the factor loadings and unique variances.[9] Table 20.1 shows the number of groups where we encountered Heywood cases and the factor number at which they occurred.[10] Note that Heywood cases occurred more frequently as more factors were extracted.

Our results for estimating the number of factors present in the return generating process are shown in Table 20.2. There are three sections: one

Table 20.1
Distribution of Heywood cases for alternative numbers of extracted factors

	Number of factors extracted						
	2	3	4	5	6	7	8
Actual returns	1	2	4	17	26	33	42
Wilshire beta					not	not	not
Simulated returns	2	10	17	31	run	run	run

Table 20.2
Number of factors and P-levels

Number of factors	P-levels 0.9	0.8	0.7	0.6	0.5	0.4	0.3	0.2	0.1	0.0
Actual returns										
RR*	.38	.17	.07	.02	.12	.02	.05	.05	.10	.02
5	.03	.02	.05	.00	.02	.09	.16	.07	.12	.45
6	.09	.03	.09	.10	.14	.09	.09	.09	.14	.16
7	.26	.03	.14	.16	.12	.05	.07	.05	.07	.05
8	.50	.09	.10	.07	.07	.05	.03	.03	.03	.01
Wilshire beta simulated returns										
1	.03	.07	.05	.09	.14	.07	.05	.03	.14	.33
2	.18	.17	.07	.05	.07	.09	.09	.14	.07	.07
3	.41	.09	.09	.12	.07	.10	.05	.00	.03	.00
4	.53	.14	.12	.07	.05	.03	.02	.00	.03	.00
5	.72	.12	.07	.03	.00	.02	.02	.02	.00	.00
Historical beta simulated returns										
3	.02	.00	.02	.05	.07	.03	.05	.16	.10	.48
4	.03	.05	.05	.14	.10	.05	.09	.19	.10	.19
5	.14	.12	.10	.10	.12	.16	.05	.10	.05	.05
6	.28	.17	.16	.17	.05	.07	.05	.02	.02	.02
7	.47	.22	.17	.05	.02	.03	.02	.00	.02	.00

* This row reproduces the Roll and Ross result for 5 factors.

for actual returns; one for simulated returns using Wilshire betas; and one for simulated returns using historical betas. The rows under the section for actual returns are analogous (for our time period) to Table 20.2 in [6]. For convenience, the results of Roll and Ross are reproduced in the row denoted by RR. Recall that Roll and Ross used five factors.

The column headings are *P*-levels. These are the probabilities of samples that are expected to yield χ^2 greater than that of our particular sample for a given hypothesized number of factors. If these *P*-levels were small compared to some critical level, then we would reject the hypothesis that a given number of factors is sufficient. Thus, we may interpret these *P*-levels as the probability of a certain number of factors being sufficient. The rows are the fractions of 58 groups that yielded the corresponding *P*-levels at a pre-specified number of factors. For example, the 0.03 in the row for five factors and under the column 0.9 in actual returns is the fraction of 58 groups, i.e., two groups in which we observed a probability of over 0.9 that no more than five factors were needed to explain returns.

Our results with actual returns show that we seem to require more factors than Roll and Ross. Roll and Ross decided that five factors were sufficient. At the same level of significance they used, we have a very high probability that more than five factors are required. We do not have an explanation for this finding other than the use of a different time period and different groupings of stocks. This finding is not due to adjustments for Heywood cases. Before we made adjustments, we still required more than five factors. In a subsequent analysis, we used seven factors. This level gives us a distribution of *P*-levels that roughly corresponds to that used by Roll and Ross.

When we simulated returns either using historical or Wilshire betas, fewer factors were found. With a simulation using historical betas, six factors had a higher probability of being sufficient than seven factors did using actual returns. With a simulation using Wilshire betas, three factors were more likely to be sufficient than seven factors were using actual returns. In subsequent analyses, we used six factors for the case of historical beta simulated returns and three factors for the case of Wilshire beta simulated returns.

The Roll and Ross procedure led us to believe that there were more factors present in the return generating process than in fact were present for our simulated data. However, the real test of their procedure is to examine how many factors are priced.

II Testing the APT

The next step involved examining the effect of factors on equilibrium returns. Once again, a methodology directly parallel to that employed by Roll and Ross was used. Cross-sectional generalized least square regressions were employed using Roll and Ross's equations (10) to (13).[11] In applying this general procedure, there are two ways of estimating a value of the zero beta coefficient λ_0. This value can be set from external data (Roll and Ross used 6 percent) or can be estimated using the augmented factor loading matrix.[12] The advantages and disadvantages of above procedures are described in [6], p. 1091. An external estimate of λ_0 is less arbitrary for our simulated returns than that used by Roll and Ross for actual returns. Since we have generated the data by simulations, we know the "true" value of λ_0. From the last section, λ_{0t} is equal to R_{zt} for any period t.[13] This value was used in the cross-sectional tests. Given that we know the value of λ_{0t} in our simulated returns at any time, the estimating procedure using the augmented factor loading matrix is of less interest. Nevertheless, we present the results for purposes of comparison with Roll and Ross.

Let us examine the two methodologies one at a time. Panel A of Table 20.3 presents the percentage of groups with at least a specified number of risk premiums being significant at the 95 percent level. Roll and Ross concluded that at least three factors were important for pricing but that it was unlikely that more than four factors were important. The results they obtained are reproduced as row "Roll and Ross" in table 20.3. When we repeated their methodology on actual returns during our sample period, we found evidence of larger numbers of factors being priced. If five factors were in fact significant, we would expect to find the sixth factor to be significant 5 percent of the time. Since six factors were significant slightly more than 5 percent of the time, it seems reasonable to assume that either five or six factors were affecting returns over this period. Recall that we tested over a different time period from that used by Roll and Ross. The fact that a different number of factors is significant in a different time span is not surprising. The covariance structure of returns can and does change over time.

The cross-sectional results where returns were simulated by the zero beta CAPM employing changing parameters are striking. Whether returns were simulated from a model employing fundamental betas or historical betas, we conclude that fewer than three factors were generat-

Table 20.3
Cross-sectional generalized least square regressions of arithmetic mean sample returns on factor loadings: percentage of groups with at least these many factors significant at the 95 percent level.

A: λ_0 computed by adding the adjustment factor to R_{ft} as in simulations							
	Factors						
	1	2	3	4	5	6	7
Roll and Ross	88.1	57.1	33.3	16.7	4.8	n.a.	n.a.
Actual returns	100.0	100.0	86.2	55.2	32.8	8.6	0.0
Wilshire betas	100.0	13.8	0.0	n.a.	n.a.	n.a.	n.a.
Historical betas	100.0	33.3	0.0	0.0	0.0	0.0	n.a.

B: λ_0 estimated using augmented factor loading matrices							
	Factors						
	1	2	3	4	5	6	7
Roll and Ross	69.0	47.6	7.1	4.8	0.0	n.a.	n.a.
Actual returns	58.6	17.2	1.7	0.0	0.0	0.0	0.0
Wilshire betas	100.0	100.0	12.1	n.a.	n.a.	n.a.	n.a.
Historical betas	100.0	66.3	33.3	0.0	0.0	0.0	n.a.

ing returns. If one factor were generating returns, we would expect to find a second factor to be significant 5 percent of the time. Since, in either model, we find a second factor significant more than 5 percent of the time we conclude that two factors may have affected equilibrium returns. The fact that a second factor was unnecessary for 86.2 percent of the cases when fundamental betas were used, and 66.7 percent of the cases when historical betas were used, indicates that one factor was sufficient for the majority of the cases. The zero beta CAPM has often been called the two-factor CAPM with the two in the title referring to the fact that both the return on the market and the return on the zero beta portfolio affect the expected return on any stock. The reader may wonder why, when we generate returns from the zero beta model, one factor explained equilibrium returns in such a large percentage of the cases. The explanation is that one factor, R_z, was set externally and removed from returns before the tests were conducted. Thus, we should find only one factor priced. The fact that, having removed R_z, we found two factors priced for some group indicates that the methodology had a small tendency to overestimate the number of factors at work. Later, when we discuss the results obtained using the augmented factor loading matrix where λ_0 was not set externally, we expect to see one additional factor (two factors) priced.

Before turning to this analysis, we wish to point out what is perhaps the major conclusion of this paper. We have examined the cases where returns with similar expected values and variances as actual returns were generated by a two-factor equilibrium model with parameters changing. In these cases, the Roll and Ross methodology found many less factors being priced than those found when the methodology was applied to actual returns. Thus, it seems that there may be more than two factors in the market that influence the equilibrium returns.

Panel B of Table 20.3 is analogous to Panel A. The difference is that augmented factor loading matrices were employed to arrive at estimates of λ_0. The results are not surprising. The fractions of cases where a third factor is needed, under either simulation, to explain returns is roughly the same as it was for two factors in the previous cases (Panel A). We can conclude then that, when returns are generated by a two-factor model, equilibrium returns are explained by two factors most of the time although occasionally three factors are needed.

As a reference, we categorize some of our findings according to the 58 groups in Table 20.4. Observe that, because of Heywood adjustments, not all of the 58 groups had 30 securities and that, due to missing observations, not all of the 58 groups had the same number of observations. Columns under the headings of "*P*-level" present the probabilities of seven factors being sufficient for actual returns and of three factors being sufficient for Wilshire beta simulated returns. Columns under the headings of "Priced" present the number of factors that are significant at the 95 percent level when cross-sectional regressions were carried out with λ_{0t} set externally.

III Conclusion

Roll and Ross [6] present important evidence that the structure of equilibrium returns cannot be explained by a zero beta form of the CAPM. In two simulation experiments, we find that while their procedure has a slight tendency to overstate the number of factors at work in the market, this tendency cannot account for the large number of factors they found in their original article. This is true even though the parameters of the two-factor CAPM were linearly related to other variables and changed over time in response to changes in these variables.

Table 20.4
Summary findings for all 58 groups

Group order	Stocks used	Number of observations	Actual returns P-level	Actual returns Priced	Wilshire simulations P-level	Wilshire simulations Priced
1	29	1292	.404	2	.853	1
2	29	1618	.922	3	.944	1
3	29	1721	.145	3	.486	2
4	29	1697	.918	4	.744	1
5	30	1670	.357	3	.997	1
6	29	1703	.901	3	.994	1
7	30	1696	.451	4	.450	1
8	30	1596	.327	3	.650	1
9	30	1689	.258	3	.819	1
10	30	1697	.503	3	.493	1
11	28	1655	.567	4	.939	1
12	30	1732	.272	4	.980	1
13	29	1606	.645	5	.529	1
14	27	1694	.622	5	.442	1
15	29	1709	.047	4	.627	1
16	28	1587	.999	5	.817	1
17	29	1705	.803	4	.585	1
18	30	1683	.684	3	.379	1
19	30	1680	.105	5	.609	2
20	28	1695	.978	5	.905	1
21	29	1688	.882	3	.534	1
22	28	1700	.965	2	.198	1
23	29	1748	.107	6	.770	1
24	30	1684	.776	5	.951	1
25	29	1701	.658	5	.977	1
26	28	1276	.448	2	.686	1
27	29	1703	.712	5	.765	1
28	29	1537	.744	5	.059	1
29	29	1711	.670	3	.031	1
30	30	1692	.567	4	.422	1
31	30	1668	.900	5	.998	2
32	29	1621	1.000	2	.954	2
33	30	1172	.338	3	.165	1

Table 20.4 (continued)

Group order	Stocks used	Number of observations	Actual returns P-level	Actual returns Priced	Wilshire simulations P-level	Wilshire simulations Priced
34	30	1707	.691	2	.936	1
35	29	1547	.530	6	.754	1
36	29	1704	.528	4	.924	1
37	29	1666	.273	4	.779	1
38	29	1710	.993	5	.399	1
39	28	1708	.708	4	.866	1
40	29	1670	.058	6	.991	1
41	29	1564	.628	4	.830	1
42	30	1646	.718	4	.966	1
43	29	1686	.108	3	.999	1
44	30	1703	.761	3	.979	1
45	28	1667	.951	5	.902	1
46	28	1609	.720	3	.440	1
47	30	1671	.906	3	.996	1
48	28	1691	.737	2	.901	1
49	30	1676	.646	3	.661	1
50	29	1658	.622	5	.984	2
51	30	1668	.597	2	.915	2
52	30	1636	.548	6	.632	1
53	30	1699	.361	2	.305	2
54	30	1681	.006	5	.572	2
55	28	1621	.914	3	.870	1
56	30	1686	.994	4	.974	1
57	29	1663	.987	3	.942	1
58	29	1657	.996	6	.641	1

NOTE:
1. "P-level" presents the probabilities of seven factors being sufficient for actual returns and three factors being sufficient for Wilshire beta simulated programs.
2. "Priced" presents number of factors significant at the 95% level.

Notes

1. Data were supplied to the authors by Wilshire Associates. We wish to thank Wilshire and in particular Dennis Tito and Gill Hammer for their cooperation.

2. Ross [9] has shown that existence of variables that affect the influences of market returns on securities' returns can lead to a multi-index model. Particularly, see his equations (9.16) through (9.21).

3. Daily rates were calculated as the 90th root of one plus the 90 day rate minus one; i.e., the geometric mean over 90 days.

4. This grouping procedure is different from that of Roll and Ross who grouped stocks according to the alphabetical order of company names. However, this difference should not affect the results.

5. An intercept α_i was allowed in each regression. In determining these historical estimates, we made sure that there were more than 30 observations in each quarter. Otherwise, we used the estimates of the adjacent quarter.

6. We assumed that betas are stationary within each quarter.

7. We used the subroutine GGNML from International Mathematical and Statistical Library (IMSL) computer subroutines for these random numbers.

8. Variance-covariance matrices were calculated using the subroutine BECOVM of IMSL computer subroutines.

9. This procedure has been advocated by Schönemann and Wang [10] and Brown and Weinstein [1].

10. We ran three different factor analyses for each group; one based on the actual return data and the other two based on simulated return data. This means that for each group we have to find those stocks that do not encounter Heywood problems in all three cases. Since there is no systematic way of searching these stocks except by trial and error, we decided to search for those stocks that eliminate Heywood problems for the cases of actual return data and Wilshire beta simuated return data.

11. There are several misprints in the Roll and Ross article. Equation (10) is $\hat{\lambda}_t = (\hat{B}^t\hat{V}^{-1}\hat{B})^{-1}\hat{B}^t\hat{V}^{-1}r_t = \Gamma r_t$ while equation (12) is $\bar{\lambda} = \Gamma\bar{r}$. Note that equation (11) should have been $(B^tV^{-1}B)^{-1}$ and equation (13) should have been $(B^tV^{-1}B)^{-1}/T$. Also, one should readjust factor loadings and unique variances by multiplying with σ and σ^2, respectively, where σ^2 is one-half the largest variance of the 30 individual stocks in each group. Otherwise, t-statistics will be underestimated by σ. This is so because Roll and Ross did not use the variance-covariance matrix but a matrix that is scaled down by σ^2 in carrying out factor analysis.

12. One should note that $\hat{V}$ used in this latter estimation should be the same as that used in the previous case where the nonaugmented factor loading matrix was used.

13. This need not, of course, be the true value for actual historical returns.

References

[1] Brown, S. J., and M. I. Weinstein. "A New Approach to Testing Asset Pricing Models: The Bilinear paradigm." *Journal of Finance*, Vol. 38 (June 1983), pp. 711–743.

[2] Dhrymes, P. J., I. Friend, and B. Gultekin. "The Contribution of Arbitrage Pricing Theory to Capital Asset Pricing." Working Paper, University of Pennsylvania (1982).

[3] Elton, E. J., M. J. Gruber, and J. Rentzler. "Equilibrium Returns on Assets under Inflation: An Application of the APT." *Journal of Finance* (forthcoming).

[4] Jöreskog, K. G. "Some Contributions to Maximum Likelihood Factor Analysis." *Psychometrika* Vol. 32 (December 1976), pp. 443–482.

[5] ———. "Factor Analysis by Least Squares and Maximum Likelihood Methods." In *Statistical Methods of Digital Computers*, K. Enslein, A. Ralston, and H. S. Wilf, eds. New York: John Wiley & Sons, Inc. (1977).

[6] Roll, R., and S. A. Ross. "An Empirical Investigation of the Arbitrage Pricing Theory." *Journal of Finance*, Vol. 35 (Decemeber 1980), pp. 1073–1103.

[7] Rosenberg, B., and V. Marathe. "Common Factors in Security Returns: Microeconomic Determinants and Macroeconomic Correlates." *Proceedings of the Seminar on the Analysis of Security Prices*, University of Chicago (May 1976), pp. 61–115.

[8] Ross, S. A. "The Arbitrage Theory of Capital Asset Pricing." *Journal of Economic Theory*, Vol. 13 (December 1976), pp. 341–360.

[9] ———. "Return Risk and Arbitrage." In *Risk and Return in Finance*, I, Irwin Friend and James L. Bicksler, eds. Cambridge, Mass: Ballinger Publishing Co. (1977).

[10] Schönemann, P. H., and M. Wang. "Some New Results on Factor Indeterminancy." *Psychometrika*, Vol. 37 (March 1972), pp. 61–91.

V Taxes and Portfolio Composition

In this section we discuss our work on the impact of taxes on asset prices. The first chapter has generated more subsequent work than any other article we ever wrote. Even though it is now almost thirty years old, we still receive two to three articles a year using our methodology to estimate tax rates. It has been replicated in the United States and over a dozen other countries. The subject: measuring the impact of changes in the tax law. A careful reading shows that we were very careful to deal with the impact of market movements. We controlled for them by using the change in the market and carefully selecting a time period where the market had as many up days as down days (weighted by the number of dividends) and where the magnitude of the up and down moves balanced out. We also carefully examined transaction costs to see if short-term trading was possible. It always surprises us that people have copied our methodology without using the same care in following our testing. We show that taxes affect prices of common equities and provide an estimate of the marginal rate. We also show that there are dividend clienteles where investors in high or low tax brackets cluster.

The second chapter is a reply to a paper by Avner Kalay. He argues that short-term trading around the ex-dividend day could have an impact on prices and the estimate of the marginal stockholder tax rate. We show that at the time of our article, transaction costs were such that short-term trading to take advantage of the ex-dividend day drop in price was unprofitable, even for broker dealers with the lowest transaction costs. Short-term trading had no impact on our estimates. After fixed transaction costs were eliminated, there was a possibility of short-term trading having some impact for the most extreme differences between the size of the dividend and the size of the ex-dividend day price movement. The impact of short-term trading is to reduce this difference and to make the estimated tax rate slightly less than the true marginal rate if all firms are used.

The alternative approach requires the researcher to eliminate firms where the ex-dividend day drop could be affected by short-term trading.

The third chapter explores the relationship between residuals from a zero beta CAPM and dividend yields. We find a strong relationship. There are many more direct tests of the post-tax CAPM. What is distinctive about this article is that we document that stocks that pay zero dividends do not fit any conventional model of tax effects. We explore whether the differences could be explained by a low-price stock effect and find there is still a substantial amount that is unexplained.

The final chapter in this section examines the optimal portfolio to hold if an investor wishes to solve the portfolio problem using after-tax returns, when either the standard or post-tax CAPM describes the world. Under either model, the market portfolio is not the optimal portfolio for most investors. The optimal portfolio is a function of the investor's tax rate, the dividend yield, and the risk characteristics of the various securities.

21

Marginal Stockholder Tax Rates and the Clientele Effect

Edwin J. Elton and Martin J. Gruber

The determination of marginal stockholder tax brackets is an important and unresolved issue in the economic literature. Marginal stockholder tax brackets play an important role in stock valuation models [1, 6, 14], in normative investment and dividend policy models [11, 16], and in descriptive capital allocation models [7, 8, 10, 12].

The purpose of this paper is to present and test a method of determining marginal stockholder tax brackets and to explore the implications of our findings for corporate investment policy, corporate dividend policy, and the assumption of market rationality.

In the first section of this paper we expand upon the reasons for studying marginal stockholder tax brackets. In the next section we show how marginal stockholder tax brackets can be inferred from the ex-dividend behavior of common stock. In the third and fourth sections we compute marginal stockholder tax brackets and discuss their implications for capital theory.

Reasons for the Study

While stockholder tax brackets are interesting in themselves, they are of primary importance because of the role they play in establishing the firm's cost of capital. In capital theory the cost of retained earnings is defined as that rate which makes a firm's marginal stockholders indifferent between earnings being retained or paid out in the form of dividends. Because dividends are taxed at a different rate than capital gains the cost of retained earnings is a function of the marginal stockholder's tax bracket. This tax rate is therefore necessary in order to accurately determine the firm's optimal investment policy.

Knowledge of marginal stockholder tax brackets will also allow us to draw inferences about the importance of dividend policy.[1] Such inference could be made if we find a strong relationship between corporate dividend policy and investor tax rates. The establishment of this relationship would provide evidence that supports the clientele effect of Miller and Modigliani [13] (each firm is assumed to have a body of stockholders who find its dividend policy optimal). Furthermore, such a finding means that a change in dividend policy might cause a change in clientele and this could be costly.[2]

The final reason for studying the ex-dividend behavior of common stock is that it can provide evidence of rationality. Most of the work in investment theory assumes rationality on the part of stockholders (for example, almost all valuation models). This paper provides evidence that a theory based on rational stockholder behavior is really descriptive of their behavior.

Despite the importance of marginal stockholder tax rates to financial theory and practice there have been few attempts to identify stockholder tax brackets. Those attempts which have been made have relied on either a survey of a firm's stockholders or the collection of tax data for all stockholders in the economy. Neither of these methods attempts to identify tax rates for stockholders at the margin. In addition, the latter method implicitly makes the assumption that the tax rates of stockholders in all corporations are identical.

The Relationship between Ex-dividend Behavior and Stockholder Tax Rates

The ex-dividend behavior of a corporation's common stock should be related to the tax rates of its marginal stockholders.[3]

A stockholder selling stock before a stock goes ex-dividend loses the right to the already declared dividend. If he sells the stock on the ex-dividend day he retains the dividend but should expect to sell it at a lower price (because of this dividend retention). In a rational market the fall in price on the ex-dividend day should reflect the value of dividends vis-à-vis capital gains to the marginal stockholders. Since dividends and capital gains are taxable at different rates, the relative tax rate on these two types of income affect the decision. If this formulation of the ex-dividend behavior of common stocks is correct, then one can infer marginal stockholder tax brackets from observing the ex-dividend behavior of common stocks. This will now be done more formally.

Starting with the premise that the stockholder wishes to maximize his after-tax wealth we can derive an expression for the relationship between the ex-dividend behavior of common stock prices and the marginal tax rates of marginal stockholders.

Let:

P_B = Price on the day before the stock goes ex-dividend.

P_A = Price of the stock on the ex-dividend day.

P_C = Price at which the stock was purchased.

t_o = The tax rate on ordinary income.

t_c = The capital gains tax rate.

D = The amount of the dividend.

If a shareholder were to sell his stock in a corporation before it goes ex-dividend his per share wealth would be equal to the price he receives for the stock (P_B) minus the tax he must pay on any capital gain incurred by owning the stock ($t_c(P_B - P_C)$).

If he were to sell on the day the stock goes ex-dividend his wealth per share would be equal to the dividend (D) times one minus his marginal tax rate on ordinary income ($1 - t_o$) plus the after tax return on the sale of the share ($P_A - t_c(P_A - P_C)$). For him to be indifferent as to the timing of his sale, the wealth received from either course of action must be the same. This is:[4]

$$P_B - t_c(P_B - P_c) = P_A - t_c(P_A - P_c) + D(t - t_o) \tag{1}$$

Rearranging (1) we get[5]

$$\frac{P_B - P_A}{D} = \frac{1 - t_o}{1 - t_c}. \tag{2}$$

The statistic $(P_B - P_A)/D$ represents the ex-dividend behavior that would cause a stockholder with a particular set of tax rates t_o and t_c to be indifferent as to the timing of purchases and sales of common stock. For the market to be in equilibrium the price movement on the ex-dividend day must be such as to leave prospective (marginal) buyers and sellers of the stock indifferent as to whether they buy before or after the stock goes ex-dividend. If the expected ex-dividend price was either too high or too low marginal buyers and/or sellers would change the timing of their purchases or sales until stock prices were in equilibrium. That is, until their after-tax wealth would be the same whether they sold before or after the stock went ex-dividend. The statistic $(P_B - P_A)/D$ must then reflect the marginal tax rates of the marginal stockholders and one should be able to

Table 21.1

	Number of observa- tions	Mean	Standard deviation of mean	Probability true mean is one or more	Implied[b] tax bracket
Raw data	4148	.7767	.0990	.013	36.4
Data adjusted by index	4148	.7868	.0875	.0075	35.1

a. $\frac{P_B - P_A}{D} = \frac{(1 - t_o)}{(1 - t_c)}$.

b. t_c will be one-half of t_o or 25 per cent, whichever is lower. For any particular ordinary income tax rate one and only one capital gains tax rate is appropriate. For example, in table 1 the assumption that the capital gains tax is one-half the income tax rate holds because the implied ordinary tax rate is less than 50 per cent.

infer these tax rates by observing $(P_B - P_A)/D$. This is what we shall do in the next section.

Tests of Our Statistic

In order to test our hypothesis, we examined the behavior of all stocks listed on the New York Stock Exchange that payed a dividend during the period April 1, 1966 to March 31, 1967, and were traded on both the ex-dividend day and the prior day.[6] We defined P_B as the closing price on the day before a stock went ex-dividend. P_A was measured by the closing price on the ex-dividend day. We used closing rather than opening prices because all orders on the specialists' books are adjusted by the amount of the dividend. Consequently, the first trade is likely to be a biased estimate of the equilibrium market price. Since we had no way of handling this bias, we had to reject opening prices.[7]

Table 21.1 lists the average value of the statistic $(P_B - P_A)/D$ for our entire sample. The probability that the statistic has a value of one or more (price fell by the amount of the dividend) is less than 0.015.[8] Furthermore, the implied average marginal tax bracket for stockholders on the New York Stock Exchange seems reasonable. Our estimate of 36.4 per cent agrees closely with the results reported by Jolivet [9]. He attempted to determine the marginal tax rates that would be paid by analyzing historic tax returns. He estimated the tax rate to be 36 per cent for the year 1965.[9]

Our use of closing prices on the ex-dividend day might raise questions of bias. A whole trading day has elapsed since the stock went ex-dividend and part of the price movement we attribute to tax effects might actually be due to a systematic shift in market prices. For example, if the market increased in price on the day a stock sold ex-dividend, P_A would tend to

Table 21.2

Date		Index value	Date		Index value
April	1 1966	48.76	November	1 1966	43.49
May	1 1966	49.23	December	1 1966	43.42
June	1 1966	46.51	January	1 1967	43.74
July	1 1966	46.36	February	1 1967	47.24
August	1 1966	44.60	March	1 1967	48.03
September	1 1966	41.94	March	31 1967	49.52
October	1 1966	40.42			

increase, decreasing the value of our statistic, and contributing to the fact that our statistic appears to be significantly different from one.

The presence of a bias favorable to our hypothesis was checked in two ways. First, the movement of the New York Stock Exchange index during the period we calculated our statistic was examined.[10] As can be seen from table 21.2, the index increased during six months and decreased during six months. Furthermore, its ending level 49.52 is quite close to its opening level of 48.76. These two reasons are in fact why we selected this period of time. However, it is still possible that stocks went ex-dividend primarily on days the market was increasing. To check this we did the following. We counted the number of stocks that went ex-dividend on a particular day and multiplied this number times the change in the New York Stock index.[11] For the sample year this yielded a net positive change of $8.30 in 4,148 observations or about two tenths of a cent per stock. Although this would tend to decrease our statistic this is so small that it should have a minimal influence on our results.

To further control against any problem of bias we adjusted our data by the market index. That is, we took the price on the ex-dividend day and multiplied it by the ratio of the index on the day before the stock goes ex-dividend to the index on the ex-dividend day. We then recomputed the results. As can be seen from table 21.1, our results remain essentially the same. The test statistic is significantly less than one at the 0.01 level and the inferred marginal tax bracket becomes 35.1 per cent.[12]

Clientele Effect

Having inferred the average marginal tax rate for New York Stock Exchange firms let us see if we can disaggregate the results and find the marginal stockholder tax rates for firms with different characteristics. In particular, let us see if the dividend policy of a firm affects the tax rate of its marginal stockholders. This would be useful information for it would aid in predicting the tax rate of any firm's marginal stockholders, and at the same time it would provide strong evidence as to the existence of the Miller and Modigliani clientele effect.

In order to test the presence of the clientele effect, two variables were hypothesized which should affect stockholder's desire to invest in a company. The first was the firm's dividend yield. The lower a firm's dividend yield the smaller the percentage of his total return that a stockholder expects to receive in the form of dividends and the larger the percentage he expects to receive in the form of capital gains. Therefore, investors who hold stocks which have high dividend yields should be in low tax brackets relative to stockholders who hold stocks with low dividend yields.

The second variable that we hypothesized might affect the ex-dividend behavior of common stocks was the payout ratio. Firms that paid out a high percentage of their earnings as dividends would, all other things being equal, grow (both in terms of market price and earnings) at a slower rate than firms which retained a larger percentage of earnings. Thus, the high payout firm should attract stockholders in relatively lower tax brackets than the low payout firms.

Tables 21.3 and 21.4 present the tests of these two hypotheses. In each table all observations were divided into deciles according to the variable which was supposed to account for the ex-dividend behavior of the stock (dividend yield in table 21.3 and payout in table 21.4). For each decile the mean of both the variable hypothesized as accounting for ex-dividend behavior and the statistic used to measure ex-dividend behavior were computed. Spearman's rank correlation coefficient was then used to judge the extent of the relationship between these two variables. If the relationship is statistically significant we can conclude that there is a clientele effect present in the market.[13]

In tables 21.4 and 21.5 we have also calculated the implied tax bracket associated with each decile. Once again, we employed the central limit theorem to calculate the probability that the ex-dividend price really fell by less than the amount of the dividend.

The results presented in table 21.3 are quite striking. The relationship between the dividend yield and the statistic measuring ex-dividend behavior is positive and statistically significant at the one per cent level.[14] In fact, with the exception of the first and eighth decile the test statistic rose continuously as the dividend yield went up.[15]

Table 21.3
$((P_B - P_A)/D)$[a]

Decile	D/P mean	Mean	Standard deviation	Z value	Probability true mean is one or more	Implied tax bracket
1	.0124	.6690	.8054	.411	.341	.4974
2	.0216	.4873	.2080	2.465	.007	.6145
3	.0276	.5447	.1550	2.937	.002	.5915
4	.0328	.6246	.1216	3.087	.001	.5315
5	.0376	.7953	.1064	1.924	.027	.3398
6	.0416	.8679	.0712	1.855	.031	.2334
7	.0452	.9209	.0761	1.210	.113	.1465
8	.0496	.9054	.0691	1.369	.085	.1747
9	.0552	1.0123	.0538	.229	.591	b
10	.0708	1.1755	.0555	3.162	.999	b

a. Spearman's rank correlation coefficient between D/P and $(P_B - P_A)/D$ is .9152 which is significant at the 1 per cent level.
b. Indeterminate.

Table 21.4
$((P_B - P_A)/D)$[a]

Decile	D/E mean	Mean	Standard deviation	Z value	Probability true mean is one or more	Implied tax bracket
1	.204	.677	.801	.403	.3446	.4883
2	.316	.674	.197	1.655	.0485	.4945
3	.371	.756	.134	1.818	.0344	.3889
4	.409	.730	.124	2.179	.0146	.4254
5	.447	.741	.104	2.486	.0064	.4108
6	.486	.680	.108	2.959	.0015	.4848
7	.533	1.024	.125	.191	.5754	b
8	.594	.896	.092	1.133	.1292	.1889
9	.674	.925	.080	.933	.1762	.0806
10	1.040	.899	.086	1.173	.1210	.2245

a. Spearman's rank correlation coefficient between D/E and $(P_B - P_A)/D$ is 0.7939 which is significant at the 1 per cent level.
b. Indeterminant.

The relationship between implied tax brackets and dividend yields can be seen by examining the third and last column of table 21.3. The tax bracket in general decreases as the dividend yield at which the stock sells increases. The fact that the first is out of line may simply be a result of chance alone given the magnitude of its standard error.[16]

The implied tax rates for the last two deciles cannot be computed. In both deciles the market exhibits a preference for dividends over capital gains, with the preference being stronger and in fact statistically significant at the 1 per cent level for the 10th decile.[17]

The explanation of this preference for dividends over capital gains may be at least partially attributed to our tax structure. While many institutions are indifferent as to capital gains and dividends (tax free institutions such as pension funds or educational institutions) corporations actually prefer dividends. For example, corporations are taxed at a rate of 25 per cent on their capital gains but they only pay a tax on 15 per cent of the income they receive as dividends from another corporation. Thus, a corporation would pay a lower tax on dividends (7.8 per cent) than it did on capital gains (25 per cent). While corporations might account for some of the dividend preference exhibited by the last two deciles, the authors do not believe that this phenomena is widespread enough to account for the extent of dividend preference. Part of the preference for dividends might result from behavioral patterns which, while not wholly rational, have become widely recognized over time. One behavioral pattern that could account for part of the preference for dividends is the propensity for the beneficiary of trust accounts to be restricted or to restrict himself to dividend income from the account. Since capital gains cannot be used as income, the trust manager would prefer to retain the right to the dividend. This type of behavior along with the tax advantage of dividends for a few types of institutional investors could account for the dividend preference exhibited by the last two deciles.

Table 21.4 contains the same type of data that is contained in table 21.3 except that the analysis has been performed in terms of the firm's payout ratio. The relationship between our test statistic and the firm's payout ratio is significant at the 1 per cent level, adding support to the findings discussed earlier. Furthermore, as expected, the implied tax bracket declined with an increase in the firm's payout ratio.

The close relationship between both measures of a firm's dividend policy and the implied stockholder tax bracket suggests that Miller and Modigliani were right in hypothesizing a "clientele effect." As our results show, firms not only seem to attract a clientele but they attract a *rational* clientele—one which should prefer their dividend policy.

Summary

In this paper, we have derived marginal stockholder tax brackets by studying the ex-dividend behavior of common stocks and have shown that these tax brackets are related to a firm's dividend policy. These findings.

1. Provide data that is necessary in order to calculate a firm's cost of retained earnings and to test investment models.
2. Provide evidence in support of Modigliani's and Miller's clientele effect, suggesting that a change in dividend policy could cause a costly change in shareholder wealth.
3. Illustrate one form of market rationality in that stockholders in higher tax brackets show a preference for capital gains over dividend income relative to those in lower tax brackets.

Notes

This paper has been presented at the Econometric Society Meetings, Fall 1968 and Operations Research and Management Science Meetings, May 1, 1969. The research for this paper was started at the Harvard Seminar on Research in Finance, sponsored by the Ford Foundation in 1967 and continued support was provided by the Office of Research, Schools of Business, New York University. Computational assistance was provided by William O'Neill and Constantine Fliakos. We would like to thank Michael Keenan and William O'Neill for helpful comments and suggestions.

1. A distinction has been drawn between investment policy and dividend policy. The same investment policy can be met by using different combinations of retained earnings and external financing. The question remains as to whether dividend policy per se affects firm value. See [13].

2. One type of cost would be the transaction costs incurred by both buyers and sellers as the firm's clientele changes. Furthermore, there should be at least a short run unfavorable price movement as the change in dividend policy is more apparent to those investors who find it less favorable (present stockholders) than to those who find it more favorable. For an estimate of the effect of a change in clientele on a firm's cost of retained earnings, see Elton and Gruber [5].

3. Discussion of the ex-dividend behavior is not new in the financial literature [see 2, 3, 15]. A large part of the literature states that the price of a share of stock should, and does, fall by the amount of the dividend on the ex-dividend day. The proponents of this approach usually state that the assets per share fall by the amount of the dividend, and thus the price per share should fall by this amount. The wide acceptance of this approach is best illustrated by its being institutionalized in the regulation of the New York Stock Exchange. At the opening

of the ex-dividend day all buy and sell orders on the specialists' books are lowered by the amount of the dividend. If our model is correct, this should in general work to the disadvantage of those individuals with offers on the specialists' books. If the seller has an ordinary income tax rate greater than zero the value of his stock should have dropped by less than the amount of the dividend.

Although most theoretical analysis would indicate otherwise, the published empirical work on the ex-dividend behavior of common stock indicates that the price has fallen by less than the amount of the dividend. This tendency while present in all previous tests has not proved to be statistically significant.

4. Actually, both sides of this equation should be adjusted for the transaction costs incurred in selling stock. The incremental transaction costs are the transaction costs on the decrease in stock price. Elsewhere [4] we have argued that 1 per cent might be a reasonable estimate of transaction costs. Since the reduction in price on the ex-dividend day is our statistic, our statistic could be off by 1 per cent.

5. A similar conclusion is reached if the decision is analyzed from the buyer's side. In this case if the buyer purchases the stock before the ex-dividend day then he receives the stock and the after-tax value of the dividend. If he buys the day the stock goes ex-dividend he receives the stock, pays a reduced price and incurs an increased tax liability. Setting up the above in equation form and rearranging we would again derive (2) with one qualification. Since the payment of the tax liability is delayed, the denominator of (2) is reduced. Given reasonable time horizons this should not significantly affect the magnitude of the implied tax bracket. Evidence that time horizon is generally short is contained in Ortner [14].

6. Foreign corporations and closed end mutual funds were eliminated from the sample.

7. Problems, because of movements in the market between opening and closing prices, will be discussed shortly.

8. From the central limit theorem, the mean is normally distributed with a standard deviation equal to the standard deviation of the population divided by the square root of the number of observations. This result is used to test the statistical significance of our statistic.

9. Weston and Brigham [17] made an earlier attempt to define stockholder tax brackets using a method analogous to Jolivet. They found a rate of 46 per cent for the year 1965. Neither of these results are fully comparable to ours. Both authors exclude institutional investors from their studies and both look at a weighted (by ownership) average tax rate. Nevertheless, their estimates can be considered as defining a general area in which we would expect to find marginal tax rates.

10. The New York Stock Exchange index is not the ideal index for our purposes. We would like to have an index that weights equally a movement in any stock's price. Unfortunately, the New York Stock Exchange index weights price movements by the total market value of the firm's stock. Although this means the index is not ideal, it is closer to what we need than any daily index we know of.

11. One could argue that since the ex-dividend day affects the index, the index understates the "true" movement of the market. Fortunately, the number of stocks going ex-dividend on a particular day are just not that large. For example, in the last quarter the largest day had 63 stocks meeting our criteria, 7 days had more than 40 stocks and the majority had 20 or less.

12. For firms paying very small dividends $(P_B - P_A)/D$ is occasionally very large. We eliminated various groups of low dividend paying stocks and examined the effect on our results. The only effect was to reduce the variance.

13. The possibility of bias arises in our rank correlation because of the use of dividends in the denominator of one of our variables and in the numerator of the other. To check for the presence of bias, data were collected on a random sample of stocks (during our test period) on days on which they did not go ex-dividend. Rank correlations were run on the dividend price ratio versus our statistic and the dividend earnings ratio versus our statistic with the data arranged into 10 groups (deciles), 20 groups, 25 groups, 50 groups and 100 groups. The rank correlation coefficients ranged from positive to negative with no value significant at the 45 per cent level (as we report shortly, Spearman's rank correlation coefficient on the ex-dividend day is always significant at the 1 per cent level).

14. Because deciles are an arbitrary way of grouping data, we tried a number of other groupings to show that our findings were insensitive to the method of grouping used. In particular, we divided the data into 10, 20, 25, 50, and 100 groups. In every case, the relationship between our test statistic and the dividend price ratio was found to be significant at the 1 per cent level. The relationship between our statistic and the dividend earnings ratio is always significant at the 5 per cent level and usually significant at the 1 per cent level.

15. The standard deviation of the mean of the ex-dividend statistic for the first decile is so high (relative to the standard deviation of the mean within other deciles) that we can place little confidence in the ranking of this mean relative to other means. The extremely high value of the standard deviation for the first decile is explained by the presence of several low dividend stocks in this decile. The first decile contained some stocks with quarterly dividends of a few pennies which experienced ex-dividend price movements of several times the amount of the dividend.

16. See footnote 15.

17. In order to imply a marginal tax rate we would need a structural relationship between the capital gains tax rate and the ordinary income tax rate for individuals or institutions who prefer dividends to capital gains.

References

[1] Arditti, F., "Risk and the Required Return on Equity," *Journal of Finance*, XXII (Mar. 1967), 19–36.

[2] Campbell, J., and W. Beranek, "Stock Price Behavior on Ex-Dividend Dates," *Journal of Finance*, X (1953), 425–429.

[3] Durand, D., and A. May, "The Ex-Dividend Behavior of American Telephone and Telegraph Stock," *Journal of Finance*, XV (Mar. 1960), 19–31.

[4] Elton, E., and M. Gruber, "The Effect of Share Repurchase on the Value of the Firm," *Journal of Finance*, XXIII (Mar. 1968), 135–149.

[5] Elton, E., and M. Gruber, "The Cost of Retained Earnings—Implications of Share Repurchase," *Industrial Management Review*, 9 (Spring, 1968), 87–105.

[6] Gordon, M., *The Investment, Financing and Valuation of the Corporation* (Homewood, Ill.: Richard D. Irwin, 1962).

[7] Griliches, Z., and D. Jorgenson, "Source of Measured Productivity Change: Capital Input," *American Economic Review* LXI (May, 1966), 50–62.

[8] Jorgenson, D., and C. Siebert, "Theories of Corporate Investment Behavior," *American Economic Review*, LVIII (Sept. 1968), 681–712.

[9] Jolivet, V., "Tax Rates on Dividends," *American Economic Review*, LVI (June 1966), 473–477.

[10] Kuh, E., *Capital Stock Growth: A Micro-Econometric Approach* (Amsterdam: North-Holland, 1954).

[11] Lindsay, R., and A. Sametz, *Financial Management: An Analytical Approach* (Homewood, Ill.: Richard D. Irwin, 1967).

[12] Meyer, J. R., and E. Kuh, *The Investment Decision* (Cambridge, Mass.: Harvard University Press, 1957).

[13] Miller, M., and F. Modigliani, "Dividend Policy, Growth and the Valuation of Shares," *Journal of Business* (Oct. 1961), 411–433.

[14] Ortner, R., "An Estimate of the Time Horizon and Expected Yield for a Selected Group of Common Shares 1935–1955," *International Economic Review*, II (May 1961), 179–198.

[15] Rendett, P., *The Price Behavior of Stocks on Their Ex-Dividend Dates* (unpublished masters thesis, Massachusetts Institute of Technology, 1956).

[16] Solomon, E., *The Theory of Financial Management* (New York: Columbia University Press, 1963).

[17] Weston, J. F., and E. F. Brigham, *Managerial Finance* (New York: Holt, Rinehart and Winston, 1966), 309.

22

The Ex-Dividend Day Behavior of Stock Prices; A Re-examination of the Clientele Effect: A Comment

Edwin J. Elton, Martin J. Gruber, and Joel Rentzler

In a recent article in this journal, Kalay [5] has written an extensive comment on our 1970 article [2] concerning "Marginal Stockholder Tax Rates and the Clientele Effect." While we are flattered that our article is viewed of sufficient importance to gain this attention 12 years after it was written, we do have reservations about Kalay's comments. We are principally concerned with his interpretations of relevant transaction costs and the role they play in setting equilibrium.

I Equilibrium and Ex-Dividend Day Prices

A major issue in the Kalay article is his assertion that the actions of short-term traders rather than tax effects may determine the size of the price decline on the ex-dividend day.[1] In the absence of transaction costs, a risk neutral investor would eliminate any drop in price not equal to the amount of the dividend by buying and selling around the ex-dividend day. Kalay recognizes transaction costs and argues that if the actions of short-term traders are important the size of the changes in price may reflect transaction costs rather than tax effects.

Kalay recognizes that consistent evidence of a fall in price less than the dividend is evidence of tax effects. If there were no tax effects, short-term traders in the presence of transaction costs would cause the fall in price on the ex-dividend day to be randomly distributed around the amount of the dividend. This is certainly not the pattern found by Kalay, by us, or in any of the previous research in this area. Another possibility is that tax rates are important but that short-term trading limits the amount of the fall in price that would occur due to pure tax effects. If this were true then our article would have contained a downward biased estimate of tax rates particularly for very high dividend paying stocks.

Table 22.1
Critical level of transaction costs for deciles ranked by dividend yield

Group	Critical level of transaction costs (α) in percent
1	0.103
2	0.277
3	0.314
4	0.308
5	0.192
6	0.137
7	0.089
8	0.117
9	−0.017
10	−0.311
Average	0.210

The question of whether or not short-term trading limits the decline on the ex-dividend day rests on the size of the transaction costs facing traders. Kalay in his Table II presents estimates of the level of transaction costs at which short-term trading becomes important.[2] This table is based on adjusting the ex-dividend day closing price by the prior period's return. We will argue shortly that this adjustment is less appropriate than the adjusted estimate we used. Thus, to analyze the potential for profitable short-term trading, we have presented the critical levels below which transaction costs would have to be in order for traders to affect the price decline using data from our original article. These are shown in Table 22.1. This table presents the results from our original sample both on average and for 10 equally sized groups ranked on dividend yield. These numbers are in percent. For example, round trip transaction costs would have to be less than 0.21% on average for the actions of short-term traders to affect ex-dividend day behavior.

Whether short-term trading could be the equilibrating mechanism depends on whether transaction costs are lower or higher than these values. We believe that the estimates of the level of transaction costs which Kalay presents in his Table II are in fact much too low and that true transaction costs make it clear that short-term traders are not setting equilibrium prices on the ex-dividend day.

Kalay recognizes that transaction costs are sufficiently large for individuals that they are not potential short-term traders. He points out that transaction costs are much smaller for broker dealers and argues that they are potential short-term traders.[3] Thus, it is transaction costs for his group that we will analyze.

Kalay uses as his estimates of round trip transaction costs for a broker dealer (his Table III) the execution costs for a broker dealer as shown in the New York Stock Exchange Constitution and Rules published in 1975. There are two problems with Kalay's estimates of transaction costs to broker dealers.

1. Kalay used the wrong version of the New York Stock Exchange Constitution and in addition misused the version he chose.

2. Execution costs are not the only costs to broker dealers and Kalay ignored other major components of transaction costs.

We'll discuss each of these two points in turn.

A Minimum Transaction Costs as Determined by the Exchange

Recall that our study used data for the period April 1966 through March 1967. At this time the New York Stock Exchange published minimum execution costs for broker dealers. Kalay has utilized the minimum commission schedule for execution in force in the early 1970s. This schedule was different from and in general lower than the schedule in force during 1966 and 1967. In addition, Kalay has misinterpreted the transaction costs from his own schedule. Transaction costs have breakpoints, e.g., a certain dollar cost per share is applicable to stocks selling at $20 or above. Kalay has consistently misunderstood these breakpoints and used the incorrect (and in general lower) transaction costs for prices at the breakpoint. While both of these errors in Kalay's analysis lead to an underestimate of transaction costs, the errors are small in magnitude. The errors of omission he has committed in estimating transaction costs are a more serious matter.

B Omitted Transaction Costs

There are three types of transaction costs that were not included in Kalay's Table III but are incurred by a broker dealer.

These are

a. transfer taxes and registration fees

b. bid-ask spreads

c. clearance costs

Table 22.2
Round trip transaction costs (in percent)

Price of stock	1 Execution	2 Execution costs plus transfer taxes	3 Column 2 plus a bid-ask spread of 1/8	4 Column 2 plus a bid-ask spread of 36¢*	5 Column 3 plus a clearance cost	6 Column 4 plus a clearance cost
2	1.40	2.03	8.28	20.03	9.13	20.88
8	0.53	0.84	2.40	5.34	2.75	5.69
14	0.44	0.71	1.60	3.28	2.05	3.73
18	0.34	0.55	1.24	2.55	1.59	2.90
25	0.29	0.49	0.99	1.93	1.28	2.22
30	0.24	0.41	0.83	1.61	1.08	1.86
35	0.21	0.35	0.71	1.38	0.92	1.59
40	0.19	0.32	0.63	1.22	0.83	1.42
50	0.15	0.25	0.50	0.97	0.66	1.12
60	0.13	0.21	0.42	0.81	0.55	0.94

* For low priced stocks we expect a bid-ask spread closer to 1/8. Thus, column 3 is probably more representative for these stocks.

During the time period studied in our original article, there was both a transfer tax and registration fee in existence. This cost was incurred by broker dealers as well as individuals. In Table 22.2 we have reproduced execution costs in effect for a broker dealer at the time of our study and have added the transfer taxes and registration fees. As can be seen from this table, transfer taxes are quite large and result in an over 60% increase in transaction costs.[4]

Another transaction cost that must be considered is the bid-ask spread. If we were to buy and sell a stock at an instant in time, we would expect on average to have the prices differ by the bid-ask spread.[5] We would expect the same costs for a purchase and sale differing in time by a fraction of a day. Hamilton [3] has estimated that only 15% to 20% of transactions take place within the bid-ask spread. Thus, the bid-ask spread represents a reasonable estimate of another transaction cost in addition to execution fees and transfer taxes. Several estimates have been made of the bid-ask spread on the New York Stock Exchange.[6] Most studies find values at or slightly above 36¢.

In table 22.2 we have calculated the impact of bid-ask spreads of 36¢. In addition, we have examined the impact if the bid-ask spread is $\frac{1}{8}$. This is certainly the lower limit for actual bid-ask spreads. It should constitute a reasonable lower limit for the transaction cost due to bid-ask spreads even if we recognize that some trades take place well within the normal bid-ask spread.

The final type of transaction cost that must be considered is the cost of clearance. Clearance is a cost that can't be avoided. There is a large amount of paperwork that accompanies any trade. The SEC estimated that a trade during the time period under study generated 33 different documents. At that time many broker dealers cleared through other broker dealers and there were set rates for this clearance activity. For broker dealers who cleared through other firms, these rates reflect clearance costs. For those firms who cleared themselves, these costs depend on the efficiency of their back office. While this was presumably less than published rates, the costs were positive. In Table 22.2 we use published rates with the understanding that actual costs to some broker dealers might be less.

An examination of Table 22.2 reveals clearly that transaction costs are of a sufficient order of magnitude even for a broker dealer that it would not pay a broker dealer to attempt to trade away differences between the fall in price on the ex-dividend day and the amount of the dividend. The addition of transfer taxes and any reasonable clearance cost is more than sufficient to insure that short-term trading is not setting equilibrium prices on the ex-dividend day. Consideration of bid-ask spreads makes this even clearer.[7] From Table 22.1 it is clear that price changes on the ex-dividend day are so small that short-term trading is unprofitable. Once we recognize that ex-dividend behavior lies well inside the no profit area, it becomes apparent that tax rates are determining price behavior.

II The Adjustment for Ex-Dividend Day Price Changes

Kalay and we use adjusted closing prices to estimate the price after a stock goes ex-dividend.[8] Kalay took exception to our adjusting closing prices by the price change in the NYSE index. He adjusted in two ways: using the market model and using the historic return for each stock over a preceding estimation period. We have investigated the ability of all three of these techniques to estimate previous day's closing prices and same day opening prices from a set of closing prices. We find almost no difference in the accuracy of estimates prepared by the market model and the method we used. We do find that using the historic rates of return for each stock tends in this time period to lead to an underestimate of both the opening and the prior day's closing prices. We believe the reason for this is that prices went up $2\frac{1}{2}$ times as much during the period Kalay used to estimate historic returns as they did during the period of our ex-dividend day study. Thus, in analyzing the effect of transaction costs we used data from our original article. However, it should be emphasized that similarities in our results far exceed the differences. Kalay and we find a decline less than the amount of the dividend despite differences in adjustment procedures.

III Conclusion

We believe that Kalay has seriously underestimated transaction costs and has adjusted closing prices in a way that is no better than the method we used in our original article. The fact that he still finds results which are "consistent with a tax effect and a tax induced clientele effect" is powerful evidence of the robustness of these influences.[9]

Notes

1. This assertion is also used uncritically by others. See, for example, Miller and Scholes [8] or Copeland and Weston [1]. Kalay calls this short-term strategy arbitrage. It is not arbitrage in the usual use of the term since it involves positive investment with a positive probability of negative returns.

2. The column he labels $(P_B - P_A)/D$ in Table II is really $(P_B - \bar{P}_X)/D$ as properly described in the text following his Table II.

3. Kalay argues that for broker dealers both dividends and capital gains are taxed as ordinary income. Thus, for this group the form of the return does not affect taxes. While corporations are taxed at a higher rate on capital gains than on dividends, the transaction costs encountered by corporations precludes them from engaging in profitable short-term trading.

4. Transfer taxes were paid on transactions that took place in New York. Regional firms paid these taxes in full until the law changed in June 1, 1969. After that point they paid a nonresident tax which was very close to but lower than the resident tax.

5. There is obviously both a buyer and seller on all transactions. The party initiating a trade incurs the bulk of the transaction costs associated with the bid-ask spread. Thus, an investor putting in a market order to buy on the day before the stock goes ex-dividend and selling on the ex-dividend day would likely pay a bid-ask spread.

6. See [3], [4], [6], [9], and [11].

7. Even if one accepts Kalay's Table II as appropriate there is at most one group (group 20) for which ex-dividend behavior may be affected by short-term traders and this only occurs for a small sample of high priced stocks selling at very high dividend yield.

8. Some of the differences between Kalay's results and ours may be accounted for by the difference in our sample. Our sample included all stocks which paid a dividend in our test period except for those companies with dividends subject to special tax treatment. Kalay

uses a *sample* of stocks from the period and does not mention any attempt to eliminate stocks with special tax treatment of dividends.

9. See Kalay [5, p. 1059].

References

1. T. E. Copeland and J. F. Weston. *Financial Theory and Corporate Policy*. Reading, Mass.: Addison-Wesley, 1979.

2. E. J. Elton and M. J. Gruber. "Marginal Stockholder Tax Rates and the Clientele Effect: A Reply." *Review of Economics and Statistics* 52 (February 1970), 68–74.

3. J. Hamilton. "Competition, Scale Economics, and Transaction Costs in the Stock Market." *Journal of Financial and Quantitative Analysis* (December 1976), 779–802.

4. ———. "Market Place Organization and Marketability: NASDAQ, the Stock Exchange and the National Market System." *Journal of Finance* 33 (May 1978).

5. A. Kalay. "The Ex-Dividend Day Behavior of Stock Prices: A Re-Examination of the Clientele Effect." *Journal of Finance* 37 (September 1982), 1059–70.

6. A. Kraus and H. Stoll. "Price Impacts of Block Trading in the New York Stock Exchange." *Journal of Finance* 27 (June 1972), 569–88.

7. R. Litzenberger and K. Ramaswamy. "The Effect of Personal Tax and Dividends on Capital Asset Prices: Theory and Empirical Evidence." *Journal of Financial Economics* 7 (June 1979), 163–95.

8. M. H. Miller and M. S. Scholes. "Dividends and Taxes: Some Empirical Evidence." Unpublished manuscript, University of Chicago.

9. F. Reiley and W. Slaughton. "The Effect of Dual Markets on Common Stock Market Making." *Journal of Financial and Quantitative Analysis* (March 1973), 167–82.

10. *Securities Industry Study*. Government Printing Office, 1972.

11. S. Tinic and R. West. "Marketability of Common Stocks in Canada and the USA: A Comparison of Agent versus Dealer Dominated Markets." *Journal of Finance* 29 (June 1974), 729–46.

23

A Simple Examination of the Empirical Relationship between Dividend Yields and Deviations from the CAPM

Edwin Elton, Martin Gruber, and Joel Rentzler

I Introduction

Several papers have been published in recent years dealing with both the theoretical and the empirical impact of dividend yields on security returns. Dividends have been postulated as affecting stock returns because of tax effects [see Elton and Gruber (1970, 1978), Litzenberger and Ramaswamy (1979)], information effects [see Aharony and Swary (1980), Taub (1976), Pettit (1972, 1976) and Watts (1973, 1976)], agency costs [see Jensen and Meckling (1976)], and the Wealth Transfer Hypothesis [see Kalay (1980)].[1] In this paper we perform a purely empirical examination of whether and to what extent deviations from the zero beta form of the CAPM are explained by dividend yields. The paper demonstrates that dividend yield has a large and statistically significant impact on return above and beyond that explained by the zero beta form of the CAPM. This is consistent with the findings of Litzenberger and Ramaswamy (1979). In addition our results are consistent with the findings of small firm effects which are documented by Roll (1980), Banz (1981) and Reinganum (1981). The next section of this paper describes our procedure while the following section presents the results.

II Methodology

The study utilizes the monthly data on dividends, prices and returns for New York Stock Exchange securities available on the University of Chicago's CRSP tape. The period covered by this study is from January 1927 through December 1976. Since we are interested in examining the relationship between deviations from the zero beta CAPM and dividend yield, we must calculate estimates of each of these variables.

Our first step was to estimate the zero beta CAPM. In order to reduce the error in measuring beta which is used as input in estimating the CAPM, the portfolio grouping procedure employed by several previous researchers was employed [see Black, Jensen and Scholes (1972), and Fama and MacBeth (1973)]. The beta for each stock was calculated based on five years of data (e.g., 1927–1931) and using the CRSP value weighted index.[2] All stocks were ranked and grouped into twenty portfolios on the basis of these betas. The beta for each portfolio was then calculated using data for the next five years (e.g., 1932–1936). This beta was then employed as the best estimate of the beta of each portfolio for 1937. This procedure was repeated changing each of the 5 year periods by 1 year so that we had beta estimates for 20 portfolios for 40 yearly periods (1937–1976).[3] For each of these years the average return on each portfolio j was calculated and the following cross-sectional regression was run:

$$\bar{R}_j^t = \gamma_0^t + \gamma_1^t \beta_j^t + \tilde{\varepsilon}_j^t, \qquad j = 1, \ldots, 20, \qquad \text{where}$$

$\bar{R}_j^t$ = average return on portfolio j in year t,

β_j^t = estimated beta for portfolio j in year t,

γ_0^t, γ_1^t = cross-sectional coefficients estimated for year t,

$\tilde{\varepsilon}_j^t$ = random error term in year t.

The excess return α_i^t for each security i in year t was then defined as

$$\alpha_i^t = \bar{R}_i^t - (\hat{\gamma}_0^t + \hat{\gamma}_1^t \beta_i^t), \qquad i = 1, \ldots, N,$$

where β_i^t is the estimated beta of the portfolio to which security i belongs, $\hat{\gamma}_0^t$, $\hat{\gamma}_1^t$ are the estimated cross-sectional coefficients for year t. This value for alpha was used as the best estimate of alpha for each of the securities in a particular portfolio.

Our next step was to obtain a forecast of the dividend yield for year t (year 11) where the first forecast of dividend yield was made when year 11 was 1937. In order to obtain this estimate we decided to use the dividend yield on a portfolio of stocks rather than on each individual stock. There is substantial forecast error in the estimate of a security's yield. By utilizing the dividend yield for a portfolio of stocks rather than an individual security we hoped to reduce this forecast error. Stocks were grouped by their dividend yield in year 9—two years before the forecast year.[4] Twenty groups were formed. The first 19 groups were formed by ordering all stocks which paid positive dividends from highest to lowest

Table 23.1
Percent of stocks with zero dividend yield in grouping year.

Grouping year	Forecast year	All stocks	Stocks under $5 eliminated
1935	1937	54.4%	45.4%
1939	1941	44.0	32.0
1943	1945	23.6	17.8
1947	1949	13.6	10.6
1951	1953	11.3	9.3
1955	1957	11.5	10.6
1959	1961	14.5	13.8
1963	1965	13.2	11.5
1967	1969	9.1	9.1
1971	1973	16.2	14.8
1974	1976	11.0	6.1

and then dividing these stocks into 19 equal groups. The 20th group contained all stocks that paid zero dividends during year $t-2$ (year 9).

Placing all stocks with zero dividends into one group is in contrast with the procedure used in some prior studies [e.g., Black and Scholes (1974)]. Our purpose in grouping was to reduce forecast error while at the same time obtaining portfolios with a wide range of dividend yields. In some periods stocks with zero dividend yields were so numerous that if we had an equal number of stocks in each portfolio grouping, then a large number of these portfolios would have had zero dividend yields. Table 23.1 shows the percentage of stocks in our sample that did not pay a dividend in year $t-2$. For example putting an equal number of stocks in each group would have resulted in about half the portfolios having zero dividend yield in the early years and two or three with this zero yield in later years. Having formed the 20 portfolios we then had to forecast the dividend yield for year t (year 11). We used as our forecast the actual dividend yield in year $t-1$ (year 10).[5]

The next step was to relate excess return to dividend yield. First the average excess return, $\bar{\alpha}_j$, and average forecasted dividend yield, $\bar{\delta}_j$, for each portfolio j was computed. The average was taken over the 40 forecast years (1937–1976). Then a cross-sectional regression of the form

$$\bar{\alpha}_j = A_0 + A_1\bar{\delta}_j + \bar{\varepsilon}_j, \qquad j = 1, \ldots, 20$$

was run to obtain estimates of A_0 and A_1. This averaging process was repeated using all eight non-overlapping 5-year subperiods in our 40 year sample giving eight other estimates of A_0 and A_1.

As will become clear later, there were reasons to suspect that the zero dividend group of stocks would behave perversely. To test this, a regression of the following form was run:

$$\tilde{\alpha}_j = A_0' + A_1'\bar{\delta}_j + A_2'D + \tilde{\varepsilon}_j, \qquad j = 1, \ldots, 20$$

In this regression D is a dummy variable having a value of 1 for the portfolio of stocks which paid zero dividends in the grouping year and a value of 0 for all other groups.

Note that this methodology is designed so that forecasts of both the betas and the dividend yields employed in the analysis use only data which is available prior to the dates over which the returns are calculated. Thus, the existence of an excess return with respect to dividend yield indicates that an investor in the absence of transaction costs could have acted in a way to earn an extra return using available information. This would not necessarily indicate that he could have earned an excess return because of the presence of transaction costs and additional non-market risk incurred. However it does indicate an additional influence on equilibrium returns. Note also that our procedure is designed so that if there is a bias it is *against* finding a dividend influence. If betas are correlated with dividend yields then our two step procedure would have a bias towards finding no dividend effect even when one was present. This was a deliberate choice on our part. As has been discussed in the literature, there is considerable disagreement on the reasonableness of the procedures used for the joint estimation of dividend and beta effects. Our procedure, while biased against observing dividend effects, avoids the estimation controversy. Thus, finding a dividend effect with this procedure would provide strong evidence in support of such an effect.

III Results

Table 23.2a summarizes the statistical relationship between the average yearly excess return (alpha) and the average dividend yield in each of the 20 groups where the averages are taken over the entire forecast period 1937–1976. By examining the first row of data in table 23.2a we see that although there is a significant positive relationship between excess return and dividend yield over the entire period, the relationship is small. The R^2 for the relationship is only 0.188.

Table 23.2a
Cross-sectional regressions of average excess return on dividend yield over 40 year forecast period (*t*-values in parentheses).

Forecast period	Intercept	Dividend coefficient	Dummy variable coefficient	R^2
1937–1976	−2.263	0.344		0.188
	(2.59)	(2.04)		
	−4.774	0.794	6.189	0.874
	(−10.87)	(9.60)	(9.64)	

As examination of the data used in obtaining these regression results (table 23.3) shows that the weak positive association may be due to the presence of two distinct relationships.[6] Note that portfolio 20, which was formed two years before the forecast year using all stocks which did not pay a dividend, has a high positive excess return (alpha). The return on this group is considerably higher than the return on any other group though it has by far the lowest yield in the year prior to the forecast (year 10) and so the lowest forecasted yield. These zero dividend stocks constitute an outlier group. This finding is not surprising and has been noted earlier by Blume (1979). Later in this section we will examine some possible explanations for the observed high excess return in this group. Before turning to this discussion we will first eliminate the effect this group has on the dividend yield-excess return relationship. This could be accomplished either by deleting this group from the data or by adding a dummy variable which has a value of one for the non-dividend portfolio group (number 20) and zero for all other groups. These two procedures are identical in their effects on the intercept and slope term. The advantages of using a dummy variable is that it allows a direct measurement and a test of significance for the difference of behavior of the excess return in the zero dividend group. The results of including this dummy variable in the regression for the entire forecast period are shown in the second line of table 23.2a. Notice that now the positive relationship between excess return and dividend yield is both large (0.794) and statistically significant at the 1% level. Furthermore the portfolio constructed from stocks which had paid zero dividends has an excess return beyond what one would expect given the behavior of the other portfolios. The value of 6.189 is statistically significant at the 1% level. The inclusion of the dummy variable also raises the coefficient of determination on the regression from 0.188 to 0.874.

Table 23.2b
Cross-sectional regressions of average excess return on divident yield, over five year periods (t-values in parentheses).

Forecast period	Intercept	Dividend coefficient	Dummy variable coefficient	R^2
1937–1941	1.078	−0.091	−0.204	0.002
1942–1946	−13.790	1.076	25.745	0.853
1947–1951	−1.298	0.221	1.211	0.037
1952–1956	−1.082	0.216	−0.419	0.077
1957–1961	1.425	−0.337	−0.299	0.082
1962–1966	−1.448	0.218	5.588	0.477
1967–1971	−4.907	1.457	2.059	0.570
1972–1976	−11.868	2.629	10.727	0.883
Mean	−3.986	0.673	5.551	
	(2.075)	(2.062)	(1.862)	

As a further check on the form of this relationship, the regression including the dummy variable was run for each of the eight five year non-overlapping subperiods between 1937 and 1976. These results, reported in table 23.2b, are supportive of the overall relationship. The relationship between excess return and dividend yield is positive in six of the eight periods and on average the regression coefficient is significantly different from zero at the 5% level. The impact of the dummy variable is positive in five of the eight periods and its average value is positive and significant at the 5% level.

The high positive excess return associated with zero dividend stocks is important and worthy of additional attention. Is this an effect caused by low dividends or is there an alternative explanation? The most obvious alternative is that the result is due to a small firm effect. Small firms make up a much higher proportion of zero dividend stocks than they do of other groups and a number of authors have found that small firms on average have positive excess returns [see Roll (1980), Banz (1981) and Reinganum (1981)]. Thus the zero dividend effect we observe may be, in part or total, a small firm effect. At present there is no adequate explanation of the small firm effect. Roll has an argument that surely explains part of the phenomena. He shows that small firms have many more non-trading days then do large firms. He then demonstrates that non-trading leads to a downward bias in the beta. A downward biased beta leads

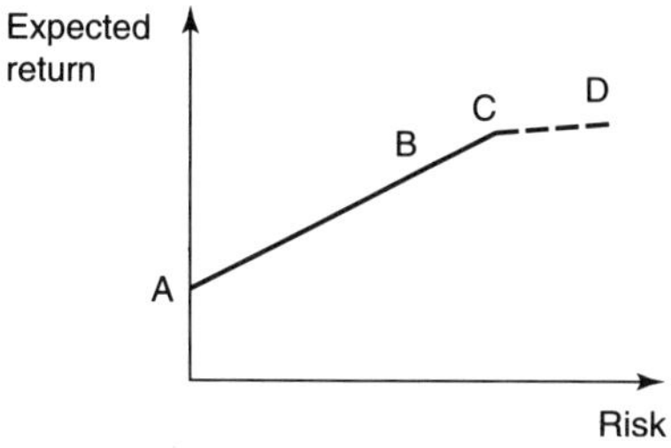

Figure 23.1

to a positive excess return if a zero excess return would exist using the unbiased beta.[7]

An alternative explanation of the positive excess return on the zero dividend stocks involves their price. Stocks under $5 in price are treated differently by brokerage firms and financial institutions and the zero dividend group of stocks contain a much higher proportion of these low price stocks than do the other dividend groups.[8] Stocks which sell for less than $5 are not considered as appropriate collateral for margin. Thus, in figuring the amount of assets in an account for purposes of margin, stocks under $5 are eliminated. Therefore, an investor who borrows or uses margin would find these stocks less attractive unless they offered a higher return. A similar argument can be seen by examining fig. 23.1.

The efficient frontier with borrowing restricted to margin is *ABCD*. The position of *CD* depends on the maximum borrowing that is available. If the borrowing limit is lowered then, *ceteris paribus*, the efficient frontier involving borrowing is lowered. Thus, stocks that reduce the amount that can be borrowed will be held only if their return compensates for this lowering of the frontier.

Low capitalization stocks in general sell for less than $5. Thus low price can serve as a proxy for low capitalization and it is difficult to be sure which factor might be causing positive excess returns. Roll's argument concerning infrequent trading of low capitalization stocks holds equally well for stocks selling under $5. However, the margin restrictions apply to stocks selling for less than $5 and not to low capitalization stocks. Thus we decided that, in order to separate the effect of low priced small capitalization stocks from the effect of zero dividend payment, it was most relevant to eliminate stocks selling for under $5 from our population.[9]

Tables 23.4 and 23.5 are analogous to tables 23.2 and 23.3 except that all stocks selling for less than $5 per share were eliminated. Examining the first row in table 23.4 shows that eliminating such stocks had a major

Table 23.3
Average portfolio dividend yield and average excess return over 40 year forecast period 1937–1976.

Portfolio number	1	2	3	4	5	6	7	8	9	10	11	12	13	14	15	16	17	18	19	20
Average dividend yield	7.48	7.31	6.89	6.53	6.41	6.09	5.86	5.58	5.37	5.13	4.80	4.62	4.40	4.25	3.89	3.67	3.32	3.08	2.40	0.73
Average excess return	1.23	0.61	−0.63	1.38	0.39	0.51	0.02	−0.31	0.11	−1.22	−0.37	−1.02	−1.41	−1.52	−1.78	−1.59	−2.23	−2.85	−2.89	1.99

Table 23.4a
Cross-sectional regressions of average excess return on dividend yield over 40 year forecast period with under $5 stocks eliminated ($t$-values in parentheses).

Forecast period	Intercept	Dividend coefficient	Dummy variable coefficient	R^2
1937–1976	−2.623	0.549		0.471
	(3.69)	(4.00)		
	−4.398	0.865	4.445	0.841
	(8.95)	(9.36)	(6.28)	

Table 23.4b
Cross-sectional regressions of average excess return on dividend yield over five year subperiods with under $5 stocks eliminated ($t$-values in parentheses).

Forecast period	Intercept	Dividend coefficient	Dummy variable coefficient	R^2
1937–1941	−0.789	0.369		0.044
1942–1946	−5.054	0.632		0.139
1947–1951	−0.518	0.101		0.012
1952–1956	−0.612	0.111		0.016
1957–1961	1.119	−0.269		0.051
1962–1966	0.416	−0.192		0.029
1967–1971	−4.631	1.437		0.602
1972–1976	−8.869	2.085		0.734
Mean	−2.367	0.534		
	(−2.072)	(1.951)		
1937–1941	−0.093	0.246	−1.341	0.052
1942–1946		1.402	15.063	0.765
1947–1951	−1.316	0.218	1.665	0.043
1952–1956	−1.185	0.201	1.246	0.036
1957–1961	1.176	−0.281	−0.132	0.052
1962–1966	−1.451	0.260	5.046	0.415
1967–1971	−4.838	1.488	0.733	0.604
1972–1976		2.450	8.181	0.845
Mean	−3.707	0.748	3.808	
	(2.337)	(2.443)	(2.102)	

effect. The impact of dividend yield on excess returns as measured by the regression coefficient has grown from 0.344 to 0.549 and is statistically significant at the 1% level. The coefficient of determination between dividend yield and excess return has changed from 0.188 to 0.471. Eliminating stocks under $5 per share reduced the unexplained excess return associated with the zero dividend group. This indicates that part of the peculiar behavior of this group was due to the inclusion of these low priced firms.

However not all of the peculiar behavior of this group is eliminated by removing $5 stocks from the sample. Table 23.5 shows that the return on portfolio 20 which had previously paid a zero dividend is 0.86% whereas the behavior of the other 19 groups would lead us to expect a negative excess return for portfolio 20. To test for perverse behavior on the part of the zero dividend portfolio, the regression was rerun with a dummy variable. The results again improved. As seen in the second line of table 23.4a, the t-value of the intercept and dividend yield coefficient both increase, the coefficient of determination increases, and the dummy variable enters with a positive and statistically significant (at the 1% level) coefficient.

Table 23.4b presents the regression results for all five year nonoverlapping periods with and without the dummy variable. The results continue to support the earlier findings that there is a strong positive association between excess returns and forecasts of dividend yield except for the group of stocks which had previously not paid a dividend. These stocks seem to earn a real premium above that which one would expect based on their forecasted beta and dividend yield.

IV Conclusions

In this article we have examined the relationship between residuals from the zero beta form of the capital asset pricing model and dividend yields. We have found a persistent relationship between dividend yield and excess returns. In particular, except for those stocks which had previously paid zero dividends, the higher the dividend yield the higher the excess return. One group of stocks, those which had previously paid no dividends, had excess returns which were above that we would expect from this relationship. Part of this differential was shown to be due to the effect of low priced stocks but an influence beyond that still seems to exist. There seems to be persistent patterns in excess returns which are related to dividend yield. Some of these differences may be due to tax effects. Others have not as yet been adequately explained.

Table 23.5
Average portfolio dividend yield and average excess return over 40 year forecast period 1937–1976 with under $5 stocks eliminated.

Portfolio number	1	2	3	4	5	6	7	8	9	10	11	12	13	14	15	16	17	18	19	20
Average dividend yield	7.56	7.28	6.91	6.55	6.41	6.10	5.83	5.59	5.39	5.15	4.81	4.60	4.42	4.27	3.93	3.69	3.31	3.11	2.37	0.94
Average excess return	2.12	1.29	0.45	2.15	1.14	1.64	1.13	0.41	0.91	−0.64	0.72	−0.67	−0.85	−1.17	−1.05	−1.00	−1.41	−2.20	−2.34	0.86

Notes

The authors would like to thank Dexter Corporation, Windsor Locks, Connecticut for funding this research.

1. The Wealth Transfer Hypothesis refers to the ability of stockholders to transfer wealth from creditors to stockholders by paying out assets in the form of dividends.

2. The analysis in this paper was also conducted using the CRSP equal weighted index. These results were indistinguishable from those reported in this paper.

3. The composition and size of each of these portfolios changed from year to year. The number of stocks which had the required data over each 11 year period and so were placed into portfolios varied from a low of 419 to a high of 880 with an average number of 740.

4. The arguments behind grouping on dividend yields are directly analogous to the arguments used in grouping on betas to provide better estimates. In forming groups we defined dividend yield as dividends in year 9 divided by the ending price. Our purpose was to obtain a set of portfolios with a wide range of yields in year 10.

5. We have employed the simplest possible forecast model in this paper setting next year's dividend yield equal to last year's dividend yield. If we had found no dividend yield effect it might have been due to the use of this naive forecasting model. However, the fact that we do get strong results with this naive model highlights the importance of the dividend effect. A more sophisticated forecasting model might lead to even stronger results.

6. In examining table 23.3 recall that group 20 has many more members than other portfolios. Thus although most groups have negative alphas, the average overall alpha is close to zero.

7. The use of monthly data rather than daily reduces the importance of this effect.

8. Many financial institutions will not hold low priced stocks due to either transaction costs or perceived risk.

9. At a number of points in the study we eliminated low capitalization stocks rather than those selling for less than $5. This didn't have a significant impact on the results and so these results are not reported.

References

Aharony, J. and I. Swary, 1980, Quarterly dividend and earnings announcements and stockholders' returns: An empirical analysis, *Journal of Finance* 35, no. 1, March, 1–12.

Banz, R., 1981, The relationship between return and market value of common stocks, *Journal of Financial Economics* 9, no. 1, March, 3–18.

Black, F. and M. Scholes, 1974, The effects of dividend yield and dividend policy on common stock prices and returns, *Journal of Financial Economics* 1, no. 1, March, 1–22.

Black, F., M. Jensen and M. Scholes, 1972, The capital asset pricing model: Some empirical tests, in: M.C. Jensen, ed., *Studies in the theory of capital markets* (Praeger, New York).

Blume, M., 1979, Stock returns and dividend yields: Some more evidence, Rodney L. White Center for Financial Research, Working paper no. 1–79.

Elton, E. and M. Gruber, 1970, Marginal stockholders' tax rates and the clientele effect, *Review of Economics and Statistics* 52, no. 1, Feb., 68–74.

Elton, E. and M. Gruber, 1978, Taxes and portfolio compensation, *Journal of Financial Economics* 6, no. 4, Dec., 399–410.

Fama, E. and J. MacBeth, 1973, Risk, return and equilibrium: empirical tests, *Journal of Political Economy* 81, no. 3, 607–636.

Jensen, M. and W. Meckling, 1976, Theory of the firm: Management behavior, agency costs and capital structure, *Journal of Financial Economics* 3, no. 4, Oct., 305–360.

Kalay, A., 1980, The dividend decision and the conflict of interest between bondholders and stockholders, Working paper (New York University, New York).

Litzenburger, R. and K. Ramaswamy, 1979, The effect of personal taxes and dividends on capital asset prices: Theory and empirical evidence, *Journal of Financial Economics* 7, no. 2, June, 163–195.

Pettit, R., 1972, Dividend announcements, security performance and capital market efficiency, *Journal of Finance* 27, no. 5, Dec., 993–1008.

Pettit, R., 1976, The impact of dividend and earnings announcements: A reconciliation, *Journal of Business* 49, no. 1, Jan., 86–96.

Reinganum, M., 1981, Misspecification of capital asset pricing: Empirical anomalies based on earnings' yields and market values, *Journal of Financial Economics* 9, no. 1, March, 19–46.

Roll, R., 1980, A possible explantion of the small firm effect, U.C.L.A. Graduate School of Management, Working paper, Oct.

Taub, M., 1976, On the information content of dividends, *Journal of Business* 49, no. 1, Jan., 73–80.

Watts, R., 1973, The informational content of dividends, *Journal of Business* 46, no. 2, April, 191–211.

Watts, R., 1976, Comments on "The informational content of dividends," *Journal of Business* 49, no. 1, Jan., 81–85.

24 Taxes and Portfolio Composition

Edwin J. Elton and Martin J. Gruber

I Introduction

The implication that under the Sharpe–Lintner–Mossin form of the CAPM all investors should hold the market portfolio is well known. When one considers the fact that income and capital gains are taxed at different rates, then except under the special circumstances derived by Long (1977), one will get (1) a different equilibrium relationship for the capital markets (the post-tax CAPM of Brennan), and (2) a different model of optimal investor behavior.

This paper addresses the following problem. Assume an investor recognizing his tax liability wishes to select portfolios on the assumption that either the Sharpe–Lintner–Mossin form or the post-tax form of the CAPM holds. Then what is the optimum portfolio for him to hold? Under what circumstances is it the market portfolio? When it differs from the market portfolio, what are the characteristics of securities that should be held in greater or lesser proportions by any investor?

More precise answers to these questions can be reached if we are willing to make simplifying assumptions about the variance-covariance structure of returns. We shall explore the answers to these problems under two specific models of how covariance structure is determined: the single index model and the constant correlation model. The single index model is standard and needs no introduction here. The constant correlation model is based on the assumption that the correlation coefficient between each pair of securities can be considered to be constant.[1]

II The General Case

In this section of the paper, we examine the optimal portfolio holdings of investors when no special assumptions are made about the variance-covariance structure of returns. We first assume that investors act as if prices are determined by the capital asset pricing model that results from portfolio decisions being made on the basis of post-tax returns. We then briefly review the results when investors are assumed to act as if the Sharpe–Lintner–Mossin form of the CAPM determines prices. The conclusions we can reach in this section are quite limited and add further motivation for examination of models which assume simplified forms of the covariance structure.

In appendix B we derive the following expression for the portfolio behavior of an investor who is subject to taxes and believes that prices are determined by the post-tax CAPM,

$$Z_{k,i} = HX_k + (T_i - T_m)C_k, \tag{1}$$

where

$Z_{k,i}$ = a number which is proportional to the fraction of the ith investor's portfolio which should be invested in stock k.

X_k = the fraction of the market portfolio which consists of stock k.

H = the market price of risk for the post-tax capital asset pricing model (see appendix A).

T_i = the difference between the ith investor's marginal capital gains tax rate and his income tax rate divided by one minus his capital gains tax rate.

T_m = the effective average value of T_i for the market (see appendix A).

C_k = a constant for the kth security; C_k is defined in appendix B.

In appendix B of this paper we also derive the optimal portfolio behavior for investors under the assumption of the Sharpe–Lintner–Mossin form of the CAPM. We show that

$$Z_{k,i} = H'X_k + T_iC_k, \tag{2}$$

where H' is the market price of risk for the pre-tax capital asset pricing model.

We will now proceed to examine the implications of eq. (1) for the composition of an investor's portfolio. If the tax rate for the market is equal to the individual's tax rate, then the optimal investment for the individual is the market proportions in each security. This conclusion follows from noting that if $T_i = T_m$, then the second term in eq. (1) is zero. Furthermore, Z_{ki} is proportional to the optimal fraction of the ith investor's portfolio and dividing $Z_{k,i}$ by a constant does not affect this property of $Z_{k,i}$. Hence, dividing both sides of eq. (1) by H yields a new $Z_{k,i}$ which is equal to $Z'_{k,i}$. However, the $Z'_{k,i}$ are already scaled to add to one so that no further scaling is needed for the new $Z'_{k,i}$'s.

Consequently, when investors desire to make investment decisions on the assumption that the post-tax capital asset pricing model generates returns in the market place, they hold the market portfolio if the individual's tax rate equals the market tax rate. Making a parallel argument for eq. (2) if investors wish to make investment decisions based on the assumption that the pre-tax capital asset pricing model reflects risk–return opportunities in the market, then they invest in the market portfolio if the individual's tax rate is zero.

We can use eqs. (1) and (2) to examine the portfolio composition of investors with different tax rates. In particular, we will examine two questions. First, which securities are held in greater than market proportions and which are held in less? Second, what are the characteristics of a security which determine how 'unbalanced' the investor's portfolio will be with respect to it? For example, if securities A and B are held in greater than market proportions which deviates more from its market proportion? To examine the first of these questions, we will compare the percentage of security k in investor i's portfolio with the percentage security k represents of the market. Let X_k represent the market proportion of security k and recognize that $Z_{k,i}/\sum_k Z_{k,i}$ is the fraction of his portfolio that investor i holds in security k. An investor holds more than the market proportion in security k if

$$Z_{k,i}\Big/\sum_k Z_{k,i} > X_k.$$

Substituting in eq. (1) yields

$$\frac{HX_K + (T_i - T_m)C_k}{H + (T_i - T_m)\sum_k C_k} > X_k.$$

Rearranging and simplifying shows that security k will be held in greater than market proportions, if

$$C_k\Big/\sum_k C_k \begin{cases} > X_k & \text{if} \quad T_i > T_m, \\ < X_k & \text{if} \quad T_i < T_m. \end{cases} \tag{3}$$

The value of all terms except T_i are independent of the investor under consideration. All investors with the same relationship of T_i to T_m will hold the same stocks in greater than market proportions. In essence, there are three sets of investors. Investors with $T_i = T_m$ hold market proportions. Investors with $T_i > T_m$ hold stocks with $C_k/\sum_k C_k > X_k$ in greater than market proportions, stocks with $C_k/\sum_k C_k = X_k$ in market proportions and all other stocks in less than market proportions. Finally, the third group of investors for which $T_i < T_m$ act exactly opposite to the second group.

The analysis when the investor wishes to act as if the Sharpe–Lintner–Mossin C.A.P.M. holds is similar. Utilizing eq. (2) in analysis parallel to that just undertaken yields a set of equations identical to eq. (3) except that zero replaces T_m in the right-hand set of inequalities. Given the predominance of income tax rates above capital gain tax rates, most investors will tilt their portfolio in favor of stocks with low dividends and it is unlikely that markets will clear at the prices determined by the Sharpe–Lintner–Mossin form of the CAPM.[2]

The second question worth examining is the condition under which one stock will be held in a higher percentage relative to its market proportions than will a second. Stock j is held in a greater percentage of its market proportion if

$$\frac{Z_{j,i} \Big/ \sum_j Z_{j,i}}{X_j} > \frac{Z_{k,i} \Big/ \sum_k Z_{k,i}}{X_k}.$$

Substituting, rearranging and cancelling yields

$$C_j/X_j > C_k/X_k \quad \text{if} \quad T_i > T_m, \tag{4}$$

$$< C_k/X_k \quad \text{if} \quad T_i < T_m. \tag{5}$$

The values of the C's and X's are independent of the investor under consideration. Therefore the relationship of T_i to T_m determines the extent of the deviation of investor i's portfolio from market proportions. If stock j is held in a greater proportion of its market percentage than stock k for an investor in a tax bracket above the market average tax bracket , then this is true for all investors in tax brackets above the average.

Similar results hold if the no tax CAPM model adequately describes returns. In this case, the analysis follows from setting $T_m = 0$.

We now know that most investors will not hold the market portfolio. To make more precise statements about optimal portfolio composition we must know C_k. But C_k depends on both the excess dividend yield on all stocks and the properties of the inverse of the variance–covariance matrix. More can be learned about investor behavior if we introduce simplifying assumptions about the variance covariance structure of security returns.

III The Single Index Model

In this section of the paper we examine the optimal portfolio holdings of investors under the assumption that they estimate the joint movement of securities employing the assumptions of the single index model. Eq. (3) still holds and the implications of this equation as discussed in section 2 remain valid. However, the special form of the single index model allows us to get more insight into the problem.

In particular, utilizing eq. (B-3) from the appendix, eq. (3) becomes[3]

$$\left[\begin{array}{ll} \dfrac{\beta_k}{\sigma^2_{\varepsilon,k}}\left[\dfrac{\delta_k - R_F}{\beta_k} - C_0\right]\dfrac{1}{C_1} > X_k & \text{for} \quad T_i > T_m \\ \qquad\qquad\qquad\qquad\quad < X_k & \text{for} \quad T_i < T_m \end{array}\right] \tag{6}$$

Eq. (6) represents the case where general equilibrium is derived in terms of after tax returns. Setting $T_m = 0$ would make eq. (6) appropriate for the case where general equilibrium is derived in terms of pre-tax returns (the Sharpe–Lintner–Mossin CAPM).

Note that C_0 and C_1 are constants with respect to both all stocks and all investors. Assume for the moment that $T_i < T_m$ or that the investor is subject to a higher tax rate than the effective tax rate in the market. It is clear from eq. (6) that for positive Beta stocks, the lower the dividend yield, all other things being equal, the more likely the stock is to be held in more than market proportions. Also we see from eq. (6) that if two stocks have identical Betas, residual risk and dividend yields an investor who pays a tax rate higher than the effective average in the market is more likely to hold more than market proportions of the stock which represents a larger share of the market (has a higher X_k). An investor with a tax rate lower than the effective rate in the market will act in the opposite manner.[4]

If we employ the pre-tax equilibrium model, all of the above analysis holds except that zero should be substituted for T_m. That is, the investors' reaction to dividend yield is determined by whether his tax rate on ordinary income is greater than or less than his tax on capital gains, rather than the effective average tax rate in the market.

We can learn about the characteristics of stocks in which an investor unbalances the most by substituting eq. (B-3) in eqs. (4) and (5). For an investor with a tax rate above the average rate in the market, we find that for stock j to be held in a larger proportion relative to its market weight than stock k is held relative to its market weight,

$$\frac{\beta_j}{\sigma^2_{\varepsilon,j}}\left[\frac{\delta_j - R_F}{\beta_j} - C_0\right] < \frac{\beta_k}{\sigma^2_{\varepsilon,k}}\left[\frac{\delta_k - R_F}{\beta_k} - C_0\right]\frac{X_j}{X_k}.$$

It is clear from the above expression that for positive Beta stocks, the lower the dividend yield on a stock the more likely (other things being equal) it is to be held in a higher percentage of its market proportion. If an investor is subject to a tax rate which is lower than the effective average rate in the market, the above inequality is reversed and the investor is likely to unbalance in favor of high dividend paying stocks.[5]

IV The Constant Correlation Model

This section of the paper will parallel the previous section but will make an alternative assumption about the mechanism generating the covariance structure of security returns. Specifically, we will assume that the correlation coefficient between the returns on all pairs of stocks is the same.

Employing eq. (B-4), eq. (3) can be written as[6]

$$\frac{1}{\sigma_k}\left[\frac{\delta_k - R_F}{\sigma_k} - C_0\right]\frac{1}{C_1} > X_k \quad \text{for} \quad T_i > T_m, \qquad (7)$$
$$< X_k \quad \text{for} \quad T_i < T_m.$$

A similar set of expressions follow with respect to the pre-tax CAPM model. The difference is that T_m is replaced with zero in the inequalities on the right side of eq. (7). Once again, as in section 3, we see that the investor who pays a higher tax than the average for the market is more likely to hold stocks with low dividend yields in more than market proportions. Furthermore, for two stocks with the same characteristics, he is more likely to hold the one which represents a large share of the market in more than market proportions.[7] Investors who pay taxes at a rate below the market average will act in the opposite manner.

We can learn more about which of two stocks will be held in larger proportions relative to their market proportions by making use of the special properties of the constant correlation model. In particular, eq. (3) can be written as

$$C_j^* < C_k^* \frac{X_j}{X_k} \quad \text{where} \quad C_j^* = C_j(1-\rho).$$

Making use of eq. (B-4) the C_j^*'s can be interpreted as a very good approximation of the amount by which a stock's dividend yield minus the risk-free rate divided by the stock's standard deviation exceeds the average of the same ratio for the market, with the difference divided by the stock's standard deviation.[8] This inequality then says that an investor who has a tax rate higher than the average tax rate in the market will hold less of a stock (relative to its share in the market) as compared to a second stock if the first stock has a higher C^* relative to its market share than does the second. Thus, the investor with the higher than average tax rate will not hold the market portfolio but will tilt his portfolio in favor of stocks with lower dividends and lower standard deviations.

The analysis for an investor with a tax rate lower than the effective average tax rate in the market is directly analogous and this investor should behave in the opposite manner from the case discussed above.

There is one more case than can further clarify the implications of this analysis for optimum investor behavior. Let us identity the stock k such that $C_k^* = 0$. This stock k is a stock which has a $(\delta_k - R_F)/\sigma_k$ (excess dividend yield to risk) approximately equal to the average excess dividend yield to risk of all stocks in the market.[9] If $C_k^* = 0$, eq. (9) becomes $C_j^* < 0$ for investors with tax rates above the average effective tax rate in the market. Thus investors with tax rates above the effective average should all place a higher fraction of their funds (relative to market proportions) in stocks which have a ratio of excess dividend yields to standard deviation below the average than they place in the stock which has an excess dividend yield to standard deviation equal to the average. Since the inequality is reversed for investors with tax rates below the average, they will hold more of their portfolio in high dividend paying stocks and less in low dividend paying stocks. Once again, in the case where the standard CAPM is believed to hold, the above analysis follows if zero is substituted for the average market tax rate.

V Conclusion

In this paper, we have investigated the impact of personal taxes on the optimum portfolio composition of individual investors. We have demonstrated that even if the investor believes that the standard form of the CAPM is an exact description of returns in the market, he might not hold a market portfolio if he must pay taxes. We have investigated the properties of those stocks that he will hold in more than market proportions and those that he will hold in less than market proportions. The results indicate that if investors look at post-tax returns the market is unlikely to clear at prices set by the standard CAPM model. We have then derived a post-tax CAPM model and demonstrated the optimum portfolio holdings for investors if this model describes returns in the market. Under the post-tax capital asset pricing model as under the standard CAPM, the optimal portfolio holdings of investors becomes a function of the investor's tax rate, the dividend yield on alternative securities, and the risk characteristics of alternate securities. Pettit and Stanley (1977) use survey data on individual investor portfolio composition to analyze whether taxes influence portfolio choice. Consistent with the predictions of this analysis, they find that there is a significant relationship between investor tax rates and portfolio choice.

Appendix A

In this appendix we derive a Capital Asset Pricing Model assuming investors make portfolio decisions on the basis of post-tax returns. An alternative proof of the post-tax capital asset pricing is contained in Brennan (1970). We shall make the normal assumption of homogeneous beliefs about pre-tax returns. However, since different investors are subject to different tax rates, beliefs about the post-tax returns will be different.

As shown in Lintner (1965) the portfolio problem can be viewed as maximizing the ratio of excess returns to risk.[10] Expressing this is after-tax terms,

$$\max \frac{X_i' R(1 - t_{gi}) + X_i' \delta(t_{gi} - t_{oi})}{X_i' \Sigma X_i (1 - t_{gi})^2}, \tag{A-1}$$

where

R = a vector of excess returns on securities.

δ = a vector of excess dividend yields on securities (divided yields minus the risk-free rate).

t_{gi} = the marginal capital gains tax rate for investor i.

t_{oi} = the marginal ordinary income tax rate for investor i.

X_i = the vector of the fraction of his risky portfolio which investor i places in each stock.

Σ = the variance covariance matrix of returns.

From first-order conditions

$$R + T_i\delta = K_i \Sigma X_i,$$

where

$$T_i = (t_{gi} - t_{oi})/(1 - t_{gi}),$$

and K_i is a constant for investor i which is equal to the maximum value of (A-1) times $(1 - t_{gi})$.

Rearranging

$$X_i = K_i^{-1}\Sigma^{-1}(R + T_i\delta). \tag{A-2}$$

Recognizing from market clearing conditions that

$$\sum_i W_i X_i \bigg/ \sum_i W_i = X_m, \tag{A-3}$$

where W_i is the amount of wealth which the ith investor places in his portfolio of risky assets, and X_m is the vector of market weights.

Substituting eq. (A-2) into (A-3)

$$\left(\sum_i (W_i/K_i) \bigg/ \sum_i W_i\right)\Sigma^{-1}R + \left(\sum_i (W_i T_i/K_i) \bigg/ \sum_i W_i\right)\Sigma^{-1}\delta = X_m,$$

or

$$R = H\Sigma X_m - T_m\delta, \tag{A-4}$$

where

$$T_m = \sum_i (W_i T_i/K_i) \bigg/ \sum_i (W_i/K_i), \qquad H = \sum_i W_i \bigg/ \sum_i (W_i/K_i).$$

T_m is a weighted average of investor tax rates. Since eq. (A-4) must hold for all assets and portfolios including the market portfolio

$$H = \frac{\bar{R}_m - R_F}{\sigma_m^2} + \frac{\delta_m - R_F}{\sigma_m^2} T_m.$$

Appendix B

Define the $N \times 1$ vector

$$Z = K_i X.$$

As pointed out by Lintner, the objective function (A-1) is homogeneous of degree zero. Thus, the solution to the problem with the Z's is the same as the solution to the problem involving the X's. Eq. (A-2) can be written as

$$Z = \Sigma^{-1}(R + T_i\delta).$$

If the after-tax version of the capital asset pricing model holds, eq. (A-4) holds. Substituting into the above expression

$$Z = HX_M + (T_i - T_m)\Sigma^{-1}\delta.$$

With homogeneous expectations, the value of $\Sigma^{-1}\delta$ is independent of the particular investor under consideration. Defining the $N \times 1$ vector C as $\Sigma^{-1}\delta$ yields

$$Z = HX_M + (T_i - T_M)C. \tag{B-1}$$

If the pre-tax capital asset pricing model holds, then

$$R = H'\Sigma X_M$$

where

$$H' = (\bar{R}_M - R_F)/\sigma_M^2,$$

and

$$Z = H'X_M + T_iC. \tag{B-2}$$

If one is willing to make special assumptions about the variance–covariance matrix then simplified forms of the inverse of the variance–covariance matrix exist and C has some interesting special forms. Two assumptions about the variance–covariance matrix are known to yield simple structures for the inverse of the variance-covariance matrix; these are the variance–covariance matrix that result from assuming the single index model and the variance–covariance matrix that results from assuming the correlation coefficient is a constant between any pair of securities. If the single index model is assumed, the main diagonal element of the inverse of the variance-covariance matrix in row k has a value equal to

$$\frac{1 + \sigma_M^2\left(\sum_{j=1}^{n}(\beta_j^2/\sigma_{\varepsilon,j}^2 - \sigma_M^2(\beta_k^2/\sigma_{\varepsilon,k}^2)\right)}{\sigma_{\varepsilon,k}^2\left(1 + \sigma_m^2\sum_{j=1}^{n}(\beta_j^2/\sigma_{\varepsilon,j}^2)\right)},$$

where $\sigma^2_{\varepsilon,k}$ is the variance of the residuals from the single index model for the kth stock. The off-diagonal element k, j for $j > k$ is equal to

$$\frac{-\sigma_M^2\beta_k\beta_j}{\sigma^2_{\varepsilon,k}\sigma^2_{\varepsilon,j}\left(1+\sigma_M^2\sum_{p=1}^{n}(\beta_p^2/\sigma^2_{\varepsilon,p})\right)}.$$

The off-diagonal element k, j for $k > j$ is

$$\frac{-\sigma_M^2(\beta_k^2/\sigma^2_{\varepsilon,k})}{\sigma^2_{\varepsilon,k}\left(1+\sigma_M^2\sum_{p=1}^{N}(\beta_p^2/\sigma^2_{\varepsilon,p})\right)}.$$

Using these expressions to determine C yields for the kth row

$$C_k = \frac{\beta_k}{\sigma^2_{\varepsilon,k}}\left[\frac{\delta_k - R_F}{\beta_k} - \frac{\sigma_M^2\sum_{j=1}^{N}\{(\delta_j - R_F)\beta_j/\sigma^2_{\varepsilon,j}\}}{1+\sigma_M^2\sum_{j=1}^{N}(\beta_j^2/\sigma^2_{\varepsilon,j})}\right]. \tag{B-3}$$

This expression was derived in another context in Elton, Gruber and Padberg (1976).

If one assumes that the correlation coefficient between any two securities is the same and is equal to ρ, then the element jj of the inverse of the variance–covariance matrix is equal to

$$\frac{(1+\rho)(1/\sigma_j^2)}{(1-\rho)(1+(N-1)\rho)},$$

the off-diagonal elements in row k, column j are equal to

$$\frac{-\rho(1/\sigma_k\sigma_j)}{(1-\rho)(1+(N-1)\rho)}.$$

Using these expressions to determine C yields for the jth row

$$C_j = \frac{1}{(1-\rho)\sigma_j}\left[\frac{\delta_j - R_F}{\sigma_j} - \frac{\rho}{1-\rho+N\rho}\sum_{k=1}^{N}\frac{\delta_k - R_F}{\sigma_k}\right]. \tag{B-4}$$

Once again, this was derived in another context by Elton, Gruber and Padberg (1976).

Notes

The authors would like to thank the Institute for Quantitative Research in Finance for their generous financial support, and Michael Brennan for his comments and suggestions.

1. See Elton and Gruber (1973) for an empirical justification of this model.

2. Long (1977) presents the necessary and sufficient conditions for this to happen, and finds empirical evidence is inconsistent with markets clearing at the standard CAPM prices.

3. This inequality assumes that C_1 is positive. C_1 can be negative, in which case the inequality in each of these equations is reversed. However, since C_1 is negative with the inequality reversed, all of the discussion which follows still holds.

4. Whether an investor invests in more than market proportions in high Beta stocks depends on the sign of C_0. If $C_0 < 0$ (a likely case) investors in high tax brackets will favor low Beta stocks—ceteris paribus.

5. Once again, if the pre-tax CAPM is assumed to hold the above analysis follows except that the effect of dividend yield is found by comparing the investor's differential tax rate with a rate of zero, rather than the average effective rate in the market.

6. The mathematical expressions for C_0 and C_1 are different from those in the last section of the paper. They follow directly from eqs. (B-4) and (3).

7. For the case where investors make decisions based on pre-tax equilibrium, the analysis holds with the market average tax rate replaced by a zero tax rate.

8. To be more exact,

$$C_j^* = \frac{1}{\sigma_j}\left[\frac{\delta_j - R_F}{\sigma_j} - \frac{\rho}{1-\rho+N\rho}\sum_{k=1}^{N}\frac{\delta_k - R_F}{\sigma_k}\right]$$

$$= \frac{1}{\sigma_j}\frac{(N\rho + (1-\rho))((\delta_j - R_F)/\sigma_j) - N\rho\,\mathrm{AVG}((\delta_k - R_F)/\sigma_k)}{N\rho + (1-\rho)}$$

$$\approx \frac{1}{\sigma_j}\left[\frac{\delta_j - R_F}{\sigma_j} - \mathrm{AVG}\frac{\delta_k - R_F}{\sigma_k}\right].$$

9. To be more exact,

$$\frac{\delta_k - R_F}{\sigma_k} = \frac{N\rho}{N\rho + (1-\rho)}\mathrm{AVG}\frac{\delta_k - R_F}{\sigma_k} \approx \mathrm{AVG}\frac{\delta_k - R_F}{\sigma_k}.$$

10. Lintner's equations are presented in terms of return. Since we are assuming investors are concerned with post-tax returns, the equations hold with respect to post-tax returns for each investor.

References

Brennan, Michael, 1970, Taxes, market valuation and corporate financial policy, *National Tax Journal*, 417–427.

Elton, Edwin J., Martin J. Gruber and Manfred Padberg, 1976, Simple criteria for optimal portfolio selection, *Journal of Finance*, 1341–1348.

Elton, Edwin J. and Martin J. Gruber, 1973, Estimating the dependence structure of share price—Implications for portfolio selection, *Journal of Finance,* 1203–1232.

Lintner, John, 1965, The valuation of risky assets and the selection of risky investments in stock portfolios and capital budgets, *Review of Economics and Statistics* 47, 13–37.

Long, John, 1977, Efficient portfolio choice with differential taxation of dividends and capital gains, *Journal of Financial Economics* 5, no. 1, 25–54.

Pettit, Richard, 1977, Consumption-Investment decisions with transactions costs and taxes: A study of the clientel effect of dividends, *Journal of Financial Economics* 5, no. 3.

VI The Past and the Future

25 Modern Portfolio Theory, 1950 to Date

Edwin J. Elton, and Martin J. Gruber

I Introduction

One of the key issues facing an individual is how to allocate wealth among alternative assets. Almost all financial institution have the same problem with the added complication that they need to explicitly include the characteristics of their liabilities in the analysis. While the structure of these problems varies somewhat, they are similar enough that we classify both as portfolio theory.

Portfolio theory is a well-developed paradigm. There are excellent textbooks on the subject. Of course, we are especially partial to our own *Modern Portfolio Theory and Investment Analysis.*[1] There are also good reviews in more advanced doctoral-level texts such as Ingersoll (1987) or Huang and Litzenberger (1988). There are also some careful mathematical treatments (Szegö, 1980). Finally, good review articles such as Constantinides and Malliaris (1995) exist. Therefore, instead of writing one more general review article, we will be more selective and our discussion will be rather eclectic. This paper will present four topics we find of particular interest. Rather than attempting to survey all articles or all issues on each topic, we will discuss what we find of special interest and importance. We will attempt to convey where the field is today and where it is headed in the future.

This paper is divided into four sections, each covering one topic. Section 2 presents a historical review of the basic theory and its current state of development. Section 3 discusses issues in estimating the key inputs for portfolio theory and Section 4 discusses the special issues that arise when portfolio theory is applied to financial institutions.[2] Section 5 will review portfolio evaluation techniques.

II Historical Development and Current State of Theory

Markowitz (1952, 1959) is the father of modern portfolio theory. His original book and article on the subject clearly delineated, for the first time, modern portfolio theory. The book was filled with insights and suggestions that anticipated many of the subsequent developments in the field. Markowitz formulated the portfolio problem as a choice of the mean and variance of a portfolio of assets. He proved the fundamental theorem of mean variance portfolio theory, namely holding constant variance, maximize expected return, and holding constant expected return minimize variance. These two principles led to the formulation of an efficient frontier from which the investor could choose his or her preferred portfolio, depending on individual risk return preferences. The important message of the theory was that assets *could not* be selected only on characteristics that were unique to the security. Rather, an investor had to consider how each security co-moved with all other securities. Furthermore, taking these co-movements into account resulted in an ability to construct a portfolio that had the same expected return and less risk than a portfolio constructed by ignoring the interactions between securities.

Considering just the mean return and variance of return of a portfolio is, of course, a simplification relative to including additional moments that might more completely describe the distribution of returns of the portfolio. Early work developed necessary conditions on either the utility function of investors or the return distribution of assets that would result in mean variance theory being optimal (see, for example, Tobin, 1958). In addition, researchers (see Lee, 1977; Kraus and Litzenberger, 1976) offered alternative portfolio theories that included more moments such as skewness or were accurate for more realistic descriptions of the distribution of return (Fama, 1965; Elton and Gruber, 1974). Nevertheless, mean variance theory has remained the cornerstone of modern portfolio theory despite these alternatives. This persistence is not due to the realism of the utility or return distribution assumptions that are necessary for it to be correct. Rather, we believe there are two reasons for its persistence. First, mean variance theory itself places large data requirements on the investor, and there is no evidence that adding additional moments improves the desirability of the portfolio selected. Second, the implications of mean variance portfolio theory are well developed, widely known, and have great intuitive appeal. Professionals who have never run an optimizer have learned that correlations as well as means and variances are necessary to understand the impact of adding a security to a portfolio. Borrowing a concept from the next section, risk measures such as beta, which have been developed based on mean variance analyses, add information and are recognized and used by investors who have no idea of the theory behind them. The precepts of mean variance theory work. Thus, we will concentrate on mean variance portfolio theory.

Mean variance portfolio theory was developed to find the optimum portfolio when an investor is concerned with return distributions over a single period. An investor is assumed to estimate the mean return and variance of return for each asset being considered for the portfolio over the single period.[3] In addition, the correlations or covariances between all pairs of assets being considered need to be estimated. Once again, these estimates are for the single decision period. One of the major theoretical problems that has been analyzed is how the single-period problem should be modified if the investor's true problem is multi-period in nature. Papers by Fama (1970), Hakansson (1970, 1974) and Merton (1990), and Mossin (1969) have all analyzed this problem under various assumptions. The papers found that under several sets of reasonable assumptions, the multi-period problem can be solved as a sequence of single-period problems. However, the optimum portfolio would be different from that selected if only one period was examined. The difference arises because the appropriate utility function in the multi-period case is a derived utility function that takes into account multiple periods, and this differs from the utility function that is appropriate for decision-making over a single period.

One assumption underlying most multi-period portfolio analysis is independence of returns between periods. There has been a substantial amount of research in the last decade showing that mean returns and variances are related over time and are functions of easily observable variables (Fama and French, 1989; Campbell and Shiller, 1988). A major research topic for the future will be how this empirical literature should effect optimum multi-period portfolio decisions.

Another strand of theoretical research has been the study of separation theorems. It is easy to show that if an investor has access to a riskless asset, the choice of the optimum portfolio of risky assets is unequivocal and independent of the investor's taste for expected return or variance. This is the separation theorem. It has three implications. First, it facilitates calculation in that the portfolio problem can be stated as finding the tangency portfolio to a ray passing through the riskless asset in expected return standard deviation space. The tangency portfolio is the portfolio that maximizes the ratio of expected return minus the return on the riskless asset to the standard deviation. Second, it leads to a mutual fund theorem, namely that all investors can obtain their desired portfolio by mixing two mutual funds, one made up of the riskless asset and one representing the tangency portfolio. One of the areas of theoretical research deals with how many mutual funds are needed and what is the nature of the portfolios that comprise them under alterative assumptions about the nature of asset returns or utility functions (See for example Ross, 1978). This is important because it provides guidance to investors and the mutual fund industry on what kinds of portfolios should be attractive. Furthermore, for financial institutions such as banks or insurance companies, mutual fund theorems provide guidance with respect to which types of commingled funds to offer. As the assumption of a constant riskless lending and borrowing rate is relaxed, other assumptions more funds and new types of funds enter the decision set. For example, if there are different riskless lending and borrowing rates but short sales of risky assets are allowed, four funds are needed. Two of the portfolios are any two portfolios of risky assets that lie on the efficient frontier and the remaining two portfolios are the instruments which yield the riskless lending and borrowing rates. While a substantial amount of work has been undertaken on mutual fund separation, and we will discuss it again in later sections, more still needs to be done. In particular, a reconciliation between theory and the actual array of mutual funds which exist would be useful.

There are two other types of theoretical research that have received substantial attention in the literature but have not had a major impact on the implementation of portfolio management. First, a number of articles have been written that analyze the portfolio problem in continuous time (see Merton, 1990). In the continuous-time formulation, the portfolio problem and consumption investment problem are solved simultaneously. The primary result of the continuous-time framework has been to confirm the discrete-time results. The confirmation in some cases assumes a somewhat more realistic set of assumptions such as lognormal rather than normal returns and more general utility functions, but the results constitute in large part a confirmation of standard discrete-time results. The major exception is Merton's results concerning hedging portfolios. Merton finds that in the intertemporal continuous-time framework an investor needs to hold hedging portfolios to protect against changes in the state variables.

The other type of theoretical research that has received some attention is attempts to understand how current holdings and transaction costs should affect portfolio rebalancing. Again, this analysis, while interesting, has had little impact on practice.

An applied area of research that has been of concern is computational efficiency. With the enormous improvement in computer speed and memory, early computational concerns about solving large-scale problems have disappeared. What still has value are the insights into the composition of the optimum portfolio that can be obtained by simple solutions to the portfolio problem. In a series of papers, Elton et al. (1976, 1977, 1978a, b) showed how optimum portfolios could be selected by a simple ranking device. This ranking device clarified the characteristics of securities that would lead to their inclusion in an optimum portfolio. The basic insight that made the EG&P algorithms work is the following: most analysts who solve portfolio problems use a model to estimate the covariances between securities. Portfolio problems can be solved by inverting a matrix. Often the structure of the model used to estimate the covariances is such that the covariance matrix can be explicitly inverted and a closed form solution written down. This solution clarifies why a security enters into the optimum portfolio and provides a simple ranking device that allows easy solution. In the single-index case, the ranking is by the excess return (expected return minus riskless rate) divided by the security's beta. If the covariance is estimated by assuming that the correlation among securities is constant, the ranking is by excess return to standard deviation of return. Similar ranking devices exist for more complicated assumptions about how the covariance is estimated. A number of papers have elaborated on the original EG&P analysis. These have suggested ways of speeding up the computations and incorporating more realistic short sales assumptions, and have led to improved understanding of the effect of estimation error on optimum portfolios (see Chen and Brown, 1983). A useful extension would be to pursue the solution where multi-index models describe the return-generating process. EG&P have done some of the analysis (see Elton et al., 1977, 1979). However, they made some simplifying assumptions that, while consistent with models used at the time they derived their results, are less typical of models used today. The use of multi-index return-generating models is standard in today's investment community. A solution that is consistent with the types of models used today would be useful.

The final area that has received a great deal of attention is estimation of the inputs to the portfolio selection problem. We will not attempt to discuss all of this literature. Rather, we will concentrate on the literature that is unique to the portfolio selection area, namely the estimation of the covariance or correlation structure. It is to this discussion that we now turn.

III Index Models and Covariance Estimates

After mean variance portfolio theory was first developed, there was an enormous amount of work on estimating inputs. For the first time in the literature of financial economics, estimates of correlation coefficients (or alternatively covariances) were required. The principal tool developed for estimating covariances was index models.[4] These models have found wide application beyond estimating covariance structures, and are worth reviewing on their own.

A *Index Models*

The earliest index model that received wide attention was the single-index model, and in particular one variant of the single-index model, the market model. This was first discussed in Markowitz, but was developed and popularized by Sharpe (1967). The market model is

$$R_{it} = \alpha_i + \beta_i R_{mt} + e_{it},$$

where R_{it} is the return of stock I in period t, α_i the unique expected return of security I, β_i the sensitivity of stock I to market movements, R_{mt} the return on the market in period t, and e_{it} is the unique risky return of security I in period t and has a mean of zero and variance σ_{ei}^2.

From the point of view of portfolio inputs, the important characteristics of the use of the market model were that the number of estimates required was reduced, the type of inputs needed was easier for analysts to understand, and the accuracy of portfolio optimization was increased. Even when using historical data to estimate the market model, the accuracy of the market model in estimating covariances was higher than direct estimation (see, for example, Elton and Gruber, 1973). Furthermore, if subjective estimates are used or if subjective modification of historical data is used, the reduced data requirements of the single-index model should lead to improved forecasting. Finally, a steel analyst can better understand the relationship between steel and the market than between steel and General Foods, and therefore is likely better able to meaningfully estimate betas than covariances.

The single-index model quickly took on a life well beyond its use in estimating inputs. A large number of firms were started whose principal business was estimating betas. These firms developed sophisticated techniques that improved estimation over simply fitting a regression to historical data.[5]

In addition, many financial institutions estimate or use others' estimates of beta. Although many of the estimates found their way into portfolio algorithms, more commonly they were used to understand and manage the market exposure of the portfolio. In particular, since betas are additive, security betas help a manager ascertain the impact of adding a security on the overall market exposure of the portfolio.

Shortly after the market model was developed, a number of researchers started to explore whether multi-index models better explained reality. The prototype multi-index model is

$$R_{it} = \alpha_i + \sum_{j=1}^{J} \beta_{ij} I_{jt} + e_{it}, \qquad i = 1, \ldots, N,$$

where β_{ij} is sensitivity of security I to index j, I_j the jth index, J is the total number of indexes employed, and other terms as before.

The basic issue was what were the indexes and how many were there. Early work was primarily statistical in nature. Indexes were extracted from the variance-covariance matrix of returns using either factor analysis or principal components analysis (see Roll and Ross, 1980; Dhrymes et al., 1984; Brown and Weinstein, 1993; Cho et al., 1984). The alternative way to estimate a multi-index model was to pre-specify a structure. Three types of pre-specifications are used:

1. Market-plus-industry indexes (see Cohen and Pogue, 1967).
2. Surprises in basic economic indexes (e.g., production, inflation) (see Chen et al., 1986).
3. Portfolios of traded securities (e.g., an index of small minus large securities) (see Fama and French, 1992).

The use of models in which indexes are pre-specified is gaining acceptance and is likely to be the dominant form of multi-index models in the future. Statistical estimates of factors are likely to be used primarily to help confirm that the pre-specified indexes capture all of the major influences and that they are important in explaining returns.

Multi-index models can be used to provide inputs for a portfolio optimization technique. The analyst needs to have estimates of N times J betas and the variances of the J indexes. However, as with single-index models, multi-index models are widely used in other ways. Multi-index models are the building blocks for arbitrage pricing theory. Multi-index models are also used by portfolio managers to understand the sensitivity of the portfolio to various economic influences and to allow the manager to make active bets on how the indexes will change in the next period. As shown in a later section, multi-index models are the basic tool for evaluating fund managers. Finally, multi-index models can be used to reformulate mean-variance portfolio theory in a way that may be more meaningful to managers. This use is discussed in the next section.

Currently, different types of multi-index models have been used for different applications, and this will likely continue in the future. A manager interested in understanding the sensitivity of the portfolio to basic economic influences needs a multi-index model that captures these influences. The same manager is likely to use a model expressed in terms of tradeable portfolios of securities when evaluating performance, and may use a market-plus-industry model in deciding on sector rotation.

Multi-index models also are useful in understanding and visualizing the portfolio choice. This is the topic to which we now turn.

B Portfolio Analysis in a Multi-index World

In the previous section we saw that single and multi-index models not only simplify the inputs to the portfolio selection problem, they also can lead to better forecasts and make the selection process easier to comprehend. If we accept index models as a sufficient description of reality, they also allow us to simplify the construction of the optimal portfolio.

In the previous section we reviewed portfolio selection when the single-index model is employed. If we make the additional assumption that the Capital Asset Pricing Model (CAPM) holds and we ignore the insight of Fama (1968) that the residuals from the market model cannot be uncorrelated and we allow short sales, then the Elton et al. (1976) solution reduces to the Treynor and Black (1973) solution that the investment in any stock should be proportional to the ratio of alpha to the variance of residual risk.

The reformulation of the portfolio problem for multi-index models was first analyzed by Ross (1978) and Ingersoll (1987). When returns are generated by a multi-index model, the portfolio problem can be viewed as choosing among portfolios in multi-dimensional space with one dimension for expected return and an additional dimension for each beta. When some securities are mispriced, an additional dimension must be added for residual risk. Although this is equivalent to the mean variance problem, managers may relate better to this choice. In particular, a manager may find it easier to think in terms of choosing exposures to risks and how much residual risk they will accept rather than total risk. The general case where indexes cannot be exactly replicated (e.g., they may be macroeconomic influences), where securities exist which are priced out of equilibrium and indexes are not necessarily normally distributed, is analyzed by Elton and Gruber (1992b).[6] They show that in this case each investor can form an optimum portfolio by choosing from among an investment in the riskless asset plus a number of portfolios equal to the number of indexes generating returns plus one. The solution involves forming one replicating portfolio for each index (simple rules are presented for forming those portfolios) plus one portfolio which is made up of mispriced securities. Elton and Gruber (1992b) prove that the optimum proportions in the portfolio of mispriced securities are proportional to the product of the inverse of the variance-covariance matrix of residuals and the vector of alphas. If we assume that the coviarance between residuals is equal to zero, this reduces to the ratio of each alpha to the variance of each residual risk.[7]

Fama (1996) develops models of equilibrium and portfolio optimization in the world of Merton's Intertemporal CAPM. While Fama's results are analogous to those presented above, the multi-period nature of the problem requires the addition of one more portfolio, the market portfolio, to be included in the set of portfolio choices given to the investor.

IV Portfolio Optimization with Investor Liabilities

We believe that one of the important future directions for portfolio theory involves the explicit inclusion of liabilities into the asset allocation decision. While conceptually easy to solve, the implementation of a system to include both liabilities and assets in a manner that produces real insight is much more difficult.

At one extreme, liabilities have been treated in the immunization literature. The idea of simply holding a set of bonds that has the same duration as, or that will have the same cash flows as, a set of liabilities has been treated in great detail in the literature of financial economics. At the other extreme, the idea of simply treating liabilities as assets with negative cash flows and constraining them to be present in the QPS solution to a portfolio optimization problem has been proposed. The first idea assumes that the user is interested in a minimum variance solution. The second provides little insight into what is of necessity a problem with a multi-period time dimension. Neither takes into consideration the fact that cash flows from liabilities are uncertain and subject to systematic risks which are similar to those for asset returns.

Elton and Gruber (1992a, b) formulate the asset liability problem, where both assets and liabilities are related to a one-index model, and develop an equilibrium model and a portfolio theory where equilibrium exists but some assets are out of equilibrium. The special role of duration and cash flow matching is developed and the analysis shows robust conditions under which cash flow matching some, but not all, of the liabilities is desirable.

We believe that the extension of this analysis employing a multi-index framework has great potential. Liabilities are usually not certain, but often depend on influences such as inflation and changes in interest rates. Similar influences affect the return in assets. By formulating both liabilities and asset returns as a function of indexes which affect these returns (and in the case of liabilities affect the amounts), solutions to the portfolio problem can be reached that allow investors to make tradeoffs in terms of not only expected return and total risk but in terms of the type of risk to which they will be exposed.

V Portfolio Evaluation

Up to this point we have been concerned with how to construct an optimal portfolio. We have also discussed the fact that the payoff from portfolio management models is in large part a function of the type and quality of the data used. It would be inappropriate to end this review article without a discussion of portfolio evaluation. Not only do evaluation models follow naturally from the theories of portfolio management, it is only by employing evaluation measures that we can find whether the combination of portfolio management techniques and the type of data used add value. If managers cannot add value to passive portfolios, why bother with portfolio management models at all?

Concern with portfolio performance predates the advent of modern portfolio theory. One of the early interesting studies on performance evaluation was published by Cowles (1933). In this study he compared the average performance of a set of managed portfolios to a passive portfolio and concluded that the managed portfolios underperformed the passive benchmark. Cowles examined return but ignored any consideration of risk.

What modern theory has taught us is that we need to be concerned with risk as well as return in examining performance. It was not long after Markowitz's path-breaking contribution that techniques were developed and applied (primarily to mutual fund data) for evaluating performance based on risk and return.

Early studies employed a variety of evaluation techniques. These included the Sharpe ratio (Sharpe, 1966), the Treynor ratio (Treynor, 1965), the alpha of Jensen (1968, 1969), the use of randomly generated passive portfolios of the same risk of Friend et al. (1970). Each of these studies evaluated performance adjusting for a measure of risk. Some used total risk (Sharpe, and Friend et al.) as the correct measure. Others (Treynor, Jensen, and Friend et al.) used beta as the correct measure of risk. While Friend et al. evaluated a managed portfolio against randomly generated unmanaged portfolios of the same risk, each of the other authors used the fact that combinations of any portfolio and the riskless asset lie along a straight line in either expected return beta space or expected return standard deviation space to evaluate performance.

Because these measures are discussed in most books of portfolio management or investment analysis, we will not review them in detail.[8] Instead, we will use Jensen's measure as a benchmark for further discussion. Jensen's alpha is the intercept from the following time series regression:

$$R_{Pt} - R_{Ft} = \alpha_p + \beta_p(R_{mt} - R_{Ft}) + e_{Pt},$$

where R_{pt} is the return on the portfolio being evaluated at time t, R_{Ft} the riskless rate in period t. R_{mt} the return on the reference portfolio. β_p the sensitivity to the reference portfolio, and e_{Pt} is the mean zero random error.

The alpha from this regression can be defined as the abnormal return above what would be earned if the CAPM held and thus the non-equilibrium return the manager earned. There is a simpler and more intuitive explanation. Alpha represents the return the manager earned over a combination of an index fund (the market portfolio) and Treasury bills, where the combination is selected to have the same risk as the managed portfolio. Since the investor is free to place some money in an index fund and some in riskless assets, this is an appealing way to justify this model.

In the remainder of this article we will discuss some of the problems and progress that have occurred in employing the early models of portfolio performance.

A *Jensen's Measure and Benchmark Identification*

The problem with identifying the correct index to use in the Jensen model has been discussed in detail in Roll (1978). The efficiency of the index is of key importance. If the index is not efficient, then performance attributed to any fund becomes a function of the particular index selected. Relying on the defense that alpha simply represents the abnormal return over holding the portfolio of an index fund (e.g., the S&P 500 Index) and Treasury bills with the same beta also fails because it ignores the choices available to the manager. For example, small stocks (low market value stocks) have outperformed the S&P 500 Index for long periods of time. A small stock mutual fund manager with no selection ability or even negative selection ability would show superior performance during such periods when compared to a combination of riskless assets and an S&P 500 index fund.

The problems inherent in the use of a single-index model have led to the development of multi-index performance measures. In answer to Roll's critique, we know that if returns are generated by no more than N factors, then N diversified portfolios are sufficient to describe relative returns and a linear combination of the N diversified portfolios will be efficient (see Ross, 1978; Grinblatt and Titman, 1987). A second defense for a multi-index model comes directly from arbitrage pricing theory, which postulates that expected returns can be expressed as a linear function of sensitivities to more than one index. Thus, deviations from this linear function are a measure of a manager's selection ability.

Finally, returning to viewing the manager relative to a passive fund or funds, it is clear that comparing active funds in total or a particular active fund to a passive strategy is inappropriate if these funds hold very different types of securities from the passive portfolios with which they are being compared.

This is made very clear in a series of articles. Ippolito (1989), using data for 1965–1984, found that a sample of mutual funds had positive alphas from the Jensen model. In addition, mutual funds with higher expenses had at least as good performance as those with lower expenses, even after fees were deducted in computing performance and, finally, load funds outperformed no-load funds. An examination of Ippolito's sample showed that funds in his sample had much more money in small stocks than that implied by the composition of the S&P 500 Index and the weighting of stocks in the S&P 500 Index. In fact, a number of the funds had as their objective the construction of a portfolio of small stocks. It is easy to correct for small stocks by introducing another index into a Jensen-type model. In the simplest case the model becomes

$$R_{Pt} - R_{Ft} = \alpha_p + \beta_p(R_{mt} - R_{ft}) + B_{ssp}(R_{sst} - R_{Ft}) + e_{pt},$$

where R_{sst} is the return on an index of small stocks in period t and other terms as before.

During the period studied by Ippolito, small stocks had a much bigger return than large stocks, in excess of 10% annually. Furthermore, the average mutual fund had a large positive beta with the small stock index. When this multi-index model is used to determine abnormal returns (α), the results indicate that funds on average have negative alphas and funds which have higher expenses tend to do worse than funds with smaller expenses, and load funds underperform no-load funds.[9] Thus, the use of an appropriate model reversed the conclusions.

On a theoretical and practical basis, multi-index versions of the Jensen measure are more appropriate than single-index versions. This still leaves us with the problem of which multi-index models to use. In a sense this is a return to our earlier section on multi-index models where we discussed alternative ways of specifying them. Several authors (e.g., Lehmann and Modest, 1987; Connor and Korajzcyk, 1991) have examined the use of multi-index models derived statistically to evaluate mutual fund performance.

A second approach to developing multiple indexes is to find portfolios of securities which span the types of investments held by mutual funds. This approach has been used by Sharpe (1992), Elton et al. (1996a), and Blake et al. (1993). For example, Elton et al. (1996a) employ a four-index model involving the S&P 500 Index, a size-related index, a bond index, and a growth-value index to explain the return on domestic non-specialized mutual funds. Sharpe uses a 12-index model to explain the return on a broader set of mutual funds including domestic as well as international bond funds and stock funds.[10]

The appropriate set of indexes to use to evaluate portfolio performance has not been completely resolved. However, recent papers by Sharpe (1992) and Elton et al. (1996b) indicate that good models already exist. In particular, Elton et al. (1996b) show that no more than five indexes are sufficient to explain the returns on domestic stock funds and suggest that performance can be meaningfully evaluated in terms of these five easily identifiable indexes.

B Return Ratio

Up to now we have been describing multi-index forms of Jensen's alpha as the appropriate measure to use for portfolio evaluation. In fact, Sharpe (1994) has formalized a generalized version of the Sharpe ratio as a useful alternative for performance measurements in a multi-index world. Rather than measure the ratio of difference between average return on a portfolio and the riskless rate to the standard deviation of the portfolio as in the original Sharpe ratio, the generalized ratio suggested by Sharpe uses the ratio of the difference between the average return on the portfolio and the benchmark portfolio (which can be a combination of several portfolios, e.g., a multi-index model) to the standard deviation of difference.[11] While there are several ways to identify the benchmark portfolio and estimate sensitivities to it, if this is done via a time series analysis of a multi-index model, the Sharpe measure becomes α_p/σ_{sp}.

Notice that both the multi-index Sharpe measure and a multi-index version of the Jensen measure will identify the same funds as having superior performance. However, they can rank funds in different order.[12]

C Forecasting

We have examined some alternative measures of performance, but we have not yet faced an important issue. The major purpose in analyzing past performance is to gain insight into the future. If past performance is unrelated to future performance, then performance evaluation is of no help when selecting a fund or a manager. Four recent studies have found persistence in mutual fund performance: Hendricks et al. (1993), Grinblatt and Titman (1992), Sharpe (1994), and Elton et al. (1996a). The last two studies use multi-index models based on portfolios of securities. Elton et al. (1996a) document that the top 10% of funds ranked on past alpha over one- and three-year periods not only provide superior risk-adjusted return in future one- and three-year periods, they produce positive alphas in a period when alphas are negative for the fund industry as a whole. Finally, when modern portfolio theory is followed and funds are weighted proportionally in the top decile by α_p/σ_{sp}^2 rather than equally weighted, the subsequent alpha is significantly increased.

Past performance when risk adjustment is done carefully through the use of an appropriately designed multi-index model allows investors to select funds that have superior future performance.

D Timing

The use of a single or multiple index model to judge performance and to forecast performance assumes that betas (sensitivities) are reasonably constant and that management does not change them to gain added return through market timing. There are a number of papers (e.g., Treynor and Mazuy, 1966; Lehmann and Modest, 1987; Henriksson, 1984) that examine the reasonableness of this assumption. The general conclusion is that timing does not increase risk-adjusted returns and may even lower them.

The more immediate question for this article is whether changing betas cause the betas on multi-index models to be so unreliable as to be of no value. The answer appears to be "no". Large changes in the portfolio betas in the multi-index model would cause betas to be poorly estimated and should cause past alphas to be unrelated to future alphas. This does not seem to be the case for most funds. Both Sharpe (1994) and Elton et al. (1996a) find that past alphas have some predictive power. However, Elton et al. (1996a) show that alphas are more predictable if funds for which the model has low correlation ($R^2 < 0.80$) during the fit period are eliminated. This does suggest that these funds for which the model does not fit well, which may include funds attempting to time the market, should be examined separately and are worthy or further study.

E Why Bother with Performance?

In closing this section, we want to discuss why we bother with performance. In a perfectly efficient market we would expect performance to be random over time. While some funds might outperform an appropriate passive strategy and others underperform it, the difference would be strictly random over time. On the other hand, if superior management exists, then unless this performance is reflected in higher fees, we would expect to find persistence in performance. The facts that mutual funds (and, we suspect, managers in general) do not raise fees to reflect performance and that fees as a percent of assets tend to be lower for good performing funds mean that, if superior management exists, it should be reflected in persistence in performance. The fact that performance shows persistence suggests that at least some managers have superior information and give us hope that modern portfolio theory can be used to benefit the investor.

Final Comments

In this article we have attempted to review modern portfolio theory and to highlight some topics and areas of future research. Because of constraints on time and space, we have not included references to many areas of interesting research. We apologize to the authors of the hundreds of interesting papers in portfolio theory that we have not cited in this paper.

Acknowledgements

The authors would like to thank Giorgio Szegö for helpful comments on an earlier version of this paper.

Notes

1. Elton and Gruber (1995).

2. One of the early discussions of this problem is presented by Szegö (1980), chs. 15, 16.

3. The appropriate length of the period in a single-period solution is a topic of significance on which very little research has been done.

4. Index models fitted to historic data produce the same estimates of historic average returns and historic variance as do using the raw data itself. The only difference is in the estimates of correlations.

5. See Elton and Gruber (1995), ch. 5.

6. When indexes cannot be replicated exactly, there is no mathematical inconsistency in assuming residuals from the model are not correlated.

7. This solution reduces to that presented by Ross (1978) and Ingersoll (1987) when indexes can be replicated perfectly (e.g., when they are tradeable portfolios).

8. See, for example, Elton and Gruber (1995), ch. 24.

9. See Elton et al. (1993).

10. Another advantage of using these models is that the measured betas indicate the type of securities each fund is holding. Elton et al. fit their model via regression analysis. Sharpe uses quadratic programming. Sharpe's approach, like regression analysis, fits the betas to minimize squared deviation from the regression plane, but by using QPS, Sharpe introduced constraints so that the sum of the betas equals 1 and no beta is negative. He interprets the betas from these constrained regressions as being investment proportions.

11. Sharpe uses QPS rather than regression analysis to identify differential return and risk, and requires the betas to sum to one. The results from this estimation well be somewhat different, since the weights are different and this affects both α_p and σ_{ep}.

12. It is worth noting that Elton and Gruber (1992b) show that under reasonable sets of assumptions the optimal amount to invest in an actively managed fund in an actively managed portfolio of funds is proportional to α_p/σ_{ep}^2.

References

Blake, C. R., Elton, E. J., Gruber, M. J., 1993. The performance of bond mutual funds. *Journal of Business* 66 (3), 371–403.

Brown, S., Weinstein, 1993. A new approach to testing asset pricing models: the bilinear paradigm. *Journal of Finance.*

Campbell, J. Y., Shiller, R., 1988. The dividend-price ratio and expectations of future dividends and discount factors. *Review of Financial Studies* 1 (3), 195–228.

Chen, S., Brown, S., 1983. Estimation risk and simple rules for optimal portfolio selection. *Journal of Finance* 38, 1087–1093.

Chen, N., Roll, R., Ross, S., 1986. Economic forces and the stock market. *Journal of Business* 59, 386–403.

Cho, D. C., Elton, E. J., Gruber, M. J., 1984. On the robustness of the Roll and Ross arbitrage pricing theory. *Journal of Financial and Quantitative Analysis* 19 (1), 1–10.

Cohen, K., Pogue, J., 1967. An empirical evaluation of alternative portfolio selection models. *Journal of Business* 46, 166–193.

Connor, G., Korajzcyk, R., 1991. The attributes, behavior and performance of U. S. mutual funds. *Review of Quantitative Finance and Accounting* 1, 5–26.

Constantinides, G., Malliaris, A., 1995. Portfolio theory. In: Jarrow et al. (Eds.), *Handbooks in O.R. and N.S.*, vol. 9. Elsevier, Amsterdam.

Cowles, A., 1933. Can stock market forecasters forecast? *Econometrica* 1 (3), 206–214.

Dhrymes, P. J., Friend, I., Gultekin, N. B., 1984. A critical reexamination of the empirical evidence on the arbitrage pricing theory. *Journal of Finance* 39 (2), 323–346.

Elton, E. J., Gruber, M. J., 1973. Estimating the dependence structure of share prices—implications for portfolio selection. *Journal of Finance* 8 (5), 1203–1232.

Elton, E. J., Gruber, M. J., 1974. Portfolio theory when investment relatives are lognormally distributed. *Journal of Finance* 29, 1265–1273.

Elton, E. J., Gruber, M. J., Padberg, M. W., 1976. Simple criteria for optimal portfolio selection. *Journal of Finance* 11 (5), 1341–1357.

Elton, E. J., Gruber, M. J., Padberg, M. W., 1977. Simple rules for optimal portfolio selection: the multi group case. *Journal of Financial and Quantitative Analysis* 12 (3), 329–345.

Elton, E. J., Gruber M. J., Padberg, M. W., 1978a. Simple criteria for optimal portfolio selection: tracing out the efficient frontier. *Journal of Finance* 13 (1), 296–302.

Elton, E. J., Gruber, M. J., Padberg, M. W., 1978b. Simple criteria for optimal portfolio selection with upper bonds. *Operation Research.*

Elton, E. J., Gruber, M. J., Padberg, M. W., 1979. Simple criteria for optimal portfolio selection: the multi-index case. In: Elton, Gruber (Eds.), *Portfolio Theory: 25 Years Later.* North-Holland, Amsterdam.

Elton, E. J., Gruber, M. J., 1992a. Optimal investment strategies with investor liabilities. *Journal of Banking and Finance* 16, 98–112.

Elton, E. J., Gruber, M. J., 1992b. Portfolio analysis with a non-normal multi-index return generating prices. *Review of Quantitative Finance and Accounting* 2 (1), 5–16.

Elton, E. J., Gruber, M. J., Das, S., Hlavka, M., 1993. Efficiency with costly information: a reinterpretation of evidence from managed portfolios. *Review of Financial Studies* 6 (1), 1–22.

Elton, E. J., Gruber, M. J., 1995. *Modern Portfolio Theory and Investment Analysis,* 5th ed. Wiley, New York.

Elton, E. J., Gruber, M. J., Blake, C. R., 1996a. The persistence of risk-adjusted mutual fund performance. *Journal of Business* 69, 153–157.

Elton, E. J., Gruber, M. J., Blake, C. R., 1996b. Common factors in mutual fund returns. Unpublished working paper, New York University.

Fama, E. F., 1965. Portfolio analysis in a stable Paretian market. *Management Science* 11, 409–419.

Fama, E. F., 1968. Risk return and equilibrium: some clarifying comments. *Journal of Finance* 23 (1), 29–40.

Fama, E. F., 1970. Multiperiod consumption-investment decisions. *American Economics Review* 60, 163–174.

Fama, E. F., French, K. R., 1989. Business conditions and expected returns on stocks and bonds. *Journal of Financial Economics* 25 (1), 23–49.

Fama, E. F., French, K. R., 1992. The cross-section of expected stock returns. *Journal of Finance* 47, 427–465.

Fama, E. F., 1996. Multifactor portfolio efficiency and multi-factor asset pricing. *Journal of Financial and Quantitative Analysis* 31, 441–465.

Friend, I., Blume, M., Crockett, J., 1970. *Mutual Funds and Other Institutional Investors,* McGraw-Hill, New York.

Grinblatt, M., Titman, S., 1992. The persistence of mutual fund performance. *Journal of Finance* 47, 1977–1984.

Grinblatt, M., Titman, S., 1987. The relation between mean-variance efficiency and arbitrage pricing. *Journal of Business* 60, 97–112.

Hakansson, N., 1970. Optimal investment and consumption strategies under risk for a class of utility functions. *Econometrica* 38, 587–607.

Hakansson, N., 1974. Convergence in multiperiod portfolio choice. *Journal of Financial Economics* 1, 201–224.

Hendricks, D., Patel, J., Zeckhauser, R., 1993. Hot hands in mutual funds: the persistence of performance, 1974–1988. *Journal of Finance* 48, 93–130.

Henriksson, R., 1984. Market timing and mutual fund performance. *Journal of Business* 57, 73–96.

Huang, C., Litzenberger, R., 1988. *Foundations for Financial Economics,* North-Holland, Amsterdam, The Netherlands.

Ingersoll, J., 1987. *Theory of Financial Decision Making,* Rowman and Littlefield, New York.

Ippolito, R., 1989. Efficiency with costly information: a study of mutual fund performance, 1965–1984. *Quarterly Journal of Economics* 104, 1–23.

Jensen, C. M., 1968. The performance of mutual funds in the period 1945–1964. *Journal of Finance* 23 (2), 389–415.

Jensen, M., 1969. Risk, the pricing of capital assets, and the evaluation of investment portfolios. *Journal of Business* 42 (2), 167–247.

Kraus, A., Litzenberger, R., 1976. Skewness preference and the valuation of risky assets. *Journal of Finance* 21 (4), 1085–1100.

Lee, C. F., 1977. Functional form, skewness effect and the risk return relationship. *Journal of Financial and Quantitative Analysis* 12, 55.

Lehmann, B., Modest, D., 1987. Mutual fund performance evaluation: a comparison of benchmarks and benchmark comparisons. *Journal of Finance* 42, 223–265.

Markowitz, H., 1952. Portfolio selection. *Journal of Finance* 7, 77–91.

Markowitz, H., 1959. *Portfolio Selection: Efficient Diversification of Investments,* Wiley, New York.

Merton, R. C., 1990. *Continuous Time Finance,* Basil Blackwell, Oxford.

Mossin. J., 1969. Optimal multiperiod portfolio policies. *Journal of Business* 41, 215–229.

Roll, R., 1978. Ambiguity when performance is measured by the securities market line. *Journal of Finance* 33, 1051–1069.

Roll, R., Ross, S., 1980. An empirical investigation of the arbitrage pricing theory. *Journal of Finance* 35 (5), 1073–1103.

Ross, S. A., 1978. Mutual fund separation in financial theory—The separation distributions. *Journal of Economic Theory* 17, 254–286.

Sharpe, W., 1992. Asset allocation: management style and performance measurement. *Journal of Portfolio Management* 18, 7–19.

Sharpe, W., 1967. A simplified model of portfolio analysis. *Management Science* 13, 277–293.

Sharpe, W., 1966. Mutual fund performance. *Journal of Business* 39, 119–138.

Sharpe, W., 1994. The Sharpe ratio. *Journal of Portfolio Management,* 49–57.

Szegö, G., 1980. *Portfolio Theory with Applications to Bank Asset Management,* Academic Press, New York.

Tobin, J., 1958. Liquidity preference as behavior toward risk. *Review of Economic Studies* 25, 65–86.

Treynor, J., 1965. How to rate management of investment funds. *Harvard Business Review* 43, 63–75.

Treynor, J., Black, F., 1973. How to use security analysis to improve portfolio selection. *Journal of Business* 46, 66–86.

Treynor, J., Mazuy, K., 1966. Can mutual funds outguess the market? *Harvard Business Review* 44, 131–136.

Index